PALGRAVE MACMILLAN SERIES IN
INTERNATIONAL POLITICAL COMMUNICATION

Series editor:

Philip Seib, University of Southern California (USA)

From democratization to terrorism, economic development to conflict resolution, global political dynamics are affected by the increasing pervasiveness and influence of communication media. This series examines the participants and their tools, their strategies and their impact. It offers a mix of comparative and tightly focused analyses that bridge the various elements of communication and political science included in the field of international studies. Particular emphasis is placed on topics related to the rapidly changing communication environment that is being shaped by new technologies and new political realities. This is the evolving world of international political communication.

Editorial Board Members:

Hussein Amin, American University in Cairo (Egypt)
Robin Brown, University of Leeds (UK)

Eytan Gilboa, Bar-Ilan University (Israel)
Steven Livingston, George Washington University (USA)

Robin Mansell, London School of Economics and Political Science (UK)
Holli Semetko, Emory University (USA)

Ingrid Volkmer, University of Melbourne (Australia)

Books Appearing in this Series

Islam Dot Com

Contemporary Islamic Discourses in Cyberspace

Mohammed el-Nawawy
and
Sahar Khamis

First published in hardcover in 2009 by
PALGRAVE MACMILLAN®
in the United States—a division of St. Martin's Press LLC,
175 Fifth Avenue, New York, NY 10010.

Where this book is distributed in the UK, Europe and the rest of the world,
this is by Palgrave Macmillan, a division of Macmillan Publishers Limited,
registered in England, company number 785998, of Houndmills,
Basingstoke, Hampshire RG21 6XS.

Palgrave Macmillan is the global academic imprint of the above companies
and has companies and representatives throughout the world.

Palgrave® and Macmillan® are registered trademarks in the United States,
the United Kingdom, Europe and other countries.

ISBN: 978–0–230–33815–9

Library of Congress Cataloging-in-Publication Data

El-Nawawy, Mohammed, 1968–
    Islam dot com : contemporary Islamic discourses
  in cyberspace / Mohammed el-Nawawy, Sahar Khamis.
        p. cm.—(Palgrave macmillan series in international political
            communication)
    Includes bibliographical references and index.
    ISBN-13: 978–0–230–60035–5 (alk. paper)
    ISBN-10: 0–230–60035–2 (alk. paper)
      1. Islam—Electronic discussion groups. 2. Islam—Computer network
  resources. 3. Muslims—Blogs. 4. Internet—Social aspects. I. Khamis,
  Sahar. II. Title.

BP40.5.E46 2009
025.06′297—dc22   2008047885

A catalogue record of the book is available from the British Library.

Design by Newgen Imaging Systems (P) Ltd., Chennai, India.

First PALGRAVE MACMILLAN paperback edition: December 2011

10 9 8 7 6 5 4 3 2 1

Printed in the United States of America.

Transferred to Digital Printing in 2011

Contents

FOREWORD

Much of the social and political dynamism within the Islamic world today is attributable to the growing pervasiveness of new media, particularly Internet-based communication. Islam's public sphere is increasingly active. Although in many countries discourse is far from totally free, boundaries are being pushed back. Previously taboo topics are being discussed openly; previously silent voices are being heard. Lively discussion, often a precursor of at least some level of democratization, abounds.

Mohammed el-Nawawy and Sahar Khamis provide a detailed examination of Internet-driven change within this important part of the world community. Their analytical and theoretical approach to understanding the Internet's relationship to Muslim identity construction brings solid evidence and thoughtful interpretation to a topic that has often been addressed with more conjecture than proof.

Principal among the issues they consider is the existence of a virtual *umma*. Is it reality or illusion? Do Internet-based media provide a platform on which new connectivity among Muslims is being built? The long-established conventional wisdom was that because the Muslim in Djakarta, the Muslim in Cairo, the Muslim in Dakar, and the Muslim in Toronto had so little in common the *umma* was at best a theoretical concept. But the Internet—featuring websites such as those el-Nawawy and Khamis examine—may be changing that. In the world of the Web, national boundaries become less relevant and shared cultural identity may supersede parochial interests.

A special relationship exists between religion and the Internet. Through interactive websites, individuals can connect at anytime to philosophy, advice, social activities, and other aspects of organized religion and do so as a very private exercise. While the Internet is reshaping social connectivity in other aspects of life, it is also altering the connection between the religious establishment and the individual believer.

For Islam, the Internet provides a forum in which those who want to construct new, modern interpretations of Islam (such as Amr Khaled) may do so. The new technology of the Web also encourages the building of new linkages between Islam as institution and the individual Muslim. As the world's Islamic population becomes more dispersed, this is an essential part of retaining a sense of religious community.

Just as the Internet pulls Islam together, it also allows a dispersion of influence. With easy access to a global online audience, new opportunities are provided to those who may wish to challenge the role of the *ulama*, the men of knowledge who have long had great power to explain tenets of Islam. With the Internet, centrality is less necessary. For good or ill, influence comes from many different directions, and the *ulama* may even be circumvented when aspects of Islam are being considered in online forums.

The Internet also brings a kind of populism to *ijtihad*, independent reasoning. The exercise of that independence ripples outward in concentric rings and a truer form of intellectual autonomy takes root. The breadth of participation in thinking and talking about Islam extends outward along the almost infinite facets of the Web.

This is not to say that Islam has become atomized. The Internet also accelerates cohesion. The pan-Islamic nature of numerous popular websites makes the *umma* less nebulous. Through the Internet, individual Muslims—including those in diasporic populations—can directly connect to the greater community of Islam. The potential geopolitical ramifications of this enhanced connectivity within a virtual *Dar al-Islam*—territory of Islam—are only gradually being recognized by Muslim and non-Muslim governments around the world.

All these matters contribute to this book being an exceptional contribution to scholarship in this field. El-Nawawy and Khamis present an examination of Islam on the Internet that is thorough and culturally sensitive. It suggests answers to many of the questions about how Muslims see themselves and how they view the rest of the world.

PHILIP SEIB
University of Southern California

Acknowledgment

The authors would like to thank the following people for their valuable contributions through different stages of producing this book: Philip Seib, Professor of Journalism in the Annenberg School of Communication at the University of Southern California and the editor of the Palgrave Macmillan Series in International Political Communication, for his unsurpassed encouragement and support and his belief in the idea of this book; Adel Iskandar, a visiting researcher in the Center for Contemporary Arabic Studies at Georgetown University, for his precious contribution and advice in the initial stages of developing the book proposal; Karen Walker, a doctoral candidate in the Department of Communication at the University of Maryland, College Park, for providing useful and relevant sources for the literature review, mapping some of the discussion forums in the three Islamic websites under study, and providing thorough edits and thoughtful remarks on the first draft of this book; Catherine Romero, an undergraduate student in the Department of Communication at the University of Maryland, College Park, for her stylistic revisions and for compiling the book's bibliography and index; Caiyan Luo, a former graduate student in the Department of Communication at Georgia State University, and Jasmin Al-Baghdadi, an undergraduate student in the Department of Biology at Queens University of Charlotte, for their help with compiling academic literature for this book; as well as Curtis Grooms, an undergraduate student in the Art Department at Queens University of Charlotte for designing the book cover.

The authors are also thankful to the current and former editorial staff at Palgrave Macmillan, especially Farideh Koohi-Kamali, the editorial director for the academic program; Kristy Lilas, production associate; Robyn Curtis, editorial assistant, and her predecessors Asa Johnson and Toby Wahl, for their continuous assistance and valuable editorial advise.

Finally, both authors would like to express their gratitude and appreciation to their families for their unconditional love and support.

Introduction

There are numerous Islamic websites that have had a great impact on mainstream Islamic discourses in recent years. Some of these sites were launched by authoritative religious clerics as virtual extensions of conventional Islamic institutions, while others are simply attempts by ordinary individuals, with no formal religious education or training, to create an online public space for discourse about Islam. The current trends in online Islamic websites pose several pressing and foundational questions: What are the general patterns and trends of these sites' discourses? Have these sites weakened or consolidated the control of the mainstream Islamic establishment over the production and distribution of religious information? Can these sites provide a platform for alternative voices, which can diverge from, or even challenge, the traditional authority of the *'ulama* (religious scholars)? Can they also provide a forum for resistant voices that can challenge sources of internal political authority, such as governments in the Muslim world, as well as forces of external hegemony and domination? How far do these sites act as a platform for the display of collective identities within the realm of the "virtual *umma*" (Islamic community) in the digital age? How far can they also provide a forum for divergent identities to freely express themselves? Do these sites play a divisive or an integrative role, or both, between different Muslim identities, on one hand, and Muslim versus non-Muslim identities, on the other hand? What types and levels of identity (re)construction and resistance(s) manifest themselves through these sites? How do these sites contribute to the creation of an Islamic public sphere(s)?

This book will attempt to address these questions, which deserve further investigation in the academic literature, through analyzing the discourses and deliberations in the discussion forums of three of the most popular Islamic websites. In doing so, it will explore the potential impact of the new Islamic virtual public sphere, and the reconfiguration of the virtual *umma* online, on the creation of multiple identities and resistances, which manifest themselves through various Islamic sites, producing varying degrees of consensus, divergence, and negotiation in multiple contexts and across different discourses.

In other words, one of the main objectives of this book is to test the degree to which "the Internet may be bringing a degree of virtual cohesion to the *ummah*, giving members of the world-wide Islamic population some easily accessible common ground despite the many differences within this global community."[1] This is particularly important since the extent to which Islam "may prove to be a transcending unifying factor is not known"[2] and the degree to which "there might be an as yet unformed cohesion within the *ummah* that new media can galvanize"[3] is still unexplored. In exploring this relatively new terrain, however, it is wise to bear in mind that "the Internet as a unifying tool does not require uniformity. Members of dispersed groups can tie themselves tightly or loosely, as they choose, to a central cultural identity. The Internet connects on its users' terms."[4]

Therefore, this book attempts to examine the different ways through which members of the Muslim *umma* are capable of creating, intersecting, overlapping, or clashing identity positions and subjectivities around various issues and discourses in cyberspace today. This is especially significant taking into account the fact that the plethora of Islamic websites available today constitutes a virtual community that is similar to "a bustling marketplace [*souq*] in which diverse 'goods'—in the form of ideas and concepts about Islam and Muslims—are exchanged, bought and sold."[5] It is this online marketplace that "can give rise, even inadvertently, to new formulations and critical perspectives on Islam and the status of religious knowledge."[6] Today, many Muslims, especially those who seldom have access to formal information from conventional Islamic institutions, utilize various newsgroups, e-mail discussion lists (listservs), and live discussion forums to solicit information about mainstream Islamic discourse on different issues. "Instead of having to go down to the mosque in order to elicit the advice of the local *mullah* [revered religious figure], Muslims can now receive [traditionally] 'authoritative' religious pronouncements via the various e-mail *fatwa* [religious edict] services."[7] It is in this milieu that mainstream and alternative interpretations of Islamic doctrine and scripture find their competing voices in the world of cyberspace.

Some scholars argue that the ability of the Islamic community online to give instant access to Islamic teachings and thoughts has accelerated the information delivery of major issues, such as interpretations of the Qur'an, and has created new discourses where the power of the traditional sources of religious authority could be decentralized and contested by the general public.[8] "The proliferation of actors able to assert a public role [through Islamic websites] leads to a fragmentation of authority, and it increases the numbers of persons involved in creating and sustaining a religious-civil public sphere."[9]

But there are dangers associated with the Islamic environment online or as Bunt (2000) calls it the "digital *umma*" (Islamic community in cyberspace).[10] Due to the fact that many of the Islamic websites are anonymous, "one can never be sure whether the 'authoritative' advice received via these services is coming from a classically trained religious scholar or an electrical engineer moonlighting as an amateur *'alim* [religious scholar]."[11]

The above-mentioned issues have been marginally investigated in the published literature, so far. In fact, the research conducted by the authors showed that the work done to date on Islamic websites is quite limited in scope and rarely analyzes the content of these sites or the discourses on Islamic discussion boards online. This can be contextualized within the relative shortage in studies of new media, including the Internet, so far, since as Dow and Condit (2005) rightly observe "There is little work on the internet... although it is certainly the most influential technological development in media of the late 20th century, and it has dramatic implications."[12]

In this book, we attempt to fill that void, theoretically as well as empirically, through investigating the extent to which the current Islamic Internet sites have provided a venue for Muslims to freely engage in vibrant deliberations and constructive discussions among themselves, as well as with Others, that is, non-Muslims, about issues related to their religion, in particular and various political, economic, and social issues, in general. Here, it is important to highlight that the introduction of the Internet and "the birth of Arab satellite channels signified the start of a new era of self-definition and self-representation for Arabs and Muslims."[13] Therefore, we are keen to highlight the capacity of online Islamic sites to serve as platforms for "self-definition" and "self-representation" on three different levels, namely, individual, communal, and global levels, since the Internet offers the opportunity for "the emergence of new and intersecting forms of local, global, regional, and religious affiliations that transcend national identity."[14]

The previous point clearly explains our decision to keep our analysis specifically focused on the discussion forums in these Islamic websites. Although we provide the reader with a succinct background about the various websites under study, their similarities and differences, as well as their various sections and contents, we decided to focus on the discussion forums in these sites. We believe that these forums provide an ideal platform for the emergence of contesting, or even conflicting, views, identity positions, and resistance mechanisms, as well as competing deliberations between various participants.

The importance of painting this rich, deep, and comprehensive picture of diverse Muslim identities, with such a broad brush, is of utmost importance in light of the international developments and tensions in the post 9–11 era, especially the ongoing discourse of clash of civilizations, the war on terror, and the war in Iraq, which have all had a profound impact on the (mis)perceptions of Islam and Muslims. Therefore, although the distorted images of Arabs and Muslims in the west have existed and have been studied for a long time:

> the new international events and developments that took place in recent years, starting with the September 11 attack and ending with the current troubled conditions in postwar Iraq, the violence in the occupied Palestinian territories, and the war on Lebanon, necessitate (re)addressing and (re)visiting this issue.[15]

The significance of this point stems from the fact that "After September 11, Arab and Muslim identities became politicized through the ascribed interrelationship between Islam, Arab identity, and terrorism."[16] As a result, most Muslims now find themselves (mis)perceived, at best, as an isolated and excluded minority of "anti-western fanatics," who resist integration, or even interaction, with other cultures and faiths, or, at worse, as a group of "terrorists," who can violently attack Others and threaten their safety and security. This, in turn, pushed many Muslims to adopt one of the following three positions in dealing with "non-Muslims": to *inform* other people in the hope of increasing their awareness and correcting their (mis)perceptions about the essence of their identity and the true nature of their religion, or to *explain*, and even *justify*, to others *why* they are Muslims, and *what* it means to be a Muslim, or to *defend* themselves and their religion against unfounded attacks and accusations. This could be explained in light of the fact that "after September 11 ... Muslims made their identity more salient, mainly because they felt the need to educate people about Islam but also to justify being Muslim."[17] These themes will be given further in-depth analysis and exploration later in this book.

Interestingly, the post 9–11 era also had its implications on the development of academic literature dealing with the formation and expression of Arab and Muslim identity, which could be divided into two main discipline areas, namely "terrorism studies" and "communication studies," whose "approaches to issues of identity, deliberative democracy, civil society, and media serve different aims."[18] On one hand, "the terrorism studies literature advances policy and strategy development, supports information analysis, and improves operational capability,"[19] while on the other hand, "Work within the communication discipline strengthens civic engagement, promotes capacities of social agency, and bolsters community resilience."[20]

Analyzed within this context, this book falls under the category of "communication studies," since it provides an in-depth analysis of the complex processes through which meaning(s) could be individually and collectively produced, shared, contested, negated, and negotiated through different discursive frameworks, and how they contribute, in turn, to the equally complex processes of identity construction and manifestations of resistance(s). Through providing such a thorough and deep analysis of these overlapping, complex processes of meaning production, identity (re)construction, and manifestations of resistance(s) in different forms and on different levels, this book challenges the previously discussed stereotypical negativism and reductionism, which clouded and diminished the multiple realities of Muslims today by projecting negative and distorted images painted with the single brush of fanaticism and/or terrorism.

In fact, we argue that acknowledging the diverse and multifaceted social, political, cultural, ideological, and gendered Muslim identities, which reveal themselves throughout this book, has special value and significance "in the current climate of tension between Arabs and non-Arabs as well as Muslims and non-Muslims as evidenced, for example, in the global discourse on terrorism or the ongoing conflicts in Iraq and Palestine."[21]

This last point clearly explains and justifies our decision to focus our analysis and investigation on the discussion forums of moderate, mainstream Islamic websites, which focus mainly on providing a platform for argumentation, debate, and exchange of ideas between the various participants around issues of common concern, as well as spreading knowledge and awareness of the Islamic faith, since the analysis of such sites can provide the reader with a more comprehensive and well-rounded view of the multiplicities, complexities, and diversities exhibited by Muslim identities today, rather than focusing on the so-called Jihadi or extremist websites, which would be better analyzed within the domain of "terrorism studies."

The significance of analyzing these mainstream Islamic websites emanates from the fact that most of these websites' audiences are young Muslims, whose lives are largely shaped by new media, particularly the Internet. This implies that the ongoing discourses in many of these sites could have a large impact on shaping the subjectivities and identities of current and future Muslim generations. Based on these facts, this book could be regarded as an invaluable source for analyzing and forecasting contemporary and future currents of Islamic thought.

The sensitivities and complexities involved in accomplishing this challenging task require us to shed some light on our own personal and professional backgrounds, and, therefore, hopefully help the reader to gain a better understanding of the multiple factors that contributed to the construction of our own identities and subjectivities, as authors. Both of us are Arab-Muslim, western-educated, scholars, who were born and raised in Egypt, but who have been exposed to western culture through receiving western education throughout our lives, as well as through our frequent travels, and the fact that we are both currently residing in the

United States and occupying academic positions in major American institutions of higher education. Therefore, we believe that our rich intercultural experience, and the fact that we have one foot in each world, best enables us to grasp the nuances and intricacies of the multiple identities, which emerged through the discussion forums under study in this book, particularly the competing Muslim and/or Arab identities, on one hand, and the non-Muslim and/or western identities, on the other hand. Furthermore, we believe that our own hybrid, diasporic identities provide us with the necessary insights to deeply analyze the complexity of the dynamics and interactions, as well as the demarcations and overlaps, of multiple identities within the contexts of transnationalism, globalization, and "deterritorialization (the severing of the relationship between a religion or culture and a defined territory or society)."[22]

However, we were also fully aware of the necessity of separating our own ethnic, religious, and cultural identities from our academic role as analysts and investigators, through striving to maintain a high degree of academic integrity, objectivity, and balance in approaching the sensitive and controversial issues, which we didn't shy away from tackling in this book, and through avoiding any manifestation of religious and/or political advocacy or affiliation. In other words, we tried to maximize the benefit of utilizing our own identities and backgrounds in analyzing the discourses explored in this book, without allowing our subjectivities to obfuscate our judgment and analysis of these discourses.

Moreover, the complexity and interrelatedness of the issues tackled in this book also require drawing upon an equally complex set of theoretical frameworks, encompassing both identity and public sphere theories, to contextualize and interpret the findings. This mainly stems from the fact that

> The questions of *where* one forms, expresses, and negotiates identity, and how one *represents oneself* to the world, link inextricably the identity-subjectivity and public sphere moves of contemporary rhetorical theory...the search for community by those who name themselves Arab, Muslim, and Islamic offers a challenging and complex landscape for theorists and rhetorical critics employing identity and public sphere theory.[23]

Therefore, the book draws upon Habermas' theory of the public sphere, which calls for a "rational-critical" communication, outside the institutional boundaries of the authority, as "the ideal standard of modernity."[24] Habermas (1989) defined the public sphere as "a sphere between civil society and the state, in which critical public discussion of matters of general interest" took place.[25] While there has been much succinct and valid criticism of the Habermasian public sphere, both in its application to modern society and its appropriation to explain the role and impact of the Internet, it remains a compelling situational approach for the study of divergent views online. No longer viewed as an avant-garde theoretical conception, we have decided to incorporate it to the study of Islamic websites because we believe it can provide a useful theoretical framework for the conceptualization of mainstream discourses in Islam. Therefore, one of the key notions under investigation in this book is whether the expansive *umma* today gave birth to general tendencies for consensus within Islamic communities, which can provide the level of mainstreaming required for a Habermasian public sphere.

In analyzing the content of various Islamic discussion forums, we compared the discourses in these forums with a set of requirements of the public sphere developed by Habermas. We used these requirements to investigate whether "the public sphere of rational-critical discourse [is] extended"[26] through these Islamic websites and to have a measure of the extent to which varying discourses are facilitated through these websites' discussion boards.

However, despite the appropriateness of the public sphere notion, as it is theoretically formulated by Habermas, as a general theoretical framework for this study, we are, nonetheless, fully aware of some of its limitations, which do not allow its full applicability across all the analyzed Islamic forums and discourses in this book, as will be fully explained later.

In exploring the above-mentioned notions, we are also keen to compare some of the opinion formation and consensus building mechanisms within an Islamic context, such as *ijtihad* (independent interpretation), *shura* (consultation), and *ijma'* (consensus), which will be fully explained in chapters 1 and 3, to the concepts of communicative action, rational-critical debate, and consensus within the Habermasian public sphere context, in terms of examining the applicability of these concepts to the discourses in the discussion forums under study.

The significance of comparing these parallel concepts within both the Islamic and the Habermasian contexts lies in the fact that "there would appear to be some degree of discursive overlap between a new *ummah* consciousness and recent thinking in western critical theory. The notion of dialogue and some form of 'communicative action' (informed by tradition) within a 'public sphere' seem to be intrinsic to both."[27]

The book also incorporates in its theoretical framework the requirements of the public sphere discourse, which were outlined by Lincoln Dahlberg (2001)[28] as follows:

1. "Exchange and critique of reasoned moral-practical validity claims"[29] (i.e., participants are engaged in reciprocal assessment of "normative positions" that are provided reasonably, not assertively);
2. "reflexivity"[30] (i.e., participants reevaluate their cultural norms as well as the values of the society at large);
3. "ideal role taking"[31] (i.e., participants are committed to a constructive dialogue where differences in opinion are respectfully considered and attended to);

4. "sincerity"[32] (i.e., each participant would "make a sincere effort to provide all information relevant" to the issues being discussed);
5. "discursive inclusion and equality"[33] (i.e., each participant is "equally entitled to introduce and question any assertion." This inclusion maybe limited by "inequalities from outside of discourse," such as access restrictions; or by "inequalities within discourse," such as a discourse being dominated by one voice).
6. "autonomy from state and economic power"[34] (i.e., discourse is a reflection of the "concerns of publicly oriented citizens" rather than "money or administrative power").

Here again, while including the above-mentioned requirements outlined by Dahlberg in our analytical framework in this book, we are equally keen to highlight the various factors that may limit their full applicability in the context of the Islamic discussion forums under study.

However, it is important to mention that in tackling the notion of the public sphere in this book we view it as a complex, multidimensional, and dynamic concept, which is highly shaped by the "active arguments before an audience about issues of shared concern."[35] This, in turn, implies the potential formation of numerous public spheres around different issues of argumentation, providing a platform for varying degrees of agreement or disagreement, disputes, controversies, and resolutions, to be expressed among different publics, who exhibit interests, fears, concerns, or problems, related to these issues. Most importantly, we are sensitive to the fact that "The expansion of analysis from the inner workings of one sphere to its relationship with other publics (as a counter-public) presupposes a perspective toward either constitutive negotiation and social interchange, or domination and resistance."[36] Thus, we are keen to analyze how this complex process can, in turn, lead to the creation and proliferation of a number of "mini-public spheres"[37] manifesting multiple identity positions and subjectivities.

Therefore, to best analyze this phenomenon, the book also incorporates theoretical insights into the process of identity (re)construction, among the participants in these Islamic discussion forums, on different levels and through different stages of identity formation and expression "as an individual within a familial or kinship group; a citizen in relationship to a nation-state; and a member of a global community of believers."[38] In analyzing these multifaceted, multilayered, dynamic identities, we argue that their development and movement from one stage of identity construction to the next, as well as between these different identity positions, is a "cyclical," rather than a linear, process:

The progression from one stage to the next is non-linear. Consider instead a sphere with the individual at the center. The sphere possesses elasticity.

It expands and contracts through identity negotiation and discourse, with varying degrees of openness and vulnerability to internal forces (e.g., the search for security and belongingness) and external circumstances (e.g., a conflict that forces an identity choice, or conflicting sources of civil and religious authority).[39]

Therefore, in exploring the manifestations and contestations of these diverse identities, which are defined by gender, marital status, religious affiliation, cultural experience, political orientation, as well as varying degrees of localization or globalization, we are keen to highlight their demarcations and overlaps on the identity map, bearing in mind that "identity expression is not a linear act of encoding and decoding but a complex process in which avowed and ascribed meanings are expressed, evaluated, affirmed, and refuted between interactants."[40]

The importance of incorporating the dimension of identity construction in our analytical and theoretical framework in this book lies in the fact that "Muslim communities are...embroiled today in complex debates about the very nature and boundaries of their religion. What does Islam mean to Muslims living in the west? From whom can reliable knowledge about Islam be gained? How can one differentiate reliably between 'good' and 'bad' interpretations of Islam?"[41] When such important questions are addressed in the modern era of globalization they urge Muslims to "come face to face with the myriad shapes and colors of global Islam, forcing their religion to hold a mirror up to its own diversity."[42] Such experiences "often play an important role in processes of identity formation, prompting Muslims to relativise and compare their self-understandings of Islam."[43]

To better understand the complex interaction between the politics of identity construction, on one hand, and public sphere formation, on the other hand, we adopt the view undertaken by scholars, such as Marc Lynch (2006), who, in his analysis of the emergence of the 'new' Arab public sphere, has highlighted the role of modern means of communication, including new technologies, such as the Internet, in fueling and accelerating the formation of a new and vibrant public sphere, but has maintained that the ongoing arguments, debates, and discussions between the participants within this sphere, who exhibit multiple identity positions, are the driving force behind its formation.[44] Commenting on this line of analysis, Walker (2007) draws our attention to the fact that "Lynch puts technology in the category of centrifugal force, amplifying but not creating the public sphere. Identity is the centripetal or unifying force."[45] Analyzed within this context, it could be said that "Identity-subjectivity...is aligning itself with a more charitable view of the public sphere."[46] It is indeed this view of the interrelationship and overlap between identity-subjectivity and the politics of the public sphere that forms one of the main pillars of our theoretical framework in this book.

Another analytical and theoretical concern in this book is the degree to which these overlapping, contesting, or competing identities gave birth to a wide array of resistances on different levels and in different forms, starting from the intimate, familial level of resisting dominant male figures in the household, to the global, politicized level of resisting foreign hegemony and domination.

We argue that these multifaceted resistances are clear manifestations of the complex process of multiple identities' construction, which is, in turn, a direct outcome of the "renegotiation between the personal and the collective approach to religious practice."[47] This phenomenon of renegotiating personal and collective identities is made possible today due to "The development of deterritorialized cultures and communities based on categories of race, gender, religion, and even lifestyle"[48] and it clearly highlights the importance of "developments on the Internet, as they are significant gauges of individual Muslim self-perception and specific group expression,"[49] as will be fully explored in this book.

The book also explores the process through which these emerging "media-aided and issue-driven"[50] multiple identities actually constitute what Henry Jenkins (2006) describes as "knowledge communities," since "the age of media convergence enables communal, rather than individualistic, modes of reception"[51] and, therefore, "Online forums offer an opportunity for participants to share their knowledge and opinions."[52] Therefore, in line with Jenkins' (2006) analysis and observations, one of the aims of this book is to further explore how the process of "media convergence" today is equally paralleled by a process of "cultural convergence," which enables media "consumers" to become "producers," through exercising more control over the media content that is being created and exchanged freely, especially in cyberspace, and through modern forms of communication. In doing so, the book also contemplates the notion of how these "knowledge communities," in turn, create the phenomenon of "collective intelligence," which refers to "the ability of virtual communities to leverage the combined expertise of their members"[53] through employing "the ethics of shared problem-solving in an online community."[54]

Three Islamic Websites: General Background

On the empirical level, this book relies on a qualitative textual analysis of the discussion boards of three of the most popular Islamic websites (in terms of the number of visitors or the amount of traffic) to examine the current discourses and the ongoing deliberations on these sites' boards.

The three websites are www.islamonline.net; www.islamway.com; and www.amrkhaled.net.

Our selection of these sites was based on the ranking of Alexa.com, a website traffic ranking service that provides the ranking of any site based on the total number of visits over a three-month period. The sites mentioned above had rankings ranging between 500 and 1,500, over the three-month period that preceded the writing of this book, which are very high by religious websites' standards, or by any website's standards for that matter. These high rankings indicate that these three websites are considered among the most significant platforms in terms of framing the ongoing discussions and deliberations about Islam in cyberspace and, hence, are most appropriate for the purpose of this study.

In our analysis of these three websites, we looked at both the Arabic and the English discussion boards of islamonline.net and islamway.com, and the Arabic discussion board of amrkhaled.net, since this website does not have a discussion board in English. Here, it is worth mentioning the fact that both authors are bilingual, since their native language is Arabic, and have also fully mastered the English language, helped them to analyze the content of the discussion forums in both languages.

We provide below basic background information about these three websites, followed by a discussion highlighting their similarities and differences.

www.islamonline.net

This site, which was established in 1997, has been one of the leading Muslim sites on the Internet, and among the most popular, professionally produced religious websites worldwide.[55] The mission of islamonline.net, as displayed on the site's webpage, is "To create a unique, global Islamic site...that provides services to Muslims and non-Muslims in several languages; to become a reference for everything that deals with Islam, its sciences, civilization and nation; and to have credibility in content, distinction in design, and a sharp and balanced vision of humanity and current events."[56] The site aims at promoting "a unified and lively Islam that keeps up with modern times in all areas...[under the] motto...: credibility and distinction."[57]

Islamonline was created thanks to the encouragement and inspiration of Sheikh Yusuf Al-Qaradawi, who heads a committee of prominent Muslim scholars that oversees the operations of Islamonline. This committee, which includes experts from various fields, such as political science, economics, arts, and media, makes sure "that nothing on this site violates the fixed principles of Islamic law (*Shar'ia*)."[58]

The most prominent Muslim preacher, who belongs to the Sunni sect of Islam, Al-Qaradawi was born in Egypt, but currently resides in Qatar.

Al-Qaradawi's popularity among Muslims has skyrocketed over the past ten years thanks to his regular appearance in a weekly show titled "Al-Shari'a wal Hayat" (Islamic Canonical Law and Life), which is broadcast on Al-Jazeera satellite channel.[59] Al-Qaradawi's fame and credibility spilled over to Islamonline. The fact that this website has been associated with his name and established under his guidance secured its huge popularity among Muslims everywhere, "since they perceive it as affiliated with a renowned figure of indisputable authority."[60]

Al-Qaradawi, who is an Al-Azhar-educated ʿalim is widely regarded as moderate in the Islamic world.[61] He is "classically-trained but positively engaged with the world and with middle-class concerns, styles and outlooks."[62] The Sheikh belongs to a school of thought known as *Al-Wassatiya* (moderation), which advocates modern and flexible "interpretations of Islam that...incorporate new social developments."[63] Therefore, "he sees no contradiction in using modern technology— indeed he regards it as his duty—to spread his *fatwas*."[64] Al-Qaradawi believes that the ʿulama have a responsibility to educate the lay Muslims about their religion, using various means, such as the Internet. "Otherwise, [he says], Muslim societies and Islam run the risk of being hijacked by extremists."[65] Another reason behind his passionate support of the Internet is his belief that "its transnational nature protects the online Islamic community from pernicious government meddling."[66] Al-Qaradawi's condemnation of the September 11 attacks against the United States has been disseminated to millions of Internet surfers through various Islamic websites and translated to several languages.[67]

Al-Qaradawi authored more than ninety books, most of which address the issue of awakening the Muslim *umma* and trying to solve its current social and political problems with the guidance and advice of the ʿulama. According to Al-Qaradawi, "The ʿulama...are not a priesthood but simply people who have had the privilege of studying Islam and who have a duty to [publicly] share their understanding with laymen, and with each other. Islam...is only realized in critical and public discussion. Freedom of thought and speech is thus a prerequisite of true Islam."[68]

Al-Qaradawi's belief in the role of the new media in the awakening of the *umma*[69] was one of the reasons that made him initiate the idea of launching Islamonline website. Among Islamonline's main objectives, as outlined in an e-mail that was sent to us by the site's webmaster, are to enhance the Muslim *umma*'s openness to the world through facilitating acquaintance between Muslims and non-Muslims in a globalized era; awaken and inspire the Muslim *umma* by increasing information about Islam and providing a forum for dialogue and discussion of various issues and concerns; and bridging various kinds of gaps between theory and practice, the opinion and the counteropinion, the present and the desired future, and the self and the other.[70]

According to the webmaster, who preferred to remain anonymous, Islamonline tries to address all people from all age groups, but it focuses on the Muslim youth (ranging between the ages of 15 and 40) since young people are "more enthusiastic and more capable of initiating change [in the *umma*]."[71] The webmaster also noted that Islamonline's officials often print selected sections of the site to reach out to audiences who have no access to the Internet. This takes place in various Arab and Islamic countries, such as Jordan and Yemen.[72]

In addition to the basic religious offerings that are provided through Islamonline, as mentioned above, the site provides a continuously updated news section of interest to Muslims, as well as pragmatic information that is needed for the everyday life of a contemporary Muslim, such as offering advice on the religious education of children, interfaith marriages, and social relations within an Islamic context.[73] Many of the issues addressed through Islamonline revolve around women's issues, such as raising children and the wife's relationship with her in-laws.[74] The material presented through Islamonline is "modern in expression, orthodox in theology, and middle-of-the-road in interpretation."[75] It can be argued that the Islamonline site provides material that is a hybrid between preservation and reform in Islam.

www.amrkhaled.net

This site was launched in 2002 by Amr Khaled, an Egyptian-born accountant-turned preacher in his early forties, who has developed a huge popularity, particularly among the 15–35 age group across the Arab world.[76] Considered a lay reformer, and one of the "new religious intellectuals,"[77] Khaled openly admits that he is not qualified to provide *fatwa* since he is not a *'alim*, and he does not have the classical religious credentials, particularly the *ijaza* (teacher's authorization or license), that would qualify him to do so.[78] Therefore, "Khaled does not preach, lecture, or offer religious opinions according to the norms of Islamic scholarly discourse."[79] Rather, he has been utilizing the new media to reach out to young Arab-Muslims from the upper and middle classes, who have often felt alienated by the traditional *'ulama*. Those young people found in Khaled what they have been looking for in a preacher: someone who looks like them, dresses like them, and addresses them in a language and a manner to which they can relate. "Gone are the turban and cloak of the *'alim*, replaced instead by a young, clean-shaven man attired in designer Western suits."[80]

Through his website and his regular shows on Saudi-owned satellite channels *Iqra'* and Arab Radio and Television (ART), Khaled was able to enhance the young Arab youths' confidence in their abilities to improve their lives and achieve their goals in life through a balance between piety and hard work. Khaled's flagship show "Life-Makers" has embodied his message to the Arab and Muslim youth, which is that "True change [can come] into existence, not by restricting thought and forcing direction, but by accepting accountability and believing in one's ability."[81] Therefore, his message is one of "hope, prosperity, and the possibility of gaining God's love, favor, and forgiveness."[82] He emphasizes a type of piety, which does not simply stress ritual obligation, but incorporates personal success and affluence.[83] This approach highlights the "essentially 'post-Islamist' character of Amr Khaled's approach,"[84] which does not challenge the political order or its keepers, rather, it attempts to promote gradual transformation through social change and collective action.

Although Khaled's message does not have a direct political connotation, he was banned from public preaching by the Egyptian authorities in 2002; the ban forced him to leave Egypt and launch his website.[85] Currently, Khaled resides in London, where he is working on his doctorate degree in Islamic studies. He is invited to many countries inside and outside the Arab world to give lectures to young Muslims.

Khaled has been using his website to reach hundreds of thousands of young Arabs and Muslims. The change that he has been urging the young Arab and Muslim youth to undertake "is a change of personal attitude and belief, and it is first acted out virtually, on the [discussion] forums, where everyone can have a voice and everyone is empowered to speak."[86] Khaled's popularity earned him a spot in *Time Magazine*'s top 100 most influential figures in 2007.[87] He has also been ranked among the world's top ten public intellectuals in an online voting process organized and sponsored by *Foreign Policy* magazine in 2008.[88]

In a personal interview with Ne'mat Awadallah, the webmaster for amrkhaled.net, in Egypt in spring 2007, she mentioned that the issues debated on the website's discussion board are not just religious, but also historical, social, and cultural. Awadallah heads a committee that revises entries on the discussion board to make sure that there is no profanity or material that is offensive to religion, political parties, or public figures. She noted that Amr Khaled is not part of this committee, and his opinion regarding the site's content is taken into consideration, but it is not mandatory. According to Awadallah, Khaled sets the site's general direction and philosophy, but he does not micromanage the content. Awadallah also noted that the site's policy is to encourage the usage of classical Arabic and reduce colloquial Arabic and slang in the material posted on the website. The site's future goal, according to Awadallah, is to be ranked the number one website worldwide.[89]

www.islamway.com

Islamway.com enjoys a very high ranking, ranging between 500 and 800, in terms of the average number of visitors over a 3-month period as reported by Alexa.com. However, we could not find any background information on this site beyond what is included in its homepage. Moreover our attempts to interview the site's webmaster have been unsuccessful. We sent several e-mail messages, including our questions about the site, but received no answer.

According to the site's webpage, the site follows "the traces of...*al-salaf as saleh* (Righteous Predecessors), [and it]...aims at [providing a] sound and clearer perception of Islam."[90] It is also noted on the webpage that islamway.com, which addresses all Muslims, has no affiliation to any "political party, group or any other governmental guardianship."[91]

The fact that this particular website is not affiliated with a well-known scholar or a renowned figure, such as Al-Qaradawi or Amr Khaled, means that it does not enjoy the high degree of "source credibility," which the affiliation with such figures brings to islamonline.net and amrkhaled.net respectively, since both these sites derive most of their popularity, credibility, and high online traffic from their association with these prominent figures.

SIMILARITIES AND DIFFERENCES AMONG THE WEBSITES

The main similarity between the three websites under study is the fact that they are all mainstream Islamic websites that focus on the spreading of *da'wa* (propagation of faith), which is also defined as "God's invitation, addressed to humankind and transmitted through the prophets, to live in accord with God's will,"[92] as one of their main objectives. To fulfill this objective, they offer a variety of services, such as providing *fatwa*, audio and video lectures by prominent Muslim figures, religious counseling and advice, articles about Islam, religious sermons, and audio Qur'anic recitations, which has special importance due to the fact that "The Qur'an in cyberspace also represents a continuity of the obligation of *da'wa* or propagation of Islam"[93] and that "The Internet now forms part of this process, with the Qur'an a central feature of Islamic computer landscapes."[94] In achieving their main objective of spreading *da'wa* the three websites appeal to varied audiences including "the curious non-Muslim, existing Muslims, and/or Muslims from outside the specific traditional and interpretative practices endorsed by a website's authors."[95]

Another area of similarity between these three websites is the fact that they are all Sunni websites, which is particularly important due to some of the distinctions between the Sunni and Shi'ite Islamic sects, which are, in turn, reflected in the nature and content of their respective websites. For example, unlike Shi'ite websites that are mostly dominated by a handful of leading religious figures, who enjoy the supreme and sacred power to issue religious edicts or rulings that become binding to their followers,[96] in most Sunni websites there are usually multiple, but influential, religious voices, which results in a greater dislocation and fragmentation of religious authority.[97] This last point was certainly found to be true in the analyzed websites in this book, which exhibited a high degree of fragmentation of the *'ulama's* traditional authority, and even a replacement of their role by so-called "new religious intellectuals,"[98] as will be fully explained in the rest of this book.

In addition, all three websites adopt a dialogical approach that allows for civil engagement in debates and deliberations revolving around issues of common concern to contemporary Muslims living in Muslim-majority societies, as well as in the diaspora. The three sites also provide discussion boards (*montadayat* or *sáhát lel hewar*), which serve as platforms for their visitors to express their views on various Islamic issues and to participate in lively deliberations online. We decided to focus our analysis on these discussion boards since they can exemplify the deliberative skills of participants in communicative action and the rational-critical debates that form the gist of the public sphere concept as envisioned by Habermas and Dahlberg, as well as enabling the examination of the notions of *ijma*, *shura*, and *ijtihad*, as defined in an Islamic context.

As for the differences between the three websites under study, it is worth mentioning that while islamonline.net has only Arabic and English versions, islamway.com and amrkhaled.net are multilingual, providing their services in languages such as Arabic, English, French, German, Turkish, and Spanish among other languages.

Furthermore, although the three websites had access to rules and regulations banning certain behaviors, such as using strong language and profanities, naming and offending public figures, attacking other participants' values and beliefs, as well as insulting governments, it is clear that the degree of the participants' adherence to these rules, as well as the moderators' ability to enforce these regulations on the participants, varied widely across a broad spectrum.

On one end of the spectrum, islamway.com English forum exhibited maximum regulation and control, due to the highly homogenous nature of its participants, who were all Muslim women,[99] most of whom were either new converts to Islam or living in the west. Therefore, they exercised a remarkable degree of self-censorship and self-regulation, due to their high sense of uniformity and collectiveness, based on the unity of gender, faith, and experience. On the other end of the spectrum, islamonline.net English forum exhibited the least degree of regulation, due to the highly heterogeneous nature of its participants, who represented both genders, as well as different religious, ethnic, and cultural identities, and due to the absence of the moderators' role in regulating the ongoing discussions and debates in this forum.

Therefore, it can be concluded that there were clear differences between the three forums in terms of the degree of strictness or flexibility in enforcing access to rules and regulations, the degree of supervision and regulation exercised by the moderators, the dominant tone and style, as well as the characteristics of the participants. Not surprisingly, the audience composition in terms of gender, ethnicity, and religious affiliation affected the nature of the forums, in terms of tone, style, focus, and content, as well as the degree of regulation, as will be fully explained in chapters 4 and 5. In addition, there were differences based on the degree of "source credibility," or lack thereof, in each website, as well as the degree of "agenda-setting," which can be exercised by a prominent figure, such as Amr Khaled, through designing the general framework of the website and prioritizing the key issues to be discussed in its forum.

The wide array of differences between these websites clearly indicates that "Cyber Islamic Environments represent one barometer of diversity within the Islamic spectrum,"[100] a theme that will be further investigated and developed in the rest of this book.

The next section discusses how we used the method of textual analysis in this book, how we selected postings from the discussion boards, as well as our time frame for conducting the study.

Textual Analysis

We used textual analysis in this book to study the dimensions of the Islamic virtual public sphere, as represented in the deliberations taking place on the discussion boards of the three Islamic websites mentioned above. Our analysis of the discussion forums stretched over a period of six months: from February to July 2008. Textual analysis, which can also be referred to as "interdiscursive analysis," entails "seeing texts in terms of the different discourses, genres and styles they draw upon and articulate together."[101] Conducting textual analysis requires studying the actual text and interpreting the meaning(s) constructed through that text. Meanings in a text can either be explicit (i.e., overtly stated) or implicit (i.e., assumed or implied).[102]

According to Norman Fairclough (2003), interpretation of meanings in a text is

> Partly a matter of understanding...what words or sentences or longer stretches of text mean, understanding what speakers or writers mean (the latter involving problematic attributions of intentions). But it is also partly a matter of judgment and evaluation: for instance, judging whether someone is saying something sincerely or not, or seriously or not; judging whether the claims that are explicitly or implicitly made are true; judging

whether people are speaking or writing in ways which accord with the social, institutional etc. relations within which the event takes place, or perhaps in ways which mystify those relations.[103]

Context plays a critical role in textual analysis in the sense that the meanings in a text have to be interpreted with the cultural context in mind.[104] Since various cultures have different interpretive approaches, a particular text does not necessarily have to produce one correct interpretation. In other words, there can be multiple interpretations of the same text, and these interpretations may not be the same as the one intended by the creator of that text.[105] This post-structuralism or cultural relativism, which is the basic characteristic of textual analysis, means that "different ways of thinking about the world might be equally valid."[106]

Furthermore, as Acosta-Alzuru and Kreshel (2002) rightly point out, "Textual analysis recognizes that meaning is a social production. The method is different from content analysis. Whereas the latter is interested in the recurrence of patterns in the manifest content, the goal of textual analysis is the study of the latent content of texts through a study of their signification. The object of a textual analysis is not the meanings of the texts, but rather the construction of those meanings through the text."[107]

This complex process requires, according to Stuart Hall (1975), three distinctive stages, namely "a long preliminary soak in the text, which allows the analyst to focus on particular issues while preserving the 'big picture'; a close reading of the chosen text and preliminary identification of discursive strategies and themes; and an interpretation of the findings within the larger framework of the study."[108] We are keen to adopt this deep, sensitive, and comprehensive approach in applying textual analysis to analyze the discourses in this book.

The results of our textual analysis of the discourses on the discussion boards of islamonline.net, amrkhaled.net, and islamway.com and our interpretation of their contextual meanings will show the extent to which they facilitate a rational and critical public sphere in the virtual Muslim *umma*, as highlighted in the six requirements or criteria that were derived from Habermas' theories of the public sphere and communicative action and outlined by Lincoln Dahlberg (2001),[109] as well as their compatibility with the Islamic concepts of *shura*, *ijtihad*, and *ijma*.

In conducting this interpretation of the discourses and deliberations on these three websites, we are careful not to detach the analyzed threads in these discussion boards from their overall context, and we are equally careful to give the participants in these discussion boards a true "voice," through using direct quotations from the actual threads in these forums. We are also equally keen not to lose the original meaning of the participants' own words while conducting the translation from Arabic to English.

The value and significance of adopting this approach lies in its ability to highlight "the rhetorical resources of individuals and groups—that is, how they exercise voice and social agency to negotiate relationships and public discourse,"[110] which is one of the main objectives of this book.

However, it is equally important to highlight some of the stylistic and ethical issues, which sometimes influenced our decision to either edit some of the quoted material, or to exclude it altogether. Despite our strong commitment to best reflect the genuine and true "voices" of the participants in the forums under study, there were some cases that necessitated some form of editing, either for the purpose of modifying and improving the phrasing to make it more clear and understandable to the readers, or for the purpose of excluding and avoiding some of the profanities and offensive expressions, which were sometimes exchanged between some of the participants, either to attack and insult one another, or to attack and insult some of the public figures, especially when they were identified by name. This editing process stems from professional and ethical concerns to avoid any form of defamation or poor taste.

It is also important to highlight the fact that we were selective in choosing the analyzed threads from the three websites under study, as well as choosing the most important and meaningful parts of each thread, which best represent the thrust of the main arguments in the thread, the multiple views expressed in it, and the general tone of the discussion. This selectivity was mandatory due to the massive magnitude of the threads on the three websites under study, as well as the length of some of the threads.

The fact that we were faced with this challenge of selectivity highlights the limitations of this study in terms of representation and generalization. We would like to emphasize that the discussed threads in this book provide the reader at best with a "snap shot" or a "flavor" of some of the ongoing debates and deliberations in some Islamic websites today. However, they are not meant to provide a comprehensive overview of all the ongoing debates in all Islamic websites, which is beyond the scope of this book, and, therefore, they cannot be representative of or generalized to all the ongoing discourses in all Islamic websites in cyberspace.

Another equally important issue is our decision to conceal the identities of the posters in these discussion forums. Although many of them do not post with their real names—the majority use "nicknames" online—we felt that it is important to protect the privacy of the posters on these forums, especially since many of them are well known to each other, and many have gained some degree of popularity and recognition through being regular and long-time posters on these forums. Therefore, we decided to replace their posted names with pseudonyms to protect their privacy. In doing so, we were sensitive to the fact that being anonymous is not always the same as being "identity-less"[111] in cyberspace.

CHAPTERS OUTLINE

This book consists of six chapters. The first three chapters are devoted to providing the reader with the necessary theoretical, conceptual, and historical background that is much needed to grasp the essence of the contemporary discourses in Islamic cyberspace. Chapters 4 and 5 are devoted to presenting the results of the textual analysis of the ongoing discourses in the discussion forums in the three Islamic websites under study. Chapter 6 provides an overall summary of the main themes and findings of the book. We provide below a more detailed overview of the content of each chapter.

Chapter 1, "The Public Sphere in an Islamic Context," starts out by providing a brief background of the notion of the public sphere and its critics. The chapter then applies the public sphere notion to the Islamic context through analyzing the dynamics of the complex relationship between political authority and religious authority in the Muslim world, on one hand, as well as exploring the traditional structures of authority in this world, such as the mosque and the 'ulama, on the other hand. In doing so, it provides an in-depth analysis of the factors that led to the fragmentation of traditional religious authority in postmodern Islam and the emergence of "new religious intellectuals."[112] The chapter also discusses how these factors resulted in a reconfiguration of Islamic identity and, therefore, the birth of new Islamic public sphere(s), which led to the emergence of alternative voices within the Islamic arena, and changing the boundaries of who sets the agenda on key Islamic debates and who is entitled to give *fatwa*.

Chapter 2, "Religion in the Virtual Public Sphere: The Case of Islam," sheds light on the limited scholarly literature that analyzes religious websites, with a specific focus on Islamic websites. The chapter also investigates the role of the Internet and new media in creating and maintaining the ideological, ritualistic, and social functions of a traditional religious community, with a special focus on the Islamic community. It also provides a brief background on how Islam was brought to cyberspace. The chapter also touches on the plurality of Muslims' voices online to explain how Islamic websites and online discussion groups have provided new forums for *da'wa* and for participation in communal ritualistic acts that represent new, virtual communities of worship.

In addition, the chapter deals with the Muslim public's trust, or lack thereof, toward the information delivered through Islamic websites. It also provides an outline of debates surrounding the role of new media in contemporary societies, and it addresses the notion of the "digital divide" and the extent to which it impacts accessibility to the Internet in the Muslim world today.

Chapter 3, "Is the *Umma* a Public Sphere?" addresses the concept of the *umma* to examine the applicability of the public sphere criteria to it. The chapter provides an overview of the historical context behind the development of the concept of the *umma* through different phases of Islamic history. In doing so, it explains how the concept of the *umma* evolved and developed over time, and how it is different from the concept of the "nation." Furthermore, it explores how the concept of the *umma* oscillated between the poles of moral unity and political fragmentation, as well as the factors behind each of these complex processes and their significant implications. The chapter also investigates the challenges that are currently confronting the *umma* within the international public sphere, and how these challenges developed and crystallized, due to various political, historical, and social factors. Special attention is paid to the challenges of the emergence of "re-Islamization,"[113] the capacity of the *umma* to accommodate democratization and pluralism, as well as the potential of constructing effective dialogue between the Muslim *umma* and its Others, that is, those who are outsiders to it, especially in the western world.

Chapter 4, "The 'Virtual *Umma*': Collective Identities in Cyberspace," explores how new media, especially the Internet, (re)formulated and (re)defined the concept of the *umma* in cyberspace. Special focus is given to the creation of "collective Muslim identities" around key issues and debates in cyberspace, and how this phenomenon is directly related to the emergence of a virtual *umma* that exemplifies collective Islamic consciousness online. In doing so, the chapter starts by introducing the contemporary currents that gave birth to the concept of the virtual *umma*, as it manifests itself in cyberspace today in the form of a "transnational" or "digital" *umma*, within the international, global sphere. The chapter then provides a theoretical background of the concept of identity, in general, and the concept of collective identity, in particular, and the multiple factors contributing to it.

The rest of this chapter is devoted to a detailed textual analysis of some of the postings in the discussion boards of the Islamic websites under study, in an effort to examine how they reflected collective Muslim identities online. In doing so, the chapter groups the themes in the various threads under two general categories, namely, "religio-political" topics and "religio-social" topics, in an effort to detect the formation of collective Muslim sensibilities around the themes under each of them.

Chapter 5, "Islamic Websites: Divergent Identities in Cyberspace," analyzes how different, or even conflicting, identities emerged through the various discussion boards in the three analyzed websites, whether among different groups of Muslims, such as Sunni versus Shi'ite Muslims, or between Muslims and non-Muslims, as well as around different gender discourses and political discourses.

Unlike chapter 5 that focused on analyzing the aspects of conformity and unity within the boundaries of the Muslim *umma*, this chapter analyzes how diverse online identities can diverge, contrast, or compete with each other, creating different types of resistance(s) on different levels, such as resistance to traditional religious authority, to governments in the Arab and Muslim world, to foreign hegemony and domination, and even to male figures in the family, to mention only some examples.

Before indulging in the detailed textual analysis dealing with the previous points, the chapter provides some theoretical insights related to exploring the concept of identity in the realm of divergence to provide the necessary conceptual contextualization for the analysis of the arguments and debates in the rest of the chapter.

Chapter 6, "Virtual Islamic Discourses: Platforms for Consensus or Sites of Contention?" provides an overview of the analyzed discourses and deliberations in the discussion boards of the three Islamic websites under study, and how and why they provided a platform for displaying different positions of unity, divergence, or negotiation. In doing so, it examines the applicability of the notions of the rational-critical public sphere and communicative action, on one hand, as well as the Islamic concepts of *shura*, *ijtihad*, and *ijma*, on the other hand, to the results of the textual analysis of these online discourses and deliberations.

CHAPTER 1

The Public Sphere in an Islamic Context

The Habermasian public sphere provides the theoretical foundation for our exploration of Islamic online discourse. Since its development in the 1960s, the "public sphere" has elicited several controversial discussions and lively debates, especially among academics, intellectuals, and historians. Despite the fact that it has been criticized for its rather idealistic approach,[1] it continues to be useful—at least in its normative form—in "thinking about how wider social and cultural issues are addressed; and for trying to make sense of how agreement about what is acceptable in a culture is reached."[2] In this chapter, we will provide a brief background of the public sphere concept, which was developed by the contemporary German philosopher Jürgen Habermas, and we will touch on the arguments of its main critics. Theoretical implications of Habermas' work and its evolution inform and enrich our understanding of the functioning of public sphere in multiple contexts, including the Islamic community. We apply the public sphere concept to the Islamic context by investigating how it shapes community acceptance of political and religious authority, with particular attention to the role of the 'ulama (religious scholars) within and in response to the "new Islamic public sphere" emanating from a variety of factors, such as greater access to education and information and communication technologies.[3]

WHAT IS THE PUBLIC SPHERE?

The term "public" was defined by John Dewey (as cited in Salvatore and Eickelman, 2005) as "an institution with recognized common goals and at least an informal leadership...[The public] is organized and made effective by means of representatives who as guardians of custom, as legislators, as executives, judges, etc., care for its special interests by methods intended to regulate the conjoint actions of individuals and groups."[4]

A public has to function in an environment or a sphere. Habermas' analysis of the public sphere, which is based on the Frankfurt School tradition of Critical Theory,[5] envisions an "unrestricted" and "uncoerced" environment "operating on the 'universal' pragmatics of communicative rationality."[6]

In his book *The Structural Transformation of the Public Sphere*, which was published in Germany in 1962 and translated into English in 1989, Habermas referred to the normative notion of the "bourgeois public sphere," which was formed for a relatively brief period in the late seventeenth- and early eighteenth-century Europe, and which comprised a group of "private people [coming] together as a public; they soon claimed the public sphere regulated from above against the public authorities themselves, to engage them in a debate over the general rules governing relations in the basically privatized but publicly relevant sphere of commodity exchange and social labor."[7]

Habermas emphasized the importance of separating the public and the private spheres. "The model of the bourgeois public sphere presupposed strict separation of the public from the private realm in such a way that the public sphere, made up of private people gathered together as a public and articulating the needs of society with the state, was itself considered part of the private realm. To the extent that the public and the private became intermeshed realms, this model became inapplicable."[8] The ideal situation for Habermas "is one where public life—what he calls the 'systems world,' the world of external, bureaucratized machine life—would have no impact on our private lives—the 'lifeworld.' [This] 'lifeworld' is the space of organic humanity...where people develop their personalities, their identities, their opinions...[without] state intervention."[9]

Habermas noted that members of the bourgeois public sphere often convened at salons and coffeehouses (especially in Germany, Britain, and France) to engage in rational and critical debates about social and cultural matters of common concern. The issues that were debated covered a wide array of subjects, mostly on the serious side, such as politics, economics, and literature. Participation in these debates, according to Habermas, was supposedly open and accessible to anybody who wanted to have a voice in the discussions outside the realm of the state control.[10] The desired objective of these discussions was to reach a consensus or a collective agreement on the issues being debated among equals.

So, according to Habermas, the bourgeois public sphere, which coincided with the development of capitalism in Western Europe,[11] did not consider status as a criterion for joining the critical debates. "The tendency replaced the celebration of rank with a tact befitting equals. The parity on whose basis alone the authority of the better argument could assert itself against that of social hierarchy...[was that] of 'common humanity.' "[12] It is worth mentioning here that the ideal public sphere that Habermas envisioned included a unified and homogeneous group rather than a fragmented audience.[13] From Habermas' perspective, homogeneity within the public sphere would help reach a consensus on the issues being discussed.

One important aspect in the process of debating to reach an agreement is what Habermas described as "communicative action"—a process through which participants communicate by using language to reach a mutual understanding and coordinate their actions. In this process, various participants utilize "argumentative speech" by setting aside their subjective views and "owing to the mutuality of rationally motivated conviction, assure themselves of both the unity of the objective world and the intersubjectivity of their lifeworld."[14] In the communicative action process, the speaker tries to rationally, rather than coercively, convince the hearer to accept what Habermas referred to as "validity claims" or claims made by the speaker to validate certain issues by associating them with truth, rightness, and sincerity.[15]

According to Habermas, "we can argumentatively agree on what is in the general interest only if every participant adopts an impartial standpoint from which his or her own particular interests count for no more nor less than those of any other participant."[16]

For Habermas, communicative action represents an "ideal speech situation," where participants try to defend their claims based on rational thinking.[17] Habermas believed that the members of the bourgeois public sphere had the ability, through their deliberative powers, to engage in communicative action. They expressed these deliberative powers mainly through face-to-face interactions and small-scale print media. "On the basis of his linguistically based [communicative action] model, Habermas has been able to provide a substantive foundation or free debate as the rationale and goal of social existence."[18]

To further illustrate the bourgeois public sphere, Curran (1997) argued that it is "the space between government and society in which private individuals exercise formal and informal control over the state: formal control through the election of governments and informal control through the pressure of public opinion."[19] Along the same lines, Eisenstadt (2002) argued that the public sphere lies between the official and the private spheres, but for its membership it relies on the private sphere. "It expands and shrinks according to the constitution and strength of those sectors of society that are not part of the rulership."[20]

In a way, Habermas' notion of public sphere illustrates "how a private sphere of society could take on a public relevance...Civil society came into existence as the corollary of a depersonalized state authority."[21] The bourgeois public sphere represented "an institution mediating between private interests and public power...[It was] based on a fundamental ideological obfuscation: the fictional identity of the property owner (*bourgeois*) and the human being pure and simple (*homme*)."[22]

The discursive environment of the bourgeois public sphere received its greatest support from the print media represented in newspapers, journals, newsletters, and periodicals that existed in eighteenth-century Europe, and that provided a space through which members of the literary public were able to publish their opinions using critical reasoning.[23] These print media outlets grew out of the traders' need to publicize businesses and to have access to information about other markets. The newsletters and journals started out under the strict censorship of the state, but soon enjoyed more freedom.[24]

The bourgeois public, which was a "reading public," became "the abstract counterpart of public authority and came into an awareness of itself as the latter's opponent, that is, as the public of the now emerging public sphere of civil society."[25]

One may argue that universality (i.e., "access is guaranteed to all citizens") and equality (i.e., citizens convene and participate in discussions with no restrictions)[26] characterize the ideal public sphere. The Habermasian public sphere seeks synthesis and resolution, and seeks to regulate forces of fragmentation. Wherease Habermas called for the right of all citizens to have equal access to the public sphere, he was reluctant to have those citizens "bring their distinct cultures and identities with them, for he [thought] this works against equality. In order for everybody to be equal in public debate...they must leave their differences at the door and agree to all speak the same language."[27] That might have been the reason as to why the "bourgeois public sphere," according to Habermas, worked best when it was limited to "educated white males."[28] In Habermas' opinion, that helped keep the public sphere homogeneous and intact rather than fragmented.

This ideal public sphere is not a physical sphere. "It is a metaphorical term that is used to describe the virtual space...where people's conversations, ideas and minds meet."[29] Despite the fact that the ideal public sphere, as described by Habermas, was crystallized mainly through face-to-face interactions, what matters for Habermas is not the physical space where the deliberations are taking place, but rather the presence of "shared social spaces."[30] This means that the normative standards of public discourse do not favor one form of dialogue over another as long as there is a rational-critical deliberation focused on matters of common concern to the participants. These standards "can be applied to assess the democratic potential of face-to-face dialogue, mediated deliberation, and more complex, hybrid forms like those found in Internet discussion forums."[31]

The End of Bourgeois Public Sphere and the Rise of Commercialized Mass Media

Habermas made the argument that the commercialization and commodification of the mass media, along with the rise of modern propaganda, led to the disintegration of the bourgeois public sphere and the deterioration of the rational-critical debates.[32] According to Habermas, unlike the small-scale intellectual journals that allowed for meaningful exchanges of opinions and debates, the mass media failed to enrich the public critical discussions because they have ended the demarcation between the public and the private spheres, which was necessary for preserving the intellectual quality of the public sphere. "When the laws of the market governing the sphere of commodity exchange and of social labor also pervaded the sphere reserved for private people as a public, rational-critical debate had a tendency to be replaced by consumption, and the web of public communication unraveled into acts of individuated reception, however uniform in mode."[33]

The main problem in the current media sphere, according to Habermas, is the absence of high-quality political information and the citizens' increasing inability to participate in public deliberations.[34] Other factors that contribute to the problem are the "news media's propensity for episodic, as opposed to thematic, news reporting, focus on the personal attributes and private lives of political actors rather than their positions on substantive policy issues, and horse-race coverage of strategies, tactics and polls."[35]

In this context, Habermas coined the term "re-feudalization of society," which he used to describe as "a retreat to an earlier form of public life in which its only function was to act as an arena for the display of power."[36] Under such circumstances, the private organizations take on more public power and the government interferes in the private realm.[37] According to Habermas, the public sphere has been transformed into "an arena for advertising than a setting for a rational-critical debate."[38]

Commenting on the public sphere's decline, Thompson (1990) argued that "this re-feudalization of the public sphere turns the latter into a theater and turns politics into a managed show in which leaders and parties routinely seek the acclamatory assent of a depoliticized population."[39]

In this environment, where the agents of power are marginalizing the less dominant voices and where the public relations firms are shaping political debates, "public opinion comes less to generate ideas and hold power accountable and more simply to register approval or disapproval in the form of opinion polls and occasional elections."[40]

These factors have led to a situation where

the relationship of the individual to the state has increasingly become one of client or consumer of services, rather than citizen. Individuals have become increasingly dependent upon the state, losing the independence that is central to the citizen role...Public opinion is no longer the ultimate authority, as democratic theory demands. It is an object and target for intervention strategies designed to manipulate and control it in a variety of ways.[41]

This is not an ideal situation for an intellectual discourse in which the "best" argument finds its way to peoples' minds; it is a situation where the "loudest" voices, rather than the "most reasonable" voices, are heard.[42]

Although today's expanding media sphere encompasses wider segments of the audience compared to the limited segment included in the bourgeois or literary public sphere in eighteenth-century Europe, Habermas is pessimistic about the prospects for a vibrant public sphere where everybody is allowed equal access to useful knowledge that enables them to monitor the government actions. Habermas laments what he considered to be the mass culture's appeal to the lowest common denominator leading to a decline in the general taste and a "dumbing down" of the level of debate.[43] He observed the transformation of the small newspapers into large-scale media institutions, whose main goal is to make profits rather than to enlighten the general public.[44] He expressed his dissatisfaction with the current commodification of culture:

> To the degree that culture became a commodity not only in form but also in content, it was emptied of elements whose appreciation required a certain amount of training—whereby the "accomplished" appropriation once again heightened the appreciative ability itself. It was not merely standardization as such that established an inverse relationship between the commercialization of cultural goods and their complexity, but that special preparation of products that made them consumption-ready, which is to say, guaranteed an enjoyment without being tied to stringent presuppositions. Serious involvement with culture produces facility, while the consumption of mass culture leaves no lasting trace; it affords a kind of experience which is not cumulative but regressive.[45]

According to Habermas, the "critical activity of public discourse" was replaced by an environment that is conducive to passive cultural consumption and political apathy. Therefore, today's mass media world "is a public sphere in appearance only."[46] In this context, Habermas (1989) argued that "the deprivatized province of interiority was hollowed out by the mass media; a pseudo-public sphere of a no longer literary public was patched together to create a sort of superfamilial zone of familiarity."[47]

In his comment on the decline of the political debates in the mass media era, Goode (2005) argued that today's deliberations are centered around the market philosophy of supply and demand:

> Today's ethic of good citizenship does not demand that our opinions are "tested out" in the argumentative crossfire of the coffee house or, for that

matter, the Internet discussion group. Rather, the governing logic is that of the market: the analogy is the educated consumer who, before plucking goods from the supermarket shelf, carefully considers the range of choices on offer and the cases that competing corporations make for their products.[48]

CRITICISM OF HABERMAS' PUBLIC SPHERE

Habermas was criticized for idealizing the bourgeois public sphere and exaggerating its potential for consensual deliberations. According to Gunaratne (2006), the consensus-oriented nature of Habermas' public sphere represents a "hopelessly inadequate response to the complex issues that arise in highly differentiated postindustrial societies."[49]

Along the same lines, McCarthy (1992) argued that individuals' interpretations of their needs stand in the way of their reaching a consensus in public deliberations. "Even if we outfit our good-willed participants with the intelligence and sensitivity to understand and appreciate the needs, interests and points of view of others, we are still far from rationally motivated consensus."[50]

Habermas claimed that the bourgeois public sphere was inclusive and that the rational-critical debates were open to anybody who had access to books, journals, and other cultural products. He adopted "the idea that the best rational argument and not the identity of the speaker was supposed to carry the day."[51]

Despite Habermas' claims in that regard, several academics argued that the bourgeois public sphere was not really accessible to everybody, but was limited to members of the elite—mainly rich people who owned property and had access to the literary sources. In this context, Goode (2005) noted that "illiteracy and poverty excluded much of the rural and the property-less urban populations, and the literature that was energizing the bourgeois specifically addressed the bourgeoisie in both form and content."[52] Along the same lines, Calhoun (1992) argued that members of the European bourgeois public sphere were mostly "educated, propertied men, and they conducted a discourse not only exclusive of others but prejudicial to the interests of those excluded."[53] Calhoun further explained that it was not Habermas' intention to imply that the only factor that made the public sphere bourgeois was the socioeconomic class of its members. "Rather, it was society that was bourgeois, and bourgeois society produced a certain form of public sphere."[54]

Looking at the issue of equality and accessibility in the public sphere from a different perspective, Schudson (1997) argued that it is "publicness" rather than "egalitarianism" or equality that ought to characterize conversation in any public sphere. Schudson is opposed to the norm of equality among members of a public sphere, as, according to him, it undermines the richness of the deliberations. He argued that in order for a public sphere to result in useful and enlightening deliberations, it has to include members of various inclinations and diverse backgrounds who hold differing opinions. "An individual must have 'cultural capital' to participate effectively in conversation. One might even argue that the actual relationship of talk and equality is not one of affinity but of paradox. The more that talk is among true equals, the more it fails to make assumptions clear, fails to state premises, fails to be accessible to all, lapses even into silence."[55]

Fraser (1992) noted that it was not just the lower socioeconomic classes that were excluded from Habermas' bourgeois public sphere, but also women. According to Fraser, previous feminist research has shown that men have a tendency to interrupt women and to speak more than them in any public deliberation. And so, the debates in Habermas' public sphere served "as a mask for domination [by men]."[56] Echoing Fraser's argument, Roberts and Crossley (2004) noted that Habermas' "neglect of public spheres other than the male bourgeois public sphere...establishes all sorts of false and misleading dichotomies."[57]

Fraser believed that Habermas has idealized the bourgeois public sphere to the extent that it failed to incorporate what she referred to as other "competing public spheres"[58] within society. In the course of her argument, Fraser posed a critical question about Habermas' homogeneous public sphere: "Under conditions of cultural diversity in the absence of structural inequality, would a single, comprehensive public sphere be preferable to multiple publics?"[59] In her answer to that question, Fraser called for the necessity of having various public spheres to accommodate the interests, needs, and identities of the different members of "subordinated social groups," such as women, people of color, blue-collar workers, and gays and lesbians. She proposed to call these various spheres "subaltern counterpublics"[60] that would help expand the discursive environment and enrich the rational deliberations. Fraser also called for a "postbourgeois conception"[61] that can allow for envisioning a more vital role for the public spheres that have often been marginalized in society.

Other scholars criticized Habermas for what they described as his "print-media bias"[62] that is expressed in Habermas' argument that the new broadcast media's immediacy might discourage distanced reflection and critical discussion among their audience. Habermas (1989) argued that "in comparison with printed communications, the programs sent by the new media curtail the reactions of their recipients in a peculiar way. They draw the eyes and ears of the public under their spell but at the same time, by taking away its distance, place it under 'tutelage,' which is to say they deprive it of the opportunity to say something and to disagree."[63]

Habermas warned against the immediacy of the electronic media, but he fails to account for the fact that these media have been more accessible to the general masses compared to the print media.[64] In this context, Thompson (1990) argued that "the development of mass communication has created new opportunities for the production and diffusion of images and messages…This new situation endows the communicator with unprecedented opportunities for reaching and influencing a large number of individuals."[65] According to Thompson, electronic media can enhance creative interaction among individual audiences, even when "they do not share a common spatial-temporal setting."[66]

One of the main criticisms of Habermas' public sphere is its "Eurocentric" bias[67] in the sense that it has its roots in Western Europe during the seventeenth century, and it derived its meaning from the Enlightenment values of modernity that characterized that era. Among these values were that "all citizens were of equal worth…(equality); everyone should be treated fairly (justice); everyone should have control over their own lives (freedom); and everyone had a right to a basic level of material welfare (comfort)."[68] In response to this criticism, we take the stand that the values are universal, but that societies differ in how these values are defined, weighted, and put into practice. There are several nonwestern societies that enjoy at least some of these values, and even people in nonwestern societies that are deprived of these values yearn to attain them. The public sphere ideal that originated in the west, and that calls for facilitating deliberations over issues of shared interest for the common good of the public, can still be applied to other nonwestern contexts that do enjoy rational and critical deliberations in discursive environments.

There are, however, some aspects related to Habermas' public sphere that are culture-bound in the sense that they would not fit nonwestern societies. One such aspect is the distinction between public and private spheres, which prevents matters related to the family and the household from coming under public scrutiny. In this context, Benhabib argued that the vagueness associated with the term "privacy," as used by Habermas, has excluded many issues from the public sphere, even though they deserved to be part of it. Included in these issues are "female spheres of activity like housework; reproduction; nurture and care for the young, the sick, and the elderly."[69]

Echoing Benhabib's argument in that context, Fraser noted that "discursive contestation" should be the only way to decide whether the topics belong to the public or the private domain. This means that nothing should be determined or taken off the table before such contestation. "On the contrary, democratic publicity requires positive guarantees of opportunities for minorities to convince others that what in the past was not public in the sense of being a matter of common concern should become so."[70]

Along the same lines, Gunaratne (2006) argued that in several nonwestern, and particularly collectivistic societies, the family is a cooperative entity that contributes to the community in a way that makes it practically impossible to limit its role to the private realm or to separate it from the community or the public sphere.[71]

Another aspect related to Habermas' notion of public sphere that cannot be applied to nonwestern cultures, especially Islamic cultures, is the total neglect of religion as a possible factor in the public deliberations. This is partly explained by the Enlightenment thinkers' philosophy that modernity develops at the expense of religion.[72] Those thinkers argue that religion belongs more to "the private sphere of individual preference and individual practice" rather than to the public sphere and public life.[73] We will deal with this argument in more detail later in this chapter.

This latest criticism of Habermas' public sphere leads us into the next section on the public sphere in Islam. As mentioned above, we believe that the public sphere notion should not be limited to the western world, and that there are vibrant, rational and critical deliberations taking place in offline and online Islamic communities.

THE ISLAMIC PUBLIC SPHERE

The public sphere concept can be best applied to the "classic era of Islamic reform," which took place in the late nineteenth century through the "structural transformations" of religious authority during the 1960s and 1970s,[74] on to the present time that is witnessing the emergence of a new Islamic public sphere that is formed by increasingly open debates through the new media, particularly the Internet.[75]

Throughout these various eras, the term that can be used to describe the Islamic public sphere is "public Islam," which refers to the diversity of intellectual contributions, thoughts, practices, and civic debates initiated by Muslim scholars, academics, students, engineers, and many others in the realm of Islamic public life.[76] In this public space, "Islam makes a difference...not only as a template for ideas and practices but also as a way of envisioning alternative political realities, and increasingly, in acting on both global and local stages, thus reconfiguring established boundaries of civil and social life."[77]

Multiple discourses of public Islam represent the various sociopolitical paths and ideological trends of Muslim communities.[78] Members in the sphere of public Islam participate in open discussions and critical negotiations of various issues in a way that eventually leads to achieving *al-maslaha al-ʿamma* (common good).[79] Although the nature and substance of these discussions are different from those adopted in the west, the definition of the "common good," and the requirements and principles that are needed to achieve it converge with the western understanding of such a concept.[80] Given that the ideal of common good is reached through continuous public debates and contestation, "there can scarcely be a single conception of it, nor can it simply be equated with that which is best for most people."[81]

Because Islam is not just a religion but a way of life, all aspects of a Muslim's life are possibly subject to deliberations in the Islamic public sphere. This means that the Habermasian distinction between the public and the private cannot be applied to the sphere of public Islam.

Unlike Habermas' "bourgeois public sphere," where equality had to be accompanied by homogeneity among participants in order to facilitate the process of reaching a consensus, in the Islamic context, homogeneity is not required of all the participants in the public deliberations and debates to reach a common good.[82] Those participants can come from different backgrounds and still engage in constructive dialogue.

In order to make sure that justice and freedom of opinion prevail in the deliberation process, the Qur'an calls for adopting *shura* (consultation). "The meaning of '*shura*' is the solidarity in society based on the principle of free consultation and genuine dialogue, reflecting equality in thinking and expression of opinion."[83] In this context, the Muslim Prophet Mohammed said, addressing his companions: "Do not be a conformist, who says I am with the people, if they do good I do good, and if they do harm, I do harm."[84] Several scholars argued that *shura* is "the equivalent of parliamentary democracy."[85]

The premise of the *shura* in public Islam is the idea of inclusiveness rather than exclusiveness. This means that the *shura* is open to people from all walks of life and all segments of the society. In this sense, the process of *shura* is different from the process of *ijtihad* (independent interpretation), which has been classically limited to the *fuqaha* (experts of jurisprudence).[86]

Participants in the *shura* process, like their counterparts in Habermas' communicative action, should reach *ijma'* (consensus). *Ijma,'* which is reached through rational-critical debates, is an integral aspect of public deliberations since "it supports collaborative and consensus-building process rather than authoritative, competitive, or confrontational procedures for dealing with differences."[87] Salvatore (2006) argued that the Muslim participants who interact in public deliberations to reach *ijma'* go through the process of reflexive rationalization[88]—a process through which they use various modes of engagement to frame and analyze issues in a reasonable manner. The concept of "reflexivity" was introduced by Anthony Giddens, whose definition of the concept was cited in Hoover and Lundby (1997) as "the conscious, monitored dimension of social life that is constantly assigning meaning to the transactions of everyday life."[89]

The intellectual contributions, reflexive rationalizations, and rational-critical debates in public Islam derive their meaning from religious authority. Islam, like any other mainstream, monolithic religion, has various sources of authority that have contributed to the definition of Islamic identity.

It has often been hard to define religious authority. According to Max Weber, "authority describes the ability or 'chance' to have one's rules and rulings followed, or obeyed, without recourse to coercive power."[90] Religious authority helps identify practices and beliefs that guide the conduct of followers of any religion. It also sets the ground rules for the interpretation of religious text.[91] In Islam, religious authority emanates from knowledge of the Qur'an and the *sunna* (Prophet's Muhammad's sayings and deeds). Dealing with the Qur'an and the *sunna* as the main guidance sources in Islam requires extensive religious training and in-depth expert knowledge. In Islam, "persons matter more than institutions as sources and mediators of religious knowledge and authority."[92] The articulation and expression of authoritative knowledge in Islam can take place through both formal and informal networks that form the Islamic public sphere.

However, to better grasp the historical construction of this Islamic public sphere, it is of utmost importance to take a closer look at the previously mentioned concepts of *maslaha, shura, ijtihad, ijma,* as well as other relevant concepts in this domain, and to examine their diverse roots, manifestations, and limitations.

Albert Hourani (1993) draws our attention to the fact that, over the course of time, there emerged from the Qur'an and *hadith* a "comprehensive system of ideal morality, a moral classification of human acts which would make clear the way (*Shari'a*)."[93] He explains that when there was a clear and highly valid text in the Qur'an or the *hadith* regarding a certain issue, it was easy to just refer to the Islamic law in this case to arrive at a conclusion regarding this issue. However, when this was not the case, "those who possessed the necessary intellect and training must deduce the answer from the texts, by using their minds in accordance with the rules of strict analogy or some other processes of reasoning (*ijtihad*)."[94] When the results of this process earned the general acceptance or consensus of the most wise and learned people in the community, they earned a power and "...an authority no less binding than that of *Qur'an* or *hadith*."[95]

However, Hournai (1993) makes it clear that there were still many differences of opinion about how *ijma* could be reached, how it could be best defined, what it validated, and most importantly, "beyond the bounds of the *ijma*, about the ways in which human reason could be used and the results its use would lead to."[96] He contends that these differences, over the course of time, gave birth to "a number of systems (*madhab*), all of them equally legitimate for a believer to accept."[97]

Explaining the birth of these different Islamic schools of thought, Mansoor Moaddel (2005) points out that "Four schools of Islamic jurisprudence laid the methodological foundation of Islamic laws in the Sunni sect,"[98] and that they "came to fruition in order to address the problems

Muslim administrators and generals faced as a result of the passage of time and the expansion of Islam into new territories. For these problems, there were no specific guidelines in the scripture or in the tradition of the prophet."[99] Yet, it is important to bear in mind that each of these four Islamic schools of thought also had a different view on the degree of *ijtihad* that can be allowed or tolerated, and how the concept of *ijma* can be best defined, and how it can be arrived at. Moaddel (1995) clarifies that the founder of the first school "Abu Hanifa, was the first to introduce a new rule of reasoning known as *qiyas* (analogy), which went beyond the literal meaning of the Quranic text to its causal (*'illa*) underpinnings."[100] The founder of the second school, Malik Ibn Anas, upheld the value of following the Prophet's tradition and, therefore, adopted the position that *qiyas* should only be used as a last resort. Yet these two positions, according to Moaddel (1995), did not satisfy the founder of the third school, Muhammad al-Shafi'i, "who extended the principle of *ijma* beyond the jurists of Medina to include all the ideas and decisions that were agreed upon by all the competent authorities in Islam."[101] Therefore, the four sources of Islamic jurisprudence in the Shafi'i school were the Qur'an, the *hadith*, *ijma*, and *qiyas*. However, the fourth and final authoritative figure in Sunni jurisprudence, Ahmad Ibn Hanbal, attacked the concept of *qiyas*. "For him, rationalist interpretation of the *Qur'an* and tradition was permissible, and thus *ijma* was unlawful innovation (*bid'a*). After the death of Ibn Hanbal, the gate of *ijtihad* was considered closed among the Sunnis, and all the jurists were instructed to follow one of these four orthodox schools."[102]

Although the door of *ijtihad* was officially closed among those who represent authoritative religious knowledge, however, "the popular mind consoled itself with the belief that in each century there would arise a renovator (*mujaddid*), and with the expectation of a *mahdi*, one sent by God to restore the rule of the saints and prepare the coming of Jesus and the end of the world."[103] This view, according to Hourani (1993), is based on the notion that although "For Muslims, the great age of early Islam served as an image of what the world should be";[104] however, this glorification of the past does not always "take the form of a desire to reconstruct the whole of the past."[105] Rather, it usually relies on a "selective approach," which adopts the most relevant and meaningful aspects of this glorious past, and excludes other aspects that are perceived as less relevant or meaningful in the modern context. At the heart of this process of selectivity

stands the living tradition of *ahl al-sunna wa'l-jama'a*, the self-appointed, self-recognized, unorganized body of "concerned" Muslims, believing in the revelation of Muhammad, wishing to preserve it unaltered amidst the changes of time, seeking in it guidance in the new problems cast up by those changes, defending it and drawing out its implications not so much by a rejection of what was new as by a discrimination between what could be absorbed into Islam and what could not.[106]

Another very compelling issue in our understanding of the Islamic public sphere is the relationship between the ruler and the ruled and the general guidelines that define it. Here it is important to highlight the fact that according to the Sunni school of thought "The *Khalafah*—which is the highest authority in the state—was based on consultation (*shura*), choice (*ikhtiyar*), contract (*aqid*) and allegiance (*bay'a*), and never on heredity."[107] The purpose of this position, according to Tareq and Jacqueline Ismael (1985), was to ensure that societal authorities and the state will not have a religious claim and that "what is temporal, political and legal which were not dealt with by the Qur'an...are left to *ijtihad*, the determining criteria and purpose of which should be the public interest—the interest of the entire community."[108] This vision is, of course, very different from the notion of *Imamah* that was adopted by the Shiites, and combined both political and religious authority in the descendants of the Prophet. A detailed discussion of the notions of *Khalafah* and *Imamah* and the differences between them will be provided in chapter 3.

Mona Abul-Fadl (1990) draws our attention to the fact that in Islam "The fundamental relationship between the ruler and the ruled is essentially of the contractual variety, embodied in the oath of allegiance, or a *bay'ah*, which delegates power from the community to its leaders. In this *bay'ah* the community pledges its support, and obedience, as long as its political leadership, its *imarah*, observes the spirit of its founding 'constitution.'"[109] She further explains that under this arrangement "Ideally, the spirit of the Islamic polity combined elements of the authoritative and the consensual. It drew its authoritativeness from the principles enunciated in *wahy*—(Qur'an and Sunnah)...; its consensuality was itself contingent on the authority mandated its community by these very principles."[110]

Presenting another view on the issue of *bay'a*, Hournai (1993) points out that while some caliphs were designated by their predecessors, others were chosen by a group of leaders in the community, and "the idea of a choice was always preserved, and symbolized by the ceremony of *bay'a*, the formal acknowledgment of a new caliph and the pledge of loyalty to him."[111] However, he alerts us to the fact that after the first age this became no more than just a formality and it did not really represent a process of election. "It was rather a recognition than a choice;...in the *bay'a* the community acquiesced its authority, it did not confer it. By implication, the first duty of the community towards the ruler was one of obedience."[112] Yet, Hourani (1993) also highlights the fact that "obedience should be neither passive nor without conditions...the ruler should consult the leaders of the community (*shura*) and they should give him moral advice and exhortation (*nasiha*), although there was no clear idea who exactly should be consulted and should warn, and how far the ruler should be bound by what they said."[113]

The previous point draws our attention to one of the major challenges in the ruler and ruled relationship within the Islamic context, which is the vagueness of the principle of *shura*, and the elusiveness of its practical applicability. Elaborating on this point, Abdelwahab El-Affendi (2006) points out that "Shura in the context of the traditional Islamic political practice did not...represent a device of convenience for the ruler in order to perfect decision making...It was in fact a vehicle for political participation. The Prophet and his immediate successors used to consult with their followers specifically to ensure that they were on board with major policy decision."[114] However, he points out that "The problem...has been that the practice of *shura* was not institutionalized...the ad hoc procedure was suitable for a small community, like that of Medina. Once the community expanded to span several continents, the procedure proved inadequate. It will be equally inadequate today."[115]

The vagueness surrounding the concept of *shura* and the lack of formal political institutions or structures through which it can be practiced led Muslim theoreticians, according to Tareq and Jacqueline Isamel (1985), to search for a solution. "The solution was the concept of *ahl al-hal wa al-'aqd* (Council of Notables), to be the basis for a legitimate method of choosing a leader."[116] They indicate that at the beginning the only ones qualified to belong to this category were the religious leaders who exhibited a high degree of knowledge and justice. Later on, however, this criteria changed and this category started to encompass "the elite and prominent members of the Muslim community, irrespective of their religious merits. This concept of *ahl al-hal wa al-'aqd* was never clearly defined: How were the members to be chosen? What was their role? What was the relationship of this group to the rest of the Muslim community?"[117]

The fact that these and other important questions, such as "what were the qualities essential in a ruler, how many people should belong to *ahl al-hal wa al-'aqd*; how many constituted a legal *bay'a*, and what constituted *ijma* (consensus),"[118] were never clearly answered and "led to political turmoil throughout Islamic history."[119] This could be attributed to the fact that "under the doctrine of *ahl al-hal wa al-'aqd*, the Muslim community was constantly...prevented from playing an active political role in choosing the ruler. As a result, dissension, rebellion and factionalism erupted with each succession."[120]

This was particularly the case whenever the community was faced with a Khalifah "who puts himself up as an absolute authority,"[121] according to Abdelwahab El-Affendi (2006), since this, in turn, implies that he is claiming divine powers to himself, which can lead to a much greater danger, since a "person who claims to embody divine authority by being the final arbiter on divine law very soon moves...to put himself above divine law."[122] The ascription of this role to an individual, as El-Affendi (2006) points out, negates the central ethical and legal principle of *ijma'* or consensus, which is "considered the most authoritative source of Islamic legislation after the two main sources, the Quran and the Sunna (sayings and practice of the Prophet)."[123] This important principle gains more significance due to the fact that "Islam has left a very wide array of discretion to the community. The importance is even more in case of the political realm, where the endemic disagreements over how to conduct affairs betray an underlying agreement that no definitive prescriptions existed in this area."[124]

These challenges became even more pressing, according to Tareq and Jacqueline Ismael (1985), with the expansion of the Islamic community and the establishment of a stretching Islamic empire, which brought about a widening gap between the ruler and the ruled, and, therefore, "the increasing distance between the ruler and the community made the problem of the public interest a central concern in these issues: what was the public interest; how was it be best served; what if it was violated?"[125]

Here again, we are left with more questions than answers, which opens the door for further challenges, debates, and even confrontations, within the realm of the expanding and changeable Islamic public sphere, with many implications on the development of the modern Islamic public sphere, on one hand, as will be discussed later in this chapter, as well as the development of the notion of the *umma* (Islamic community) into a public sphere, on the other hand, as will be discussed in chapter 3.

Meanwhile, an integral aspect of the development of the *umma* and the crystallization of the Islamic public sphere is the centers of oral communication in Muslim communities and their multiple manifestations and impacts on the formation of Islamic consciousness, as will be discussed in the next section.

Centers for Oral Communication in the Islamic Public Sphere

In the mid-nineteenth century, the Ottoman Empire in Istanbul, Turkey, witnessed flourishing public sociability sites, represented in coffeehouses. These coffeehouses, which were as many as 2,500 spread throughout Istanbul, attracted mostly male customers to exchange information and opinion. Cengiz Kirli (2006) described these coffeehouses as follows:

> the coffeehouse as a ubiquitous place of sociability has served multiple functions. Coffeehouses were places of leisure where Istanbul men met, played

games, smoked tobacco, listened to political fables told by story tellers, and laughed at the grotesque characters of shadow theater that displayed profanity, irony, and humor with a highly political subtext. They served as commercial venues where merchants struck deals, ship captains arranged their next load, and brokers looked for potential customers. They were occupational spheres where practitioners of different professions and trades frequented…They were spheres of manifest resistance and opposition. They were used as headquarters for the janissaries, the elite soldiers.[126]

These coffeehouses can be compared to the ones that existed in eighteenth-century Europe and that were the main sites of public deliberations among members of Habermas' bourgeois public sphere. But unlike the European coffeehouse customers who were mainly members of the literary community, customers of the Turkish coffeehouses were predominantly illiterate. One possible explanation for oral information networks in nineteenth-century Istanbul is the fact that print media, particularly newspapers, did not exist in the Islamic world until the late nineteenth century and the earlier part of the twentieth century.[127] The strong oral tradition in the Muslim world has to do with the method of transmitting knowledge in Islam. The Qur'an, which is believed to be "God's Word" revealed to the Prophet through Angel Gabriel, has always been transmitted orally, and the oral recitation of the Qur'an has been the predominant method of Islamic education, especially at the *madrasas* (Islamic schools).[128] "Even to this day, the process of learning the Qur'an is first and foremost an exercise in memorization and oral repetition. This goes some way to explaining why the Muslim world hesitated to embrace the technologies of 'print capitalism' even when they were readily available."[129]

So, it can be argued that while the coffeehouses in Europe strengthened the literary tradition by allowing for a sphere that was an extension to the deliberations on the pages of newspapers, journals, and newsletters, the mid-nineteenth century coffeehouses in a place like Istanbul reinforced the oral tradition in the Islamic world. "Every individual opinion articulated [at the Turkish coffeehouses] incited comment from others, then further disseminated through the word of mouth, and ultimately contributed to the formation of public opinion."[130]

Understanding the Islamic public sphere also requires shedding some light on another equally important center for oral communication, which is the mosque and its role in the domain of public Islam. The mosque in Islam is the main prayer center where the preachers deliver their sermons and the Islamic scholars teach the principles of Islam. Of symbolic importance at the mosque are the *minbar* (pulpit), from which the preacher addresses the community of Muslims and the *mihrab* (the decorated empty niche that marks the direction of Mecca). For Muslims, the mosque is not just a building or a physical space where they perform their religious rituals, but it is a representation of the "central value system"[131] to which they adhere and which defines their collective identity as Muslims. The importance of mosques also emanates from the fact that they are not just sacred places for worship, but vibrant public sphere centers where rational-critical deliberations around the common good ideal often take place.

" 'Ulama" in the Islamic Clerical Networks: The Core of the Islamic Public Sphere

The core of the Islamic public sphere is the Islamic clerical networks that have traditionally included well-trained 'ulama (religious scholars) with extensive authoritative knowledge of the Qur'an and the *sunna*. The 'ulama's principal goal has been to teach Islam and to disseminate religious information to Muslims and non-Muslims. They can also serve as sources of social as well as emotional support. The position of a network leader or 'alim (singular of 'ulama) has its foundation in his "claim to have esoteric knowledge of Islam"[132] that is unmatched by any other network member. He attains this knowledge after many years of formal Islamic studies at any distinguished traditional institution of Islamic law, such as Al-Azhar institution in Egypt.

The degree that a network leader gets at the end of his studies is called *ijaza* (teacher's authorization or license), and it is the evidence of his religious authority. This license allows the 'alim to pass on his religious information to others. This authority is often reflected in a network leader's ability to transmit Islamic knowledge and create a large following. The religious authority of a network leader or 'alim is also expressed in his ability to interpret the principles of *shari'a* and to teach Muslims how to apply these principles to their daily lives.[133] In other words, it could be said that the *shari'a*, as the main foundation of the Islamic public order, "had its qualified and publicly acknowledged experts, the 'ulama, whose task was to develop a derivative legislative corpus, a *fiqh tashri'i*, that would be contingent on the evolution and needs of society."[134]

In this sense, the 'ulama "are considered '*marja'-i-taqlid*' or source of practices, whose authoritative guidance is followed in matters of Islamic polity, law, economics, and culture."[135] It is known that in Islam, there is no ordained clergy, but there are authoritative religious specialists represented in the 'ulama.[136] In a way, the 'ulama, who are mostly males, are considered the "religious elite" in the Islamic public sphere thanks to their credentials and their formal training at prestigious religious institutions. They have always enjoyed a "*de facto* hegemony on religious debate"[137] in the discourse on Islam.

This elevated and distinguished status, according to Ira Lapidus (2002), was based on the fact that the "'Ulama were commonly organized into schools of law, which were associations of scholars, teachers, and students adhering to the codes of law developed by discussion and debate among legal scholars...Through the law schools, the scholars organized higher education and trained teachers and judicial administrators. From the law schools came *muftis*, or legal consultants, notaries, and judges."[138]

Hourani (1993) describes the *'ulama* as "the doctors of religion,"[139] who were treated with a high degree of respect, because they played a number of important roles extending beyond the religious sphere, "They were the guardians of Islamic morality and law, and of the Arabic language and culture which went with them...The *'ulama* were not only judges, teachers, and officials; they were consulted and used for foreign negotiations, they took part in the politics and revolutions...they served in a sense as leaders of the indigenous opinion."[140]

Likewise, Lapidus (2002) highlights the fact that "In every Islamic society *'ulama*...were the teachers, exemplars, and leaders of Muslim communities. The *'ulama* were the scholars knowledgeable about Muslim hadith, law, and theology. Their primary function was instruction and judicial administration."[141] However, he also draws our attention to the fact that "The *'ulama* performed different political roles, depending upon their class level and the type of political system in which they were embedded. Higher-ranking *'ulama* were commonly state-functionaries, while lower-level teachers were often spiritual counselors for the common people."[142]

In his comment on the role of the *'ulama* in enhancing the concept of the common good, Muhammad Qasim Zaman (2005) noted that

> inasmuch as they are part of this landscape, and are often loud, even artic-
> ulate, contributors to public debate, the *'ulama* help shape the public
> sphere. Indeed, their discourses contribute in practice to precisely the sort
> of contestation that constitutes not just the public sphere but also notions
> of its common good. For all the *'ulama*'s wish simply to discover and
> enunciate concepts rather than acknowledge creating them, it is precisely
> through a long history of discourse and contestation that the tradition in
> terms of which they define themselves has been constituted. The *'ulama*'s
> discourses in the present are not just articulated in contestation with other,
> rival voices in society but are also in constant dialogue and argumentation
> with the resources their own tradition offers.[143]

The *'ulama* have traditionally relied on oral transmission of their knowledge. The relatively low literacy rates among Muslims during the years preceding the advent of print technology in the Islamic world have contributed to the *'ulama*'s monopoly over the production and dissemination of religious knowledge. The *'ulama* were among the selected few scholars who had exclusive access to religious literature until the introduction of print technology in the Islamic world in the second half of the nineteenth century.[144]

The shared intellectual discourse of the 'ulama had allowed them to form "interpretive communities"[145] through which they had no problem communicating with each other. Where they had trouble was their ability to communicate with the laymen, especially before the introduction of print technology to the Muslim world (premodern era). The 'ulama's intellectual elitism made them out of reach for the average Muslims. "The majority of pre-modern Muslims were villagers or rural agriculturalists; they did not concern themselves with judicial values or the custodians of those values, the 'ulama. Pre-modern networks were expansive, but they were traveled by the elite."[146]

Some 'ulama have played an active role on the political front on local, regional, and national levels. Those who are too close to the state have been referred to as "establishment 'ulama" and those who chose to distance themselves from the political life and even criticize the politicians have been described as "oppositional 'ulama."[147] Eickelman and Piscatori (2004) cited a former Tunisian cabinet minister, who made a distinction between "the power of the 'ulama" and the "'ulama of power."[148] While the 'ulama belonging to the latter type enjoy intellectual autonomy, speak their mind, and provide religious advise, even if it angers members of the political regime, the 'ulama belonging to the former type often appease the political authorities. According to the former Tunisian minister, the "'ulama of power [prefer] the flickering light of the candle to the blazing flame of the spirit."[149]

The Fragmentation of the 'Ulama's Authority

For more than a millennium, the 'ulama had served as the main source of interpretation of the Qur'an thanks to their formal religious training and their exclusive access to specialized Islamic education.[150] However, several factors have contributed to putting an end to the 'ulama's monopoly over the dissemination of religious information, and have eventually led to the weakening of their position and the fragmentation of their authority. These factors could be best understood within two different contexts, namely the historical context and the modern context.

The historical context takes us back to some of the unresolved dilemmas and unanswered questions regarding the issue of political leadership and the relationship between the ruler and the ruled in Islam, such as "The question of who had the necessary qualifications to be the leader of the Islamic community and how the Islamic conception of authority was to be reconciled with changing political reality."[151] These questions became especially more pressing after the death of Prophet Muhammed and after the end of the golden age of his four successors, since, as Manssor Moaddel (2005) points out,

> The Sunni theorists were unanimous about the legitimacy of the first four caliphs, given the honorific title of the *Rashidun*—exemplars of rightful Muslim rulers. Nevertheless, the changing political realities of the post-Rashidun caliphate under the Umayyads (661–750), the Abbasids (750–1258), and thereafter provided serious problems for Muslim jurists: How is one to reconcile the Islamic notion of sovereignty with the claims of a self-made caliph among the continuously emerging military leaders and tribal chiefs in different parts of the Islamic world?[152]

The dilemma posed by the previous question stems from the fact that "the community at large which gave allegiance to Islam seemed mostly devoted in fact to enjoying the fruits of conquest under the leadership of men whose position in power had resulted largely from force and from tribal alliance."[153] This, in turn, led to the birth of a "semi-political, semi-cultural body of opposition to the ruling trends."[154] This "piety-minded"[155] opposition, as Hudgson (1974) points out, consisted "primarily of the religious specialists, later called *'ulama*, who provided much of the leadership. At the same time, the more pious of their followers are to be included, for there was no sharp line, at first, between *'ulama* scholars and others. Only gradually did the social element…the 'Piety-minded' resolve itself later into sharply differentiated Sunni and Shi'i *'ulama*, followed with lesser or greater sectarian devotion by partisan groups in the wider population."[156]

The previous discussion highlights two equally important facts regarding the origins of the fragmentation of the *'ulama's* authority. The first one is that the *'ulama*, who originally started as a unified and powerful group in the early history of Islam, later on split among themselves and became divided under the two major Islamic sects, namely Sunni and Shi'ite. The second one is that a parallel split also took place between the *'ulama* and their followers among the general Muslim population. The latter point was a direct outcome of the fact that many *'ulama* started to endorse and legitimize the rule of some of the unjust political leaders in the Islamic world under the assumption that "A despotic ruler is better than anarchy."[157] The rational argument (*ijtihad*) behind this, according to Tareq and Jacqueline Isamel (1985), "derives from the basic premise that human beings are not capable of running their affairs harmoniously without the presence of a mediating authority"[158] and, therefore, the presence of a leader or an Imam among Muslims becomes of utmost importance in order to protect their interests and their religion, to ensure the spread of peace and justice, and to prevent anarchy and disruption in society.[159]

Henceforth, out of this line of thought emerged the belief that "Trying to unseat the sultan by declaring his power illegal would result in lawlessness and chaos (*fitnih*), a condition more detrimental to the welfare of Muslims than having a tyrant in power."[160] In light of this view, it is assumed that ideally a Muslim ruler or Imam "must obey God just as his officials obey him, and for this reason he should consult the *ulama*, the guardians of God's law. But if he does wrong he should not be deposed as an official is dismissed, because of the disturbance of conditions."[161] Again, this was based on the perception that "even an unjust ruler was better than strife and the dissolution of society."[162]

Hourani (1993) explains that this perception stemmed from defining "the caliphate as being a necessity derived from the divine law rather than from reason; the Quran enjoins men to obey those set in command over them, and this implies that there should be a caliph, to replace the Prophet so far as the maintenance of religion and the administration of worldly interests are concerned."[163] The most serious challenge posed by this perception, however, lies in the fact that "For thinkers of the early period, the duty of obedience only held so long as the caliph ordered nothing which was contrary to the Shari'a. In later thought...obedience tended to become an absolute duty, and even an unjust ruler was regarded as better than none at all; only a minority of late thinkers taught that revolt could be legitimate."[164]

Another driving force behind the adoption of this perception was the desire to maintain the legal and political unity of the Muslim community, which "prompted the majority of Muslim jurists to support the office of the *khalifa*, despite the character and disposition of its incumbent, so long as he proclaimed in public loyalty and submission to the *shar'ia*."[165] Therefore, "In order to preserve this unity, they were willing to compromise with the political realities of their time, which often included giving allegiance to less than ideal rulers."[166]

Moreover, "Further development of the *shari'a* was seriously limited when Abbasid jurists curtailed legal innovation in order to prevent political meddling from the rulers. As a result, the *shari'a* became less and less relevant to Muslim practice, especially in administrative or constitutional matters."[167] Here it could be said that closing the door of *ijtihad*, and the consequently shrinking role of the *shar'ia* in the political and constitutional domains, were additional factors that contributed to the already diminishing role of the *ulama* in public life.

However, it is important to highlight the fact that there were some cases in which *ulama* and jurists "played the role of the loyal opposition to corrupt caliphs."[168] In other cases, some groups of *ulama*, such as the "Hanbalis in Egypt and Syria, Malikis in North and West Africa, and Naqshbandis in India not only maintained their autonomy, but were the active opponents of state elites in the name of Islamic principles."[169]

Moreover, some prominent *ulama*, such as Ibn Taymiyya and Ibn Khaldun (1333–1406), "Noting a poor fit between the ideal Islamic state and the political reality of their time…conceded that the caliphate had ceased after the fourth caliph and that the sovereignty exercised by the Umayyads and the Abbasids had never been more than a 'royalty.' "[170]

Despite these manifestations of opposition and resistance to political authority on the part of some ʿulama, the overall picture that emerges from the previous discussion is that of an increasingly fragmented and diminishing role for the ʿulama in many facets of public life, mainly because their credibility in the public's eye has been shaken by their acceptance to compromise with corrupt or unjust rulers, or even to endorse and legitimize their practices, which resulted in widening the gap between them and their followers.

After providing this overview of the historical context of the fragmentation of the ʿulama's authority, it is now important to shift our attention to the modern context, which also encompasses a number of equally important factors behind the weakening of the ʿulama's authority and monopoly over knowledge. First among these factors was the introduction of print technology to the Islamic world in the second half of the nineteenth century. The Muslim world adopted newspapers, newsletters, and pamphlets to defend itself against the European missionaries. This step, which marked the beginning of modernity in the Islamic world, resulted in a gradual rise in the literacy rates among the average Muslims, which eventually increased the number of lay people who could read and interpret the religious texts beyond the realm of the ʿulama.[171]

To help explain the consequences of this development, Mandaville (2002) cited Robinson as saying that "books…could now be consulted by any Ahmad, Mahmud or Muhammad, who could make what they will of them. Increasingly from now on any Ahmad, Mahmud or Muhammad could claim to speak for Islam. No longer was a sheaf of impeccable ijazas the buttress of authority; strong Islamic commitment would be enough."[172]

Another factor that challenged the ʿulama's knowledge and led to the fragmentation of their authority was the massive-scale education that resulted from the print technologies. Modern pedagogical methods have started to get incorporated in the religious curricula at various schools. These methods highlighted the importance of understanding and interpretation, rather than just memorization and recitation of Qur'anic texts.[173] In addition, secular fields of study, such as medicine, engineering, and political science have become an integral part of the studies many Islamic universities, including Al-Azhar University in Egypt. This "mass education" trend has created new types of public space in Islam and has encouraged an increasing number of educated Muslims to expand their intellectual horizons in unprecedented ways. "A once fairly unified and restricted area of knowledge has now been called into question"[174] thanks to the increasing educational levels.

It is worth mentioning in this context that many Muslim modernists have accused the traditional *ulama* of intellectual stagnation, narrow-mindedness, and of lacking the creative abilities that are needed to cope with various aspects of modernity.[175]

Still, another factor that challenged the *ulama*'s knowledge and compromised their position was the Muslim governments' interference in the Islamic affairs, leading to the politicizing of several aspects of religious thinking. "In every country of the Muslim world, Islam is either a State religion or under State control...In light of this fact, the State is almost always the primary agent responsible for the authoritative interpretation of tradition."[176]

This could be explained in light of the fact that "The religious authority of the *ulama*, their expertise in law, and their social leadership made it important for states to control them."[177] This control, however, took different forms, in some cases the *ulama* were bureaucratized,[178] while in other cases, "the *ulama* were not bureaucratically organized but were still couriers and clients of the political elites."[179]

A case in point, which exemplifies this state control over the *ulama*, was the step taken by the late Egyptian president, Gamal Abdel Nasser, to reform the Al-Azhar institution in Egypt in 1961 in a way that allowed his regime to exert more control over the *ulama* affiliated with Al-Azhar. The Nasser regime reorganized the Al-Azhar administration and placed it under the direct supervision of the head of state. The regime also introduced new subjects at Al-Azhar without involving the *ulama* in the decision-making process. It also dispossessed the *ulama* of their judicial authority and made them more economically dependent on the state. So, the Al-Azhar *ulama* became a group of "civil servants" subject to complete state authority, and even receiving their salaries from the state.[180] The bottom line was that they lost their legitimacy and identity as autonomous religious scholars.

Another stark manifestation of this process of state control and hegemony over the *ulama* lies in the fact that there were instances when " *ulama* supporting a particular state have justified its pursuit of its own interest (which was in fact the interest of the ruling regime) in religious terms. Saudi *ulama* justified support for secularist Iraq in its war with Iran, and later legitimized Saudi Arabia's participation in America's war against Iraq. When Iran and Taliban Afghanistan nearly went to war in 2000, both justified their rival claims in religious terms."[181]

Given the above-mentioned factors, the *ulama*'s authority has been fragmented; their authority has not completely dissipated, but they have lost much of their privileged access to and monopoly over religious knowledge to alternative voices and "new interpreters"[182] of the religion or "new religious intellectuals,"[183] who are contributing to the religious deliberations in the Islamic public sphere without having the *ulama*'s traditional religious training. Those new voices have been given an opportunity through the tremendous development of modern media technologies to contest the 'ulama's discourses. Thus, a "new Islamic public sphere"[184] has been created. The next section will shed some light on this.

THE "NEW ISLAMIC PUBLIC SPHERE"

The expression of religious authority in the Islamic public sphere has been affected by the expansion and increasing accessibility of mediated forms of mass communication, such as satellite television and by interactive new media, such as the Internet. These media have created new grounds for deliberations and have allowed for a proliferation of voices in a way that has not been witnessed before in the discursive public sphere of Islam. Deliberations about Islamic issues are no longer limited to the mosque, the *madrassa*, and the print media, but have taken on a new form through the mediated means of mass communication that have contributed to a new Islamic public sphere. The impact of the new forms of media, particularly the Internet, on the Islamic public sphere can be compared to the tremendous effect of the print revolution that was witnessed during the early years of modernity.[185]

According to Eickelman (1999), the modern means of mass communication "[involve] people on a mass scale...[and] facilitate an awareness of the new and unconventional. In changing the style and scale of possible discourse, they reconfigure the nature of religious thought and action, create new forms of public space, and encourage debate over meaning."[186] Thompson (1995) highlighted the new media role in what he described as "the mediazation of tradition"[187] (i.e., freeing tradition from the restrictions of face-to-face interaction). The media help facilitate the production, consumption, and dissemination of religious messages to the point where the spheres of media and religion are "interpenetrated by one another. Religion as a symbolic universe or universes of ultimate values and knowledge and media as mediators in communication, constitute fundamental dimensions of culture in their own right."[188]

A category of "new religious intellectuals," mostly comprised of young professionals with academic degrees in various secular fields, such as medicine, engineering, and anthropology, has been utilizing the modern mass media to challenge the role of the 'ulama and to try to play an active role in the emerging Muslim public sphere.[189] Those new religious intellectuals "take it upon themselves" to provide interpretation, through *ijma'*, of the classical and modern textual sources in Islam.[190] In this context, Eickelman and Anderson (1999) noted that "opening up *ijma'*—the creation of authoritative legal and moral consensus—to a range of educated persons and not just scholars formally trained in Islamic jurisprudence alters the ground rules for Islamic legal interpretation, introducing 'lay' interpreters and heightening public scrutiny to the judicial process."[191] So, in this increasingly discursive environment, the religiously trained *ulama* are facing fierce competition from the nonconventional newcomers to the public sphere of Islam—the secularly trained new religious intellectuals.

Along the same lines, Muhammad Qasim Zaman (2002) noted that, "the new religious intellectuals often define themselves against the *ulama*, compete for authority with them, and sometimes dismiss them either as stooges of the government or as utterly mired in an anachronistic tradition."[192]

Eickelman and Piscatori (2004) predicted two possible outcomes of the fragmentation of the *ulama*'s authority as a result of the rising levels of mass education and mass communication in the Islamic public sphere: Either the conflict on the Islamic arena will become more intense and the parties involved in the deliberations will become more polarized, or the authority contenders will reach a compromise and accommodate each others' needs through peaceful deliberations.[193]

The new media are creating what Mandaville (2002) referred to as "media Islam" or "soundbite Islam,"[194] which has the ability to reach out to major segments of the public across time and space. One segment of the Muslim public that is becoming more involved in the new Islamic message disseminated by the "new religious intellectuals" is the young generation. Many of those young Muslims may not attend religious sermons at mosques regularly, but they spend hours using the new media—either watching shows presented by the new religious intellectuals on satellite television or surfing the Internet, where several of those nontraditional intellectuals have their websites. Those young crowds have often felt a "disconnect" with the traditional *ulama*, because of what they perceived as the alienating nature of their preaching methods, the complexity of their messages and their inability to understand the developments of modern society. The new, nontraditional religious intellectuals have broken the barriers that used to exist between the religious establishment and the younger people. They have the ability to reach out to the young Muslims; they dress like them, speak their language, and understand their mentality. In this context, Reza Sheikholeslami (2006) noted that "No longer is the turbaned Azharite [scholar from Al-Azhar] the trademark of the Muslim image; Islam is now available in far more accessible format, open to everyone."[195]

The strong presence of the Islamic message in the modern media technologies, such as the Internet and satellite television, in the new Islamic public sphere is "one of the main characteristics of Islamic revival"[196] in the twenty-first century. This goes against the argument made by several secular modernists in the west, who predicted that religion in general, and Islam in particular, will diminish in the modern era.[197] The next section will address the importance of religion in the modern public sphere and the meaning and role of postmodernity in public Islam.

The Islamic Revival in the New Public Sphere: From "Modernity" to "Postmodernity"

Habermas' "bourgeois public sphere" neglected the role of religion as previously mentioned in this chapter. This is part of a trend by the western "hegemonic discourse of modernity,"[198] which has its origins in Europe's Enlightenment era, and which argued that secularism is a prerequisite for modernity, and that religion would eventually disappear from the modern public spheres since it is not compatible with modernity.

Casanova (1994) was among the first scholars who challenged the modernity theorists' argument in that context through his "deprivatization of religion" thesis. The core of Casanova's thesis is that "religion abandons its assigned place in the private sphere and enters the undifferentiated public sphere of civil society to take part in the ongoing process of contestation, discursive legitimation, and redrawing of the boundaries."[199] Casanova argued that religion is not antimodernity since it has the ability to be "reflexively reconstructed"[200] by becoming integrated in the public sphere of modern civil societies. He supported his thesis by citing several incidents that reflected the rise, rather than the demise, of religion in the 1970s. The most notable of these incidents was the Islamic Revolution in Iran, which overthrew the secular and monarchical regime of the Iranian Shah in 1979.[201]

According to Casanova, the revival of religious movements in various public spheres may be taken to be "a sign of the failure of the Enlightenment to redeem its own promises in each of these spheres. Religious traditions are now confronting the differentiated secular spheres, challenging them to face their own obscurantist, ideological, and inauthentic claims."[202]

Echoing Casanova's argument, Thompson (1995) argued that religious traditions have not weakened in the modern world because they are an integral part of everyday life, and they are providing individuals with a sense of collective identity and of being part of a community that has the same destiny.[203]

Many western secularists, who have written about the subject, mainly during the 1960s, have doubted that Islam is compatible with modernity. This trend, described as the "secular bias of modernization theory,"[204] has questioned Islam's openness or ability to change and predicted its demise. It has also noted that new technologies would have to weaken any religious faith. Proponents of this trend criticized religious tradition, and considered it an antithesis to modernity. "To them, the label 'traditional' *taqlidi* [in Arabic] implies being chained to the past and unwilling to participate in debates concerning the reform of existing social and political institutions."[205]

Daniel Lerner (1963), one of the prominent western modernity theorists, argued in his classic book *The Passing of Traditional Society*, which has set the tone for subsequent scholarship in that area, that the Middle East (mostly an Islamic region) has to adopt the western model of modernization in order for it to have any hope of achieving progress. Lerner gave the Middle East two choices: "Mecca [as a symbol for religion since Mecca is the holiest place for Muslims and the site of the annual Muslims' pilgrimage] or mechanization [as a symbol for western modernity]."[206]

The flaws of secular theorists' argument have been highlighted by several scholars. For example, Eickelman and Piscatori (2004) noted that those theorists' presumption that tradition and modernity cannot go hand-in-hand "oversimplifies a complex process of interaction in which religion and tradition coexist with economic development and the needs of a modern society."[207] Along the same lines, John Thompson (1995) argued that individuals who seek modernity and enlightenment do not have to give up their tradition.[208] "To view the renewal of religious belief as merely a defensive reaction to the process of modernization is to fail to see that there are certain aspects of tradition which are neither eliminated nor made redundant by this process—aspects which provide a foothold for the continued cultivation of religious and other forms of belief in the modern world."[209]

Wilkins (2004) dismissed the western secularization theory as "ethnocentric, hierarchical and patriarchal."[210] Wilkins alluded to the importance of considering the cultures, norms and traditions that are unique to the Middle East region rather than assuming that this region will have take the same path to modernity that the west has taken, regardless of the critical differences between the west and the Middle East.[211]

Two main questions should be addressed in this context: What does tradition mean? and What does modernity mean? Thompson (1995) defined tradition as "a set of background assumptions that are taken for granted by individuals in the conduct of their daily lives, and transmitted by them from one generation to the next. In this respect, tradition is not a normative guide for action but rather an interpretive scheme, a framework for understanding the world."[212]

Peter Mandaville (2001) argued that there is no clear definition of modernity, but it has often been discussed in the western context. According to Mandaville, modernity does not have to be associated exclusively with the west, but its nature has to be renegotiated to make it fit any cultural context, and not just the western context. It is possible "to construct an Islamic modernity, one which retains modern features but which elaborates them without reference to or conjunction with Western political theory, a modernity divorced from the West."[213]

Echoing Mandaville's argument, Pernilla Ouis (2002) argued that Muslims are trying to achieve "modernization without Westernization."[214] This means that Muslims are willing to adopt certain aspects of modernity, such as scientific progress and technology, but they are not open to adopting western secular values or to giving up their religious traditions. Ouis suggested a strategy called "Islamization," which means integrating Islam in the different sectors that characterize a modern society, such as science and technology without offending the Islamic traditional values. This strategy would "[resolve] the paradoxes between tradition and modernity as it creates a discourse of coalition between the traditional and modern discourses."[215] Islamization would be the consequence of having the process of modernity go through a "cultural filter"[216] to make it more suitable to an Islamic context.

Responding to the western modernity theorists' criticism of tradition, Hobsbawm (1983) was cited in Ouis (2002) as arguing that the best of past traditions can be reconstructed and used in today's modern cultures. This is part of a process described as "invented traditions"[217]—a term that encompasses both tradition and modernity through justifying current developments by past practices.[218]

Many voices of reform in the Islamic world today are adopting the "invented traditions" process by invoking Islam's "Golden Age" to justify their calls for more developments within Islamic societies. This "Golden Age," as previously mentioned, refers to the Prophet's lifetime and the era of his first four successors who were described as *al-Khulafa al-rashidun* (the rightly guided caliphs). That era witnessed "little divergence between ideals and reality"[219] since Muslims at the time were abiding by the state law voluntarily, without state coercion, and there was justice in the community.[220]

The most prominent Islamic trend that adopted the "invented traditions" process by finding inspiration in the Muslims' "Golden Age" was the *Salafiyya* (from *salaf,* the ancestors of Islam). One of the proponents of that trend, Sheikh Muhammad 'Abduh, who lived in the nineteenth century, argued that "Muslims' neglect of the common good in legal matters and rulers' emphasis on obedience above justice engendered intellectual confusion, legal stagnation, political corruption, and the decline of Islam."[221]

The "invented traditions" process can be applied to the current developments in the Islamic world. It is becoming obvious today that the traditional Islamic message, which originated in the heart of the Arabian desert during the "Golden Age" more than fifteen centuries ago, has not weakened or disappeared, but it has acquired further strength and attracted more followers through its appearance in the new media. It can be argued that the flaws of the western secularization theory have been proven by the fact that Islam is currently witnessing the emergence of a new public sphere, where the media technologies, such as the Internet, are assigned a vital role without marginalizing the Islamic traditions. In fact, these new media technologies are being utilized to fit the Islamic context. If technology is one aspect of modernity, then the fact that media technologies operate in an Islamic context has two implications: that Islam is not opposed to modernity and that modernity can exist alongside religious traditions in nonwestern environments.

The new Islamic public sphere that is taking place through the new media is highly complex, and it includes new voices competing in a fast-paced, multifaceted environment. Some observers argue that making sense of the tremendous changes that have been taking place in this new public sphere is beyond the scope of modernity. "More complex ways of inculcating and negotiating background understandings are needed to provide the 'connecting tissue' of information, expression, and solidarity."[222] That is why, the new Islamic public sphere can be described as "postmodern," allowing for the preservation of Islam's foundational core, while giving way for the revitalization and "reinvention"[223] of values and beliefs. The postmodern nature of the new media, particularly the Internet, "is characterized by features such as the eclectic mixing of hitherto antagonistic spheres such as high and low culture, the breakup of national consensus and paternalism, and individual constructions of identities."[224] The postmodern philosophy leans toward resisting the status quo to the point of approaching anarchy.[225]

Like modernity, the literature does not seem to provide a clear or comprehensive definition of postmodernity. In this context, Akbar Ahmed, one of the most prominent thinkers in political Islam, argued that even though "the postmodern [as its prefix indicates] comes after the modern, their boundary is blurred and each is mutually implicated in the other. This makes it rather difficult to determine just how 'new' the changes allegedly typical of postmodernity are and whether they must be subjected to a new 'postmodernist' form of analysis."[226] Postmodernity, according to Ahmed, is associated with "pluralism," "a greater tolerance of difference" and "a heightened skepticism of traditional orthodoxies."[227]

The sense of skepticism that Akbar referred to in the context of postmodernism is a common characteristic among the new breed of participants in the "new Islamic public sphere," who are using media technologies to question basic elements of their religious identity and redefine many of their ideologies. Skepticism is one main aspect of the "objectification" of Islam, which will be discussed in the next section.

"Objectification" of Islam in the New Media Environment

The new media, such as the Internet, have paved the way for the "new religious intellectuals" in Islam to be continuously inquisitive, ask questions about the Qur'an and the *hadith* and reinterpret aspects about their faith that they used to take for granted. This is part of the "objectification of Islam"[228]—a term coined by Eickelman and Piscatori (2004) to help redefine what it means to be a believer or a member of the Islamic faith in a postmodern environment. Mass education and mass communication have become important factors in the process of objectifying Islam, especially during the last third of the twentieth century, and getting into the twenty-first century. The Islamic world today is witnessing an "increased scrutiny of received ideas as Muslims realize the diversity of [the voices in their religion] and the multiple 'Islamic' ways of doing things."[229] Today's Muslims, by redefining their religious identity, "assert their continuity with the past while coming to terms with a modern intellectual terrain."[230]

Objectification involves objectively assessing basic premises and parameters of the religion through asking broad questions, such as "What is Islam? How does it apply to the conduct of my life? and "What are the principles of faith?"[231] Asking these kinds of questions on the Internet has created "a public space that is discursive, performative, and participative, and not confined to formal institutions recognized by state authorities."[232]

Olivier Roy (2004) has argued that the objectification process is a natural and logical consequence of two factors: the fragmentation of traditional Islamic authority, represented in the *'ulama* and the "deterritorialization of Islam" (i.e. "Islam is no longer embedded in territorial cultures").[233] According to Roy, objectification is characterized by "the dilution of the pristine culture, where religion was embedded in a given culture and society; the absence of legitimate authorities who could define the norms of Islam, coupled with a crisis of the transmission of knowledge; and the impossibility of any form of legal, social or cultural coercion."[234]

We believe that the objectification of Islam through a discursive environment like the Internet can be a double-edged sword. On one hand, it can democratize the religious debates and encourage participants in these debates to develop a reflexive approach by re-evaluating their norms and values in a postmodern context, rather than blindly accepting them without question or argument; but on the other hand, asking broad and general questions about the basics of Islam through online discussion boards can lead to further confusion and even misperceptions about Islam, especially in an environment where the "lay" people are playing a more active role in the religious deliberations. This environment is marked by what Olivier Roy (2004) has described as the "crisis of authority,"[235] in light of the diminishing role of traditional Islamic institutions, like Al-Azhar, the marginalized role of the *ulama* in religious debates, and the rise of "new religious intellectuals" with no formal religious training, as previously explained.

The important questions that ought to be addressed in this context are: What role, if any, do the classical sources of Islamic knowledge play on the Islamic websites, and who speaks for Islam in the new public sphere online? Chapter 2 will deal with these questions in detail by researching the nature of Islamic websites, and how the Islamic virtual community has impacted the nature of deliberations about Islam.

Religion in the Virtual Public Sphere: The Case of Islam

We start this chapter by shedding some light on the limited scholarly literature that analyzes the virtual public sphere and the Internet role in creating and maintaining ideological, ritualistic, and social functions of a traditional religious community. We then provide a brief background on how Islam was brought to the cyber world, describing the plurality of Muslims' voices online to explain how Islamic websites and online discussion groups have provided new forums for *da'wa* (propagation of faith) and for participation in communal ritualistic acts that represent new, virtual communities of worship. In this chapter, we also address the issue of the Muslim public's trust or lack thereof toward the information delivered through the Islamic websites. With an outline of debates surrounding the role of new media in contemporary societies, the chapter applies the contentious critiques of the Internet and the egalitarianization of debate to Islamic websites. The chapter also addresses the "digital divide" and the extent to which the electronic public sphere is exclusive and elitist in its accessibility to those with no Internet connectivity in the Islamic world.

The Virtual Public Sphere

The Internet has created what Howard Rheingold (2000) described as "virtual communities," which are "social aggregations that emerge from the Net when enough people carry on those public discussions long enough, with sufficient human feeling, to form webs of personal relationships in cyberspace."[1] These virtual communities accentuate several of the same values that are adopted in the physical communities, such as freedom of expression, openness, and equal access.[2] The virtual community is an extension of the real community, and the meaning and values of a virtual community are derived from the participants in that community. In other words, virtual communities do not function as isolated entities, but they are the reflections of human cultural and social values.[3]

Virtual communities "combine traditional traits of [a conventional offline] community in a new setting. They occur as individuals assemble through Internet technology to form networks of interdependent relationships based on common vision, care and communication."[4] Members of a virtual community are often strongly connected through their online experiences of engaging in mutual dialogue and the exchange of ideas.[5]

Some scholars have preferred the term "online community" over "virtual community" because the term "virtual" implies a break away from reality and provides an alternate for real relationships.[6] However, Rheingold, and other advocates of the term "virtual community," argued that "what is virtual is not the online relationships, but the environment in which such relationships are established and constructed. Online relationships are 'real' in the sense that they represent actual social interactions, though they are mediated."[7]

The Internet's virtual community can fit in Habermas's concept of the public sphere as a space where members of the public participate in rational-critical debates outside the realm of the state authority. However, unlike Habermas's "bourgeois public sphere," which was characterized by defined social boundaries through the printing press and face-to-face interactions at salons and coffee shops, the public sphere on the Internet has boundless social environments that have facilitated communicative interaction in an unprecedented way.[8] The Internet develops social networks by amplifying the individual user's communicative power. "Thus, the Internet expands human relationships beyond normal forms of everyday social interaction."[9] Thanks to its "many-to-many mode of communication,"[10] which allows the possibility for all members to engage, the Internet has extended the discursive nature of the public sphere across space and time and has enlarged the number of audience that can enjoy the new online possibilities by effectively participating in robust conversations and dynamic dialogues.

The vibrant environment created by the Internet represents "structured situations in which large numbers of individuals can produce symbolic forms for others who are not physically present, while, at the same time, no individual is receiving symbolic forms produced by others to whom they cannot respond."[11] The Internet's speed and boundary-crossing capabilities allow for an open environment where democratic deliberations and exchange of ideas are possible.[12]

Members in an online environment or a virtual public sphere often feel connected through a sense of collective identity. "Each individual...[participating in an online environment] may be alone, with only the computer screen for company, but the technology shows that each separate person is linked to a greater collective, a global community of like minds and spirits. They are alone together."[13]

In the virtual public sphere, the Internet is considered a decentralized medium at two levels: At an individual user level where anyone with Internet accessibility can compose and send a message, and at an organizational level where there is a possibility of adding new networks as long as they abide by specific Internet protocols.[14] This decentralization of the virtual public sphere gives participants in online communities more freedom of action and allows for challenging the traditional authorities in the offline communities.[15]

Jon Anderson (1995) noted that cyberspace includes varied discourses pertaining to a range of realms, such as science, culture, and religion. "Some discourses have 'migrated' to the Internet from pre-existing communities and sites; others emerge there as its 'denizens' to utilize the potentials of near-instantaneous, near-global and, to them, nearly free communication to reach out and find each other—including, just as crucially, the unlike-as well as the like-minded."[16]

The question of whether the Internet expands the public sphere has been approached differently by optimistic "utopians" and cautious "dystopians."[17] Technological utopians believe that the anonymity guaranteed by the online public sphere encourages participants to express themselves more openly and to engage in informative debates with individuals from various geographical and sociocultural backgrounds. Proponents of that argument believe that the diversity of opinions and the multiplicity of identities made possible through the online environment can serve as an effective way to improve communication among members of the humankind.[18]

Utopians also argue that the Internet helps promote Habermas' concept of intersubjective communicative action through providing a forum for open-ended communication among participants from all walks of life. "This discursive quality [of the Net] permits ongoing discussion not only of existing political issues, but holds open the possibility of introducing new issues, that is, of defining the field of the political."[19]

Some utopians, such as Rheingold (2000), have gone as far as comparing the virtual public sphere to an "electronic agora"[20]—a concept that has its roots "in the original democracy, Athens, [where] the agora was the marketplace, and more—it was where citizens met to talk, gossip, argue, size each other up, find the weak spots in political ideas by debating about them."[21]

The cyber environment, with its bulletin boards, chat rooms, and listserves, allows us to "break our public silence"[22] by articulating our views in a bolder, less restrictive manner than would be possible in face-to-face conversation. The cyber world has provided a venue for a plurality of voices and enhanced people's tolerance of hostile opinions. "Cyberspace has this 'open-minded' quality; users of all stripes flock there, with only the rules of social propriety and 'netiquette' to guide them, and engage with one another."[23] The virtual community networks have the ability to promote participatory democratic systems through ongoing dialogue, trust, and social collaboration.[24]

Technological dystopians are more cautious in their analysis of the Internet as a public sphere. Despite the fact that many dystopians admit that the Internet has accelerated the pace of human communication and made the dissemination of messages more convenient, still they warn against the possibility that too much indulgence in online debates can isolate the participants from their circles of family and friends and give them the illusion of social interaction when in reality they are being alienated from their real surroundings.[25] Some dystopians argued that the online discussion boards and chat rooms can restrict rather than expand the public sphere, as they "become spaces for bonding among like-minded individuals, with limited openings for (and civility toward) ideas that challenge basic premises."[26] Other dystopians are concerned about the likelihood that online interactions can lead to cultural misunderstandings among the participants, especially the less sophisticated and less nuanced ones.[27]

Zizi Papacharissi (2002) highlighted the necessity of differentiating between public space and public sphere online. While a virtual space provides a platform for discussion, a virtual sphere promotes democracy.[28] The fact that the Internet has created a new virtual space as a forum for deliberations does not automatically imply that the Internet could enhance an open exchange of ideas in a democratic way. According to Papacharissi, the Internet has the ability to facilitate participation in debates, but it does not guarantee a stronger democracy. Therefore, participants in online discussion forums have to be genuinely committed to expressing their opinions openly. Without that commitment, "the Internet as a public sphere merely harbors an illusion of openness."[29]

It has been argued by some dystopians that the Internet reduces its users' sense of responsible arguments since it dislocates them from their geographical location. "As the tourist may behave destructively when removed from the social constraints and responsibilities of home ground, so the virtual persona lacks social responsibility when ties to place are displaced."[30]

We take the position that the Internet has a great potential as an interactive medium. It has created an unlimited space where people are meeting in the virtual world, exchanging ideas, and engaging in discussion groups to deliberate a vast array of issues. However, we do not buy into the idea that the Internet, or any other technology for that matter, has the ability, through its transformative powers, to completely change our lives and determine our future. This is part of the "technological determinism" theory developed by the Canadian scholar Marshall McLuhan, who argued that "the medium is the message"[31] and believed that technology can change society and culture, "sometimes in unexpected ways."[32] Echoing McLuhan's theory, Neil Postman (1993) argued that media technology can lead to the loss of community and the decline of traditional values and cultural beliefs. Postman coined the term "technopoly," to refer to "the deification of technology, which means that the culture seeks its authorization in technology, finds its satisfactions in technology, and takes its orders from technology."[33] Both McLuhan and Postman have overestimated and exaggerated the technological potential at the expense of considering the circumstances and conditions in traditional social contexts that have a say in how technology is utilized.

In our assessment of the Internet environment as a virtual public sphere, we have to tie the effectiveness of that new electronic public space, not just with the technological potential of the Internet, but also with the linguistic capabilities and the intellectual qualifications of the Internet users who form discussion groups in the cyber world and who participate in online deliberations. In this context, Rheingold (2002) noted that "the technology will not itself fulfill [the democratization] potential; [the Internet] must be used intelligently and deliberately by an informed population."[34] Along the same lines, Bohman (2004) argued that online communication ought to be determined by the software rather than the hardware. The Internet hardware, according to Bohman, is "a network of networks with technical properties that enable the conveyance of information over great distances with near simultaneity."[35] Bohman defined the software as "the way in which people improvise and collaborate to create new possibilities for interaction. Software in this sense includes both the modes of social organization mediated through the Net and the institutions in which the Net is embedded."[36]

Echoing the above-mentioned arguments, Deborah Wheeler (2006) argued that the Internet impact has to be assessed in the context of its users' social practice. According to Wheeler, "the meaning and implication of the [technological] tool are found in society's use of technology, and this is why we see the same tool, the Internet, having different meanings in a variety of contexts."[37]

So, what matters is not the role of the Internet technology in enhancing public sphere as much as how the Internet is being utilized by social actors to contribute to that sphere. Internet users should not be regarded as the passive beneficiaries who are at the mercy of that technology, but as active members of their society who are capable of contributing to the construction of meanings online.[38]

This brings us to the second point that we have to consider in our assessment of the virtual public sphere, and that we will address in more detail in the next section. We should not assume that the online and the offline public spheres are totally separate. The virtual interactive community cannot survive by itself; it cannot perform in a vacuum; it is affected by the prevalent culture of the offline community. The global nature of the online community complements the local nature of the offline community. In this context, Wellman and Gulia (2003) argued that

> Operating via the Net, virtual communities are glocalized. They are simultaneously more global and local, as worldwide connectivity and domestic matters intersect. Global connectivity de-emphasizes the importance of locality for community; online relationships may be more stimulating than suburban neighborhoods. At the same time, people are usually based at their home, the most local environment imaginable, when they connect with their virtual communities.[39]

The next section sheds some light on how the Internet technology, with its discussion boards and chat rooms, has contributed to the dissemination and even restructuring of religious doctrines.

RELIGION IN THE VIRTUAL PUBLIC SPHERE

The virtual public sphere provided through the Internet creates new venues for the dissemination of religious knowledge and results in changes that revitalize the core of traditional religious communities.[40] Consequently, religious doctrines are being restructured in a virtual environment that is shaped more by individual practice than by religious institutions.[41] Religious doctrines and principles that used to fall under the control of a centralized authority are now openly debated, and even challenged by participants in various online discussion boards.[42] Members of these discussion boards are enjoying greater access to religious knowledge away from the obstacles that exist in a traditional offline environment, such as age and gender.[43]

The interactive, flexible, nonlinear, and decentralized nature of the Internet has contributed to "transferring the power of presenting religious texts from the spiritual authorities to the subordinates, the users, . . . [and] opening new prisms of interpretation to dicta imposed by the religious authorities."[44] This means that the Internet has challenged the vertical channels of communication from the religious elites to the subordinates, and has questioned the exclusive divine authority of the traditional religious institutions.[45] In this context, the religious environment in cyberspace has been described as "a community of equals,"[46] where status is not a deciding factor in who can or cannot contribute to the ongoing deliberations, and where regular individual participants can ask questions that they did not dare ask in face-to-face encounters with religious authorities.

Thanks to the Internet, we are witnessing what some scholars have described as the disembedding of ritual interaction from its clearly defined temporal and spatial conditions manifested in its original social environment.[47] Addressing this issue, Anthony Giddens, who coined the term "disembedding" in his classic work *The Consequences of Modernity* (1990), defined it as "the 'lifting out' of social relations from local contexts of interaction and their restructuring across indefinite spans of time and space."[48] Interaction among participants in religious discussion groups and other online religious forums includes participants who do not necessarily come from the same geographical area and whose communication is achieved across spatial distances.[49]

Many religious groups have been taking their message to the Net over the past few years. The number of web pages covering religion has risen from approximately 1.7 million by the late 1990s to more than 51 million by the year 2004.[50] Followers of various religions are utilizing the virtual public sphere to publicize their religions, participate in religious rituals, strengthen their spiritual lives, and form online discourses to discuss and debate various issues revolving around their faith. This is part of a process described by Heidi Campbell (2005) as "spiritualizing the Internet,"[51] or bestowing on the Internet a certain meaning that contextualizes the purpose of its use in a particular spiritual environment. "Contained within the [online] discourse of spirituality is the idea of the sacred, creating a 'holy space' that is set apart...as a sphere where religious practitioners can search for meaning and present their beliefs."[52]

The way the Internet technology is being shaped to fit the needs of various religious groups is an indication of how "a technology is cultured by the culture in which it lives and by the agents who utilize it."[53] This means that "cultures modify technologies and endow them with a communal context. The Internet thus becomes a set of varied cultured technologies in different cultural contexts."[54] This implies that the Internet technology is not capable of automatically transforming a culture unless the cultural environment is conducive to that transformation and as previously discussed calls into question the determinative power of technology.

As a cultured technology, the Internet is what its users make of it. The degree of openness, freedom, and interaction in a religious website depends on the nature of that site and the agenda of its owners and designers. In this context, Christopher Helland (2005) made a distinction between "online-religion," where participants could enjoy a high level of unrestricted freedom and interactivity and "religion-online," where participants could only receive information without having the ability to interact, express their opinions, or provide feedback.[55] Helland's distinction, which is often cited in the literature, has been very helpful in showing how the type of religious website affects the interactivity level of its members.

While religion-online "is an organized attempt to present religion through a medium for communication within a traditional top-down hierarchy,... online-religion is where a more egalitarian existence reigns."[56] Online-religion websites allow religious practitioners to creatively repackage their beliefs and practices in a way that would make them more approachable and understandable by the lay people.[57]

It is the "participatory quality"[58] of the online-religion type websites that can contribute to creating a dynamic religious public sphere over the Internet. The level of participation and interaction in the online-religion websites is determined by the extent of support and encouragement that these sites receive from the individuals and institutions in the offline religious environment.

The cyber experience of the participants in the interactive, online-religion websites should not be separated from their offline experiences. The offline religious practices of those participants are extended and given new meanings through their involvement in online-religion websites.[59] Many scholars highlighted the need to study how the openness in an online environment is determined by the availability of resources in the offline world. For example, having access to computers is a required factor for participating in an online discussion group.[60] It can also be argued that the construction of religious identity is a product of the interplay between factors in online and offline communities.[61]

The literature on religion in the virtual public sphere has not provided many details on the functions of religions websites. However, Krüger (2004) highlighted four such functions: Presentation of religious principles, doctrines, and institutions; interactive communication around religious issues through discussion forums and chat rooms; providing religious services, such as arranging online rituals; and advertising of religious material, such as books and compact discs.[62]

We can conclude in this section that the Internet has been playing a critical role in expanding the religious community beyond space and time and creating a platform through which multiple voices can contribute to religious deliberations outside the realm of centralized religious authorities. The Internet role in that regard has to be complemented and facilitated by an offline religious environment that is open to and supportive of a vibrant online religious public sphere. The next section will shed some light on the Islamic presence in the cyber world and how members of the Islamic faith have found new venues for religious expression through the virtual public sphere.

THE VIRTUAL ISLAMIC PUBLIC SPHERE

A search for the word "Islam" on the Internet would yield links to a wide variety of Islamic websites, representing multiple points of view and diverse perspectives. Some of these sites are extensions of the traditional Islamic institutions, like Al-Azhar, while others are platforms for marginalized voices and alternative interpretations of Islam. Many of these sites are not labeled in a way that reflects the values and ideologies of their authors,[63] but they provide various kinds of services in several languages to their visitors, such as chat rooms, discussion boards, lectures, commentaries, *fatwa* (religious edict), and Qur'anic recitation and translation, among others.

Islamic websites are functioning in what Gary Bunt (2000) described as "Cyber Islamic Environments,"[64] where these sites' visitors are involved in the ritual sharing, exchange, and transmission of information. These online Islamic environments serve as arenas for constructive networking and dialogue, where participants reach new levels of religious understanding and articulation in a way that helps them define, or at least, draw the preliminary parameters of their religious identity.[65]

The Cyber Islamic Environments were described by Peter Van Der Veer (2006) as "cyber salons."[66] The virtual deliberations taking place through these cyber salons can be compared to the rational-critical debates that used to take place in the salons of seventeenth- and eighteenth-century Europe. These Islamic cyber salons, many of which are operating outside the realm of governmental influence, have transcended several conventional barriers—including censorship and suppression of oppositional voices—that often exist in many offline Islamic communities.[67]

Islamic websites not only provide a new platform for the articulation of opinions, but also change the way many Muslims practice their rituals. For example, a visitor to an Islamic website can determine the beginning or ending of a particular ritual, such as reciting the *Qur'an* or listening to a sermon without having to abide by the restraints of group participation at an actual mosque in one's neighborhood.[68] This phenomenon was described by Jocelyne Cesari (2004) as "desacralization," which means that thanks to the Internet, the Qur'an "no longer belongs to the space-time of the sacred...today even a non-Muslim with no knowledge of Arabic can have access to a reading of the Qur'an [online] in English, French, or German."[69]

The main objective of most Islamic websites is to stress the *da'wa* in a way that would appeal to both Muslims and non-Muslims inside and outside the Islamic world.[70] *Da'wa* is closely associated with the concept of *jihad* (exerting one's power in the path of God).[71] Despite the association of *jihad* with violence, coercion, and terrorism in the western context, the concept entails more complexity. Even though one aspect of *jihad* refers to engaging in militaristic battles to defend God's word or to protect one's homeland, the highest form of *jihad* is more spiritually oriented, and it has to do with battling the temptations of one's own self.[72] *E-jihad* is a term coined by Bunt (2003) to refer to the online manifestations of the concept of *jihad*.[73] These manifestations are determined by how a particular Islamic group opts to define *jihad* and make its website revolve around that definition. It is worth mentioning here that Islam encourages persuasive rather than violent *jihad*, particularly when it comes to *da'wa*. In this context, the *Qur'an* states in verse number 256 in the chapter titled *Al-Baqara* (the Cow) that "There shall be no coercion in matters of faith."[74]

How Islam Was Brought to the Net?

Jon Anderson (2001) noted that the emergence of Islam in the cyber world went through three stages or phases.[75] The initial phase took place in the early 1980s through the young generations of Muslim students who left their home countries and headed to the west to enroll in computer science, engineering, and other applied science programs at universities and research centers, and to receive advanced training in these fields. This phase was described by Anderson (2001) as the "technological adepts"[76] phase. The Muslim students utilized their technical expertise to develop online archives and discussion groups revolving around Islam, and thanks to their efforts, digitized texts of the *Qur'an* and the *hadith* were brought online.[77] Many of those students were members of Muslim Student Associations at American and European universities, and they had a great interest in pushing for "a global Islamic consciousness."[78] They posted practical information to help their fellow Muslim students living in the west in locating a nearby mosque, knowing prayer times, getting moderately priced flights or finding butchers who sell *halal* meat (slaughtered according to the Islamic law).[79] At this stage, very few scholars with formal religious training had a presence online.

Then, following the advent of the World Wide Web in the early 1990s, a second phase described by Jon Anderson (2001) as "officializing strategies and activists"[80] started. It is worth mentioning here that Anderson borrowed the term "officializing strategies" from the prominent French sociologist Pierre Bourdieu. In his classic work *Outline of a Theory of Practice*, which was translated to English in 1977 and reprinted in 2007, Bourdieu defined officializing strategies as the attempt by a socially recognized public authority "to manipulate the collective definition of the situation in such a way as to bring it closer to the official definition...and thereby to win the means of mobilizing the largest possible group."[81]

In this second phase, two forms of officializing strategies took shape online. One form was represented by spokespersons for established Islamic institutions and traditional *da'wa* organizations in Muslim-majority societies, who started to make their presence felt online to correct what they perceived at the time to be misrepresentations of Islam in the cyber world. Included in this phase were several Islamic embassies, such as the Embassy of Saudi Arabia in Washington, DC, which launched its own website to publicize the Saudi role in the Islamic world; also included were various 'ulama, who wanted to make their presence felt and to have a say in the new cyber world. In fact, the prestigious religious establishment, Al-Azhar, launched its webpage in both English and Arabic in 1999 to serve as a source of authoritative religious guidance online.[82]

The second form of officializing, arising in the mid- to late 1990s, had a more oppositional and assertive tone and became associated with political Islam or "Islamism." Examples of Islamist movements that launched websites during that time were the Islamic Salvation Front in Algeria, the Movement for Islamic Reform in Saudi Arabia, and the Muslim Brotherhood in Egypt. These movements' websites were mostly devoted to criticizing the Arab and Islamic regimes.[83]

The third and current phase of Islam's cyber-evolution marked the "online advent of moderate Islam."[84] According to Anderson (2001), a sense of moderation and a less assertive middle-ground approach characterizes this phase, which may be attributed to the participation of a broad base of professionals and middle-class Muslims who move back and forth between local and transnational spheres. Most of the websites in this phase have become more interactive, rather than just educational or informational, and have developed portals in multiple languages, marking a tremendous increase in the number of Internet users who can access these sites.[85]

Diversity of Opinions on Islamic Websites

The thousands of Islamic websites that exist today do not revolve around the same theme or disseminate the same message. To the contrary, the complexity and diversity of the traditional Islamic environment are exemplified in the virtual Islamic public sphere, where the Islamic websites represent the various branches of Islam—*Sunna* (orthodox), *Shi'a*, *Sufism* (mystical Islam), and schismatic or Islamic sect sites.[86] This diversity, which leads to opinion differences among participants in the Cyber Islamic Environments, counters the notion of homogeneous Islam, which is projected and propagated by several Islamic and non-Islamic circles.[87] While there is a sense of commonality and general agreement when it comes to Islam's five pillars and the Islamic faith's main principles that are clearly outlined in the *Qur'an* and the *Sunna*, there are differences in opinion regarding other issues, which have not been directly addressed in the Muslims' holy book and the *shari'a*. In fact, Islam encourages differences in opinion as long as they are settled through civilized deliberations and dialogues. Such dialogues have been extended and facilitated thanks to the virtual Islamic public sphere.[88]

Given the diversity of opinion among Islamic websites, it maybe hard to present a neat categorization for these sites. Since—as we explained in the previous section on religion in the virtual public sphere—the Internet is what its users make of it, the online Islamic environment has been utilized by various users in drastically different ways depending on their agendas and their ideologies. Some groups have developed a violent, militant form of websites that use threat and terror to spread their messages online, while others have developed a peaceful, dialogical form of websites that allow for civil engagement in debates and deliberations revolving around issues of common concern to contemporary Muslims. In this context, Hofheinz (2005) argues, "by far the most popular [Islamic] sites...are not the militant ones, but those promoting a moral renewal of the individual, based on the Qur'anic injunction that 'Allah [God] will never change the condition of a people until they change themselves.'"[89] These websites are the focus of this book, and the three websites we chose to analyze for this study belong to the latter type.

Musa Maguire (2006) addressed the issue of the diversity of messages on Islamic websites in his classification of online Islamic activity into five clusters: (1) Radical *jihadists* (considering *jihad* to be a primary Islamic duty; within that group, there are those who advocate practicing *jihad* within the parameters of Islamic law and those who use *jihad* as a justification for acts of violence and terror); (2) *Sufi* traditionalists (claiming to represent the spiritual side of Islam as a pathway to Islamic piety, and adhering to the traditional schools of Islamic law); (3) Religious modernists (enjoying a high literacy level with regard to current events, and favoring political engagement through the modern Islamist political movements, such as the Muslim Brotherhood in Egypt); (4) Conservative *salafis* (striving to abide by the beliefs and practices of the *Salaf-us-saalih* who are the pious predecessors, or the first three generations of Muslims; (5) True moderates (knowledgeable on issues of Islamic law, and adhering to the orthodox Islamic practices, yet tolerant of opinion differences among Muslims within the limits of orthodoxy).[90]

The diversity of the Islamic message online leads one to ask whether and to what extent the Islamic websites have led to a more clearly defined Islamic identity in today's postmodern world. Of course, the tenets, pillars, and core principles of the Islamic faith are not debatable, but what is open to interpretation and reconfiguration are the complexities of today's world and how Muslims cope with them. Although the Islamic websites serve as an ideal venue through which Muslims can engage in continuous dialogue about where they stand and how they ought to define themselves within contemporary contexts, some scholars believe that these websites have been successful in helping Muslims reach an agreement on these pressing issues. In this context, Bunt (2000) argued that Muslims' participation in cyberspace is "identity-less,"[91] and that there are no strict measures defining who a Muslim is or what role he/she should play in such a complex environment.

It is not the Islamic websites' responsibility to develop an Islamic identity that is agreed upon by all Muslims. In fact, this sounds like a practically impossible goal, given the diversity of the more than 1.2 billion Muslims who live in today's complex world. What these sites ought to do is to encourage their visitors to develop a greater self-awareness of what it means to be a Muslim by giving them the opportunity to ask critical questions about their religion and engage in constructive deliberations revolving around these questions. This is what many Islamic websites are actually doing, and it is part of the "objectification of Islam," which we referred to in detail in chapter 1.

Islamic Websites: A platform for New Voices

New media, particularly the Internet, have paved the way for new voices to contribute to the Islamic discussions and interpretations and to challenge the traditional Islamic authority represented by the 'ulama and the conventional religious establishment. In this context, Hofheinz (2005) referred to the possibility that the era of "the old patriarchs"[92] (by whom he meant the key figures who have traditional religious training in Islam) is nearing its end thanks to the Internet. In this section, we will shed more light on that issue and will present its consequences on the dissemination of the Islamic message.

Jon Anderson (2002) argued that the interactive nature of the Islamic websites, which relies on a horizontal, rather than a vertical form of communication, has helped the lay Muslims become more involved in the religious discussions and reduced the dependence on 'ulama's guidance.[93] The participants and visitors to these sites are lay in the sense that they have not received the traditional religious training of the 'ulama; however, they come from upper to middle socioeconomic classes; moreover, they enjoy a high educational and intellectual level thanks to the huge increase in the modern, secular mass education that allows them to engage in online Islamic discourse in multiple languages. As we mentioned in chapter 1, several scholars refer to those new participants in the online Islamic public sphere as the "new religious intellectuals,"[94] who have been using the cyber world to provide interpretations of the Qur'an and the hadith in accordance with the practical needs of contemporary Islamic societies. Eickelman and Anderson (1999) referred to the "new religious intellectuals" as follows: "The Transnational peak of this population takes the form of mobile professionals—a Tunisian Muslim psychotherapist in St. Louis or a Somali Muslim gynecologist in Toronto or an Egyptian Muslim computer programmer in Silicon Valley."[95]

In the meantime, the 'ulama and Islamic leaders affiliated with traditional religious institutions, who were initially resistant to the Internet technology, have become more open to the new technology. A case in point is the deputy to the Grand Sheikh of Al-Azhar institution, Sheikh Omar El-Deeb, whom we interviewed in Cairo, Egypt in December 2006. El-Deeb acknowledged the Internet role in facilitating and expediting the process of issuing *fatwa* and responding to Muslims' questions, but he cautioned against accessing websites with voices "claiming falsely to be a religious authority." El-Deeb noted that the best way for a Muslim to get a *fatwa* is to seek the advice of the specialized religious authorities who are in a position to make *fatwa*. According to El-Deeb, "anybody who volunteers to make *fatwa* without having the religious knowledge or the qualifications necessary to do so will end up in hell fire because he is not being honest with his fellow Muslims." El-Deeb added that engaging in an online dialogue to discuss issues related to one's religion is "a healthy phenomenon" and is highly encouraged in Islam. El-Deeb, however, argued that several online discussion boards run the risk of involving participants who are just expressing opinions with no idea about the basics of their religion. According to El-Deeb, "Islam today is being attacked through the Internet, and so Muslims have to use the same weapon to defend themselves by developing the skills that would allow them to use the Internet."[96]

The Al-Azhar institution launched its own website (www.alazhar.org) in the late 1990s. However, that Al-Azhar site has been out of service since the launching in May 2004 of a new, educationally oriented site (www.alazhar.gov.eg), providing services in Arabic, English, and French. We interviewed the webmaster of the new Al-Azhar website, Mahdy Shaltout, in Cairo, Egypt March 2007 to get more information about the website. Shaltout noted that the current site is more educational and less interactive, and that most of its visitors are students enrolled at Al-Azhar University. Shaltout also mentioned that the current structure of the site revolves around issues related to students and teachers, such as exam models and academic training. According to Shaltout, the Al-Azhar *'ulama*, in consultation with him, are the ones who determine the general philosophy and direction of the site. As for the educational material that is posted on the site, it is decided by the professors at Al-Azhar University. Shaltout mentioned that the site does not have a *fatwa* service, and that any requests for *fatwa* are transferred directly to the *Dar al-Ifta'* (the legally recognized official *fatwa* body in Egypt), which, according to Shaltout, is the only body authorized to issue religious edicts.[97]

At the time of writing, the ranking of the new Al-Azhar website on Alexa.com, based on the average number of visitors to that site over the previous three months, was 26,000. This is a relatively high ranking compared to the other popular Islamic websites, particularly when considering that the site's visitors are mainly from the academic world, which is a very limited field. We believe that Al-Azhar should have a site that caters to the needs of the Muslims at large, and not just its students and faculty. This is especially important at a time when the online Islamic public sphere is filled with thousands of websites that provide both authoritative and nonauthoritative *fatwas* and interpretations of the *Qur'an* and the *sunna*. Having mentioned that, we also believe that it is encouraging that such a prominent Islamic institution like Al-Azhar, with all its prestigious *'ulama* and scholars has decided to create a place for itself in the cyber world.

Several *'ulama* have gone beyond just acknowledging the Internet use in an Islamic context to actually contributing to the Islamic websites. A case in point is Sheikh Samy Al-Sersawy, an Al-Azhar-certified Muslim preacher, and a member of the *Fatwa* (Edicts) Committee at Al-Azhar. Al-Sersawy, a young *'alim* in his late thirties or early forties, has posted more than eighty of his religious lectures and sermons on www.Islamway. com (one of the websites included in our analysis) after being invited to do so by the site's authorities. In our personal interview with Al-Sersawy in Cairo, Egypt in January 2007, he noted that the Internet plays a critical and vital role in serving Muslims, especially the ones who live outside the Muslim-majority societies. According to Al-Sersawy, the Islamic websites, if utilized properly, can help create a new breed of moderate, nonextremist young Muslims.[98]

Al-Sersawy said, "Instead of addressing five or ten people at the mosque, I can address ten or twenty thousand people who are able to access my lectures over the Internet." Al-Sersawy, however, noted that in some cases, face-to-face interactions with the preacher could still be needed to nurture the spirituality of the individual Muslim. He added that even though the Internet can save Muslims' time in sending and receiving *fatwas*, it cannot make up for going to the mosque to participate in certain activities, such as the Friday prayers, which Muslims are required to perform in a group at the mosque. Al-Sersawy criticized the attitude of several *'ulama* who boycott the Internet technology, and he said that the Internet "ought to complement the preacher's role." He pointed to the responsibility of the modern Muslim preachers to learn how to use the technology and to be able to reach out to the younger Muslim generations with a message that suits the contemporary environment we are living in. In that context, Al-Sersawy said that he spends hours every week checking out different Islamic websites to update himself on the kinds of sermons, lectures, messages, and services that are provided through these sites. He acknowledged that Al-Azhar website is lacking on many fronts, and it needs to be updated and modernized to suit and reflect the role played by Al-Azhar in today's Islamic world. Al-Sersawy said: "There is no doubt in my mind that the Internet has its downside, such as including Islamic sites that are not backed by qualified Islamic authorities; however, if we, as Muslims, isolate ourselves and resist new technologies, there will be serious repercussions on the Islamic community."[99]

Both the *ulama* and the new religious intellectuals participate in the virtual Islamic public sphere, which includes a variety of voices, intellectual techniques, and interpretations. These mixed discourses were described by Anderson (1997) as the process of "creolization,"[100] which refers to an intermediate "creolized discourse" on a continuum between the *ulama* on one side and the "folk" Muslims on the other. This online creolized discourse is not the exclusive privilege of the *ulama*, who used to dominate the Islamic public discourse, nor is it the property of the folk, nonliterate masses. It is "a more middle-brow Islam associated with a more middling population."[101] This population is formed by what several scholars have described as the new religious intellectuals.

The creolized Islamic discourse online, which is the product of a highly educated cadre of Muslims and a decentralized, interactive medium like the Internet, has increased access to information about Islam and enhanced pluralism in the public Islamic discourse. Anderson (1999) referred to the Internet's role in making religious information more accessible as a "down-market technology," since it has enabled Muslims to access simplified information, *fatwas,* and pragmatic interpretations that used to be out of reach for many of them, or that used to be disseminated on a very limited scale in the traditional religious settings. In the meantime, Anderson described the well-educated new religious intellectuals who possess advanced technical and linguistic skills that allow them to utilize the services provided by the Islamic websites as the "up-market people."[102] So, according to Anderson, it is an up-market people possessing special skills utilizing a down-market, widely accessible technology.

One important factor that has contributed to the increasing accessibility of the Internet technology in the virtual Islamic public sphere beyond the circle of the religious elite or *ulama* is its vernacular nature. This feature has led to the "reintellectualization of Islamic discourse." Eickelman and Anderson (1999), who coined that term, described it as follows:

> By reintellectualization, we mean presenting Islamic doctrine and discourse in accessible, vernacular terms, even if this contributes to basic reconfigurations of doctrine and practice. Reintellectualization has sometimes been thought of as the province of folk or local Islam, a category that has been criticized for deflecting attention from the presence of the global in the local throughout the Muslim world. But more is involved with new media and new people: Islamic discourse has not only moved to the vernacular and become accessible to significantly wider publics, it has also become framed in styles of reasoning and forms of argument that draw on wider, less exclusive or erudite bodies of knowledge, including those of applied science and engineering.[103]

The difference between the vernacular and the classical use of language is best exemplified in the context of Arabic-speaking countries, where "a relatively wide gulf exists between formal, written Arabic and its vernacular, spoken form."[104] Many Islamic websites that address an Arab audience have been using a vernacular, more accessible form of Arabic that has helped increase their popularity, particularly among young Muslims living in the Arab world.

The vernacular nature of several Islamic websites is not the only factor that has contributed to their popularity among a wider audience; another important factor is the wide variety of controversial issues that have not often been discussed in the conventional Islamic circles. Several Islamic websites address issues that Muslims face in the contemporary complex environment. Examples of these issues are Islam's stand on organ transplantation, the use of ultrasound scan to determine an unborn baby's sex, or in vitro fertilization.[105] Such issues are often subject to heated debates among members and participants in the online discussion boards and chat rooms provided by most Islamic websites. The anonymity guaranteed by the Internet makes it easier for many Muslims to address such sensitive issues online compared to face-to-face encounters with a religious 'alim. The fact that several Islamic websites are discussing such sensitive issues negates the concerns of some scholars that the new online Islamic environment would witness the migration of old ideas and messages from the traditional Islamic public sphere rather than the introduction of new and innovative ideas.[106] In this context, Anderson warned that "new talk [on Islamic websites] has to be distinguished from new people talking about old topics in new settings."[107]

Although the 'ulama have not been entirely marginalized in the virtual Islamic public sphere, especially when many of them have enthusiastically utilized the Internet technology, still the Internet has led to a fragmentation of the traditional religious authority in Islam and the segmentation of the Islamic public sphere. For example, many members of the new religious intellectuals' group have launched their own websites to promote their ideologies and create their own following. In this context, Cesari (2004) argued that "The proliferation of public intellectuals with their own web pages...testifies to what extent Islam is becoming 'postmodernized' on the Internet...The postmodernization of Islam is characterized by a preponderance of personal testimony, of individual experience, of the ability to express one's identity through religious discourse."[108] This has led to a tremendous increase in the number of Islamic websites that exist today and confirmed the Internet's role as a segmenting rather than a homogenizing force.

In this context, Zizi Papacharissi (2002) argued that the online environment is conducive to the fragmentation of both audience and issues. This is because Internet users subscribe to special interest discussion groups that present different opinions and create several online publics that compete to participate in dialogues and deliberations in a highly discursive environment.[109] The creation of various spheres online can be compared to what Nancy Fraser (1992) described as the "subaltern counterpublics,"[110] which was referred to in chapter1. Along the same lines, Todd Gitlin (1998) argued that the Internet technology leads to the audience segmentation, moving people away from a unitary and coherent public sphere and closer to scattered, isolated, and fragmented "public sphericules."[111] Echoing Gitlin's argument, Peter Dahlgren (2005) noted that the Internet facilitates a heterogeneous environment with various "cyber ghettos" or fragmented public spheres.[112]

The fragmentation of the virtual public sphere has led to the reconfiguration of the boundaries of Islamic authority online in a way that has made them more porous.[113] "There are still the same guideposts [in Islam]: the scripture (the Qur'an), the person (the Prophet), and the law (shari'a, and with it the custodians of Muslim standards, the 'ulama), but each—the book, the Prophet, the moral custodian—has to be defined or redefined in cyberspace."[114]

Scholars have expressed different opinions about whether a unified traditional Islamic public sphere offline is better than a fragmented Islamic public sphere online. Norton (1999) argued that the authoritative interpretation of Islam, which has been limited to a small group of Muslim male theologians, represented in the 'ulama, is now open to a larger group of creative men and women who have diversified and pluralized the Islamic public sphere online.[115] Along the same lines, Bunt (2000) argued that the various platforms for dialogues that are made possible online have given an opportunity to Muslims from all sides to present their opinions, and have opened the door for stronger competition across the religious spectrum.[116] Bunt, however, warned against the anonymous sources who can easily post their opinions online. "Sermons can...be produced by anonymous sources, and, given that any individual or organization with the appropriate computer hardware, software and access to a service provider can produce an 'authoritative' Islamic website, traditional notions of religious authority can be circumnavigated in a computer-mediated environment."[117]

The Internet has made the activity of *ijtihad* easier since ordinary Muslims do not have to go out of their way to find an independent juristic interpretation based on an Islamic source. Now, they can look it up online. As we mentioned in chapter 1, *ijtihad* means "striving for the pragmatic interpretation of Islamic primary sources [mainly the Qur'an and the custom of the Prophet] in the light of contemporary conditions."[118] *Ijtihad* has traditionally been exercised by traditional religious authorities— theological scholars who received the necessary training at institutions like Al-Azhar to qualify them for that activity. But that has changed thanks to the Internet, which has opened the door for what Bunt (2003) described as "Electronic *ijtihad*," or "*e-ijtihad*."[119] This new form of *ijtihad* has expanded the circle of individuals who can interpret the *Qur'an* and the Prophet's *hadith* or provide *fatwa* online.

In this context, Annabelle Sreberny (2002) posed a critical question regarding the fragmented virtual Islamic public sphere: Who is authorized to provide religious interpretations in this open public discourse?[120] The critical nature of that question emanates from the fact that possessing an *ijaza* is no longer a prerequisite for becoming an Islamic authority online.[121] This opens the door for any individual, with no formal religious training, to claim that he is an Islamic authority who is qualified to provide *fatwa*. In this context, Deborah Wheeler (2003) questioned the authenticity of the information provided by many Islamic websites. However, according to Wheeler, this lack of religious authenticity in the new virtual Islamic public sphere has not slowed down Muslims' access to Islamic websites.[122] In this context, Dawson and Cowan (2004) referred to a "crisis of [religious] authority" on the Internet, where there are "instant experts" that come and go without any means to verify or authenticate their religious qualifications.[123]

Göran Larsson (2005) summed up the debate as to whether the Internet, with its unlimited number of websites, discussion groups, listserves, and homepages, has a positive or negative impact on religious authority in contemporary societies. According to Larsson, "On the one hand [the Internet] can be seen as an opportunity to liberate the individual from his or her social context or cultural bonds. On the other hand [it] can be seen as a threat to theological order and religious authority. From this point of view, the Internet is merely fostering relativism and sectarianism, thus leaving the individual in an existential world."[124]

Although the Internet has opened up new venues for ordinary Muslims to participate in dynamic religious discussions in a competitive, discursive environment, visitors to Islamic websites must exercise caution in seeking *fatwas* and asking for religious interpretation. They have to get information about the background of the Islamic website they are visiting, who launched it, what kind of interpretation it presents, and who provides that interpretation.

ISSUES OF TRUST AND SECURITY OR LACK THEREOF IN THE VIRTUAL ISLAMIC PUBLIC SPHERE

The postmodern society, with its tremendous developments, multiple information sources, and continuous complexities, is beyond the grasp and control of many young people who are going through the process of identity construction. Such an environment is further complicated by the declining role of the traditional values, norms, and life styles. "Instead of a phase preparing the individual to enter a new identity, which is relatively clearly defined, by tradition and the local community, the individual [in a highly complex environment] is faced with the task of exploring and constructing the self as part of a lifelong reflexive project."[125] In this context, Anthony Giddens (1990) argued that the feeling of disorientation that many people have in the current era is a result of "the sense many of us have of being caught up in a universe of events we do not fully understand."[126] Giddens referred to this era as "radicalized modernity,"[127] not at postmodernity.

In their attempts to overcome, or at least reduce, feelings of vulnerability, anxiety, insecurity, and uncertainty in such an environment where everything seems ambiguous and uncertain, many of these young people often seek guidance in the traditional religious beliefs and rituals, which they trust.[128]

According to Giddens, trust in this context emanates from a belief in the continuity and coherence of the external social reality.[129] Trust, according to Giddens, is related to "ontological security," which he defined as "the confidence that most human beings have in the continuity of their self-identity and in the constancy of the surrounding social and material environments of action. A sense of the reliability of persons and things, so central to the notion of trust, is basic to feelings of ontological security."[130] The reason many young people tend to trust religion and believe that it will provide them with what Giddens described as "ontological security" is that they feel that religion relieves uncertainty and prescribes how individuals should deal with the challenges of postmodernity.[131] "Even though this role of religion was probably more distinct and unquestioned in pre-modern societies, where religion was less differentiated from local tradition and ways of life, religious beliefs and symbols still influence rituals of transition and initiation of young people in [today's] society."[132] Since feelings of anxiety and uncertainty in contemporary societies are generally intolerable, "any movement (not only a religious one) that promises to provide or to renew certainty has a ready market [particularly among the younger generations]."[133]

We believe that many young Muslims today live in societies that are going through transitional phases, with an uncertain future. Many of them are trying to find refuge in their religion, and they are seeking religious figures that they can look up to as role models and sources of guidance that can help them make sense of their surroundings and reconstruct their identity. We also believe that many traditional ʿulama have failed to understand the mentality of the young Muslims or to gain their trust and confidence. Part of the problem is that several ʿulama have not tried to change their message to cope with the new social and cultural developments, and so they have become stagnant and old-school in the young people's eyes. Such a situation has caused many young Muslims to flock to the Internet, where many of them have found the coherence and onto-logical trust that they have been looking for on the Islamic websites. The innovative religious messages coming from the young religious intellec-tuals on these sites, along with the dynamic and interactive nature of online deliberations, have made the young Muslims feel at ease and have encouraged many of them to engage in dialogues and debates and to pose sensitive questions that they would not have dared to ask in a face-to-face encounter with a traditional *'alim* or an Al-Azhar scholar. In the online environment, many young Muslims have also felt that they are making a difference through their input, and that their opinions are seri-ously taken into consideration—a feeling that has been totally absent for many of them in the offline Islamic community.

The academic literature has touched on the Internet role as a source of trust and security in the postmodern world. For example, James Slevin (2000) argued that the Internet technology has the potential to reduce feelings of risk and uncertainty through helping the individual users cope with the complexities of everyday life and understand the "dilemmas of the self."[134] This can be achieved through sharing and exchanging ideas with like-minded people and engaging in dialogues where individuals are con-fronted with shocking experiences and encouraged to find solutions for them.[135] Along the same lines, Mia Löveim (2005) noted that a religious website can affect young people by its ability "to restructure identities and ideas encountered in life outside the Internet,...[and] also to reintegrate the complexities and ambiguities of this life, in a structure of meaning and relevance to the individual."[136] This partly explains why many young Muslims are fascinated with several Islamic websites, and why they have trusted the religious messages in the virtual Islamic public sphere.

But the seemingly limitless number of voices expressed through thou-sands of Islamic websites can also be a reason for increasing, rather than decreasing, the feelings of anxiety, uncertainty, and insecurity among the young Muslims who access these sites. Faced with the necessity to make a large number of choices whenever they access the Net, these young Muslims, who are trying to figure out their complex societies and to identify their roles in it, may lose a sense of direction in deciding which voice to follow or which interpretation to abide by. In the process, they may become even more perplexed, and may end up with more questions, rather than more answers. In this case, those who are seeking refuge from the ambiguities in the offline community may be confronted with even more ambiguities in the online community. Such a highly pluralistic and diversified environment, with no clearly defined boundaries, and where anonymous sources are issuing nonvalidated *fatwa* and giving nonauthenticated religious advise, can be similar to an anarchy.

So, the open and diverse environment provided through the Internet can be a double-edged sword for young Muslims who access the multitude of Islamic websites that emerge every day. Access to these sites can either confirm the technological utopians' perspective by reducing feelings of confusion, anxiety, and insecurity among young Muslims trying to figure out the fast developments in their societies, or it can substantiate the technological dystopians' perspective by increasing these young Muslims' sense of insecurity.

In this context, we make the argument that the Internet, in and by itself, is not capable of solely taking on the responsibility of helping today's young Muslims develop a clearly defined self-identity in a complex postmodern environment. The offline community, represented in the home, school, and mosque, should bear part of the responsibility in guiding young Muslims and arming them with the necessary tools that would help them differentiate between an authenticated and a nonauthenticated religious message in the virtual community. It is easier to build on and reinforce a religious identity that is already established in the offline community than to create an identity from scratch in the online community.[137] Social trust thrives better in an online environment when the foundations for identity construction are already in place.

The links between online and offline communities in the Islamic world would be further strengthened if more 'ulama (like Sheikh Samy Al-Sersawi mentioned earlier in the chapter) appreciate the impact of the Internet on young Muslims by joining the online discussion boards and repackaging their religious message to suit the interactive and vibrant nature of the Islamic websites. That way, today's young Muslims would develop a highly needed sense of ontological trust and security through the virtual Islamic public sphere.

The Impact of Oral Tradition on Trust in the Virtual Islamic Public Sphere

The tradition of oral communication in Islam has its origins in the *Qur'an*, which stresses the significance of "the word." In fact, the term *Qur'an* itself is derived from the verb *qara'a*, which means "to read," and the first word that God sent to the Prophet was *Iqra'* or "read."[138] The oral tradition of dealing with the *Qur'an* was reinforced through the memorization and recitation of Qur'anic versus by the Prophet and his companions and followers.[139] Moreover, the dissemination and validation of the *hadith* (Prophet's sayings) followed the indigenous oral model of *isnad* (the oral transmission of authoritative utterances by the Prophet through "trustworthy" individuals who were either close to the Prophet during his lifetime or who had these utterances transmitted to them through individuals who were part of the Prophet's immediate circle of family and companions).[140]

Contemporary Muslims, living in Muslim-majority societies, continue to adopt oral means of communication through face-to-face interactions at mosques, bazaars, and coffeeshops.[141] In today's virtual Islamic community, many Islamic websites, in an attempt to gain the trust of their visitors, are trying to reflect the oral tradition by allowing these visitors to download Qur'anic recitations, with a high sound quality, for free.[142] However, Mamoun Fandy (2000) expressed his doubts about whether the Internet that "privileges the domain of the written over that of the oral" would be able to gain the Arabs' trust.[143] It is worth mentioning here that even though the term "Arab" is not synonymous with the term "Muslim," all Arab societies are inhabited mostly by Muslims, and Islam is their official religion. So, the use of the term "Arab" in this context clearly has relevant applications to the Muslim people.

Echoing Fandy's thought, Jenny White (1999) argued that the "orality of trust," through word of mouth and simultaneous face-to-face interactions, creates local bonds that form the backbone of social cohesion in Islamic countries. According to White, "the depersonalized language of modern media [particularly the Internet] has limited credibility in niche ecologies characterized by a culture of orality and personal interaction."[144] Along the same lines, Thompson (1995) noted that new methods of religious interaction and communication on the Internet have depersonalized the content and structure of the traditional religious message. "To the extent that the transmission of tradition becomes dependent on mediated forms of communication, it also becomes detached from the individuals with whom one interacts in day-to-day life—that is, it becomes depersonalized."[145]

Cesari (2004) countered the argument that the Internet leads to a depersonalization of the religious message. According to Cesari, the relativistic nature of the religious beliefs in the postmodernist online environment, where everybody is free to pick and choose from a wide array of religious interpretations, leads to the individualization and "re-personalization—even to the point of total subjectivity—of religious belief and practice."[146]

Our position in the context of Islamic oral tradition and the Internet is that Islamic websites combine elements of both oral communication, through the audio Qur'anic recitations, and written communication through the other services that they provide, such as lectures, discussion boards, and chat rooms. There is no question that that Islamic societies have traditionally been characterized as oral cultures, but the younger-generation Muslims, who grew up with the Internet technology and got more used to it compared to their parents and grandparents, are gradually changing that tradition. The issue of oral versus written domains, and the Internet role in either or both domains is determined by other significant factors in the Islamic public sphere, such as Internet accessibility, illiteracy rates, and economic affordability. All these factors contribute to a "digital divide" when it comes to Internet use in the Islamic world. The next section will deal with this issue.

THE "DIGITAL DIVIDE" IN THE VIRTUAL ISLAMIC PUBLIC SPHERE

Before the advent of the Internet, and the emergence of various types of Islamic websites, the Islamic public sphere was exclusively dominated by a group of theologians and religious elites—the *'ulama*—who had the ultimate say and authority over the transmission of the religious message. However, as we previously discussed, the Internet has taken the Islamic public sphere to another level: The virtual world, where the religious authority has been broadened and "alternate discursive forms"[147] have been created, bypassing the "vertical hierarchies of [traditional] authority"[148] in Islam. So, for better or for worse, the *'ulama*'s privileged access to authoritative religious knowledge is challenged by alternative voices online. As religious elitism has given way to multiple sides and competing religious interpretations in the online world, socio-cultural elitism has become magnified through the technology gap popularly referred to as the "digital divide."

Pippa Norris (2006) noted that there is a "global digital divide," which refers to the "divergence of Internet access between industrialized and developing societies."[149] She also pointed to the "social divide" between the information rich and poor in each country. The Internet, according to Norris, "has reinforced existing economic inequalities, rather than overcoming or transforming them."[150]

The 2003 Arab Human Development Report, sponsored by the United Nations, showed low levels of Internet accessibility in the Arab countries, which, as we mentioned above, are mostly Islamic-majority countries. The report attributed that to several factors such as computer and Internet illiteracy, high cost of telephone lines for dial-up access, high prices of personal computers, and high access fees.[151]

An important factor that can be added to the mix of problems leading to low Internet accessibility in Arab and Islamic countries is the language barrier. Despite the fact that many Islamic websites have developed their services in various languages, particularly Arabic, the most commonly used language on the majority of these sites is still English The three websites that we analyzed for this study have both English and Arabic versions.

The low Internet penetration and accessibility levels in the Arab and Islamic world mean that only a few selected groups of elite users are contributing to the virtual Islamic public sphere. The "new religious intellectuals," whom we referred to earlier in this book are among the elite audience who contribute to the Islamic websites. Hofheinz (2005) noted that the lower middle classes in the Arab world cannot afford to buy a computer or access the Internet due to the cost factor. This means that the Internet use in the Arab world is limited to the urban, upper and middle class, younger, educated elites.[152] According to Bunt (2000), "The nature of computer-mediated communication suggests that it is the educated elite, who are literate, use English as a primary language and have access to the web and skill in presenting their message online, who are currently dominating Cyber Islamic Environments."[153]

It is worth mentioning here that the past few years have witnessed an increase in Internet access by average Muslims thanks to the prevalence of Internet cafes that provide computer services at relatively reasonable and affordable prices. Moreover, many universities and academic institutions throughout the Islamic world have opened their computer labs for their students, allowing them free access to the Internet.

It can be argued that the elitist group of the "new religious intellectuals," whose computer skills and socioeconomic means have allowed them to contribute to the religious deliberations in the virtual Islamic public sphere, and to even launch Islamic websites, share similar traits with Habermas' literary elites, who dominated the rational-critical deliberations in Europe's "bourgeois public sphere" during the seventeenth and eighteenth century.

Just like Habermas' public sphere was criticized for excluding women (see previous chapter), it seems that women who live in Arab and Islamic countries are struggling in the current Islamic public sphere online. In this context, Cees Hamelink (2003) cited UNICEF statistics revealing that the majority of the one billion illiterates around the world who cannot use computers or access the Internet are girls. "Among these kids for whom there are no schools, two out of every three in the developing world are girls."[154]

We hope that the next few years would witness a tremendous increase in the Internet accessibility levels in the Islamic world to allow more Muslims to become active participants in the Islamic virtual public sphere in a way that could contribute to strengthening the *umma* (Islamic community).

The next chapter addresses the concept of the *umma*, its historical roots and origins, the current challenges confronting it in the international public sphere, and how the public sphere criteria apply to it.

CHAPTER 3

Is the *Umma* a Public Sphere?

This chapter discusses the concept of the *umma* and how it can be compared to the public sphere, as defined by Habermas. It starts by providing definitions of the concept of the *umma* and its historical roots and origins, and moves on to compare and contrast the unity of the *umma*, in terms of faith and morality, to its segmentation and fragmentation, due to political factors. The chapter also investigates the challenges confronting the *umma* in the "international" public sphere, such as the challenge of the emergence of Islamic resurgence movements or the "re-Islamization" trend, the challenge of whether the *umma* can accommodate democracy, the challenge of how far it can tolerate pluralism, as well as the challenge of fostering constructive dialogue between the *umma* and the "Other," especially non-Islamic, western communities, and the different views around this issue, which oscillate between the pessimistic view of clash of civilizations and the optimistic view of dialogue between civilizations.

WHAT IS THE *UMMA*?

The Arabic term *umma*, which is frequently mentioned in the *Qur'an* (at least sixty-two times) and in the Prophet's *hadith* (Prophet Muhammad's sayings), originated in the year AD 622, when Prophet Mohammed settled in Medina and set the foundation of the Islamic community.[1] The importance of the *umma* in Islam "and the significance of its establishment as a state were underscored by the fact that 622 (the beginning of the Islamic community/state at Medina) and not 610 (the year of God's first revelation to Muhammad) was reckoned as the first year of the Islamic calendar."[2]

The first and most important challenge that confronted Prophet Mohammed was the "ability to maintain the first Muslim community's unity despite the presence of very strong personalities with widely differing temperaments,"[3] a mission he was able to accomplish successfully due to his possession of "an alliance between a deep heart and a penetrating spirit, of knowing how to be reasonable in all circumstances, with oneself and among other people."[4] Therefore, it could be said that the most important political side of Prophet Mohammed's heritage was his insistence on the *jama'ah* (another word for *umma*) principle of Muslim unity.[5]

Since then, the term *umma* has been given different meanings and interpretations by various thinkers and scholars. The most commonly used, and seemingly agreed-upon, definition of the *umma*, based on the literature, is that of a "community of believers that brings together not only all Muslims currently living on Earth, but also all past and future generations."[6]

The fundamentals of this *umma* can be set out quite simply: "Islam which means submission to God is constructed upon what Muslims believe is a direct Revelation in Arabic from God: the Quran. This recitation or reading, for that is what the word Quran means, is the miraculous source of the umma, the Islamic community."[7]

Several Islamic interpreters argued that the term *umma* itself is synonymous with *dar al-Islam* (The House of Islam), which refers to the world Islamic community.[8] This is because although Muslim lands are very vast and widespread "Yet, these peoples and territories...are bound by the shared affinity of a universal creed. Muslim jurists designated their own dominions the *dar al-islam* or *bilad al-islam*—the sovereign abode of Islam, unified by one faith and a single mission."[9]

This definition reflects the global, communal, and unifying nature of Islam as a religion and a way of life, even in the current postmodern era, which is witnessing a fragmentation of religious authority and a multiplicity of interpretations of Islam in the cyber world.[10] Within the same context, Reza Sheikholeslami (2006) noted that the *umma*, as a community, since its inception in the seventh century, has been encouraging its participants to work collaboratively and collectively, rather than individually, to contribute to its prosperity and development. "Sociologically speaking, one cannot remain Islamic as an individual Muslim. It is not an act of private piety that allows for an ideal Islamic life. Rather it is living in and dedicating one's life to the community that allows for an Islamic life."[11] Echoing Sheikholeslami's argument, Cooke and Lawrence (2005) noted that the concept of the *umma* "signifies all Islam, but does so within the broadest boundaries defining Muslim collective identity."[12]

The creation of this new Islamic *umma* involved a system of "ideal morality," which created both a new society as well as a new type of individual, since Muslims performed all their religious rituals, such as the Friday prayers, the fast in the month of Ramadan, the pilgrimage to Mecca, and the payment of the stipulated alms as collective acts of worship.[13] In other words, the *Shari'a* (Islamic law) "covered men's relations with each other as well as with God."[14]

ITEMS ISSUED/RENEWED
FOR Mr Nasser Jamaaoui
ON 20/01/16 16:39:13
AT Idea Store Whitechapel (TH)

Islam dot com: contemporary Islamic di/E
91000000249886 DUE 10/02/16
1 item(s) issued

The creation of this new Islamic individual/collective identity was made possible due to the "unity of faith" that dictated that "Muslims shared a doctrine, a language, a law, and a purpose...Muslims should live together in mutual tolerance of differences of rite, although not of differences on the very bases of the faith."[15]

The above-mentioned definitions of the *umma* imply that membership transcends time, and apparently takes precedence over other factors, such as one's cultural background, nationality, location within a geographical boundary and country of origin.[16] In this context, Olivier Roy (2004) argued that the *umma* or the Muslim community "is not the product of a given culture or civilization, but of the will of individuals who experience a process of individualization through deculturation and who, explicitly and voluntarily, decide to join a new community based solely on the explicit tenets of religion."[17]

So, it can be argued that the concept of the *umma*, as a global religious community, stresses the unity of Muslims under the banner of Islam, and goes beyond any cultural differences. The universality of the *umma* is further emphasized by the use of Arabic, which is the language of the *Qur'an*. "The standardization of the Qur'an, the requirement to pray in Arabic, and the popular enjoyment of reciting and writing verses of the Qur'an promote among ordinary Muslims the sense of participation in a universal language."[18]

The *umma* is also open to diversity through dealings with other, non-Muslim groups of people. Supporting this concept, God states in the thirteenth verse in *Al-hojorat* (The Rooms) chapter in the *Qur'an*: "I created peoples and tribes so that they should get to know each other."[19] According to some modern Islamic thinkers, the *umma*, as a community, encompasses non-Muslims living in Muslim-majority societies. In fact, during the Prophet's lifetime, many Jews and Christians were living peacefully alongside Muslims in Medina.[20] The ideal Muslim *umma* is the one who encourages its members to engage in dialogue with other civilizations, and to try to find common ideologies that are agreed upon by all sides. "historically the *Umma* meant models of multi-racial, multi-cultural, multi-religious, and pluralist societies. A true *Umma* respects the rights of non-Muslims as with the original Medina state."[21]

Highlighting the *umma*'s respect for diversity and the importance of communication between Muslims and other groups, outside the realm of the *umma*, the prominent Islamic thinker, Tariq Ramadan, was cited by Nielsen (2003) as saying that the Islamic *umma* is "not a communitarianism to close in on itself...We are a community of faith with influence, not a community existing in an enclosed space."[22]

The universality of the Islamic *umma* is best exemplified in the following *hadith* (Prophet Muhammad's sayings): "Other prophets before me were sent only to their peoples, I have been sent to all humanity."

This *hadith*, according to Hourani (1993), indicates that the Muslim *umma* differed from all the previous communities of faith in two important ways: "it was a message for all mankind, and it contained within itself a guarantee of its truth and its correct transmission."[23]

This last point is again expressed in another *hadith* of the Prophet: "My community will not agree on an error," which once more indicates that the Islamic revelation is eternally true and that it supersedes all previous revelations, therefore, "Since it was universal it was also united, and its members were equal. All Muslims...were equally members of the *umma*, possessing the same rights and responsibilities."[24]

This universality and equality of the Islamic *umma* is also highlighted in the following quote by the prominent Islamic poet-philosopher Mohammed Iqbal, cited by Kramer (1980) "The law of Islam does not recognize the apparent differences of race, nor...nationality. The political ideal of Islam consists in the creation of a people born of a free fusion of all races and nationalities...The inner cohesion of such a nation would consist in the unity of the religious and political ideal, or in the psychological fact of 'like-mindedness.' "[25]

The argument that the *umma*, as a community of faith, ought not be limited to a physical, enclosed space points to a similarity with the concept of public sphere as envisioned by Habermas. As we mentioned in chapter 1, the physical coexistence of participants in the public sphere, according to Habermas, does not matter as much as the sharing of ideologies that are conducive to a rational-critical debate.[26] Comparatively, Muslim participants in the *umma* do not have to share the same physical space, as long as they are united by their adherence to the Islamic principles and their abiding by the doctrines of the Islamic faith. For example, a Muslim born and raised in Saudi Arabia and another Muslim born and raised in the United States do not share the same physical space, and they do not even have the same cultural background. However, they both pray facing the *ka'ba* (the holiest place in Islam; located in Mecca), and they both fast during the Muslim holy month of Ramadan. In a way, both of them hold the same religious values, and practice their religion in the same manner. Their sharing of religious beliefs and practices is what integrates them into the Muslim *umma*. This supports the argument that Islam is a universal religion that can be practiced in any cultural context.[27]

The previous discussion clearly highlights major similarities between the notion of the *umma* and the concept of the public sphere, as defined by Habermas, namely that it is metaphorical, rather than physical, and that it encompasses the dimensions of universality and equality. We argue that these distinctive characteristics of the Muslim *umma* qualify it to be described as a "public sphere," which binds its participants together through the unity of faith and morality. In the next section, we explore the various binding factors that united Muslims together under the banner of common faith and shared morality, on one hand, as well as the divisive political factors that fragmented this unity, on the other hand.

The *Umma* between "Moral Unity" and "Political Fragmentation"

Some scholars argued that despite the universality of Islamic practice that brings together participants in the Muslim *umma*, there can be "regional *ummas*"[28] that develop to suit the political, social, and economic characteristics that are unique to each community. Each regional *umma* would have its own public sphere that would serve as a platform for its participants to discuss the matters related to their own lives. So, rather than having one universal Islamic public sphere, there would be multiple public spheres to accommodate the needs of the regional *ummas*. This can be compared to Nancy Fraser's "subaltern counterpublics,"[29] which we referred to in the previous two chapters.

These diverse regional *ummas* should ideally exist and thrive as part of the broader *umma*, which, as Farhad Kazemi (2002) points out, in spite of its followers' divisions and differences, remains to be the source and the symbol of overriding group identity and solidarity in Islam, irrespective of time and space, because "it serves as a psychological bond that crosses boundaries and historical periods and brings Muslims together under the banner of God's unity (*tawhid*)."[30]

The concept of the *umma* might seem to have affinities to that of the nation. Both concepts have been subject to various interpretations by postmodernist theorists, particularly during uncertain times of drastic social and cultural transitions and transformation, such as the Enlightenment period in Europe and the postcolonial years in the Islamic world.

In his discussion about the nation, Homi Bhabha (1990) noted in his classic work *Nation and Narration* that there is "a particular ambivalence that haunts the idea of the nation, the language of those who write of it and the lives of those who live it."[31] Ernest Renan (1990) defined nation as "a soul, a spiritual principle,"[32] through which people are bonded by their fondness of rich memories from the past and their aspiration to live together in the present. There is no doubt that similar to the members of the *umma*, as a spiritual and religious community, people's sense of bonding to a particular nation, which makes them sacrifice their lives for the sake of that nation, also has a spiritual and sentimental aspect to it.

It can also be argued that both the nation and the *umma* have some political connotations. The people of a particular nation enjoy rights and responsibilities toward that nation. In return for enjoying the citizenship that carries with it many advantages, they have to be loyal to that nation's government and abide by the terms of its constitution. They may also have to join that nation's army to protect or defend it against its enemies. Similarly, several western and Muslim scholars have made the argument that the Islamic *umma* makes no clear distinction between the religious and political realms, and that it combines *din wa-dawla* (religion and state).[33] The inseparability between both realms was supported by the example of the Prophet himself, who was both a religious and a political leader. This inseparability has more than forty references in the *Qur'an*; for example, verse number 59 in the chapter titled *Al-Nesaa'* (The Women) states: "You need to obey God, His Prophet, and those of authority among you."[34]

Despite these similarities between the nation and the *umma*, they differ in one major aspect: unlike the nation, which is often associated with a piece of land or a territory with clearly defined geographical borders, the *umma* is determined by religious faith, rather than by belonging to a certain land. The *umma* is borderless and "deterritorialized."[35]

Therefore, "territorial nationalism," which emphasizes certain national characteristics and endorses the concept of creating territorialized nation-states, is a western concept, alien to true Islam and "enjoys only limited support among Muslim thinkers."[36] Islam's rejection of the notion of "territorialized nation-states" does not entail an alternative of a community with no boundaries. In fact, Islam provided the world with a new paradigm of social definition and identification, using the " 'Adamic' and 'Abrahamic' criteria to determine who belongs where and why"[37] and to set boundaries based on faith and belief. The "Adamic" criteria is a "universal category," which holds all human beings to be essentially the same because they are all the children of Adam and Eve, while the "Abrahamic" criteria "consists of the Islamic *umma* and... *ahl al-kitab* (peoples of the book)—a category including Jews and Christians."[38]

Another distinction between the concept of the "nation" and the *umma* is that most Arabs, if asked to define what they meant by "the Arab nation," would begin by saying that it included "all those who spoke the Arabic language...and...all who claimed a link with the nomadic tribes of Arabia, whether by descent, by affiliation or by appropriation (through...language and literature)."[39] A full explanation of this concept also includes a reference "to a certain episode in history in which the Arabs played a leading part, which was important not only for them but for the whole world."[40] In other words, the main characteristic defining the *umma* is unity of faith and belief, while the nation is a multidimensional phenomenon encompassing many aspects, such as unity of language, culture, heritage, and history.

Despite the "ideal morality" of the early Islamic *umma*, which meant that "Moral unity existed even between those who held different beliefs about the truth of Islam,"[41] the "political reality" of this *umma* today signifies a considerable degree of divisiveness and fragmentation. One of the explanations for this unfortunate reality is the rise of an international system based on sovereign nation-states, which forced Muslims to adapt Islamic principles to modern conditions.[42] The political reality today is "the existence of some fifty-six independent Muslim states that frequently find themselves bitterly divided and sometimes at war with each other...significant moral issues arise in any attempt to reconcile a world of sovereign territorial states with the Islamic ideals of a universal commonwealth including diverse races, religions, and linguistic groups."[43]

Another factor that contributed to the current condition of the *umma* is that "The ideals of the religion and the practices of Muslim governments are often in conflict in the real world."[44] Therefore, although ideally nonresident Muslims should move freely, and without any restrictions, from one country to another, yet "because of the rise of nation-states, but more so because of the rise of corrupt governments and/or ruling classes or families, the realities are just the opposite of the ideals."[45]

Therefore, although classical Islamic political theory recognized no borders or frontiers,[46] there is a wide gap today between the reality of the Muslim *umma* and the ideal principles of unity, universality, and equality upon which it was created. This gap compels us to investigate the factors that gave birth to it. To do so, we have to ask an important question: "Why didn't 'like-mindedness' and 'shared morality' continue to unite generations of Muslims politically under the banner of the Muslim *umma* till the present day?"

The answer to this question lies in the fact that "While the political governance of the community has been central to the Islamic historical experience, it has also constituted one of its weakest links."[47] This is mainly because the state in the Islamic tradition does not have a separate existence apart from, or above, the community, therefore, "it has little to do with the conception of the sovereign and autonomous territorial entity that provides the foundation of the modern European experience...its institutional expression was rarely perfected."[48]

This could be explained in light of the fact that "Islamic teachings...emphasize community (ummah), and make no mention of a state or even public authority,"[49] mainly because "The unity of the *umma* was essentially one of minds and hearts, not of political forms."[50]

However, we have to bear in mind that the enforcement of the *Shar'ia* necessitated the existence of political authority and political leadership since "The *Shar'ia* told men what right action was, but it also laid down precise penalties for doing wrong. It was a system of laws as well as a system of morality."[51] Therefore, political power, exemplified in a political leader with authority, was a must for the following reasons: "To uphold the *Shar'ia* and impose the penalties, to watch over the performance of all duties commanded by God, to defend the *umma* against the enemies, to spread the bounds of the faith by holy war (*jihad*)."[52] In brief, we can conclude that "the Islamic community could not be complete unless it was also a State."[53]

One of the main challenges that confronted the Muslim *umma* was the fact that there was no clearly defined form or agreed upon structure for this state, either in the *Qur'an* or in the *hadith* (Prophet Muhammad's sayings). This did not appear to be a problem during the lifetime of Prophet Mohammed, since he himself played the role of both the religious as well as the political leader of the Muslim community, as previously mentioned. In other words, "He was prophet, head of state, commander of the army, chief judge, and lawgiver. His authority and its acceptance were based upon his prophetic calling and the Quranic mandate: 'Obey God and the Prophet.'"[54] Throughout the years, the Prophet's exemplary character and conduct, his continued reception of divine revelations, and his effectiveness and success reinforced his position of leadership, thus, under his guidance Islam crystallized as both a faith and a sociopolitical system.[55]

However, the first and most difficult challenge that threatened the unity of the *umma* came about with the death of Prophet Mohammed, since he died "without designating his replacement or establishing a system for the selection of his successor."[56] This, in turn, "plunged the community into two successive political crises involving political authority: the issue of succession and the problem of political fragmentation or civil war."[57]

This is mainly because the Prophet's position in the early Muslim community as "God's appointed religious and temporal representative was a central factor in keeping the Muslim community united politically and religiously. The accepted infallibility of the Prophet's authority in all matters gave the community a unified outlook on life, religion, and politics."[58] Therefore, his death forced Muslims to seek answers to the following pressing questions: "How should they govern themselves? Who would be the successor? What kind of government would they have? What would be the 'Islamic' method of choosing a successor to the Prophet? Who would be best qualified to run the affairs of the community?"[59]

What added to the complexity of the issue of succession, besides the fact that it was not clearly designated by the Prophet, was the fact that "The only traditions the new Muslim community had to draw upon in choosing a successor to the Prophet were pre-Islamic, tribal customs."[60] The challenge posed by going back to this tradition is that the link between human beings in pre-Islamic society "was the solidarity of the clan or tribe (*'asabiyya*); but the link between Muslims in the *umma* was a moral link, a common obedience of the law."[61] In other words, "political power in the pre-Islamic community was natural monarchy, created by a human process...and directed towards worldly goals (*mulk*); but in the Muslim *umma* power was a delegation by God (*wilaya*) controlled by His will and directed to the happiness of Muslims in the next world even more than in this."[62]

However, despite the above-mentioned differences between pre-Islamic and Islamic concepts of political power, the fact remains that "tribal identities and tribal patterns, especially inter-tribal rivalries, were a source of tensions that became manifest immediately upon the Prophet's death, since there was no clear successor and each tribal group attempted to establish a prior claim on the position."[63]

Therefore, although most Muslims believed that to found and lead a community was part of the "essential function of the Prophet and of his legitimate successors, they did not all agree, however, about the succession to the Prophet."[64] In fact, the "conflict over the question of succession led to the creation of two major sects in Islam—Sunna and Shiah,"[65] which, in turn, led to two different concepts regarding the ideal form of the state in Islam, namely *Khalafah* or *Imamah*, and, consequently, two different schools of political thought. In other words, it could be said that "Both Sunnis and Shiites agree that the state is an essential institution. However, they fundamentally disagree over the nature of political legitimacy (*Khalafah* or *Imamah*) in the state."[66]

In their earliest usage, "the word *Caliph* denoted a temporal role, the ruler's capacity to lead the political affairs of the community after the Prophet, and the word *Imam* referred to the leader of the Muslims at prayer, or, more broadly, the spiritual role of the ruler."[67] Therefore, in upholding the concept of the *Imamat* "the Shiites...maintain that political leadership of the Muslim community is primarily a religious function that belongs to the descendents of the Prophet. Political legitimacy, in other words, fundamentally derives from religious legitimacy, which derives from God and is transmitted through the Prophet's line."[68] This is a central point of difference between the two sects, since for the Sunnis "the caliphs, in theory, possessed neither God's power of making laws nor the Prophet's function of proclaiming them. They inherited only the judicial and executive power."[69]

However, the rule of the first four caliphs of Islam, who were the immediate successors of the Prophet, and who were referred to as the "Rightly Guided Caliphs," had special importance, because during this period "the community was expanding and flourishing, the Quran and the Prophet's words were taken as principles of action, and the *umma* was one in outer manifestation as well as in spirit."[70] In other words, this era represented the "ideal *umma*" or "the golden age when the *umma* was what it should be."[71]

However, following this "golden age" came the Umayyad period "when the principles of the Islamic polity were overlaid by the natural human tendency towards secular kingship."[72] Therefore, Islamic opposition flourished during this period because "Many came to feel...that the Qur'an should play a more active role in the life of the community."[73] Those who held this view believed that "the community at large which gave allegiance to Islam seemed mostly devoted in fact to enjoying the fruits of conquest under the leadership of men whose position in power had resulted largely from force and from tribal alliances."[74]

Therefore, we can say that the political fragmentation of the *umma* took place because after the "golden age" of the Prophet and the "Rightly Guided Caliphs" who followed him "The *umma* soon split on questions of policy and doctrine: one secession was...the great schism between Sunnis and Shi'is, in origin a political dispute about the succession to the Prophet, but which gradually acquired undertones of difference in doctrine, law, and custom."[75]

However, it is important to remember that "The maintenance of the unity of the *umma* has been a moral concern of Muslim thinkers throughout Islamic history, even after in reality the Islamic world fragmented into many separate political units."[76] The logic behind this is that "To classical political theorists...the communal unity of the *umma* could only be possible under political and legal unity."[77] Therefore, this perceived necessity to maintain the unity of the *umma* prompted the majority of Muslim jurists to support the office of the *Caliph*, despite the character of its incumbent, as long as he proclaimed loyalty and submission to the *Shari'a* in public, as previously mentioned in chapter 1.

It is important to mention that if the first chapter that brought about the political fragmentation of the *umma* was the conflict over the issue of succession following the Prophet's death, the final chapter in this process was the collapse of the Ottoman Caliphate. This is due to the fact that many efforts and compromises were made for the sake of maintaining the foundations of a unified *umma* over many historical periods, however, "It was not until the colonial episode, and its aftermath, that these foundations were eventually undermined."[78] By then, "the *ummah* community had seen its civilization well into eclipse, its society in stagnation and its polity in utter decadence. The final spectacle of this ebbing tide was dramatized in the formal abrogation of the Ottoman Caliphate in 1924."[79]

The collapse of the Ottoman Caliphate had such a dramatic impact because it endured for nearly six centuries and it "remained an effective symbol of the unity of the *ummah*, and of its existence as a realizable historical entity...it still provided a structure and reference point for the impending anarchy in the region,"[80] despite its shrinking role as an effective or powerful political institution in the international context of the times. Therefore, its collapse "constitutes the record of an internal disintegration marking the collapse of the historical frame of reference of the political community."[81]

The previous discussion reveals the central role of religion and spirituality in the historical development of the Islamic state and the very existence of the Muslim *umma*, whether through periods of unity or disintegration. This interrelatedness of state and religion in the Muslim *umma* constitutes a point of distinction from the secular public sphere envisioned by Habermas, where religion did not emerge as a key factor, since it was only perceived as belonging to the private, rather than the public, sphere, as previously discussed in chapter 1. This distinction could be best explained in light of the prevailing secular context in western societies today, where "The separation of state and religion...produced a clear separation between the realms of religious and temporal affairs."[82] However, this was not the case with the Muslim *umma*, which witnessed a strong "interrelationship between the temporal and the spiritual."[83]

This explains the centrality of religion in the configuration of the Islamic public sphere and the creation of the Muslim *umma* through various historical periods, which witnessed both moral unity, as well as political fragmentation. This phenomenon is clearly in sharp contrast with the secular public sphere proposed by Habermas, where the temporal and spiritual spheres are distinctively demarcated, and where religion is an absent player, as previously mentioned.

However, this whole notion of moral and religious unity, on one hand, versus political fragmentation and disintegration, on the other hand, deserves further analysis and exploration. This is mainly because the ideal form of government in Islam has been a major issue of controversy and debate, since the demise of the Ottoman caliphate. While some Muslims upheld the ideal of a single Muslim polity cross-cutting regional and cultural differences, the majority accepted the distinction between religious and political unity. In every case, however, the question of the proper form of Islamic government remained a challenge.[84]

Yet, this lack of agreement on a single form of Islamic government is "neither a defect nor a weakness in Islamic theory. Rather it results from the fact that political theory is secondary to legal theory in Islam. It also demonstrates that unity in the Islamic community is not based on political structures but on law."[85] In other words, although the *Shar'ia* had been largely abandoned in most practical applications, following the colonial epoch and the conception of the modern nation state, as we previously mentioned in chapter 1, yet this did not eradicate its cultural relevance and ethical significance for the *umma*, since "The *shari'ah* had always meant more than the legal foundations of the community or a normative code instituted by jurists. It had always constituted the ethico-legal matrix that pervaded the life of the community and imbued it with its sense for what constituted legitimacy and what did not."[86]

It was this moral, spiritual, and ethical base that kept the *umma* together as a unified community, which is held together by "a sense of belonging and affinity with a collectivity...group bonded in faith and fate, that is both historical and transcendental."[87] Therefore, "While the state, or formal system of governance, collapsed, the ideal and the reality and promise of a Muslim polity merely lapsed; and while traditional society was subject to the forces of disintegration...the Faith, as *iman* and as *'aqidah*, continued to inspire individual Muslims at all levels of society."[88]

This phenomenon was not surprising, because the Muslim community was by no means the function of the state, rather, it was the state that had been a function of community and faith.[89]

This could be best explained in light of the fact that "Islamic unity is based on consensus regarding the sources of legislation and solidarity...in the overall effort to carry out the Qur'an's command to 'establish justice' and thereby submit to the will of God. In other words, multiple political units and diversity of political systems are not only acceptable, but to be expected, within context of spiritual or moral unity."[90]

It is this spiritual and moral unity that enabled the Muslim *umma* to survive the many challenges that threatened its very existence, "it was the living faith, together with that sense of community that both sustained Muslims as social beings and that prevented the total disintegration of their societies."[91] Therefore, we can argue that if this living community of faith has enabled the Muslim *umma* to survive in the past, today: "It is this community too which...has periodically 'resurged' to provide the impetus and the input for regenerating both society and polity."[92]

This last point provides a smooth transition to the next section, which discusses the current challenges confronting the *umma* in the international public sphere.

The *Umma* and the Challenges in the "International Public Sphere"

The increasing visibility of Islam as an international force with social, political, and symbolic weight reminds us that "Islam is very much at the center of the cultural and political stage"[93] in today's modern world. This, in turn, compels us to address some of the most pressing challenges that are currently confronting the Muslim *umma* in the international public sphere, due to the fact that "What Islam means for Muslims in the modern world is now an issue for debate and action in the context of the politics of nation states, the struggle for energy supplies, superpower rivalry, and dependency."[94] These facts, in addition to very significant, recent political events, such as September 11 and the war in Iraq, which escalated the controversies and debates around Islam and Muslims more than ever before, necessitate investigating a number of contemporary challenges facing the *umma* today internationally.

These include contextualizing and interpreting modern Islamic resurgence movements, which are sometimes referred to as the "re-Islamization" trend; questioning the ability of the Muslim *umma* to accommodate both democratization and pluralism; as well as testing the capacity of the *umma* to engage in an enlightening and constructive dialogue with outsiders, especially in the western world.

The Umma *and the Challenge of "Re-Islamization"*

One of the main areas of concern that attracted wide attention from the international community, in general, and the west, in particular, over the past few decades has been the increasing tide of Islamic resurgence, which is sometimes referred to as the Islamic revival movements, as previously mentioned in chapter 1, or the "re-Islamization" trend. There have been many different outlooks and interpretations pertaining to this rising tide, some of which have been conflicting or contradictory, as will be fully discussed below.

In attempting to contextualize this trend within its appropriate historical context, some authors, such as Michael Gilsenan (2000), remind us that "The so-called revival of Islam in the 1970s and after is not a revival at all but a continuation... There have been two hundred years of what Westerners treat as a ten-year wonder. The reference is to a long history; the forms, contexts, and relations are constantly renewed."[95]

Similarly, John L. Esposito (1987) draws our attention to the fact that "Understanding twentieth-century Islamic politics requires an understanding of the character and legacy of both premodern Islamic revivalism which addressed the internal weakness of Muslim society as well as Islamic modernism which responded to the challenges of Western colonialism."[96] In explaining this point, he mentions that "Pre-modern revivalism was primarily a response from within Islam to the internal socio-moral decline of the community. In many cases it led to the creation of Islamic states in Saudi Arabia, the Sudan, and Libya."[97]

The birth of these movements was actually an outcome of the internal weakness of the Islamic community and the European colonial domination, with responses ranging from "conservative religious militant rejectionism to wholesale western-oriented adaptationism, from *jihad* movements to modernist reform movements."[98] In every case, they were "forerunners of both twentieth century Islamic modernism and contemporary Islamic revivalism."[99]

However, in mapping these different trends and orientations, which mutually coexist under the wider umbrella of the modern Islamic revival movement, it is important to bear in mind that there is a large gap between the modernists, on one hand, and the most militant fundamentalist groups in the Muslim world today, on the other hand, and that the latter groups, "despite the media attention they receive, represent only the fringes of Islamic activism."[100] The importance of highlighting this point lies in the excessive attention that has been focused lately, especially in western media, on some of the most militant groups that advocate a violent form of *jihad*, as if they are representative of the whole modern Islamic revival movement. This (mis)perception overlooks the fact that these groups actually represent a "minority" within the mainstream re-Islamization trend, which largely advocates the principles of tolerance, coexistence, and dialogue, as will be fully discussed.

One of the most popular interpretations of the Islamic revival trend is to perceive it as a form of "resistance" to foreign colonialism in the past and western domination in the present. "In all Muslim societies...Islam played an important part in instigating the various national resistance movements...Today, the story continues as the living community strives...to combat the diverse forms of continuing subjugation and to rid itself of...subservience and humiliation.[101]

This view is explained in light of Islam's emphasis on the notion of justice, which, in turn, necessitates resisting any form of injustice in order to preserve and uphold human dignity. "It is hardly surprising then that instances of an endeavor to preserve and re-assert a threatened identity and to recover a lost dignity abound. The scope of this endeavor ranges from a militant confrontation in the face of...foreign incursion...to the...defiance of the minority regimes and thinly disguised dictatorships in power."[102]

An entirely different view on this issue perceives the emergence of these Islamic resurgence movements as a desperate attempt to reconstruct a glorious past in the face of western triumph and superiority. According to the advocates of this view "science grounded in rigorous rationalism, respect for the spirit of free inquiry, and individualism—achieved for the west that global primacy that Islam had once seen as its own manifest destiny. The rise of Europe left the promise of Islam unredeemed; the inheritance passed to others."[103] Therefore, the only two alternatives that were possible for Muslims, according to the proponents of this view, were either to fully endorse the western notions of modernization and secularization, or to turn back and adhere to their old traditions as their only line of defense in the face of this sweeping wave of western modernization.

In explaining the latter alternative, one of the advocates of this line of thought, Martin Kramer (1980), indicates that "Amid this turbulence, there are some Muslims who brood over what they once were, and believe that history must somehow right itself. They yearn to restore what nearly 200 years of abrasive contact with the West eroded: an idea of community, an equilibrium with the wider world, and a sense of 'authenticity.'"[104] In doing so, he argues that these Muslims "propose to restore those lost possessions by a faithful reconstruction of that past here in the present."[105] Moreover, he argues that despite the many differences between the various Islamic movements, which may have contrasting agendas "the collision with the West is the great shared experience of the modern Muslim world. Each polity now has its Muslim faction...Their ideas are not uniform, their visions of the future differ in very significant respects, but there are enough similarities in sentiment, vocabulary, and policy to afford a rough outline of their image of a reconstructed world of Islam."[106]

Another proponent of this school of thought, W. Montgomery Watt (1988), perceives the wave of Islamic resurgence as an attempt to promote a traditional self-image of Islam, which stresses the elements of self-sufficiency, finality, and idealization in Islam, and, therefore, invites the danger of promoting the view of an "unchanging static world," which can not be compatible with the spirit of secular modernization and scientific advancement, which is brought forward by western civilization. He indicates that one of the dangers inherent in the idealization of early Islam is that the community can become "so obsessed with recreating something past that it fails to see and deal with the real challenges and problems of the present."[107]

Similarly, other authors express their concern that "Islamists insist that Islamic law ought to be universal law,"[108] and that out of this belief "a paradox arises from the coupling of the law and culture in the sense of the proposition that at some golden period of the Muslim *umma*, the community of believers, actually lived according to the proposed law. This contention forces the lawgiver to be in perpetual conflict with the forces of change."[109]

Analyzing the inherent threats in this line of argumentation, which attempts to reduce the birth of Islamic resurgence to the simple equation of "tradition versus modernity," Michael Gilsenan (2000) highlights the complexity of the term "tradition" by indicating that it is a highly variable and shifting term. "In the name of tradition many traditions are born and come into opposition with others. It becomes a language, a weapon against internal and external enemies, a refuge, an evasion, or part of the entitlement to domination and authority over others."[110] Furthermore, he reminds us that many Islamic trends today struggle over the definition of what constitutes tradition, since it means "not only a religious interpretation but a whole form of life."[111]

It is equally important to contextualize the phenomenon of Islamic revivalism within its appropriate historical, Islamic frame of reference. This is because "Revivalism is problematic only where Islamic civilization is conceived without its Muslim human life-force. The latter becomes obscured when the prevailing political and socio-cultural realities are seen outside their Islamic referent."[112] This is the case with some Orientalists and western social scientists who overlooked the specific religious, cultural, and social framework of Muslim societies, and, therefore, reached distorted interpretations of modern Islamic resurgence movements.[113]

Moreover, it is possible to perceive these Islamic resurgence movements as an attempt to achieve "self-renewal" and "self-assertion" on the part of the Muslim *umma*, which enables it to redefine the concept of modernization in light of its own historical, sociocultural, and, most importantly, religious frame of reference, and, therefore, to respond to it according to its own specific, indigenous approaches.[114] The recognition of this fact corrects the tendency to interpret these modern movements only in negative or defensive terms, or to just see them as attempts to protest foreign domination and resist western hegemony. In fact, they could be perceived as positive attempts "to access the modern age in its own terms...which would naturally subsume creed and identity. It would be...mistaken to attribute this quest merely to a conservative urge, or to an unwillingness to break with tradition."[115]

Similarly, John L. Esposito (2003) asserts that the contemporary Islamic revival movements challenged many of the presuppositions that modernization is only possible within the framework of progressive secularization and liberal westernization. In eliciting the inherent dangers in this "ethnocentric" approach he indicates that "liberal secularism...fails to recognize that it too represents a worldview, not *the* worldview or paradigm, and can easily degenerate into a 'secularist fundamentalism' that assumes its principles to be a self-evident and universal truth or norm. Thus alternative worldviews or ideologies are easily dismissed as abnormal, deviant, irrational, and a 'fundamentalist' or extremist threat."[116]

The previous point could be best contextualized within the question of whether or not Islam is compatible with modernity and modernization, a major point of contention among Muslims and between Muslims and non-Muslims for more than a century. The Islamic modernist movement in the late nineteenth and early twentieth centuries addressed this issue intellectually, socially, and politically, through discussing and debating critical issues, such as the relationship of revelation and reason, religion and science/technology, the status and rights of women and minorities, and the nature and function of Islam in the modern state.[117] However, the prevailing (mis)conception regarding the incompatibility of Islam with modernization persisted and "The reassertion of Islam in contemporary Muslim politics led many to assert that Muslims were faced with a choice between Mecca and mechanization,"[118] as previously mentioned in chapter 1.

The view that the Islamic resurgence poses a threat to modernity led to many repressive actions, by both internal and external forces, against Islamic movements. "This belief has been used by many governments in the Muslim world to discredit and repress Islamist groups, by others (in the West) especially to warn of a clash of civilizations between Islam and the West, and by governments in Europe and America to implement anti-terrorism legislation that often targets Muslims and Muslim organizations."[119]

Another interesting explanation of the birth of political Islam, or the so-called Islamic fundamentalism, is to see it as a reaction to the failure of the secularization project that was imposed by the ruling regimes in many parts of the Muslim world, since secularism was introduced in these countries "within the context of the encounter between the Western and Islamic cultural traditions."[120]

However, most of these states "were informed by a narrow, and often distorted, conception of secularism. While the ruling elite insisted on the separation of the state and religion, that separation did not entail the ideological neutrality of the state,"[121] since most of the ruling governments attempted to suppress the religious institutions and to limit their influence in their own societies, while at the same time promoting their own discourses and ideologies as substitutes for religion.[122]

Therefore, in the name of progress and modernization, many of these regimes launched "cultural assaults on the *'ulama* and Islamic institutions...attacked various aspects of the Islamic belief system...worked zealously to limit the sphere of activity of the Islamic groups, taking away their educational and social functions...and self-righteously imposed a state feminism on their societies from above."[123]

Thus, "Secularism—be it in the form of liberal nationalism, Arab nationalism and state socialism, or monarchy-centered nationalism—then became the religion of the state. But the exclusionary policies of the state further undermined its legitimacy, giving credibility to the claims of the fundamentalist groups that the state was promoting alien ideologies."[124] These repressive and exclusionary policies were also a direct factor behind the birth of political, fundamentalist Islamic movements, which could be seen in this context as an attempt to resist state suppression, as well as to assert indigenous religious and cultural values and beliefs.

A different way of looking at these Islamic revival movements is to see them within the context of "social reform." John L. Esposito (2003) highlights this point by mentioning that "While a minority of extremists focus on revolution in their own countries and abroad, others concentrate on more peaceful political and social 'revolutions' and reforms dedicated to the incorporation and expression of Islamic values in both the public and private spheres."[125] In light of this view, Islamic activism could be perceived as a social reform movement that creates "new spaces and new terms for wrestling with the core issues of identity, history, and culture, providing new possible ways of social and political integration."[126]

Along the same line, it has been argued that the attractiveness and appeal of Islamic resurgence movements, especially in some of the countries facing economic challenges, such as Egypt, has been the ability to provide socioeconomic services and support to the underprivileged segments of society and, therefore, to help them cope with their financial and social hardships in a more effective way, through finding more collective survival strategies and coping techniques on the societal level. In other words, it could be said that "In steering individuals toward loyalty to the *umma*, or community of Muslim believers, fundamentalist ideology...ultimately encourages a reorganization of society integrated at the suprafamilial level."[127]

In every case, whether this tide of "re-Islamization" is perceived as a form of resistance to foreign domination and imperialism; as a desperate attempt to hold on to tradition in the face of western superiority; as a reaction to failed imported ideologies, such as state secularism; as a social reform movement; or as an attempt to synthesize indigenous religious beliefs with modernization to create "self-renewal," the fact remains that it did play a very significant role in increasing Islam's visibility in the international public sphere. This reminds us of the strong existence of religion in the public sphere, as demonstrated through the *umma's* historical development and contemporary experience, in contrast to Habermas' vision that confines religion to the private sphere and excludes if from public discourses and deliberations.

The Umma *and the Challenge of Democratization*

Another significant challenge confronting the *umma* today is its willingness to accept and practice democracy. This is also a challenge that attracted wide attention, because, since the dawn of colonialism, people outside Islam have tried to classify it, "as distinctly anti-democratic and inherently authoritarian."[128] The controversy around this issue still continues until today and deserves further analysis and explanation, because differences of opinion remain in the Muslim community around the acceptable form of government in Islam: "Is it one that is simply headed by a Muslim, regardless of its form? Is it one in which only Muslims participate? Is it one that is based on models derived from a particular era of Islamic history? Is it, indeed, one? Is there a single Islamic form of government?"[129]

The diverse views and debates regarding the ideal form of Islamic government are best exemplified in the reality that the Muslim world today is highly pluralistic in the forms of political systems it employs.[130] However, the one issue in which they are all similar is their struggle to accommodate and/or contend with Islam and its growing role in the Muslim public sphere."[131] This is especially true, since a growing number of individuals and governments endorsed the view that "the best solution for the political problems of the *Ummah* is the institutionalization of Islamic democracies."[132]

Recent surveys have indicated that over 80 percent of Muslims would like to see their countries democratize. Except for a rather radical brand of Islamists who reject any and every form of democracy "most Islamists are now converging with secularists and moderate Muslims on the desirability of democracy."[133] The reason for this increasing trend is the fact that many Muslims, regardless of their political orientation, do believe that Islam does have a lot of good to offer and must play a role in the public sphere.[134] However, the most pressing challenge that still confronts them is answering the question "what and how much role should Islam have in the public sphere?"[135]

The attempts to answer this difficult question culminate in three schools of thought. The first school of thought is that of the secularists who do not perceive any role for Islam in politics. The advocates of such a position asserted that "contemporary Islamic resurgence was incompatible with freedom."[136] Such an argument based on the incompatibility of Islam and liberal democracy was the main catalyst behind fueling "the discourse of civilizational incompatibility and hostility,"[137] which is more commonly known as the discourse of "clash of civilizations."[138]

The second school of thought, which represents a minority in the Muslim world, is that of the radical Islamists, who also do not see any room for compatibility between Islam and democracy, but, ironically enough, for totally the opposite reason, which is the necessity of implementing Islamic rule, without importing the notion of western democracy. Obviously, therefore, these two schools of thought advocate mutually exclusive positions.[139]

The third school of thought, however, which represents the majority of the modern Islamic revival movements, advocates a "moderate discourse that seeks to find a place for Islam as well as democracy (and to) explore the contentious domain where freedom and faith, democracy and theology negotiate a mutually compatible future."[140]

Thus, it can be concluded that "with regard to the compatibility of Islamic belief and values with democracy, some Muslims, as well as non-Muslims, assert their incompatibility."[141] However, many Muslims today believe that Islam is capable of "reinterpretation (*ijtihad*) and that traditional concepts of consultation (*shura*), consensus (*ijma*), and legal principles such as the general welfare (*maslahah*) provide the bases for the development of modern Muslim notions or authentic, more indigenously-rooted, versions of democracy."[142]

These important Islamic concepts, which were previously introduced and discussed in chapter 1, provide the most appropriate foundations of governance in Islam. This is mainly because "*ijtihad* includes all the instruments used to form judgments through human reasoning and personal effort. *Ijtihad* is, in fact, the rational elaboration of laws either on the basis of sources or formulated in the light of them. Thus...*ijma* (consensus) is the product of a collective human rational discussion."[143]

These authentic Islamic principles help in drawing a connection between religious values and current trends through proposing new readings of the sources, finding new responses, or thinking of innovative models of social and economic organization.[144] This is precisely the meaning of "the Prophetic tradition that 'God sends to this community, every hundred years, someone to renew its religion.' This renewal is not a modification of the sources, but a transformation of the mind and eyes that read them, which are indeed naturally influenced by the new social, political and scientific environment in which they live."[145]

It is for these reasons that a number of contemporary Islamic scholars argued that the doors of *ijtihad* should not be closed, since it provides an excellent basis upon which to build an authentic form of Islamic government, which is capable of addressing the many challenges of our modern time and coping with its many shifting political, economic, and social realities.[146] This, in turn, will entail adopting a "pluralistic" form of government, which incorporates the principles of democracy within a genuine Islamic context.

It is equally important to stress the role of the concept of consultation in bringing about an Islamic alternative to western democracy, since *shura* was introduced in Islam as a vehicle for political participation. "The Prophet and his immediate successors used to consult with their followers specifically to ensure that they were on board with major policy decision."[147] Therefore, if democracy is defined as a process of decision making by people following deliberation, then it becomes "almost identical" with *shura*.[148]

However, if democracy is defined as people's supreme and absolute right to freely decide on any issue with majority vote, but without abiding by any framework of moral or ethical regulations, then this form of democracy becomes "the antithesis of Islam because it puts what it calls the people in the place of God; in Islam only God has this absolute power of legislation. Anyone who claims such a right is claiming to be God."[149] Yet, in a democracy where "the right of the people to legislate is limited by what is believed by society to be a higher law to which human law is subordinate and should not therefore violate, then such a democracy can be compatible with Islam."[150] In other words, what could be "un-Islamic" is "a liberal or an unconstrained democracy. The problem is with secularism or liberalism, not with democracy."[151] It is for this reason that Sheikh Yusuf Al Qaradawi, one of the most prominent contemporary Islamic scholars, mentioned that "He who says that democracy is disbelief; neither understands Islam, nor democracy."[152]

Fortunately, there is now a growing realization of the true barriers to democratization in the Muslim world, which have nothing to do with the authentic nature of Islam and its teachings. The leading magazine *The Economist* ran an article in its issue of February 19–25, 2000, under the headline "Can Islam and democracy mix?" that indicated "it is too soon to say that democracy and political Islam are incompatible; if there are corrupt governments and autocrats, do not blame Islam, blame the rulers, the armies, bad social inheritances."[153]

Despite these optimistic views, the greatest threat to the possible reconciliation between Islam and democracy remains to be the repressive measures exercised by many governments in the Muslim world against Islamists, even those who decided to pursue a moderate and nonviolent approach. This, in turn, leads to the creation of a "self-fulfilling prophecy," because "The thwarting of a participatory political process by governments that cancel elections or repress populist Islamic movements fosters radicalization and extremism. Many Islamists who experience regime violence... conclude that seeking 'democracy' is a dead end and become convinced that force or violence is their only recourse against repressive regimes."[154]

Furthermore, what adds to the severity and complexity of this problem is the international community's silence on these repressive measures, and, even worse, the fact that some western countries offer economic and political support to some of these repressive regimes, due to a growing fear of "global Islam." The combination of repressive actions by regimes, continuous violations of human rights, and a compliant western policy toward such actions creates conditions that lead to political violence. This, in turn, "validates the prior contention and prophecy that Islamic movements are inherently violent, anti-democratic, and a threat to national and regional stability."[155]

Ironically, the picture that emerges out of this situation is that of an increasing tide of "Islamic democratization," which is paralleled by an equally escalating tide of "secular authoritarianism." This is best exemplified in the fact that many Islamic resurgence movements continue to gain a wide base of popular support in most Muslim countries, and most of them are showing greater willingness to participate in the democratic process, but are usually barred from taking part in this process and/or face all types of severe repression by secular regimes in the Muslim world, which perceive, even the most moderate Islamic groups, as a potential threat. This, in turn, convinces these groups that the only possible avenue is resorting to force and violence, which creates a vicious circle of mutual hostility and aggression.

To break this vicious circle of violence and to bring about a more genuine and authentic form of Islamic democracy, it is of utmost importance to acknowledge the existence of different meanings and interpretations of democracy, as well as the danger of exploiting democracy by authoritarian governments and demagogues alike.[156]

Finally, it is important to stress that it should remain for Muslims alone "to determine the nature of their governments, to introduce or refine forms of political participation or democratization that seem appropriate."[157] The necessity of allowing the Muslim *umma* to develop its own forms of genuine and authentic government, which can ideally reconcile the teachings of Islam with the values of democracy, within the context of the international public sphere today, is a very important challenge to address, since any attempt to impose a process of democratization on the *umma* by outside forces is most likely to fail or, even worse, to backfire. This is due to the fact that such an imposition, even if it is done in the name of promoting democracy and freedom, will be "self-defeating," because it will deprive the people, that is, the members of the Muslim *umma*, from their authentic right to choose for themselves the most appropriate and genuine form(s) of government.

The Umma *and the Challenge of Pluralism*

A closely related and equally important challenge facing the Muslim *umma* is its capability to accommodate pluralism. In addressing the question of "who speaks for Islam?" today, through an examination of the notion of religious authority in the global *umma*, Peter Mandaville (2007) reminds us that there exists "in the Muslim world today a highly pluralistic understanding of Islam, linking liberal interpretations of the Qur'an and Sunna with forms of social activism and politics usually associated with progressive causes."[158]

This highly "pluralistic" Islamic scene combines and cross-cuts different trends ranging from the moderate mainstream currents to the most extreme minority groups, which, despite exhibiting divergent sociopolitical views, all share a common religious sentiment as members of the same *umma*. However, this "pluralistic" Islamic scene also meant that there "has not been a homogenization of faith, but rather an intensified, multipolar struggle over people's imaginations—over the symbols and principles of 'Islam.' Many different voices assert that they speak for 'Islam,' and not all these voices offer a vision of tolerance and mutual understanding, either among Muslims themselves or between Islam and other religious traditions."[159] Therefore, "It would be incorrect to say that there is a single, dominant view among Muslims concerning religious and ethical pluralism."[160] To clarify this point, Dale F. Eickelman (2002) asserts that "The Qur'an offers a distinctly modern perspective on the role of Islam as a force for tolerance and mutual recognition in a multiethnic, multicommunity world."[161] To document this point, he cites the following verse in the Quran that clearly endorses the notions of "pluralism," diversity, and tolerance as not only possible or expected, but, most importantly, as approved and willed by God: "To each among you, we have ordained a law and assigned a path. Had God pleased, He could have made you one nation, but His will is to test you by what He has given you; so compete in goodness" (5:48).[162]

Therefore, he points out that "Qur'anic interpretation and the Islamic tradition can be used to elaborate a notion of civil society and a public sphere in which Islam can play a role, alongside other religious and secular perspectives, free from coercion and guaranteeing individual dignity and personal liberty."[163] He attributes this to the fact that "Islam as a moral tradition...favors ethical pluralism both because it appeals to human reason and because the value of pluralism is widely accepted."[164]

John L. Esposito (2003) reminds us that the issue of pluralism is a critical issue in Muslim politics today for two opposite, but equally important, reasons, which are "the status of non-Muslims in Islamic law as *dhimmi*, protected minorities, as well as that of Muslim minority communities living under non-Muslim rule or non-Muslim governments."[165] Therefore, this makes the issue of pluralism today "a critical concern both for Muslim majority countries and for Muslim minority communities. From Egypt to Indonesia, scholars debate and reinterpret Islamic doctrines and laws."[166] In doing so, he argues that "As with other faiths, the lines of the debate are often drawn between traditionalists, who wish to simply follow the authority of the past, and modernists or reformers who argue the need and acceptability of a fresh interpretation of Islamic sources, a reformulation of Islam."[167]

However, he draws our attention to the "need for reinterpretation (*ijtihad*) and reform (*islah*) if the rights of all citizens are to be guaranteed."[168] He explains that the realization of this urgent need was the main driving force behind "a growing body of literature that reexamines Islamic traditions and addresses issues of pluralism both at the theoretical and practical levels."[169]

Another scholar Muhammad Khalid Masud (2006) emphasized the importance of these enlightened efforts in the realm of Islamic reinterpretation and considered them vital for safeguarding the concept of "pluralism" in the Muslim world. He argues that "The multiplicity of views continues...and is regarded as a blessing. The principle of legal reasoning (*ijtihad*) encourages differences of opinion, because the struggle of the jurist to derive the right ruling is considered religiously commendable even though he may arrive at an erroneous conclusion."[170] This provides strong proof that "Islam as a moral tradition has never been monolithic. Quite early in its history it developed several approaches to moral issues. These approaches vary in their sources of authority, methods of interpretation, and emphasis. They sometimes oppose one another but often continue to function side by side, even complementing each other."[171]

While we are fully aware of the fact that a comprehensive understanding of the notion of pluralism in Muslim societies compels a discussion of a number of important issues, such as civil society, citizenship, social regulation, minority rights, life-and-death decisions, human sexuality, and women's empowerment, we will choose, for the purpose of this book, to pay special attention to the issue of women's empowerment and the emergence of pluralistic visions of women's place and role in Muslim societies, in particular, due to its relevance to some of the themes pertaining to gendered identities in the next chapters.

Addressing the notion of women's rights in Muslim countries in the Middle East, which is one of the key issues where pluralism in the Muslim *umma* is questioned and tested, Deniz Kandiyoti (1997) contends that "The basic question is whether Islamist parties, movements, and regimes have the potential to generate nonauthoritarian, pluralistic societal outcomes... Is political Islam likely to generate pluralism? Or is it inevitably locked into a religious fundamentalism that 'is based on the principle of denying the rights of the other?'"[172] In answering these questions, Kandiyoti (1997) asserts that "Opinions range from qualified optimism about Islamist movements' openness to integration into a liberal political system as components of an emerging civil society to unqualified pessimism on the part of so-called neo-Orientalists."[173]

In analyzing the Muslim *umma*'s accommodation of pluralism and gender equality, we have to bear in mind that Islam replaced tribal solidarity in pre-Islamic society with "a community whose membership was based upon a common faith rather than male blood ties; religious rather than tribal affiliation became the basis of Islamic society."[174] Therefore, under this new affiliation "All members of the *ummah* were to be equal before God. The duties and obligations of Muslim life, as well as their rewards and punishments, fall upon men and women alike."[175] This gender equality, within the framework of shared faith and common belief, is highlighted in the following verse in the *Qur'an*: "Whoever does a righteous deed, whether man or woman, and has faith, we will give him (her) a good life; and we shall reward them according to the best of their actions" (16:97).[176]

However, the issues of gender equality and women's rights and status in the Muslim world continue to be among the most controversial and widely debated topics, whenever the issue of pluralism in the Muslim *umma* is discussed. One of the authors who tackled this topic, Deniz Kandiyoti (1997) points out that her "relative pessimism concerning the possibility of pluralistic outcomes for women under Islamic regimes derives neither from the assumption of some implacable fundamentalist logic nor from... the nature of religion per se."[177] Rather, she contends that it is mainly based "on the recognition that in an increasingly interconnected world where accommodation and compromise in almost every area of social life are essential to survival, the area of gender relations and of women's conduct singles itself out as a prime terrain for social control."[178]

Yet, she sees some relative hope not only in "the realities of economic restructuring and liberalization in the Middle East and North Africa,"[179] which may "alter gender relations by mandating higher and different types of input by women into the labor force,"[180] but also, ironically, in the fact that "a significant female constituency may find not only solace and solidarity in Islamic militancy but a legitimate route to greater empowerment."[181] This could be explained in light of the fact that in many Muslim societies "the vast majority of women (and men)...face the problem of living in an increasingly 'modern' society where the mingling of unrelated men and women in public settings and new forms of consumerism created new tensions and uncertainty."[182] Therefore, within such a context "an Islamic regime may provide a welcome relief from these stresses and strains by legislating unambiguously the boundaries of the permissible and even creating areas of legitimate latitude."[183]

To clarify this point, Kandiyoti (1997) cites the example of how young women in Iran "who previously might have been denied access to education by conservative families who opposed their exposure to unrelated men, after the revolution gained access to education as veiled women."[184] She argues that the same could be said about women adopting modest dress in Turkey and Egypt, since this new attire could be used as a means of increasing women's empowerment and mobility, rather than causing their isolation or seclusion.

Other authors, such as Mahnaz Afkhami and Erika Friedl (1997), while stating their general dissatisfaction with women's status in many parts of the Muslim world, have indicated that "By the 1990s...conditions in Muslim regions had changed significantly. Socioeconomic development had helped many women to become educated, to become financially independent, and to reach positions of authority and responsibility. Women became visible. Even if only very few reached higher management ranks, their public presence could not be ignored but instead became emblematic of women's aspirations and potential achievements."[185]

Most importantly, they draw our attention to the fact that, beside this relative social and economic improvement in Muslim women's status, "many Muslim women have begun to take an active interest in theological arguments regarding women. They claim the right to interpret laws and religious texts themselves and to learn the skills necessary for such interpretations...they are determined to find in Islam justifications for demanding individual freedom and women's rights."[186] In other words, it could be said that these women have, in fact, "joined the political struggle over the right to make their religion work for them."[187]

Likewise, in addressing the notion of women's empowerment in the Muslim world, Espostio (2003) emphasizes that "Today, Muslim women, representing many ideological orientations, are increasingly writing and speaking out for themselves on women's issues. They seek to empower themselves not just as defenders of women's rights, but also as interpreters of the tradition."[188] In doing so, he argues that these "Women scholars and activists draw on the writings and thought not only of male scholars but also, and most importantly, a growing number of Muslim women scholars and activists who utilize an Islamic discourse to address issues ranging from dress and education to employment and political participation."[189]

However, Afkhami and Friedl (1997) point out that such an attempt poses a major challenge, because in discussing such issues "women are hampered by the limitations and essentialist connotations of the terms *Muslim, Islam,* and *Muslim women.* These terms are problematic because they easily make people think in stereotypes that conceal a rich variety of different beliefs, practices, life-styles, and philosophies in Muslim societies."[190] In addition, they draw our attention to the important fact that in many Muslim societies there could be a heritage of "local cultural traditions that historically cannot be justified with reference to Islam. Yet they frequently are used to deny women rights in the name of Islam."[191] This, in turn, poses another serious challenge, based on the fact that "For activists working for the advancement of women's rights in these various Muslim societies skills in separating cultural conditions that impede women's rights from 'Islam' often are crucial to success; one can argue that people are more likely to let go of mere 'customs' than of their religion."[192]

Another interesting example of pluralism within the context of the Muslim *umma* is presented by Azza M. Karam (1997) who analyzes multiple forms of contemporary feminisms in Egypt, namely secular feminism, Muslim feminism, and Islamist feminism, which are all competing in different "power contests" within the modern Egyptian political, social, and cultural arena. In distinguishing between these different types of feminisms, she argues that while the secular feminists, on one hand, "firmly believe in grounding their discourse outside the realm of any religion and place it instead within the international human rights discourse,"[193] the Muslim feminists, on the other hand, "are attempting to reconcile the discourses of Islam with human rights."[194] In doing so, "their aim is to show that the discourse of total equality between men and women is Islamically valid,"[195] and, therefore, "to steer a middle course between interpretations of sociopolitical and cultural realities according to Islam and the human rights discourse."[196]

As for the Islamist feminists, although they recognize the fact that many women are, indeed, oppressed, they attribute the cause of this oppression to the fact that they try to be "equal" to men and are, therefore, "put in unnatural settings and unfair situations that denigrate them and take away their integrity and dignity as women."[197] In other words, for these Islamist feminists "it is the demands of a Western and culturally unauthentic ideology that oppress women. For them, Western feminism, with its emphasis on total equality of the sexes, results in women striving to be 'superhuman' and in the process carrying more burdens."[198]

Therefore, as Karam (1997) points out, these women are politically active in the struggle to bring about "a just Islamic society…that strives for a recognition of and respect for compatibility between the sexes instead of competition between them."[199] In doing so, they are using their understanding and interpretation of Islam to actively participate in the public sphere and to have a strong presence in different domains, which contradicts the notion of the public sphere as envisioned by Habermas, which largely excluded women as active or visible participants.

In light of this understanding, one can safely conclude that the mission of these Islamist feminists, then, "is not merely a call for women to stay at home. It is a call to enhance and to credit traditional women's roles within the family with an Islamist feminist nuance that gives women a sense of value and political purpose in these gendered roles and a sense of confidence as well: women are not less than men but equally important in different ways."[200] This theme of Islamist feminism will be revisited in chapters 4 and 5 in our analysis of some of the gendered identities' discourses in the discussion forums under study.

In light of the previous discussion, it is clear that even among some of the feminist writers who are skeptical and/or pessimistic about the status of women in most Muslim countries, there is still a recognition of the wide umbrella of "pluralism" that is manifested in the Muslim *umma* regarding the different perspectives on gender relations, as well as the various types of feminisms that are endorsed by different groups of women within the public sphere in contemporary Muslim societies. The existence of these different feminisms in the Muslim world is in itself another manifestation of the various views, practices, and applications of the notion of "pluralism" within multiple Islamic public spheres today.

The Umma *and the Challenge of Dialogue*

The significance of addressing the challenge of engaging in a constructive, enlightening dialogue between the members of the *umma*, on one hand, and the non-Muslim world, especially the western world, on the other hand, within an international, global public sphere takes us back to the fact that "The tragedy of September 11, 2001, sparked increased questioning about Islam as a global force,"[201] as previously mentioned. In explaining the roots of this tense post 9–11 atmosphere, John L. Esposito (2003) indicates that "Perhaps more than any other religion, Islam is often associated with the violent acts of extremists, terrorism, and the oppression of women. And, perhaps more than any other religion, the combination of the lack of information and a plethora of distorted information are responsible for Western ignorance about Islam and Muslims and the perceptions of Islam as a threat to Western civilization."[202]

In examining the origins of this distorted view of Islam and Muslims, Michael Gilsenan (2000) points out that Islam became a major preoccupation of western politics and media that a lot of people in the west "are tempted to think of it as a single, unitary, and all-determining object, a 'thing' out there with a will of its own, There is a strong notion of a powerful, irrational force that, from Morocco to Indonesia, moves whole societies into cultural assertiveness, political intransigence, and economic influence."[203] This tendency to (mis)perceive Islam "as a total and threatening mysterious presence"[204] could best be combated, according to Gilsenan (2000), through "a more cautious awareness of what the term *Islam* comes to mean in quite different economic, political, and social structures and relations."[205] He argues that it is through situating "some of these religious, cultural, and ideological forms and practices that people regard as Islamic in the life and development of their societies"[206] that the West can "demystify...standard approaches to Islam."[207] This book certainly hopes to offer a valuable contribution in this direction.

Along the same lines, Sohail Hashmi (2002) indicates that "For the past fourteen centuries, Westerners have not known quite what to think of Islam...Modern Europeans puzzled over the place of Islam in their emerging 'international society.' Today, Islam still remains a source of confusion and concern for many in the West."[208] He adds that amid the literature on the "clash of civilizations" thesis, "Islamic civilization emerges in this literature as the most potent remaining threat to building a liberal international order."[209]

However, Hashmi (2002) points out, in his criticism of the "clash of civilizations" thesis, that "the greatest danger of such an emphasis on civilizations is to make them into holistic, nonporous units."[210] He argues that "There is nothing, of course, more porous than the boundaries of civilizations. Islamic civilization is no exception. Indeed, Islamic civilization has historically evinced a strong syncretistic inclination, adapting easily to specific cultural conditions as the Islamic faith spread through Africa, Asia, and Europe."[211] Therefore, Hashmi (2002) concludes that "It is utterly meaningless today to speak of an Islamic 'tradition' or 'civilization' as a monolithic force operating in international politics."[212]

The interesting irony, however, is that the "increased questioning" about Islam and Muslims after 9/11, which largely associated Islam with many misconceptions and fears, also managed, at the very same time, to increase the prominence and visibility of Islam in the global public sphere. This stems from the previously mentioned fact that after September 11 a large number of Muslims, especially those who are living in western countries, felt "an increased motivation to 'explain' themselves as Muslims. Explanations were given in various forms, such as lectures about Islam, discussion fora in organizations and schools, and interfaith services."[213] Saskia Witteborn (2007) explains this more active engagement in community outreach activities on the part of Muslims living in western societies after September 11 in light of the fact that "the expression of a Muslim identity was not a matter of choice after September 11 but also perceived as being expected by non-Muslims. Several speakers engaged in community events to educate people about Islam, build relationships with non-Muslims, and speak out against discrimination."[214]

Here, it could also be argued that the debates and deliberations in various discussion forums via the Internet, such as the ones that are dealt with in this book, offer another important avenue for expressing diverse Muslim identities and, therefore, contribute to increasing the visibility of the Muslim *umma* in the global public sphere, as will be fully explained in the next chapters.

Interestingly, therefore, the paradox about September 11 was that it acted as a double-edged sword since, on one hand, it increased the distorted stereotypes and hostilities directed toward Muslims, but, on the other hand, it also increased the awareness and knowledge about Islam and asserted its existence in the international public sphere.

The different views around the notion of dialogue today range from some of the optimists, who acknowledge the existence of this dialogue, despite all the difficult political realities and pressures today, to some of the pessimists, who believe that such a dialogue has been severely hampered by these political challenges and harsh realities, and that there is only room for an escalating confrontation.

Representing the optimistic view on this issue, Eickelman (2002) mentions that "Many Muslim thinkers interpret the Islamic tradition as enjoining a continuous dialogue over meaning, one that explicitly enjoins tolerance among Muslims and among Muslim and other religious traditions."[215] In clarifying this point, he mentions that today there are many "prominent Muslim thinkers who advocate this ongoing 'internal' dialogue of reason among Muslims, often paralleled by discussions with both secularists and the followers of other religious faiths."[216]

Along the same optimistic line, Marc Lynch (2006) argues that "The events of September 11 paradoxically have made a dialogue between Islam and the West more urgent, more possible, and more real. The eruption of a genuinely global public sphere around this issue presents an opportunity which may or may not be taken."[217] However, he sees positive hope in "at least the demand for such dialogue and the existence of a strong current within the Islamic world already engaged in such a dialogue. The voices calling for dialogue represent a broad cross-section of Islamist opinion, and cannot be dismissed as simply a marginal Westernized elite."[218]

On the other hand, other authors, such as Bassam Tibi (2002), have less optimistic views on the possibility of such a dialogue, he contends that "The confrontation between Islam and the West will continue, and it will assume a most dramatic form. Its outcome will depend on two factors: first, the ability of Muslims to undertake a 'cultural accommodation' of Islamic religious concepts and their ethical underpinnings to the changed international environment; and second, their ability to accept equality and mutual respect between themselves and those who do not share their beliefs."[219]

The above view places the burden of achieving a constructive dialogue and a reconciliatory position on the shoulders of Muslims alone. Yet, a number of authors asserted the need for a "mutual" effort to be exerted by both sides, that is, Muslims and non-Muslims alike, in order for intercultural understanding, tolerance, and constructive dialogue to be achieved. For example, Esposito (2003) points out that "the realities of contemporary life in a global society require that tolerance be based more genuinely on mutual understanding and respect, the ability to agree to disagree."[220] In stressing this point, he asserts that "One need not deny essential religious, ideological, or political differences to be able to function as neighbors domestically and internationally. Differences of opinion and opposition need not be perceived as a threat."[221]

Likewise, Muqtedar Khan (2006) argues that there is a crucial need for both Islamist scholars and western scholars to be more honest and candid in their mutual perceptions of each other's cultures. He indicates that, on one hand "Western scholars either selectively compare Western present with a highly caricatured Muslim present, or they compare Western ideals, such as democracy and religious tolerance, with the worst manifestations of Muslim realities such as the extremism of the Taliban."[222] However, on the other hand "Islamists too respond in kind. They compare a glorified Islamic past with selected aspects of Western present. For example, they contrast the explosion of science and philosophy in the heydays of the Islamic civilization with promiscuity, drugs and crime in the West."[223]

Therefore, Khan (2006) asserts that the only exception to this exaggerated and distorted vision, which perpetuates the discourse of difference, is the position of the "Islamist modernists" who "register their dissent through appreciation of democracy and arguing that there is more in common between Islam and the West. They insist that what Islam and the West share is vast and profound in comparison to what separates them."[224]

However, a realistic outlook on the potential for constructive dialogue necessitates a balance between both optimism and pessimism, or as Hasan Hanafi (2002) puts it, "Pessimism in the short run leads to optimism in the long run."[225] In explaining this point he indicates that "The major risk for the future is that Muslim societies will be offered only the fundamentalist/secularist alternatives. Unless Muslim advocates of a middle course resume the serious task of developing and implementing pluralistic and representative conceptions of state and society from within the Islamic tradition, Islam will offer no alternative conception of civil society."[226] He argues that "In constructing this alternative Islam can learn from the West, and the West can learn from Islam."[227]

Likewise, Marc Lynch (2006) rightly points out that "The absence of the conditions widely assumed to be necessary for genuine communicative action, as well as the ability of the extremists to sabotage dialogue through acts of violence, should temper any optimism. But the existence of this global public sphere, and the powerful presence of Islamist and American voices open to dialogue, should equally temper any counsel of despair."[228]

The remark concerning the absence of genuine communicative action in the international public sphere in the post-9/11 era deserves some special attention. He indicates that the adopted notions of dialogue between Islamists and the west today "depart dramatically from Habermas's communicative ideal."[229] Rather, he asserts that they fall within the domain of "strategic communication," since "the ultimate goal is always to change the other without accepting the possibility of changing one's own beliefs."[230] He rightly points out that "such persuasion has little to do with communicative action; instead, dialogue is simply one more weapon in the arsenal of spreading the faith."[231] This distinction between the notions of "communicative action" and "strategic action," as envisioned by Habermas within the realm of the public sphere notion, has special relevance to our analysis of the various themes in the discussion forums in chapters 4 and 5.

Concluding Remarks

The comprehensive overview of the concept of the *umma* in this chapter reveals a number of interesting facts about the nature of the *umma*, and how far it can fit under, or diverge from, the notion of the public sphere, as envisioned by Habermas. Throughout the discussions in this chapter, the *umma* emerged as a highly dynamic, diverse, and pluralistic public sphere, which is capable of reinventing and restructuring itself in various manifestations and throughout different historical periods, by oscillating between the poles of tradition and modernity, moral unity and political fragmentation, localism and globalization, uniformity and diversity, as well as moderation and radicalism.

In doing so, it encompassed some of the attributes of the Habermasian public sphere, in terms of exhibiting the qualities of universality, equality, and the potential for encompassing consensual aspects between its members, as will be fully discussed in the next chapter. Yet, it emerged as a more inclusive, dynamic, and flexible public sphere, through encompassing some aspects that were excluded from the public sphere notion, as envisioned by Habermas, such as the involvement of women and the visibility of religion and its major significance within the public sphere.

Overall, it is important to bear in mind that the *umma* has never been, and will never be, an isolated entity, which can remain untouched and unaffected by the surrounding developments in the rest of the world. In fact, many of the views and debates displayed in this chapter show the outcomes and consequences of the continuous process of interaction between the *umma* and the many forces of political, social, and religious change, both inside and outside the Muslim world. The significance of this continuous process of interaction is even more pressing in today's world, due to the dramatic rise in higher education, the greater ease and rapidity of travel, and the proliferation of means of communication.[232]

The many challenges confronting the *umma* today in the international public sphere, including the compatibility, or lack thereof, between the Islamic resurgence movements and modernization, the possibility of accommodating democracy and pluralism within the Muslim *umma*, as well as the prospects of constructing an effective and enlightening global dialogue between the *umma* and its Others, are currently addressed and debated by a new generation of Muslim intellectuals, who attempt to reexamine and reinterpret their faith in light of modern realities.[233] The ability of this newly emerging trend, which synthesizes faith and modernity, to succeed in the face of its internal and external opponents, namely authoritarian regimes, conservative religious authorities, and secular forces, remains to be seen.[234]

This new wave of "mass interpretation" of religion by a wider group of people, due to the rapid expansion and spread of modern technology, is of utmost relevance to the theme of this book, which deals with how members of the Muslim *umma* engage in Internet discussions and deliberations to express, shape, and influence the construction of Muslim identities. Taking into account the integration of the *umma* within the international public sphere, and the many challenges confronting it in this regard, it is of utmost importance to analyze how the "deterritorialized" and transnational nature of these Internet discourses contributes to the crystallization of the concept of the "virtual" or "digital *umma*," as an imagined community in cyberspace, and how this process can impact the equally complex process of identity construction, as will be discussed in the next chapter.

CHAPTER 4

The "Virtual *Umma*": Collective Identities in Cyberspace

This chapter investigates the extent to which the expansive Islamic community, or *umma*, today gave birth to collective identities expressed through Islamic websites' discussion forums. Furthermore, we assess whether this phenomenon reaches toward the Habermasian ideal through consensus (*ijma*), as defined within the Islamic context.

The chapter introduces the concept of the "digital *umma*" or "virtual *umma*," as an imagined community in cyberspace, and it pays special attention to the role of diasporic Muslim communities in bringing Islam to the Internet. The chapter then introduces the concept of identity, in general, and the concept of collective identity, in particular, in an effort to investigate the factors that can lead to the creation of uniform Muslim identities in the realm of collectivism.

The rest of the chapter is devoted to a detailed textual analysis of some of the selected threads from the discussion forums in the three Islamic websites under study in this book, in an effort to examine the manifestation of collective Islamic identities through the discussions in these threads, and the extent to which they fit the requirements of a public sphere as envisioned by Habermas, as well as the criteria for some Islamic principles, such as *ijma*, *ijtihad*, and *shura*, which were previously discussed in chapters 1 and 3.

The "Virtual *Umma*": An Imagined Community

Since members of the *umma* may never have the opportunity to meet most of the other members, the *umma* can be an imagined community that exists in the minds of those who envision living in it. In this context, Benedict Anderson, in his classic book *Imagined Communities*, argued that an imagined community is the one whose members "will never know most of their fellow-members, meet them, or even hear of them, yet in the minds of each lives the image of their communion."[1] Members in the Muslim *umma* may have a sense of spiritual union that is nurtured by their participation in the same religious practices, regardless of where they live. There are times when this universal practice of Islam helps transform the imagined community of the *umma* into a real community. One of those remarkable times is during the annual Muslim *hajj* (pilgrimage) to Mecca, where millions of Muslims, of different races, colors, and ethnic backgrounds, convene in the same place and meet for the first, and probably the last, time in their lives. They stand, kneel, tour the *Ka'aba*, and perform all the pilgrimage duties, shoulder-to-shoulder; their sense of communion reaches its peak. That is when the imagined *umma* that they have always envisioned being part of becomes a living reality.

As previously mentioned in chapter 3, such important events, like the pilgrimage to Mecca and Medina, play a very important role in consolidating the notion of moral unity within the boundaries of the same *umma*. These occasions not only call upon Muslims to perform the same religious rituals and practices, but also they provide unique opportunities to spread knowledge, ideas, and beliefs easily and at a great speed (among those physically present). Today, it could be argued that the social, political, and symbolic weight of such gatherings has actually increased. According to Gilsenan (2000), "The sense in which Islam forms a world ideological system has deepened and become more actual as the means of communication have developed."[2] Ideas and calls to action quickly diffuse within the Muslim *umma*, such that the "meanings of Islam were both quickened and challenged at the same moment."[3] For example, "The tape recordings of the Ayatollah Khomeini's speeches smuggled into Iran spread the revolutionary message in ways security apparatuses were unable to prevent."[4]

Likewise, Eickelman (2002) argues that "Even when Islamic thinkers advocate a separation of Islamic thought and practice from other traditions, including European colonialism and economic domination, they encourage the elaboration of habits of thought and practice that facilitate introducing new elements and practices."[5] These "new" elements and practices often include the utilization of modern forms of communication to help disseminate their messages at the highest speed to the largest segment of the public. Therefore, Eickeman (2002) points out that even when activists declare that they are engaged in the "Islamization" of their society "Such thinking is increasingly reflected at the popular level by the proliferation of catechism-like 'new' Islamic books, the printed sermons and audio cassettes of popular preachers, and books 'proving' the compatibility of modern science and medicine with the Qur'an."[6]

Here, it could be argued that the Internet, as one of the most recent and most powerful forms of communication, certainly has profound implications on the phenomenon of spreading new ideas, values, and beliefs among Muslims, bridging geographical barriers as well as social, political, and cultural differences. In other words, Internet technology is a key player in transforming the actual Islamic community, the *umma*, into an imagined community in cyberspace, because it paves the way for the creation of "imagined worlds, that is, the multiple worlds that are constituted by the historically situated imaginations of persons and groups spread around the globe. Such imagined worlds replace a passive audience recipient with a potentially active-surfing public."[7]

The Internet technology has contributed to what can be described as a "virtual *umma*," or, to use Gary Bunt's term, "digital *umma*,"[8] referring to the Muslim community online. Bunt (2000) inquires about the extent to which this "digital *umma*" is emerging and is being promoted. He draws our attention to the fact that the *umma* is a term that represents the concept of a single Muslim community, as previously discussed in chapter 3, and could be extended to describe a 'single Muslim people.' Most importantly, he points out that "In Cyber Islamic Environments, reference is frequently made to '(cyber) identities' that integrate this *umma* concept."[9] This phenomenon, in turn, raises a number of interesting theoretical questions, according to Bunt (2000), such as is the digital *umma* a real or imagined phenomenon? Does cyberspace create an idealized sense of Muslim identity? In what ways do cyber Islamic environments reflect tradition, orthodoxy, individuality, and pluralism?[10] As to consequences, Bunt also asks whether cyber Islamic environments represent a loss of traditional centers of knowledge and power through the electronic circumnavigation of conventional borders.[11]

According to Peter Mandaville (2001), the *umma* is being reimagined and reconceptualized in a way that motivates its members to ask questions and engage in critical debates about the future of this *umma* as a community.[12] This reconceptualization is taking shape and becoming more crystallized through the virtual *umma*. He points out that phenomenal developments in the technologies of travel and communication allowed people to move across distances and to communicate far more easily than ever before. This, in turn, led to the compression of space and time and resulted in the fact that "the boundaries between 'here' and 'there' become blurred and eroded."[13] The implications of such processes on the Muslim *umma* today are profound, because they "permitted a wider range of voices to enter the public sphere and to articulate different understandings of Islam,"[14] thus contributing to the creation of a new "Muslim public sphere." This was made possible through bringing "Muslims from different sociocultural backgrounds together within translocal spaces…By bridging distances, these technologies have also led some Muslims to begin reimagining the *umma* as a renewed form of political communication."[15]

This raises the question of "who speaks for Islam?" within this new Muslim public sphere, which could be a difficult question to answer, because the "new Muslim public spheres do allow for some level of pluralization in religious discourse, lowering the barriers to participation and permitting new figures to lay claim to Islamic authority."[16] Therefore, "we cannot truly understand the impact of new media on Islamic authority without placing it in the context of changing patterns in terms of how Muslims understand and consume religion, and also the control and ownership of information sources."[17] In other words, the increasing pluralization and diversity within this new Muslim public sphere makes the issue of religious authority within the realm of the global and translocal *umma* a major challenge, since many voices claim to be "speaking for Islam" at the very same time, but in very different ways.

Participation in the virtual *umma* can be "identity-less,"[18] allowing Muslims and non-Muslims to express their views without having to disclose who they are, or where they are coming from. On one hand, this identity-less nature of the virtual *umma* can encourage diversity and lead to a multitude of opinion, because the online discussion boards have been serving "as powerful mechanisms for generating new understandings or formulations of old problems and/or new solutions to problems facing the Muslim *umma*."[19] This vibrant cyber world, which has been compared to an "Islamic Internet *Souq*"[20] or marketplace, enhances constructive dialogue that is needed for strengthening the parameters of the Muslim *umma*.[21]

On the other hand, the cyber world has weakened the universality of the *umma* by allowing for "a volatile mix of competing opinions—including serious divisions over who speaks for Islam."[22] What is at issue in this argument is not that there are competing opinions—in fact, as we mentioned earlier, diversity and pluralism are encouraged within the realm of the *umma*. What is at issue, however, is that this anonymity can add to the confusion in the virtual *umma* when it comes to recognizing authoritative Islamic sources, who are qualified to address Islamic issues and to provide valid religious judgments.

Yet, there maybe occasions when the virtual *umma* has reduced confusion about certain issues. One such occasion has to do with moonsighting, since Muslims in various parts of the world used to celebrate *id al-fitr* (the concluding feast of the holy month of Ramadan) at different times because of different sightings of the moon marking the end of Ramadan. However, several Islamic websites have coordinated data on the new moon sighting, and thus have unified Muslims' celebrations of the end of Ramadan. This has helped create a sense of "uniformity" within the virtual *umma*.[23]

This sense of uniformity led to a feeling of shared identity and common destiny among the participants in the virtual *umma*, which ultimately fosters, what Alexis de Toqueville calls, "'fellow feeling,'...[that is] no longer restricted to contexts of face-to-face interaction."[24]

Therefore, it can be argued that the virtual *umma* combines feelings of uniformity, as well as diversity among its members. In fact, both aspects complement each other within the realm of the virtual *umma*, as will be fully explained in this chapter, which focuses on aspects of uniformity, as well as the next chapter, which focuses on aspects of diversity.

Diasporic Muslims and the Internet

Another important aspect to highlight in discussing the notion of the virtual *umma* is the strong impact of the Internet on diasporic Muslim communities, that is, Muslims living in non-Muslim societies, as well as the role played by these young Muslims to bring Islam to the Internet. Those Muslims can reestablish connections with their religion through the various services provided to them through Islamic websites. These services have made available to those migrant Muslims, who are living in transnational, non-Muslim communities, what previously circulated in narrow, face-to-face settings and, therefore, helped them to have a sense of religious communalism and collectivism that would allow them to reconstruct their identities as members of the Islamic faith.

The term "diaspora," according to William Safran's definition, which was cited by Samers (2003), refers to "Expatriate minority communities whose members...retain a collective memory, vision, or myth about their original homeland—its physical location, history, and achievements."[25]

Diasporic identities do not function in a vacuum, but they are, to a large extent, affected by the discursive contexts in which they are shaped.[26] The diasporic people's occasional feelings of being isolated, homesick, misinterpreted by others or marginalized may make them more inclined to get involved in online communities than nondiasporic groups. These migrants' participation in the cyber world, with its discussion boards and chat rooms, can nurture a sense of belonging and common identity with those "back home" and with fellow members of the diaspora.[27] "Instead of being the alien outsider in a strange land, the online community allows the migrant to belong and be a member of a shared community."[28] This online shared community unites the scattered members of various diasporic groups. For those diasporic members, the homepages become their virtual homeland.[29]

The process of transnational migration is not a new one, rather, it has been taking place for centuries and it "led to the growth of diasporas linked by social characteristics like ethnicity, language, religion and culture."[30] What is new in this process, however, is the speed and intensity of the modern forms of communication that these groups are relying on today, since they "have been developing intercontinental networks of communication that use a variety of media that include mail, telephone, fax, film, audiotape, videotape, satellite television and the Internet."[31]

These new forms of communication play an important role in formulating diasporic identities through "the simultaneous consumption of the same content by members of a transnational group."[32] Moreover, taking into account the marginalized and underprivileged status of many diasporic minority communities, the desire to counter this marginalization and subordination "creates the demand for cultural products that maintain and ritually celebrate the links of the diaspora with the homeland... thus, sustaining global networks."[33]

The Internet, as one of the fastest and most effective forms of modern communication today, plays a very significant role in creating and sustaining the desired links between members of diasporic communities and their own homelands, thus, enabling them to preserve their distinct religious, social, and cultural identities.

Muslims in the diaspora have played a key role in the cyber world. In fact, Muslim students who migrated to the west were among the technology pioneers who helped bring Islam to the Internet. Those early diasporic Muslims, who were mostly technicians and software engineers, have pioneered in creating and enriching the virtual Islamic public sphere through their production of various kinds of Islamic websites to serve the needs of Muslims in the west.[34] Interestingly, these new trends of "cultural globalization," deterritorialization, and transnationalism pose an interesting paradox: "On the one hand, Islam is more exposed than ever before to Western influence; on the other, it enjoys better conditions than ever for the transnational diffusion of its message."[35]

Jon Anderson (1997) referred to the highly talented and skilled diasporic Muslim pioneers as the "cybernauts...the class or group of cyberspace travelers, who...explore what to be in cyberspace as they move through it."[36] According to Anderson, those pioneers' world is one "of the best-and-brightest, in which computer scientists are the latest in a series extending back through engineers and physicians before them, and military officers even earlier, who went or were sent from their countries to acquire the latest learning in the West."[37]

The diasporic Muslims' role in the cyber sphere is still active today; in fact, recent statistics by the United Nations showed that while the percentage of people who access the Internet in the Arab Middle East ranges between three and five percent, more than 50 percent of the Muslims living in the United States and Europe access Islamic websites.[38] Moreover, the fact that English seems to be the dominant language in many Islamic websites proves that the Internet is being adapted to suit the needs of the first and second-generation Muslims in the west, who mostly speak English.[39]

Muslims in the diaspora, particularly those living in the West, face major struggles and challenges because of the little, or total absence of, information that is available to them from recognized Islamic institutions. Those diasporic Muslims, therefore, have to "[take] religion into their own hands,"[40] by forming and negotiating their religious identity and adjusting their religious ideologies and practices to suit their new lives in a non-Islamic environment.[41]

Part of that adjustment requires that the diasporic Muslims ask critical and broad questions about their religion and the role they should play as followers of the Islamic faith in non-Islamic environments. They refuse "to be assigned to an essentialized, inherited, unavoidable, fixed religious culture. Living as a Muslim now relates more to choosing a reappropriated form than to enduring an identification imposed from outside."[42] In the process of negotiating their religious identity, the diasporic Muslims develop an inquisitive approach that aims at reformulating and reinterpreting Islamic thinking in a revitalized, discursive public sphere that is part of the process of "objectification of Islam,"[43] which we referred to in chapter 1. This is possible because many young Muslims living in the west have been educated in a liberal tradition that teaches them to debate, challenge, and ask questions and, therefore, "they are deploying this inquisitiveness on the early texts in order to find in them the contours of an Islam for the here and now."[44]

It can be argued that Internet technology plays a vital role in satisfying this inquisitive desire of the diasporic Muslims to learn more about their own faith. They surf the Net to connect with each other and to get information, through the Islamic websites, on how to cope with various cultural encounters without deviating from their faith and how to set a good example for Islam in the Western world.[45] Those diasporic Muslims who are utilizing the Internet technology to serve their religion are "inserting the normative discourse of Islam into the Western discourse of information technology. In this sense the use of the Internet by Muslim diaspora groups provides one of the best examples of…'globalizing the local.'"[46] This means that the diasporic Muslims are taking local versions of Islam from their original contexts and placing them in global, diasporic contexts. For them, "globalized communication [in the cyber world] means intermingling and dialogue between disparate local interpretations of what it means to be 'Islamic.'"[47] This "portability" of Islamic interpretations from local to global contexts through the Internet reflects the fact that the Muslim virtual *umma* is not spatially restricted, just like the actual *umma*, as a community of faith, is not confined to territorial boundaries.[48]

The process of negotiating and renegotiating local religious identity in a global context that often takes place among the younger-generation diasporic Muslims in the cyber world can lead to three possible outcomes: it can unify and integrate Muslims in the diaspora under the banner of globality; it can separate them by making them more aware of their own internal differences and magnifying their sense of "otherness"; or it can create an "in-between" status, where a "hybridized political identity," embraces elements of both the diaspora and the homeland.[49]

Regardless of which of the above-mentioned outcomes would affect the diasporic Muslims' use of the Internet, there is no doubt that the Internet technology serves as a highly needed platform for communication and connectedness among members of the Muslim diaspora communities. An appreciation for the Internet's role among diasporic Muslims has prompted several international Muslim organizations to launch their own websites with the aim of allowing Muslims in the west to share their experiences with fellow diasporic members.[50]

This is especially important since "Immigrant groups, historically, have turned to religion to structure their new lives, to ease the alienation, pain, and stress of transition and transplantation, and to find meaning in a new social world."[51] This phenomenon of immigrants "re-claiming religion and building a religious life with a new vitality and vigor"[52] is certainly applicable to Muslim immigrants in the west, whether within the public sphere of formal, collective practices, such as performing the Friday prayers in mosques, or within the private sphere of domestic practices and daily rituals.

We argue that the engagement of these immigrant or diasporic Muslims in vibrant discussions and interactions via the Internet can be viewed as a "virtual ritual" of "identity-making," because they rely on this modern form of communication to preserve their religious identities. This process involves identity formulation within communities which are being continually "constructed, debated and reimagined."[53]

This last point provides a smooth transition to the next section that explores the notion of identity, in general, and collective identity, in particular, in order to pave the way for a detailed discussion of how and why different shades of collective identities manifested themselves through the analyzed on-line threads in the rest of this chapter.

Exploring Identity in the Realm of Collectivism

In defining the concept of identity, Stuart Hall (1990) indicates that it involves processes of transformation that include the positioning of ourselves and others and being positioned within narrative versions of the past.[54] Likewise, Acosta-Alzuru and Kreshel (2002) point out that "At the most basic level, identity is concerned with who we are and where we are placed in time and space. Identities create meanings as they are produced, consumed, and regulated within culture."[55] Moreover, elaborating on the link between identity construction and meaning production, they mention that "Identity alludes to how a cultural product—text, object, practice—acts as a marker identifying a particular group, that is, how meanings create an identity."[56] Similarly, Stuart Hall (1997) reminds us that the processes of the production and exchange of meanings between the members of a society or group simultaneously contribute to and reflect both culture and identity. In light of this understanding, the differences exhibited through these processes of producing and exchanging meanings could be best attributed, according to Hall (1997), to different social, historical, and temporal locations among the participants who are involved in these processes.[57] These differences influence the identity positions and ideological orientations of these participants and, thus, in turn, influence their differential meaning production processes.[58]

Acosta-Alzuru and Kreshel (2002) remind us that "Conceptualizations of identity (and issues related to identity) are underpinned by a tension between essentialism and antiessentialism."[59] In explaining the difference between these two distinct and contradictory approaches to understanding identity, they clarify that "The former looks at identity as fixed, that is, based on nature (race and gender)...Non-essentialist views see identity as a dynamic concept based on symbolic characteristics that attempt to differentiate in order to identify."[60] It is the latter nonessentialist approach that fits our understanding and applicability of the concept of "identity" within the realm of this study, as we perceive identity as a complex, dynamic, multifaceted, and interrelated concept, which cross-cuts different characteristics, such as gender, religious affiliation, and political orientation, creating different degrees of divergence or overlap between or within these various categories.

Therefore, we argue that although there can be manifestations of "collective identities" within the realm of the moral unity of the Muslim *umma*, many variations and shades of diverse identities may also prevail.

Saskia Witteborn (2007) defines collective identity as the "alignment between people who express and enact themselves as members of a group. Alignment can mean certain modes of action and life styles, orientations, and expectations of what it means to be a person and a member of a group."[61] She reminds us that "collective identity is not an essence but constituted in social interactions and social practices."[62] Therefore, "By paying attention to the ways people express, refute, and affirm collective identities in particular locales, a researcher can explore the interpersonal and communal dimensions of identity talk without identifying people and groups as ethnic, cultural, or national a priori."[63]

In applying the concept of collective identity within the context of this study, we adopt the view that "Collective identity is a heuristic concept that enables a researcher to capture a variety of we-identities that people ascribe to themselves, focus on how identities are constructed and maintained in social interaction, and study group identities as emerging and changing in particular locales."[64] This explains our focus on allowing the voices of the posters in the various threads in the online discussion forums to be clearly heard, and their views to be openly expressed, since we perceive the process of collective identity formulation as a flexible and intersecting process of self-definition and self-representation, which is shared by a group of people, who inhabit similar or overlapping identity positions and identity-related discourses.

In conducting the textual analysis of the threads in the discussion boards of the three Islamic websites under study, we rely upon Habermas' notion of the public sphere and communicative action, and the various criteria derived from it, as outlined by Lincoln Dahlberg (2001),[65] and we also test the applicability of some authentic Islamic concepts, such as *shura, ijtihad,* and *ijma,* to the context of these postings.

However, before engaging in the analysis of these threads, it is essential to highlight two critical points. First, we categorized these threads under two main thematic groupings, namely: "religio-political" themes and "religio-social" themes to make for a smoother read and a better flow from one thread to another. These themes were determined by the contents of the threads in an inductive manner.

Second, we distinguished between the terms "pan-Arabism" and "pan-Islamism" and their applications in the context of our analysis. We used these terms mostly in the context of our analysis of threads that dealt with issues that lend themselves to "consensus" among the majority of "Arab- Muslims," such as the Palestinian-Israeli conflict and the publication of the offensive Danish cartoons about the Prophet of Islam. We cannot say that all the forums under study provided platforms for exhibiting pan-Arab or pan-Islamic attitudes around key issues. In fact, only the discussion forums in Islamway Arabic, Islamonline Arabic, and Amrkhaled (which is only in Arabic, as we previously mentioned) provided such platforms and exemplified such trends. That's because these three forums attracted mainly Arabic-speaking, Muslim participants who shared similar views on key issues for political and religious reasons, as will be explained later. In other words, it was the ethnic, cultural, and religious "homogeneity" of those participants that produced highly consensual, shared attitudes of pan-Arabism and pan-Islamism around certain key issues, within the realm of collective identities.

To the contrary, the Islamonline English forum is not restricted to Arabic-speaking, Muslim participants. In fact, participants in this forum exemplified diverse ethnic, cultural, and religious backgrounds, and some of them did not have any religious affiliation. This, in turn, did not allow for any pan-Arab or pan-Islamic perspectives or attitudes to emerge among the participants in this forum, which was characterized by highly polemic, rather than consensual, discourses and attitudes around key issues, within the realm of divergent identities, as will be explained in the next chapter. As for Islamway English, it did not provide a platform for discussing any political issues, and it was limited to Muslim "women" discussing social issues, within the realm of their day-to-day lives and/or marital relations, which naturally excluded the discussion of issues that would lend themselves to pan-Arabism or pan-Islamism on that forum.

COLLECTIVE IDENTITIES IN THE
"RELIGIO-POLITICAL" CONTEXT

The threads that will be analyzed in this section address issues that have both religious and political connotations. This is particularly important given the fact that some issues, such as urging the development of the Muslim *umma* and encouraging its spiritual and moral revival, as well as publishing the Danish cartoons about the Prophet, which may seem to be purely religious, are, in fact, strongly intertwined with political implications. On the other side of the coin, an issue such as the Palestinian-Israeli conflict, which may seem to be purely political, is, in fact, loaded with strong religious connotations. Therefore, it can be safely argued that both politics and religion play a critical and interrelated role within the realm of the contemporary Islamic public sphere.

The first two threads under this section deal with an issue of high salience, which has both strong pan-Arab and pan-Islamic connotations among most Arabs and Muslims, namely the Palestinian-Israeli conflict. Each one of these two threads focuses on a different angle of this conflict, but they both exhibit the same underlying implications and attitudes.

In Support of Al-Aqsa Mosque

Jawaher, the original poster in this thread, which is pulled from Islamway Arabic, provided a very comprehensive historical background of Al-Aqsa mosque, highlighting its exact location, size, and special place in Islam, as referred to in the *Qur'an* and the *hadith* (Prophet Muhammad's sayings). Jawaher also included a very detailed chronological timeline showing how Al-Aqsa mosque has been affected by political clashes between the Israelis and the Palestinians during the time frame between 1967 and 2000. Moreover, Jawaher referred to what she described as "threats by the Israelis" to demolish Al-Aqsa mosque, and she called on the Arabs and Muslims to take action to stop these threats. She addressed the other female participants in this forum with the following words: "The best way to defend Al-Aqsa mosque against the Israelis is to abide by Islam and to explain to your children why this mosque is important to us and what the Israelis are trying to do to it."

Commenting on Jawaher's long posting, another poster, Siham, responded: "God bless you sister Jawaher for this very useful information. May God help defend our Al-Aqsa mosque from the invaders and the killers."

> Um Samer: "My heart is broken when I see what is happening to our brothers and sisters in Palestine. This is a real trial from God."
> Wafa'a: "May God glorify Islam and Muslims in Palestine and everywhere."

Azza: "Month after month and year after year, the Palestinian land is still suffering under the forces of infidelity and occupation. The scenes of dead bodies, wailing women, and screaming children are destroying our dream for a unified Muslim *umma*. I feel helpless towards the Palestinians, and all I can do is pray to God to help them gain their independence."

So'ad (one of the forum's moderators): "Last year witnessed very serious escalations on the part of the Israelis regarding Al-Aqsa mosque. They started digging tunnels underneath it and preventing Muslims living around it from entering the mosque to perform the prayers. Oh God, may you preserve Al Aqsa mosque and make us one united *umma* in the face of our enemies."

Effat: "I am willing to sacrifice my body and my soul for the purpose of freeing Al-Aqsa mosque. I hope I can pray there one day."

Several other posters expressed the same strong emotions, positive feelings, and supportive attitudes regarding Al-Aqsa mosque.

Jawaher, the original poster, responded: "God bless all of you my dear sisters; I hope your children will be able to restore the dignity and greatness of this *umma*."

The thread also used photos to make a strong emotional impact. For example, one participant posted a picture of the golden Dome of the Rock, which stands in the vicinity of Al-Aqsa mosque, in the background, with the Israeli flag in the foreground.

AbouTrika Is a Soccer Player, But...

The subject of this thread, which is selected from Islamway Arabic, is the Egyptian soccer player, Mohammed AbouTrika, who, after scoring a goal with his Egyptian team in the 2008 African soccer championship in Ghana, showed the writing on his undershirt, which read: "Sympathizing with Gaza" in both Arabic and English. This writing was a sign of his support for the Palestinians in Gaza, who were under Israeli siege, during the time the game was played. As a result of his action, AbouTrika received a yellow card from the game's referee. AbouTrika's act stirred strong emotional reactions from all the posters in this thread.

Ameena (the original poster in this thread): "AbouTrika has set a role model for how an ideal Muslim should behave... How can we play and celebrate and forget our brothers in Gaza? AbouTrika: "You taught all of us a lesson in humanity. You made me cry when I saw you show the words on your undershirt. It was a very shocking and emotional moment. You were very courageous. You did not fear the United States; you did not fear the Zionists; you feared God. You received a warning for your act, but this is the most dignified warning that a soccer player can get. AbouTrika: You did that act, knowing that it may cost you and your team a lot, but any cost is diminished if compared to the well-being of our brothers and sisters in Palestine."

Rokayya: "You cannot imagine how much popularity AbouTrika enjoys among his fans. In fact, an international poll showed that he is one of the most popular athletes in the world. He is beloved by Muslims and Christians alike for his manners, his demeanor, and his respect for his religion. The Israeli newspapers have launched a fierce war against him. We all support him. It is enough that he was able to get his noble message across."

Nada: "*Allahu Akbar* (God is the greatest). Oh God, may you honor the Muslims with more youth like AbouTrika."

Heba: "It is ironic that when AbouTrika did what he did, he received a yellow card, however, when a soccer player from Ghana showed the [Israeli] flag to celebrate winning a game, nobody warned him. This implies the Muslims' humiliation in today's world."

Asala: "AbouTrika conveyed his message to the millions of viewers from all over the world who followed the African soccer championship on their television screens. Many thanks to you AbouTrika from all the Palestinians in Gaza."

Um Ayman: "I wish all our young Muslim men and women can learn from what AbouTrika did and take him as their role model. Who knows...this maybe the beginning of an Islamic revival."

Warda: "I wasn't interested in soccer, but now I am interested, thanks to Abou-Trika, who made me feel that he was playing to defend his religion, not to be famous."

The thread included emotional pictures of the soccer player AbouTrika showing the words on his undershirt and kneeling to thank God after he scored the goal. The thread also included Hebrew headlines of articles in Israeli newspapers, which criticized Abou Trika's action, and published photos showing AbouTrika's shirt.

The unanimous agreement among posters in the two above-mentioned threads reflects a strong sense of collective consciousness that emanates from both Arab and Islamic identities. The Palestinian-Israeli conflict is a pan-Arab issue, since the overwhelming majority of Arabs sympathize with the Palestinians in their plight to establish an independent Palestinian state. This is mainly because "The question of Palestine is part of the socio-political consciousness of the Arab nation as a whole. Being the single most important political preoccupation for Arabs since World War II, the Palestinian question has been and continues to be in the minds of practically all Arabs as a cause, a symbol and a reality."[66]

The Palestinian-Israeli conflict is also considered a pan-Islamic issue, since the majority of Muslims, of Arab or non-Arab descent, are concerned about the future of Al-Aqsa mosque, which is located in East

Jerusalem. Al-Aqsa mosque has a special value among Muslims due to its spiritual connotations and religious significance. The Quran mentions the story of how Prophet Mohammed was sent by God to Jerusalem in a "night journey," during which the Prophet prayed at Al-Aqsa mosque. Al-Aqsa mosque has ever since become the third holiest site in Islam, after Mecca and Medina in Saudi Arabia, and "Palestine has become one of Islam's holy lands."[67]

Therefore, many Arabs and Muslims can hardly see any separation between politics and religion when it comes to the Palestinian-Israeli conflict. This conflict unifies Arabs and Muslims and provides them with a sense of belongingness and solidarity, as part of the same collective community that has a shared destiny.

So, we can safely argue that these two threads exemplify the unified "virtual *umma*" at its best. The explicit meaning in the first thread is that Muslims need to be aware of the threats that Al-Aqsa mosque is facing, and they need to think of ways to defend it. As for the second thread, the explicit meaning is the participants' strong admiration of a soccer player, who for them, has become a "hero" and a "role model" for showing his support to the people of Gaza. But the implicit meaning, which is derived from the political and religious contexts, is the participants' overwhelming support for the Palestinians and their elation to see a popular public figure, like AbouTrika, take the same position on this issue.

Despite the fact that these two threads imply consensus based on collective identity, they do not exemplify most of the criteria for a public sphere as detailed by Habermas and Dahlberg. As we explained in chapter 1, Habermas visualized an ideal public sphere where participants are actively engaged in what he called a "communicative action" by taking an objective approach to discussing matters and by presenting their "validity claims" rationally rather than assertively.[68] "A theory of communicative action grounded on the validity claims…provides a vehicle for criticizing the distortions of communication…[and] envisions…a state in which unconstrained, perfectly free communication occurs."[69] Participants in a communicative action deal with issues reasonably, and they "communicate on the basis of their individual interests and come to agree through rational discourse on common interests. The emphasis here is on discourse, rationality, and universality as necessary ingredients of consensus."[70]

Participants in these threads could not take an impartial stand on the issue at hand (the Palestinian-Israeli conflict) given their strong religious and emotional involvement in it and given the high stakes that they are investing in that issue. Therefore, their claims reflected more emotion than reason. Several posters expressed a form of "spiritual support" to the Palestinian cause by mentioning that they will "pray to God" to protect Al-Aqsa mosque. This is a clear example of "passive resistance," since these Muslim women expressed their strong emotional support and sympathy toward the Palestinian cause and the Palestinians in Gaza, as well as their resistance to the Israeli occupation and the Israeli actions against Al-Aqsa mosque and against the Palestinians in Gaza, but without providing any specific recommendations or suggestions to offer practical help or support to the Palestinians.

Moreover, many of Dahlberg's criteria were not put to test in these threads. For example, there was no indication of ideal role taking, where participants respectfully listen to each others' opinions, since all participants expressed the same opinion. Also, there was no reflexivity since participants did not critically examine their position regarding the discussed issues.

These threads, however, like most other threads under study in this book, exemplify two main criteria delineated by Dahlberg: discursive inclusion (all the participants are equally entitled to introduce and question any claim) and independence from institutional, economic, and religious authorities.[71] Other than the general regulations set by the moderators of these discussion forums, participants in this forum are not subject to any type of political, economic, or religious pressure, and they are all given an equal opportunity to express their opinions. This corresponds with the public sphere notion of democratic involvement and open participation.

As previously mentioned, Islamway forum is limited to female participants. This gender homogeneity may increase the probability for collective consciousness, since, according to Habermas, homogeneity can pave the way for reaching consensus in a public sphere. However, the nonchallenging, and highly consensual environment that is exemplified in the two above-mentioned threads is the result, not just of gender homogeneity, but also of political and religious homogeneity, because all the participants in these two threads share the same political and religious attitudes toward the Palestinian-Israeli conflict.

Likewise, it can be argued that although the uncritical, unquestioning type of emotional consensus, which is exemplified in the two above-mentioned threads, reflects a form of *ijma*, it does not meet the required criteria for reaching a genuine *ijma*, as defined in an Islamic context. This is mainly because this *ijma* did not result from any deliberations, or any effort to reach independent interpretation, through a process of consultation. In fact, what we witnessed here is a process of consensus based on a collective endorsement of issues of shared interest, rather than a consensus reached after negotiations and/or debates around controversial issues.

The next thread deals with another issue of serious religio-political implications, which is calling for the revival and awakening of the Muslim *umma*.

When Are We Going to Wake Up? We Are Tired of Sleeping

Shaima'a, the original poster in this thread, which is selected from Islamway Arabic, laments the passive attitude prevailing in the Muslim *umma* today, since many Muslims are, according to her, just observing "the harm that is being inflicted on their fellow Muslims in places such as Palestine and Iraq and not doing anything to help them." She also laments that many young Muslims are immersing themselves in entertainment and trivial media programs rather than doing something useful for their communities.

> Shaima'a: "If [Muslims] become more proactive, we would be able to teach Israel and the United States an unforgettable lesson, and we would put more pressure on them...We need to go out to the streets to express our resentment of what is going on in Guantanamu and Abou-Ghoreib. If we are killed doing so, we will be martyrs...Oh fellow sisters: Let's pray to God that we may become more proactive in fighting for our rights and our freedom."
>
> Amani: "My dear sister: God bless you for your words. We are living a harsh reality today: Our minds are being controlled by our enemies; our peoples are subject to the powers of dictatorial leaders who care only about their self-interests rather than the interests of their people; the prisons in our countries are filled with innocent people; and our *umma* is filled with all kinds of corruption."
>
> Afaf: "I do not have much to add to what you eloquently described. We are being fought by infidels and hypocrites, and we ask God to provide us with patience and power to be able to stand against them."
>
> Amal: "Thank you sister for your message. The only thing we can do is pray during these rough times. God is our only resort."
>
> Shaima'a (the original poster): "Many thanks to you sisters for your opinions. I was hoping to receive more opinions."

There are four more posters who shared the same feelings about the issue at hand, but they did not add much to what has already been mentioned.

Except for the one poster who emphasized the need to be proactive through going out to the streets to express a collective resentment of the atrocities in Guantanamu and Abou-Ghoreib, the thread generally did not specify a way for Muslims to wake up and be proactive, but the explicit theme in the thread is the need for the Muslim *umma* as a whole to have a sense of spiritual unity and to pray for lessening the suffering of fellow Muslims, particularly the Palestinians and the Iraqis, and to stand against Israel and the United States. The posters shared a strong sense of political resistance to, what they perceived as, the corruption of their own governments, as well as the hegemony of foreign powers, particularly Israel and the United States.

Those posters, like many Muslims today, support the resurgence of Islam, as manifested in their expressed desire to restore an Islamic form of governance, which they believe is the main solution to internal corruption, as well as the best weapon to resist foreign domination. This is mainly because the most important causes behind the birth of this wave of "re-Islamization" have been "the failure of secular nationalism...to provide a strong sense of national identity; the need for independence from foreign influence and hegemony; and the ability to produce strong and prosperous societies."[72]

Most of these factors can be inferred as an implicit meaning in this thread. The political and economic failures in many Arab and Islamic societies and the general feeling of loss of identity in a postmodern world, which is characterized by tremendous transformations and complexities, urged many young Arabs and Muslims to call for the creation of a strong and unified Islamic *umma*. This call can be described as an attempt to seek a sense of, what Giddens referred to as, "ontological security,"[73] a concept that we explained earlier in chapter 2. For these young Muslims today, Islam represents the "last resort" that can provide them with a sense of security.

Despite the significance of the discussed issue and the serious implications it has, the posters' comments in this thread were extremely short, and they lacked the elements of analytical depth and sophistication that are required to address such a significant issue. We found this to be the case in most threads on Islamway Arabic forum. Without reaching any sweeping generalizations about the participants in any of the discussion forums under study, we would like to note that our observation and analysis of many threads in Islamway Arabic revealed that the level of deliberations did not live up to the expectations of a Habermasian public sphere. Posters in this thread expressed their approval of the opinion of the original poster without providing an insightful, in-depth analysis of the evidence that supports their position. Those posters can be contrasted to members of Habermas' "bourgeois public sphere," who were capable of engaging in rational and critical debates about social and cultural matters of common concern.

There is a collective consciousness in this thread that emanates from the participants' Islamic identity, but the spirit of debate and critical argument, which is the gist of a Habermasian discursive environment is obviously absent. Ironically, Habermas cited an increasing inability on the part of citizens to participate in public deliberations and the deterioration of the level of rational-critical debate as among the main problems facing the media sphere today, particularly given what he described as the commercialization of the media,[74] which we referred to in chapter 1. Habermas highlighted the deterioration of public debates as one of the main reasons for the end of the bourgeois public sphere. "The autonomous citizen, whose reasoned judgment and participation was the sine qua non of the public sphere, has been transformed into the 'citizen consumer' of package images and messages or the 'electronic mail target' of large lobbying groups and organizations."[75]

The general preference for "passive" over "active" resistance, and the highly emotional and uncritical consensual discourse, that are reflected in this thread, do not completely fit the requirements for the Islamic concepts of *ijtihad*, *shura*, and *ijma*.

Unlike this thread, where the posters discussed the issue of the revival of the Muslim *umma* in general and broad terms and with an emotional attitude, rather than a practical approach, the next thread from the Science and Art section of Amrkhaled's forum offers some specific suggestions and practical recommendations to develop the Muslim *umma*.

The Industrial Development Project for the Umma

Wael, an Arab engineer and the original poster in this thread, proposes the idea of forming specialized teams in various fields of engineering to serve as a foundation for launching successful industrial engineering projects across the Islamic countries. Wael asserted: We, the industrial engineers, can utilize this forum to coordinate our efforts and exchange ideas and expertise in preparation for launching such projects. We have to set specific goals and strategies to avoid losing focus. I am calling on skilled Muslim engineers to join us in this idea to be able to contribute to the development and prosperity of our Muslim *umma*." Wael also posted a list of 25 engineers who volunteered to look into his idea.

Wael's idea was well-received by all the other posters, who seemed to be young Arab engineers or engineering students, as inferred from their posted names, as well as the information they gave about themselves. These positive reactions are exemplified in the following postings in this thread:

> Gamal: "Thank you very much brother Wael for your idea, and I am very excited about participating."
> Howaida: "Please put me down for the project. I am an electrical engineering student."
> Abdulhameed: "May God bless you for your great idea. We are in dire need for such a project."
> Gooda: "I tried to adopt an idea similar to yours in the past, but it failed since I did not devote enough time to it, but I am willing to put my full time and energy in the project this time."

There were a few more posters who were all complementary to Wael's idea. This thread exemplifies a consensus and a collective consciousness with regard to building a successful Muslim *umma*, through utilizing science and engineering. Although the original poster had a somewhat specific plan of action, the other posters' comments were very short, simplistic, and they lacked an insightful perspective. Again, this thread did not exemplify a Habermasian deliberative public sphere, nor did it reflect any of Dahlberg's criteria, since the participants did not engage in a rational-critical debate about the discussed issue, despite its importance and significance.

However, the main difference between this thread and the previous ones is that it adopted a more practical and proactive approach, which urged the participants to take part in a specific action plan to develop and improve the general condition of the Muslim *umma*, rather than just feeling helpless and passively expressing sad emotions through prayers alone.

This thread is a good example of a project that was stimulated by the televised programs of Amr Khaled, the founder of the site from which this thread was obtained. Khaled, whose background we alluded to earlier in the introduction, is considered one of the most popular "new religions intellectuals,"[76] and he has been utilizing the new media, particularly satellite television and the Internet, to send his messages across to the young Arab-Muslim generations. In his programs, Khaled encourages the Muslim youth to coordinate their efforts, to try to improve themselves, and to be proactive in life. Khaled has been extremely successful in uniting the Muslim youth, especially in the Arab world, around one goal: To actively contribute to the advancement and development of the Islamic *umma* as a whole.

Therefore, this thread could be said to be a "direct reflection" of the spirit of Amr Khaled's teachings and an echo of his televised message, which emphasizes the high degree of source credibility enjoyed by Khaled among his fans and followers, as well as the strong "agenda-setting" function, which he performs through his forum, as previously discussed in the introduction.

The next thread also deals with the theme of the revival of the Muslim *umma*, but from a different perspective.

Do You Support the Creation of United African States?

Al-Ma'amoun, the original poster in this thread, which is taken from Islamonline Arabic, refers to the call made by the Libyan President Mu'ammar Qaddafi to form United African States, as a way to unite the African continent politically as well as economically so that the continent can stand on its feet, utilize its resources, and have a place in this competitive market-driven environment. Al-Ma'amoun poses a question: "Would Qaddafi's call find any support?"

All posters in this thread collectively expressed their opposition to, and even sarcasm of, Qaddafi's call, which they argued is too naïve and idealistic. In fact, many of them even accused Qaddafi of being a "|******," who does not have good judgment and who should not be taken seriously. The use of this negative label to shed doubt on the Libyan President's sanity is a clear violation of the first rule in Islamonline forum's access rules and regulations that calls on participants to "refrain from offending institutions, individuals, countries, nations and religions." This also implies political resistance to Arab leaders, who were accused of corruption and dictatorship by posters in other threads.

Some posters in this thread called for the need to establish an Islamic unity rather than an African unity; in other words, they called for pan-Islamism rather than pan-Africanism. This trend is exemplified in the following postings:

> Besheir: "President Qaddafi: You need to think of a better solution that would help serve the interests of Arabs and Muslims instead of the Africans who are more prone to take the side of the spiteful West."
>
> Ameer: "President Qaddafi ought to remember how his role model, the late Egyptian President Gamal Abdel Nasser, faced a great defeat, because he called for an Arab unity, rather than an Islamic unity."
>
> Khalaf: "I do not agree with President Qaddafi since countries in the African continent do not share the same language, the same religion or the same interests. They are only united by poverty and dictatorships. However, if we look at the Arab countries, we would find that they are united by language, religion, and common interests. What separates them is the corruption of their leaders. When can we see a united Islamic *umma* that includes all the Arab and Islamic countries? The farther from Islam we get, the more humiliated we become."
>
> Ali: "I am longing from the bottom of my heart to see a peaceful and united Islamic *umma* under one banner."

Like the two previous threads, postings in this thread imply a general desire among the participants to see a collective Islamic *umma* that can stand up against, what they perceive as, western hegemony and foreign domination. Also implied in this thread is a degree of animosity on the part of some posters against the west. In fact, a term such as "spiteful West," which was used by one of the posters helps crystallize that animosity.

Also, like the previous thread, postings in this thread reflect a strong manifestation of Islamic revival. This goes against the secularization theory, which was extensively discussed in chapter 1, and which assumed "that religion in the modern world was declining and would likely continue to decline until its eventual disappearance."[77] In this context, Casanova (1994) argued that "Religions throughout the world are entering the public sphere and the arena of political contestation not only to defend their traditional turf, as they have done in the past, but also to participate in the very struggles to define and set the modern boundaries between the private and public spheres."[78] According to Casanova, "By entering the public sphere and forcing the public discussion or contestation of certain issues, religions force modern societies to reflect publicly and collectively upon their normative structures."[79]

Islam, in particular, enjoys a strong presence in today's global public sphere. In fact, the theory of secularization, according to Gellner, "does not apply to Islam. In the course of the last one hundred years, the hold of Islam over the minds and hearts of believers has not diminished and, by some criteria, has probably increased."[80]

The abovementioned arguments by Casanova and Gellner are supported by the current calls for reviving the collective Muslim identity to lay the foundations for what many posters are longing for: a Muslim *umma* that is self-dependent politically and self-sufficient economically. The implication of this thread is that the high level of dissatisfaction among those posters (who are a microcosm of the Muslims at larger) with the deteriorating political, social, and economic conditions in their countries motivates them to unite around any call for unity, even when this call is not very specific. This creates a collective consciousness that revolves around the Muslim identity that is believed by many Muslims to be in dire need for revival and resurrection.

The Muslim public's expression of this collective consciousness, which challenges the institutional authorities and calls for a proactive approach to improve the conditions in the Islamic *umma*, has been facilitated and enhanced by the proliferation of modern media technologies. The venues created through these technologies, such as the online discussion forums, have paved the way for "distinctively modern senses of religious and political identity that, rooted in specific local contexts, are also systematized on a translocal horizon opened by new forms of communication."[81] According to Eickelman and Anderson (1999), "The [Muslim] publics that emerge around these forms of communication create a globalization from below ... [where those publics are] forming communities on their own scale: interstitial, fluid, and resting on shared communications."[82]

The thread under discussion is one good example of this "globalization from below" that was highlighted by Eickelman and Anderson. In this thread, lay Muslims from various parts of the world are engaging in a discussion about a unified Muslim *umma*. Despite the fact that there is almost a consensus among participants in this thread, it does not reflect a Habermasian rational-critical debate. Participants used emotion and assertiveness rather than reason. They talked in general terms, and they seemed to agree on some key issues, but they did not provide a specific critical assessment of their situation. We have to remember that "It's not the achievement of a consensus that is the test of 'rational-critical' debate. Rather, it's the extent to which the procedures allow for the possibility of an uncoerced consensus to be tested."[83] One of the key elements in this process is "reflexivity,"[84] or the participants' ability to critically and reasonably assess their cultural values. Reflexivity was one of the main requirements for an ideal public sphere discourse online according to Dahlberg.[85]

In this context, Habermas was cited in Calhoun (1992) as saying that reflexivity involves "[coming] to terms with the questions 'Who am I?' and 'Who do I want to be?' And these two questions can only be answered simultaneously. So we are trying to come to terms with what we have done (from which we want to disassociate ourselves) and with certain future projects that we would like to identify with."[86] The thread we just discussed lacks reflexivity as defined by Habermas and Dahlberg despite the fact that it has an "uncoerced consensus."

In the same manner, we can argue that this thread exhibits a collective agreement and uniform opinions as a form of general consensus buidling. However, it does not meet the criteria for reaching a genuine, critical *ijma* in the Islamic context, due to the absence of the process required for producing this type of *ijma*, namely the lack of rational, critical deliberations, independent interpretations (*ijtihad*), as well as free, informed, and sincere consultation (*shura*), as previously mentioned.

The following thread deals with an issue that is somewhat relevant to the topic discussed in the two previous threads, which is an assessment of the Muslim *umma* today, as reflected in its leaders, and the need to enhance that *umma*.

What Do the Current Muslim Leaders Lack?

This thread, which is selected from Islamonline Arabic, has only three posters, but it is important since it reflects a high level of openness and frankness in criticizing Arab-Muslim leaders. The original poster (Akram) did not just criticize those leaders, but he provided a highly sophisticated and comprehensive analysis of the factors that have contributed to the weakened role of the Muslim leaders, and have made them unqualified to lead their countries during this critical juncture. The following are some excerpts from this thread:

> Akram: "Moderate Islamic movements have been concerned about several issues, such as ending the people's political illiteracy and enhancing their social standards; however, these movements have neglected one critical issue, which is how to select an ideal Muslim leader who would gain people's trust and lead the *umma* to the right path. We are in dire need for a leader who would follow the steps of our Prophet."

Akram added that most current leaders of Islamic countries "lack several key characteristics, such as: the rhetorical charisma and the ability to convince others; a clear vision and strategic planning for the future; and the courage to become involved in a well-planned confrontation. They have also given in to the Western ideologies which are not a reflection of the Islamic beliefs."

> Mahmoud: "We do not need terrorist leaders such as Bin Laden, but we need a leader who is politically smart, and who is capable of maneuvering his way around Israel and the United States. We need a leader who knows how to manage cold wars. We need a leader who understands that this era is for chess players rather than boxers."
>
> Sameer: "The Arab leaders have to learn from their non-Arab Muslim counterparts, such as the late Khomeini, who led the Iranian revolution in 1979, the current Iranian President Mahmoud Ahmadi Nejad, and the Turkish President Abdullah Gol. Those are the types of leaders whose skills and expertise are needed to guide our Arab countries today and put us on the correct Islamic path."

Akram, the original poster in this thread, provided a comprehensive critical assessment that exemplified reflexivity, which is one of Dahlberg's main criteria for assessing an open and engaging public discourse. The posters in this thread called for Islamic revival, but instead of throwing the blame on the non-Islamic powers, they blamed their own leaders, and they provided a critical argument that was reasonable rather than emotional.

This thread touched on the issue of democratization, which is one of the basic challenges facing the Muslim *umma* today, as mentioned in chapter 3. The posters in this thread expressed their dissatisfaction with their current leaders, and they highlighted some characteristics that they would like to see in future leaders.

The fact that this thread had only three posters, who seemed to be on the same page with regard to their criticism of their leaders, did not allow for a Habermasian-styled exchange of validity claims, or a truly critical consensus in the context of genuine Islamic principles.

An issue of critical religio-political importance to the Muslims is the image of Prophet Mohammed, due to the great respect and admiration they have for him, not just as the Prophet of Islam, but also as one of their main sources of spiritual and moral guidance, and as the best role model for them to emulate in every aspect of life. The next thread deals with the issue of republishing the offensive cartoons about the Prophet of Islam, which angered Muslims all over the world, as well as the implications of this issue on the future potentialities of effective dialogue between Islam and the West, on one hand, as well as the potentialities for the discourse of clash of civilizations, on the other hand.

Danish Newspapers Decide to Publish Ofensive Cartoons

The subject of this thread from Islamway Arabic is the decision of major Danish newspapers to reprint the cartoons that made fun of the Prophet of Islam. The posters in this thread unanimously agreed that such a decision was extremely offensive to Muslims all over the world.

> Um Ahmad: "The decision by major Danish newspapers...to reprint the cartoons that were offensive to the honorable person of the Prophet was a sign of support to the Danish authorities' wave of arrest of immigrants accused of threatening the life of the Danish cartoonist Kurt Westergard. The Danish police...announced that they arrested immigrants of Tunisian and Moroccan descent, who were suspected of plotting to kill Westergard. Westergard is one of twelve Danish cartoonists who drew these offensive cartoons. The 73-year-old cartoonist...has been living under police protection for the last three months as a result of the threat messages that he has been receiving because of his cartoons.

These developments have led to the issuing of announcements by senior Danish officials, specifically the Danish prime minister and minister of justice, saying that they were worried about the serious nature of the issue. The Islamic community in Denmark expressed its fears that these arrests may have a negative impact on the relationship between the Danish community and the Muslim immigrants. May God honor Islam and Muslims and protect the image of the Muslim Prophet."

> Lobna: "May God send his curse against those people who try to harm the image of our Prophet, and may they face disgrace in their lifetime and end up in hellfire in the afterlife. I sacrifice my parents and my soul for you our beloved Prophet."
>
> Nour: "Yes, we hate that this happens to our Prophet, but we have to think about how this has helped draw the attention of many westerners to our religion, and how many of them have decided to convert to Islam. This is a message for us to try to follow the deeds of our beloved Prophet, peace be upon him."
>
> Asma'a: "May God's curse fall upon the Danish people and all those who try to offend our Prophet, peace be upon him. May God send all those people to hellfire; Amen. We sacrifice ourselves for you our dear Prophet."
>
> Sameera (one of the forum's moderators): "May God help us become one unified *umma*, so we can stand against our enemies and become victorious. May God glorify the Muslims and disgrace the infidels, Amen."
>
> Rasheeda: "I hope that those who harmed our Prophet would end up in hell and become an example to anybody who dares to touch our Prophet's image."

Kamilia posted a link to a lecture by a prominent Muslim scholar who talked about the Prophet's life and how he was a role model.

> Samar: "I am shocked that such a small country [Denmark] would offend our Prophet, the role model of our *umma* that has one billion Muslims, and not pay the price for doing so. If any leader of an Islamic country today was subject to the same offense, the least that would have been done was to close down the Danish embassy in his country and cut what they call diplomatic ties with Denmark. It is humiliating and disgraceful that this has not happened in this case."

The unanimous agreement among posters in this thread reflects a sense of collective consciousness among the members of the Muslim *umma*, who are strongly attached to their Prophet. They are unified by their pan-Islamic identity, which makes them rally behind one banner with one objective in mind, namely defending their religion and their Prophet against any attacks. In Islam, Prophet Mohammed is more precious to Muslims than any other people in their lives, including their parents, their siblings, and their children. This explains the posters' high level of emotional involvement and their strong resentment to the publishing of offensive cartoons of the Prophet. It is highly unlikely that mainstream Muslims would disagree when it comes to defending their Prophet. Therefore, this issue lends itself more to consensus, rather than difference, among Muslims.

The general discursive tone in this thread is colored by an implicit sense of bitterness, as posters lament that their leaders are not being proactive in dealing with the publishing of these cartoons. This bitterness is exemplified in terms such as "shocked," "humiliating," and "disgraceful."

The posters' emotionality and the overwhelming sense of homogeneous Islamic identity in this thread does not leave room for true deliberations, disagreements, or controversies as envisioned by Habermas. This thread has a sense of uniformity, collective identity, and shared vision. The postings in this thread are not for the purpose of engaging in a rational-critical debate, as much as they are for reemphasizing the need for defending the Islamic identity and revitalizing the notion of the Muslim *umma* through *do'aa* (praying and appealing to God to help defend the *umma* and its Prophet). For that reason, almost all the participants support each others' comments, and there is hardly any challenge or any controversy.

The unanimity of opinion in this thread emanates from the communal and unifying nature of Islam, with all its symbols (including the Prophet), under the banner of moral unity, which holds the Muslim *umma* together and ensures its cohesion and uniformity, as we previously mentioned in chapter 3. This unanimity also emanates from the posters' willingness to defend the Muslim *umma* collaboratively and collectively.

Despite the rhetorical release of emotions in this thread, there is a manifestation of sincerity (one of Dahlberg's criteria, which refers to the participants' sincere efforts to provide all the information relevant to the issue at hand). This sense of sincerity was exemplified by Um Ahmad, the original poster in this thread, who went out of her way to present the feedback of all the parties involved in this issue, including the Danish newspapers, the Danish officials, and the leaders of the Islamic community in Denmark. Another poster also included a link to a lecture by a Muslim scholar who spoke about the life of the Prophet and why Muslims today need to defend him—a topic that is relevant to the issue at hand, which can help the posters to better understand its various aspects and implications, as well as helping to contextualize the Muslims' reactions to the publishing of these cartoons.

The posters' collective identity, which is represented in their unanimous opposition to the publishing of these cartoons is a good example of the Islamic revival in the postmodern public sphere—a subject that we discussed in chapters 1 and 3. Those posters have utilized the Internet technology to reaffirm their Islamic faith and to collectively resist any attempts (mainly from the West) that from their perspective would harm that faith.

So, we can argue that this thread has two major implied meanings. One is that Islam is compatible with modernity, since Muslims are using the new media technologies to defend their faith. The second implied meaning is that there is a prevalent, ongoing discourse of "clash of civilizations" between Islam and the west. The term clash of civilizations was coined by Samuel Huntington, as previously mentioned in chapter 3, who argued that the "differences among civilizations are not only real; they are basic. Civilizations are differentiated from each other by history, language, culture, tradition, and most important, religion."[87] According to Huntington, "As people define their identity in ethnic and religious terms, they are likely to see an 'us' versus 'them' relation existing between themselves and people of different ethnicity or religion."[88]

The postings in the thread dealing with the Danish cartoons imply that the root of the clash between Islam and the west maybe a misunderstanding (whether intentional or not) on the part of the west as to what constitutes the Islamic faith and what is acceptable versus what is unacceptable within the parameters of this faith. In this case, the Danish cartoonists obviously failed to understand how offensive these cartoons are to Muslims allover the world. This misunderstanding could contribute to a clash of civilizations between Islam and the West, which represents a serious challenge, as we explained in chapter 3.

It is worth mentioning here that some scholars have expressed their reservations about Huntington's theory of the clash of civilizations, particularly when it comes to Islam's relationship with the West. Among those scholars are Eickelman and Piscatori (1996), who argued that "The new geography of Muslim politics...precludes a 'West versus Rest' mentality because of the dissolution of prior notions of distance and frontier...Because of permanent *hijra* (emigration), Western and Muslim societies are now on the threshold of new understandings of one another."[89]

Despite such arguments against the clash of civilization concept, there is no question that the post-9/11 era has witnessed an increasing "cultural divide" between the west and Islam, as previously mentioned. The publication of the Danish cartoons about the Muslim Prophet, followed by a stream of angry emotions from the Islamic world, and an utter shock to these emotions from western circles, is one strong indication of that divide. Although we cannot fully generalize the emotions released by posters in the thread about the Danish cartoons, we cannot totally ignore these emotions, either. Implied in these emotions is a feeling that the west, represented in Denmark, is intentionally trying to undermine, and even challenge, the Islamic culture.

The consensual feeling among many Muslims regarding the necessity of resisting foreign hegemonies and domination is best exemplified in the following thread, which is selected from Amr Khaled's forum.

We Don't Want to Forget Our Brothers in Chechnya

Ahmed, the original poster, provides a detailed historical outline of the military struggle between the Chechnyans (who are Muslims), the Russians. He described the situation in Chechnya as critical, argued that the Russians are committing "ethnic cleansing" against the Chechnyan civilians. Ahmed posted: "I decided to write about this issue because I have a feeling that the media are not giving it the attention it deserves. It is also highly unfortunate that many Muslims today are not aware of the details of the Chechnyans long, honorable struggle against the Russians. May God grant the Chechnyans the support, the power to be able to stand against the atrocities of the Russians." Ahmed also presented very detailed, comprehensive contextual information that shed some light on the Chechnyans' background in terms of their history, geography, demographic characteristics.

Other posters expressed their support for the Chechnyan Muslims, and lamented that the Muslims today are struggling against foreign powers, as exemplified in the following excerpts from this thread:

> Ismail: "How can we forget our dear brothers in Chechnya? How can forget our dear brothers in Kashmire, Afghanistan, and Pakistan?"
>
> Raef: "One day, we will celebrate with the Chechnyans when they get their independence. May God enable us Muslims everywhere to overcome all our enemies, Amen."

Sherif: "The Islamic *umma* today is like a human body that is bleeding everywhere. This is going on while our infidel rulers are silent and our *'ulama* (religious scholars) are liars."

Samy: "The Chechneyan struggle against the Russians can be compared to the Palestinian struggle against the Israelis. May God grant them freedom and independence and help them overcome their cruel enemies."

Kamal: "I always look at the bright side. We may have corrupt leaders, but we also have honorable men who are willing to sacrifice their lives for the sake of Islam. We may have some corrupt *'ulama*, but there are other *'ulama* who fear no one but God."

Ali: "Chechnya is as precious to us Muslims as Iraq and Afghanistan. We will not give up even one inch of this Muslim land to our enemies."

Ga'afar: "The Russians, with their heavy artillery and advanced weapons, will not be able to defeat our brothers in Chechnya. Some Chechnyan worriers said that they are fighting 'an enemy that they cannot see.' If the Chechnyans get engaged in a face-to-face fight with the Russians, the Chechnyans can easily win this fight."

Akram: "The Russians, after failing in the battlefield, are trying to propagate false information about the Chechnyans through the media. The Russians should know that their existence in Chechnya will end soon, thanks to the honorable and courageous struggle of the Chechnyan people."

Mahmoud: "We have to make the Chechnyans feel that while they are fighting the Russian occupation, we are praying for them; while their blood is being spilled over the Muslim land, we are supporting them with our souls and our spirits."

This thread, like others analyzed in this section, exemplifies a Muslim collective consciousness and reflects a homogeneous Islamic identity under the banner of the moral unity of the larger Muslim *umma*.

Here again, there is no true Habermasian public sphere or genuine rational-critical debates, but there is a general agreement and a consensus-building that emanates from moral support, spiritual unity, and a sense of Muslim resistance to foreign hegemony and domination. The kind of consensus that characterizes postings in this thread is an emotional, rather than a rational, consensus, within the realm of collective Muslim identities. A clear exception, however, was Kamal, the poster who tried to present a more balanced, objective, and rational view, by pointing out the fact that there are both good and bad rulers, as well as good and bad religious scholars, thus, resisting the "overgeneralization" implied in the angry tone of the other posters' harsh accusations of Arab-Muslim leaders and Muslim religious figures.

Another exception was Ahmed, the original poster, who presented contextual information and background details about the crisis in Chechnya, in an effort to better inform the other posters about the issue under discussion. The other posters in this thread, however, only expressed their spiritual and emotional support to the Chechnyans in their struggle and resistance against Russian hegemony and domination in a purely rhetorical and emotional manner. This rhetoric was generally characterized by lack of sophistication in expressions, as well as the use of negative labels, such as "infidels" and "liars," to release their angry emotions. Many posters also used poetry and verses from the Quran to get the message across to their fellow participants, and to invoke strong emotional and moral support among them toward the issue at hand.

The next thread, which is selected from Islamway Arabic forum, has a clear focus on reviving the Muslim *umma* through the propagation of the Islamic faith (*da'wa*) within an "international" context, but it adopts a much more practical approach to achieve this goal.

A Message to Our Expatriate Sisters

The original poster in this thread, Om Tayseer, is an Egyptian woman, who is currently living in Canada, according to the information she shares with the other participants in this thread. She calls upon her fellow expatriate Muslim sisters, who are living in different countries all over the world, especially in the west, to spread the message of Islam and to help in propagating the Islamic faith. Her message is very well-received by all the female participants, as exemplified in the following excerpts from this thread:

Om Tayseer: "I'm sure we are all aware of the insults and offenses against our beloved Prophet, but what did we do to effectively respond to them? The least we can do is to effectively spread his message. I'm not asking you to go out to the streets and to engage in demonstrations or to chant slogans, but the least we can do as Muslims living abroad, especially in Western countries, is to distribute some pamphlets and brochures informing non-Muslims about Islam. I'm sure you can encourage your husbands to do the same and to help you in this regard. I'm also sure that there are some mosques and Islamic centers around you where you can obtain such publications about the true message of Islam."

Zobaida: "I fully support your ideas sister, but I just moved to Canada four months ago, and I don't know anybody here...so I really don't know what I can do in this regard."

Om Tayseer: "God bless you sister...I also arrived in Canada just a few months ago myself. I live in Halifax, which is a small city, but it has many mosques and an Islamic center. I'm sure if you ask around and inquire from your husband and from other people, you'll be able to find some mosques or Islamic centers where you live too."

Salma: "I also support the call for Muslim sisters to help in spreading Islam everywhere they live. In fact, I would like to draw the attention of the sisters living in Britain, especially in the city of Nottingham, that there are some regular Islamic study circles (*halaqa*) where a number of sisters from different countries teach the correct principles of Islam, as well as the correct way to read and recite the holy Qur'an (*tajweed*)."

Ayat: "I would like to share with you sisters a very successful experience we had here in Germany where I'm currently living with my husband. We hold a weekly "open day" in the mosque over here where we invite both German men and women and we teach them about Islam. We invite them to have dinner with us and we give them lectures about Islam in the German language, as well as offering them free audio cassettes, pamphlets, and brochures about the authentic message of Islam. This turned out to be a very effective approach, thank God."

Om Tayseer: "Thank you sister and may God reward you for sharing this successful experience with us. We do the same over here in Canada too, and we usually end up with at least one man or one woman converting to Islam every week. This is the very least we can do to support our religion and our dear Prophet in the face of the distorted media messages, especially in the West, which spread many misconceptions about Islam."

Zobaida: "That's a great idea sisters. I'll try to propose it to my other Muslim sisters over here in Montreal, Canada, and maybe we can also hold a similar event in one of the mosques here every week or every other week. May God bless you and reward you all."

This thread provides an excellent example of an informed, enlightened type of consensus building between a number of participants who are highly homogeneous in terms of their gender, religious orientation, and sentiment, as well as their shared experience as members of "diasporic" Muslim communities abroad. Although they do not reflect the Habermasian notion of critical-rational deliberations, since they all manifest a high degree of uniformity and agreement around the discussed issue, they certainly provide a clear example of Dahlberg's criteria of "sincerity," as discussed earlier, since they are all keen to exchange their experiences, knowledge, and ideas with each other in an effort to sincerely provide each other with the best advice and guidance.

The thread also exhibited a high degree of "active resistance," since the participants did not just express their disapproval or resentment to some of the perceived attacks and distorted media messages against their religion and their beloved Prophet, through a highly emotional and sympathetic rhetorical discourse, as manifested in previous threads. Rather, the posters in this thread came up with practical suggestions and exchanged realistic recommendations to help spread the message of Islam abroad.

The posters in this thread also provided a clear example of what Henry Jenkins (2006) described as a "knowledge community" that is formed online between a number of people who share common interests and who exhibit a high degree of "collective intelligence," as manifested in the attempts of some of these women to share their experiences with the other posters and to find answers to their questions and inquiries.

Most importantly, the posters in this thread reflect diasporic Muslim identities, which are part of the borderless and deterritorialized global *umma* today, as previously discussed in chapter 3. The emergence of this "global community of believers and praxis"[90] could be explained in light of the fact that "The search for religious authority shows that Muslims in the West aspire to a transnational community united in belief and practice. This aspiration is most ardent among younger generations."[91] The creation of this global, transnational community is also a clear indication that "The *umma* is above all, an idea or vision: the conviction to take part in a border-crossing community that includes believers worldwide and raises ambitions for what believers ought to be—unified, innately connected, characterized by profound mutual loyalty and the practice of high moral standards."[92]

The emergence of this borderless, deterritorialized, global community also indicates that "there is a new trend among younger Muslims to define collectively for themselves what it means to be Muslim. 'Rediscovery' of religion and the study of religion among the young are at a new high for Islam."[93] Likewise, this phenomenon draws our attention to the fact that "the usual correlation between spatial and social distance has been destroyed. To live 'globally' means to live in a world where social proximity is constructed over and in spite of geographic distance, and where geographic proximity no longer leads *a prior* to social ties."[94] Within this context, "the power of the *Ummah*" remains a unifying force.[95]

The online discussions between these posters clearly show that "More than anything else the Internet and other information technologies provide spaces where Muslims, who often find themselves to be a marginalized or extreme minority group in many Western communities, can go in order to find others 'like them.' "[96] Furthermore, "It is inevitable when Islam is reimagined in diasporic contexts that various processes of cultural translation are set in motion. The resulting syncretisms give rise to new religious interpretations...a continual remaking of Islam through a politics of mediated community."[97] However, one of the key questions that need to be asked here is "whether information and media technologies are the harbingers of a new *ummah* consciousness, or a force that threatens to amplify differences between Islam in the West and Islam in the wider Muslim world."[98]

In every case, "it is difficult to ignore the potential capacity of diasporic Muslim media for developing new strains of reformist discourse...It is undoubtedly the case...that new conversations are beginning to unfold, new ways of understanding what Islam can mean in a global era."[99] Taking into account the fact that most of these new discourses, conversations, and interpretations, which are being propagated via new media, especially the Internet, are mainly prevalent among the young generation of diasporic Muslims, we can predict that "The true impact of the Muslim public sphere will therefore be felt when this generation moves into majority, and takes its place within public society. In this regard, any new *ummah* of the global media will be the distinct creation of those raised on the cusp of the twenty-first century."[100] It is expected that the true impact of this new Muslim public sphere and new form of global *umma* will be profound, considering the fact that many of these new interpretations and discourses, which are mostly perpetuated by young Muslims in search for religious knowledge, often develop as separate from, or even as a challenge to, traditional sources of religious authority and political hegemony.

Here, it is important to note that we are using the terms "diaspora" and "diasporic" with maximum caution, due to the "identity-less" nature of these Internet discussion forums, as previously mentioned, which means that there is a prevailing anonymity due to the concealed identities of most posters. This makes it very hard to determine who they really are or where they are actually living. Therefore, we relied on the information that was exchanged between the posters in this thread regarding their whereabouts and their current country of residence to decide whether they can be classified under the category of "diasporic" Muslims or not.

Concluding Remarks on the Threads Dealing with Religio-Political Issues

The previous threads in this section highlight a number of important points. They clearly show that the new "Islamist public sphere has shifted from a national to a transnational focus over the last two decades, with matters of shared concern to Islamists—from Palestine to Chechnya—becoming central to local political discourses. At another level, information technology has scaled up the Islamic *umma*, facilitating mediated dialogues over the Internet."[101] Therefore, it can be argued that "These electronic networks, as with cassette sermons, have transformed the relationship between diasporas and homelands, giving substance to the abstract concept of an Islamic community."[102]

The emergence of this new Islamic public sphere also gave birth to alternative voices in both the religious and the political arenas simultaneously, as evidenced in the previous threads, which signified a highly critical and distrusting attitude toward political and religious symbols of authority in the Arab-Muslim world. This gave birth to a strong tone of suspicion and accusation of figures of political and religious authority, namely the Arab-Muslim leaders and the traditional Muslim scholars, who were either regarded as agents conspiring with foreign powers against their own people, or as too helpless and weak to stand in the face of their enemies and to defend their nation. This attitude was clearly reflected in some of the threads that emphasized "the suffering of an Arab-Muslim people inflicted with the cooperation of repressive Arab rulers in the interests of the United States and Israel."[103] Therefore, the discourses of resistance that emerged out of this line of thought were equally complex and multifaceted, namely resistance against "external" enemies, who are trying to impose their hegemony and domination over the Muslim *umma*, as well as resistance against "internal" enemies, who are either too corrupt or too weak to defend the *umma* against its enemies.

Another important point that emerges out of the previous discussion is that "Despite the difficulties in defining politics in certain religious contexts in contemporary understandings of the term, the Internet is clearly important in disseminating a broad range of Islamic political-religious opinions and concerns to a global audience."[104] To further explain this point, Bunt (2000) mentions that "The internet's application...makes a significant impact in creating a cohesive electronic identity in cyberspace for Islamic political agendas and concerns. Whether this means that it also contributes to a global electronic *umma* could be open to question."[105] This is mainly because, "many political platforms *are* interlinked, but the concept of a free-flowing dialogue and shared agendas between all shades of opinion remains an aspiration rather than a reality."[106] However, Bunt asserts that "Whilst issues regarding accessibility still remain, increasingly for participants as well as observers with access to the Internet, cyber Islamic environments are a primary medium for religious, political and ideological guidance."[107]

Moreover, the previous discussions in this section highlight the significant role new media are likely to play, especially among a young generation of educated and technically savvy Muslims, who are always trying to utilize these new forms of communication in order to come up with "spaces and languages in which to shape an Islam that is both relevant to their socio-cultural situatedness and free from the hegemony of traditional sources of interpretation and authority."[108] In this particular context, it is important to ask "How are new media affecting debates between Muslims about what Islam means today and—more importantly in the context of politics—about who possesses the authority to speak on its behalf?"[109]

Therefore, the process through which "the younger generation of Muslims...are using new media to communicate interpretations of Islam suited to the demands and concerns of their particular circumstances"[110] gives birth to another equally important process, which is "how the 'politics of knowledge' engendered by these technologies is likely to influence the emergence of alternative conceptions of Muslim identity."[111]

The next section focuses on a different angle, namely the creation of collective identities around the discussion of social issues within a religious context.

COLLECTIVE IDENTITIES IN THE "RELIGIO-SOCIAL" CONTEXT

The threads to be analyzed in this section deal with social issues, such as appropriate versus inappropriate behavior during weddings, children born out of wedlock, and problems between husbands and wives; however, these issues are discussed in an Islamic context, that is, the participants in these threads were interested in finding out the correct Islamic perspective on these social issues. According to the literature, social issues are taking precedence over political issues in the contemporary Islamic public sphere. In this context, Anderson and Gonzalez-Quijano (2006) argued that "the discourse of political Islam is receding at least partly in favor of social and psychological discourses focused more on personal and behavioral issues than on political constitution and governance."[112]

The Disease of Late Nights

Hope, the original poster in this thread, which is taken from Islamway English, posted two Friday *Khutbas* (Islamic sermons) by a prominent Muslim scholar. One sermon deals with the wrongdoing and sinful acts that many Muslims often commit during the late night hours, instead of engaging in useful activities such as reading the Quran, praying, gaining useful knowledge, or asking for God's forgiveness. The sermon also refers to a plethora of Quranic verses and *hadith* that emphasize how the Prophet used to spend his late night hours praying and seeking repentance.

The other sermon discourages Muslim women from committing certain acts during wedding celebrations, such as singing inappropriate songs, wearing tight clothes, or dancing in front of males. These two sermons elicited some positive feedback from all the other posters in this thread, and they thanked Hope for taking the initiative to post them.

> Um Saleem: "May God reward you for posting these sermons. Do you happen to have them in Arabic?"
> Um Mohammed: "These [sermons] are very beneficial and [they serve as] important reminders for us."
> Arwa: "I would also like to have them in Arabic…Do you have a link maybe?"

Hope, the original poster, posted a link to these sermons in Arabic.

This thread is particularly interesting because one would expect a discussion of the sermons, and maybe even some debate and disagreement. But instead, posters sincerely thanked the woman who took the initiative to post the two sermons, and they seemed to agree with what is mentioned in them. This thread, like almost all other threads that we found in Islamway English, is dominated by a highly consensual, rather than a deliberatory, discourse. So, obviously this thread does not exemplify any of the required criteria for Habermas' notion of the public sphere. It also provides another clear example of an overwhelmingly uncritical process of consensus, whereby consensus or *ijma* already "exists" between the participants in the thread, even before they engage in this discussion together, rather than being "produced" among them, as a result of their interactions, deliberations, or negotiations with each other.

The collective consciousness exemplified in this thread emanates from those participants' common understanding of one of the basic teachings of Islam, which discourages its practitioners from wasting their time on trivial matters or engaging in immoral or sinful acts. This collective consciousness can also be attributed to the high degree of homogeneity between the participants in this forum, who share common religious and gendered identities, as Muslim women. This homogeneity is, in turn, reflected in their shared religious orientation and, thus, their uniform views on this issue.

The initiative taken by the original poster to post the two sermons, and then to include the link to the Arabic sermons, exemplifies one of the main criteria noted by Dahlberg, which is sincerity, as this poster made a sincere effort to provide relevant information to the other participants regarding the issues at hand.

The following thread deals with another important social issue, and that is children born out of wedlock and who their guardians should be according to Islam.

Follow-Up Question Regarding Children Born Out of Wedlock...

This thread from Islamway English had only three female posters. One poster, Bonnie, inquired about Islam's position on who the guardian should be for a child born out of wedlock. The second poster, Iman, was not able to provide Bonnie with the answer, but she helped her by forwarding her question to a secondary source (Islamweb) to get the correct answer. Iman told her: "I am still searching for an answer to your question. If I cannot find an answer, insha'allah [God willing], I will send it in to Islamweb."

When the answer from Islamweb was posted by Iman, a third poster, Olfat, asked a follow-up question and requested a *fatwa* (religious edict) on this matter. Again, Iman promised that she would try to obtain the answer from Islamweb, and she did.

This thread reflects sincerity (one of Dahlberg's criteria) on the part of Iman, who made an effort to provide sufficient and credible answers to the questions posted by Bonnie and Olfat. She made up for her lack of knowledge on certain religious issues by seeking out the opinions and *fatwas* of the *'ulama* and posting these opinions on the thread. There is no imposition of views or ideas, and, in fact, these women are very conscientious about the type of information they provide each other.

It can be safely argued that these posters' attempts to help each other answer difficult questions, find solutions to problems and dig for religious *fatwas* is a strong manifestation of the concept of online "knowledge communities" as described by Henry Jenkins.[113] We previously cited Jenkins' argument that participants in online communities can have the opportunity to exchange ideas and opinions and contribute in a major way to the general understanding of complex matters such as the one at hand in this thread. Knowledge communities such as the one manifested in this thread can also strengthen "collective intelligence," as previously discussed, which refers to the process of utilizing the collective expertise of the members of online communities to reach an acceptable solution to their social problems.[114]

In addition to their manifestation of "knowledge communities," there are other important aspects that are reflected on threads from Islamway English discussion forum, and that contribute to a collective Islamic identity that is nurtured and strengthened by a sense of Islamic "sisterhood" among the female participants. This forum serves as a "virtual *umma*" for Muslim women, who offer advice and share their knowledge about Islam with their fellow "sisters" with the aim of guiding them to the straight path. In other words, there is a genuine and sincere desire among these women to help each other out, and to make sure they all stay on the right Islamic path, in a respectable, nonjudgmental way.

There is no heated debate, controversy, or conflict among these Muslim women. They are very understanding and compassionate, and, most importantly, they have a sincere craving for learning about Islam, sharing their knowledge of the religion, and utilizing this knowledge to solve their social problems. Overall, the forum has an inviting tone, and there is a general feeling that these women are part of one big family of sisters coming together and sharing their experiences in a very genuine, friendly, and relaxing atmosphere. It can even be argued that Islamway English forum, which as we mentioned earlier, is limited to the discussion of social issues, serves a "therapeutic" purpose, where female posters find solace and comfort in sharing their problems with their sisters and getting genuine advice from them on how to deal with these problems.

The interesting aspect about these women is that they are all total strangers to each other, yet they welcome one another as if they have known each other forever. They create a deep virtual relationship through this forum, hanging on the theme of a feminine Muslim identity. This helps create a strong bonding with no racial or ethnic barriers, since the poster's race or ethnicity is often unrevealed.

They also trust each other; this trust is established over time, and is made possible by the fact that each thread has relatively few participants who are regular visitors of the forum. The fact that there are few participants also makes it easier to minimize conflict and to reach consensus without critically testing, analyzing, and assessing ideas. This comes at the expense of Habermas' vision of a deliberatory public sphere, where participants are engaged in a reasoned and critical debate of public matters. It is equally at the expense of a critical, genuine type of consensus, which should be produced through a process of independent interpretation and sincere consultation.

In many threads on Islamway English forum, one woman takes on the role of a "loving big sister," or even a "role model," whose opinions are often sought by other participants. In a way, she plays the role of a liaison between religious scholars and laypeople, or she can provide the religious advice herself, which makes her an informal opinion leader in the religious domain.

This special relationship that ties these women together, within this idealistic and gated community, almost pressures the newcomers to become part of this family of faith. Because they feel like they just joined a big family, these women become reluctant to offend their fellow sisters. They provide and accept advice without being critical. In a way, they do not want to "shock" their "virtual sisters" by using any offensive language, by being too aggressive, or even by disagreeing with other "sisters." This urges them to be very cautious in what they post.

The rules and terms are posted on every section of the forum; they serve as constant reminders to the participants that they have to be decent and respectful. Although there is tight regulation of this forum (e.g., one has to accept the rules before being registered in the forum), one gets the feeling that there is no need for the moderators' regulation, since the participants practice self-moderation and self-regulation, as explained above.

It can be argued that this forum is not a true reflection of what is out there in the real, everyday lives of Muslim women. Just like Habermas' notion of a public sphere has been criticized by some as too "utopian," the English discussion forum of Islamway can be described as a "utopian" virtual community of Muslim women, where every participant is both accepted and prewired for accepting other participants. This idealized community, which is dominated by a strong sense of collective Islamic identity, is conducive for the rejuvenation of the participants' spiritual senses away from the tense and conflict-oriented atmosphere that dominates other forums, as will be discussed in the next chapter.

The following three threads, which are selected from Islamway English, deal with the issue of marital problems between husbands and wives. In these threads, the original posters either complain about their relationships with their own husbands, or they refer to stories by other women who are voicing such complaints, but the other female posters take a collective stand that reflects reason, rather than emotion, in offering sincere advice and moral support to these women. The importance of these threads lies in the fact that Muslims regard their religion, not just as a source of spiritual guidance, but also as a comprehensive way of life. This means that they can use Islam as a frame of reference to interpret a breadth of topics, ranging from public issues with serious consequences, such as the future of the Muslim *umma* or the Palestinian-Israeli conflict, to the most intimate details of their private social lives and their marital disputes.

As we mentioned in chapter 1, the sphere of "public Islam," which entails public debates of private and public issues alike is contrasted with the Habermasian public sphere, which excluded matters that were considered to be private, such as "intimate and emotional relationships between husband and wife, parents and children."[115] In fact, the supporters of Habermas' theory of public sphere argued that the discussion of what they considered to be "private matters" in the public sphere may have a negative impact on the effectiveness of public discourse, which according to them ought to be limited only to the discussion of political or economic matters. In this context, Van Zoonen was cited in McKee (2005) as saying: "the invasion of the public arena by topics, values and actions, once belonging exclusively to the private sphere is said to erode the adequacy of the public sphere and to endanger effective public discourse."[116]

This distinction between the Habermasian public sphere, which focuses solely on public issues and excludes private matters, and the Islamic public sphere, which encompasses both public and private affairs, is best exemplified in the following threads that tackle a number of private issues dealing with marital and familial concerns.

Sad Story

Kareema, the original poster, shares a story that she came across about a virgin woman who saved herself until marriage to discover that her husband is not a virgin; in addition, he mistreats her. Kareema posted: "She waited and waited till he came along; swept her off her feet and rode away with her to the night. But it was too late, for she learned that her beloved husband whom she has been waiting for, by saving herself and her desires, was not a virgin; he has had other women. She was crushed and humiliated; she felt insecure, and she asked herself 'does he like me? Am I too fat? Did he have better?' She is in distress and wished he never told her. Her marriage is dull and sex is boring, not at all what she had originally thought or imagined. She makes an effort to seduce him but he says he's tired. Tears roll down so hot they burn the pillow. She regrets saving herself, she regrets turning down all those men, she feels used because he had his fun and just got married to settle down, while she got married to have fun and live her life and fulfill her fantasies. Now she is stuck with a man who had his fun; a man who did everything he wanted to do and now the job is done; now it's time to work and produce life. Because it's time to get serious for now he has a wife."

Other posters in this thread expressed several reservations about its details. Some argued that the story included inaccurate stereotypes about men, while others criticized the wife's assumptions and her attitude, as the following excerpts from this thread show:

Eva: "She was saving herself for the sake of God not for her husband. This story has horrible assumptions and stereotypes!"

Mandy: "My aunt always says that if a woman is that good, then the man will be at least decent. He will look one day, the next day, then the following day, but after sometime he will start to reassess his treatment of his wife who is so good to him. I think after all a man is a human and not a stone. But I must add that I do not know the full situation."

Sandy: "I did feel like the other posters that this was full of typical scenarios and a lot of marriages are like that with or without the virginity thing, but then again a lot of marriages are great with or without the virginity thing. It's important to marry pious, God fearing men who fear God and hope that those men will respect you and give you your rights as a mother and a wife. If the husband in the story is not willing to put any effort into the marriage and the wife is left to get into a depressive state, she has to take a good look at her life and say how much is this marriage benefiting me for a better hereafter?"

Megan: "I think the author's main problem is that she relates all the events in her life and her marriage to her husband's previous activities, whereas the marriage she describes is actually pretty typical for many couples and probably has nothing whatsoever to do with the husband's life pre-marriage. The sooner she realizes this, the sooner she can start living in the present instead of the past."

Amy: "I saw many flaws in this story . . . For example, if your husband does something or had done something bad in the past, this does not give you the justification to do the same thing. These types of stories should be avoided. And although there was a good intention in posting such a story, I would suggest in the future thinking about the benefit and the harm of posting such stories. We as practicing Muslims don't put trash in our minds. The only thing we can do for people like those in the story is to give them advice and then it is up to them to choose."

Kareema, the original poster who shared the story, noted that the participants' comments made her revisit the whole issue in a more rational, rather than an emotional way. She posted: "I was totally emotional when I read this story. But reading your postings really made me step back and think. Many valid points were made about it, especially the bit about 'saving herself for the sake of God' that were solid. *Sigh* what can I say, I am emotional. But you guys know what? I posted this same story on another sisters' forum called 'Muslimmomscafe'—which is a beautiful site that you should join—and the replies I got from those sisters were totally different. Maybe it's a battle between single and married sisters, or married sisters who are happy and married sisters who are not so happy, or they just had a fight with their husbands and think all men are scum. But like I said very valid points were made. I need to stop being so darn emotional."

How Do You Deal with the Cultural Differences between Husband and Wife?

This thread starts with a posting by Gameela, a Canadian Muslim woman, saying that she is married to an Arab man, and that there are major intercultural differences between them. Gameela posted: "I believe that women can do almost anything as long as it's not *haram!* [forbidden in Islam]. He, however, has much more traditional ideas about women (that they should be quiet, shy, stay at home, etc.)... so as you can see, there are some big cultural differences here. Thank God, I'm not regretting my decision or anything, but do realize that stuff like this has to be dealt with—the question is, how?"

The women in this thread respond to her message not by bashing or opposing the male figure but rather by providing sound and reasonable advice on how to resolve conflicts in this type of marriage:

Daleela: "Actually with anything that comes up, it's best just to be patient and communicate, especially now when you are still getting to know each other. I'm sure other sisters can help you on this too."

Nagwa: "I know a few sisters who are married to brothers who speak completely different languages than them, and they are living with their in-laws who have unrealistic cultural expectations, so count yourself amongst the lucky ones. Compromise and patience will see you through the first years as you adjust to each other and hopefully after that things will fall into place and you two will run as smoothly as a newly bought car."

Hameeda: "My husband and I are from different cultures. He is an Iraqi (Arab) and I am Dutch. The first year was the most difficult year but that's normal because then you will start to learn more about each other. Some advice....Try to learn his language!!! This is so important. Even if he speaks your language try to learn it! That way you will be able to communicate better with him and his family (and his family will be so proud if their daughter-in-law speaks Arabic). In the beginning we had some major fights about nothing, only because we didn't understand each other well. But the communication is now better. Let him see that you are interested in his cultural background. Read books about his country, watch movies about his country, etc. (trust me he will love that). Be friends with his family (your sister-in-law, mother-in-law, etc.) Try to prepare some food from his country. I make Iraqi food now and he loves it! And read some books about the wives of our Prophet. They were and still are great examples for us Muslim women."

Samia: "It isn't about keeping firm on your ideas and opinions, accept his and try to create harmony between them. My advice would be to please your husband in order to please God."

Fatimah: "I think you'll start to change automatically after you start living together, simply because you'll have other priorities, and maybe you'll even have the desire to please your husband in order to please God, like the sister said…My husband and I also come from very different cultures and we had a lot of differences in the beginning, but with time we sort of melted together,…and I don't miss any of the things I used to do as a single…it's just that I do other activities that please both me and my husband."

Am I Overreacting?

Ayisha, the original poster in this thread, complained about the fact that her husband of three years does not know how many birthmarks she has on her body. She posted: "I just feel that those little details may seem stupid, but they mean a lot because they show that you care and you pay attention to your loved one and it hurts that he didn't care."

Other women in this thread shared their personal stories with their husbands to illustrate to Ayisha that she needed to accept her husband's flaws, as the following postings show:

Rateeba: "I think this is just a guy thing…don't be too upset about it! My dad doesn't know my mom's age, her birthday, me and my siblings' ages and birthdays…none of it! The important thing is that while he might not know/remember details, he still remembers other important things about you: what you love, what you hate, what makes you happy/sad, etc. Those are the things that really matter because if he knows those things, then he'll know how to make you happy and keep you happy. Don't make a big deal about it…guys are guys and they don't care about small things like females generally do."

Fareeda: "I don't even know how many birthmarks I have on my body. I think it is overreacting a bit. A lot of men are just like this, it is no reflection on how much they care."

Somayya: "yes you are over reacting…to me it's actually childish…no offence!….men do not pay attention to detail as much as we do…my husband wouldn't know either…who cares…as long as he is doing his job as a husband and father, no need to get upset."

The three above-mentioned threads reflect a high level of "intimacy" and "closeness," which these women experience together as members of one big family. This feeling of unity, as part of a collective "family of faith," encourages them to utilize this forum to discuss their most private issues, including even an intimate detail such as how many birthmarks they have.

These threads also show that there is not much resistance to male figures among these female posters. In fact, there is a general tendency to accept men's weaknesses and flaws, rather than to oppose men and conflict with them. The female participants do not call for escalating conflicts or disputes with husbands, rather they try to down play them. Their postings reflect a mature, responsible and rational, rather than an emotional and irrational, approach to dealing with women's personal conflicts with their husbands.

Although, on the face of it, these women may seem weak, the implicit meaning in these threads is what can be described as a "positive obedience" of Muslim women to their husbands, within the context of obeying God. It is within this context that they want to help their fellow sisters lead happy lives with their husbands, as a means of pleasing God. Therefore, their obedience to their husbands does not stem from a position of subordination or inferiority, but it stems from a position of power exemplified in their strong belief in God and their sincere desire to obey His commands.

In other words, it is not the "passive," traditional submission to the male figure that these female participants are calling for, rather they are calling on their fellow Muslim "sisters" to exercise rationality, piety, wisdom, and self-discipline in dealing with their husbands, and, most importantly, to emulate the ideal example for all Muslim women to follow, as exemplified in the Prophet's wives. They perceive these qualities and virtues as a means to "empower" themselves as strong Muslim believers.

These threads reflect an emerging pattern of "Islamic feminism"[117] that accepts, rather than rejects or combats, the traditional Muslim woman's role as a wife who makes her husband happy, defying notions that Islam inherently restricts women.[118] In fact, Muslim feminists derive their power from their religion. In this context, Miriam Cooke was cited by Karim (2005) as saying that "Islamic feminism is a form of positioning. Muslim women position themselves in their faith communities, believing them to be the primary source of their empowerment."[119] According to Cooke, supporters of Islamic feminism "are claiming their right to be strong women within this tradition, namely to be feminists without fear that they [will] be accused of being Westernized and imitative."[120] This pattern is different from the widely held assumptions of Western feminism.

Posters in Islamway English forum encourage women to please their husbands, as by so doing they would actually be pleasing God, which should be their main aim. According to these posters, women are stronger than men (e.g., they are calmer; they are better communicators; they pay attention to details), and this allows them to be in control, but not in a confrontational way. They acknowledge each others' complaints and feelings and sympathize with each others' problems, but without totally bashing their husbands or attacking male figures, in general.

The discussions in these threads assign power to women in a way that accommodates, rather than clashes with, male figures. The implicit meaning in these threads is that while the man is the head of the household, and he may think that he controls all the strings, the woman is the neck, and she actually moves the head.

Women in this forum seek spiritual refuge and reassurance through receiving rational advice, compassion, and understanding from fellow Muslim "sisters." It can be argued that there is a clear sense of collectiveness and unity among the participants in this forum, which exemplifies the "collective sisterhood" and cohesion of Muslim women under the umbrella of the Islamic *umma*. This sense of collectiveness did not allow for a dynamic, critical debate, where the participants could engage in an ongoing exchange of moral-practical validity claims. Most posters in these threads provided their claims rationally, rather than assertively or emotionally; however, there was no disagreement or debates among them at any point in the threads. In fact, the female participants in these threads were generally approving and endorsing each others' opinions, rather than contesting or denouncing the opposite views.

Here again, we can clearly find evidence of a highly uniform, uncritical type of consensus, which is based on the homogeneity of the participants in terms of both gender and faith, and which is already "preexisting" between these women, before they engage in these online discussions. Therefore, there is evidence that this consensus is not the outcome of authentic processes of deliberation, independent interpretation, or free consultation.

If we apply Dahlberg's criteria to these three threads, we would find that there was a sense of reflexivity, since most posters provided a critical assessment of the female role as a wife. They also seemed committed to providing advice in a respectful and civilized manner; moreover, they had a sincere desire to support their Muslim "sisters," in a way that advocates reconciliation in their relationships with their husbands, rather than creating a challenging and confrontational attitude with them.

However, given that hardly any disagreement existed among the posters, we could not tell if those posters were willing "to revise their positions in light of what others post[ed]"[121] in a way that would eventually lead to a consensus or a collective agreement. The only exception was the thread about the story of the virgin woman who married a nonvirgin man, since the original poster in this thread said that she changed her position regarding this story after reading the other posters' comments and remarks. Overall, however, these threads did not manifest a true rational-critical discourse or a deliberative public sphere, as previously mentioned, since they did not reflect "a vigorous exchange of position statements and rebuttals."[122]

While the threads pulled from Islamway English forum have accommodated, rather than resisted, male figures and have taken a nonconfrontational approach in dealing with the social problems between husbands and wives, the following two threads (the first from Islamonline Arabic and the second from Amrkhaled) express more resistance to male figures, particularly the husbands or the prospective husbands.

Although Islamonline Arabic forum is open to posters from both genders, all the posters in the following thread, except one, happen to be females, as inferred from their posted names.

Is Women's Money an Unearned Gain for Men?

Sohaila, the original poster in this thread, argued that it had become very common for women to be blackmailed and oppressed by men in their lives, be it their husbands, fathers, or brothers. According to Sohaila, most men are trying to exploit women and take their money. She posted: "There are many cases of fathers who did not want their daughters to get married so that they could continue to take their salaries; or wives who were divorced since they refused to hand in their full salaries to their husbands. What is the best way to stop this oppression against women?"

All, but one female poster, agreed with Sohaila's argument, and appeared to be highly critical of men, who according to them tend to be selfish and exploitative in their relationship with women. These different views are exemplified in the following postings in this thread:

> Magda: "Thank God, I haven't been subject to that myself, but I know many women who had this experience with their husbands or their fathers. I think the main reason for this problem is the man's greed. Our religion and our Prophet have advised men to take care of women, but instead those men are trying to exploit women. I think the best solution to this problem is for the woman to leave her job to stop the exploitation on the part of her husband or her father."
>
> Sawsan: "This is the problem in patriarchies, where men earn the rights to take everything. I urge women who are in such situations to seek the support of the wise figures in their families."
>
> Om Ayman: "It is a shame that many men want to marry a working woman so that they can take her salary."
>
> Elham: "My advice to all the working women out there is: Please keep your money for yourself...I had every [kind] of bad experience [with

men] and I am advising you: Please don't give [in] and be strong and do not trust men."

Shaheera: "I had a firsthand experience with my father, who used to take all my mother's salary, and refused to spend any money in the house."

Laila: "I have a different perspective on this issue. I am a working wife, and my husband of five years has been very generous with me. I willingly give him my salary every month, and he takes the responsibility of planning for our finances. So far, I am very happy and satisfied with this arrangement."

Hamid (the only male poster in this thread): "To all the female posters in this thread: I think you need to take precautions before you get married by telling your future husbands that they are not entitled to the money that you had before marriage, or the money that you will earn through work after marriage."

Most posters in this thread were highly emotional, and they did not use reasoned moral-practical validity claims; there was a sense of collective consciousness in that most of them expressed a high level of resistance to male figures, particularly husbands and fathers. It is interesting to consider the contrast between this thread and many of the threads in Islamway English forum when it comes to gender demarcations and gendered identity construction. The religio-social threads that we analyzed so far from both forums did not exemplify a true rational-critical discourse; however, the female posters in Islamway English were less confrontational and less challenging to male figures, and they presented a more reasoned and reflexive opinion compared to the posters in this thread.

The following thread that also deals with marital issues is taken from Amrkhaled forum, which is open to both men and women. The following thread is pulled from the "Sisters section."

Would You Marry a Non-practicing Muslim?

Nadia, the original poster in this thread, poses the following question to her fellow posters: "How important is it for you to get married to a religious man who abides by the principles of his religion?" She posted: "The man in our Arab and Muslim societies may commit all kinds of sins before he gets married, but when he proposes to a woman, he may pretend to have quit all these sins when in reality he is still committing them. Unfortunately many young Muslim girls cannot differentiate between a man who is a genuine Muslim, i.e., someone who abides by what Islam says and does not commit any sins, and a man who is a Muslim just by name. There are many Muslim men who cannot memorize a word in the Quran and do not perform the prayers at home, not to mention at the mosque. And when their future wives encourage them to do these things, they say they will after marriage with their wives' help, but many of them never do."

Other posters in this thread tended to agree with Nadia's opinion, as shown in the following postings:

> Afaf: "Any woman who thinks that she will have an impact on her husband's performance of Islamic rituals after marriage is mistaken. In most cases, women cannot change men's habits in life. In fact, many men do not like to marry women who give them advice, even in religious matters."
>
> Somayya: "It all depends on how the woman provides advice to her husband. A man does not like a woman who makes him feel that he is less intelligent than her. If a man is a truly practicing Muslim, he will listen to his wife's advice."
>
> Thorayya: "This is a very important issue. I would like to share a personal experience with you: Someone proposed to me, and he said during our first meeting that a religious person should not go to the movie theatre. However, during the second meeting, he told me that he had been to all the movies that were out during that summer! That same person did not want to hear my opinion on anything; he wanted to have it his way all the time. I think it is a big problem that many Muslim men misunderstand their religion. I wish I could find a husband who is both religious and open-minded, like AmrKhaled."
>
> Rokayya: "Some prospective Muslim husbands try to give the impression that they are very knowledgeable about their religion. When you ask them if they memorize parts of the Quran, they say yes, but then it turns out that they are more knowledgeable about music than their religion."
>
> Radwa: "The basic habit that a prospective Muslim husband should have is performing prayers. The engagement time is ideal for women to know if their fiancées are practicing Muslims or not."

The writing style in this thread is mostly Egyptian colloquial Arabic. This is an interesting feature of the threads in Amrkhaled's forum, given that he is Egyptian himself, and so most of his fans and followers happen to come from Egypt and to speak Egyptian colloquial Arabic. It is a well-known fact that "Egyptian colloquial Arabic is the most widely understood in the Arab world"[123] thanks to the prevalence of Egyptian movies and soap operas. The use of colloquial Arabic in this thread draws attention to the concept of Islamic "reintellectualization,"[124] which we explained in chapter 2. According to this concept, the new Islamic public sphere, represented in the new media such as the Internet, has contributed to the vernacular nature of the Islamic discourse. This, in turn, has increased the accessibility of Islamic discourse, and has made it more popular among the average lay Arabs and Muslims who may have been turned off by the use of formal, classical Arabic in the books about Islamic doctrine.[125]

In addition, the posters' comments in this thread reflect more homogenization, rather than divisiveness and critique of each others' opinions. There is also a respectful exchange of opinion that is provided reasonably, rather than assertively. Participants are committed to an ongoing dialogue, but there is hardly any reflexivity (critically examining their opinions). This lack of self-critique translates into a degree of communal resistance to male figures, mainly prospective husbands or fiancées, who are criticized by some posters in this thread for being hypocritical and not religious. As we mentioned before, it is interesting to compare the general tone in this thread to the female postings in Islamway English forum's threads that dealt with husband-wife relationships, and which exemplified less resistance to male figures, more reconciliation, rather than confrontation, and more reflexivity, as we discussed before.

The reflexivity aspect, which has been exemplified in several of the threads we analyzed so far, and which is one of Dahlberg's criteria for a dynamic public sphere, is best manifested in the following thread, which is selected from Islamway English forum.

"Soul Searching, Finding Our Weaknesses and Improving Ourselves"

Om Kolthoum, the original poster in this thread, mentioned that Muslim women have to earn paradise in the hereafter by trying to know their weaknesses and to work on improving them. She posted: "My idea is that we should all look deep within ourselves and try to identify our main weaknesses of character and personality. These weaknesses do not benefit us, rather they hold us back and prevent us from becoming better Muslim women and earning God's blessings… Once we know what our faults are, we can take the necessary steps to improve ourselves." Om Kolthoum courageously listed two of her own weaknesses and explained what she has been doing to overcome them.

Other posters in this thread also revealed their weaknesses in a very open and frank manner. For example, one poster (Warda) wrote that she did not smile enough to people. One participant admits her depression and gains the support of all the Muslim sisters who participated in this thread. Another poster (Evana) mentioned that she was about to get married, and that she thought that this was a great opportunity to assess her personality and to work on improving her weaknesses.

Another poster (Raga'a) revealed her problem with depression and lack of faith. She posted: "Right now I feel I am the worst person alive. I feel depressed about things in my life that make me sad and upset. Everyone who meets me always says good things about me, but I completely disagree. There were times when my faith was way high and I feared God, but recently my faith has weakened. Since I started to work,

I hardly have enough time for prayers; I hardly read the Quran; and I don't go to the mosque to seek knowledge. I am sitting here and I feel sorry for myself."

Many posters expressed their sympathy toward Raga'a, such as Evana, who posted: "Sister Raga'a: May God make things easy for you and increase your faith, patience and strength, Amen! I have a suggestion: Take the time to make a list of things that displease you about your character... basically, list the things that you think are wrong with you.

BUT don't stop there! Go through the list and think about how you can change those things about yourself, in a positive and Islamic manner...As for work, if you're finding it too stressful, is it possible for you to cut down the amount of hours you're working? It'll take longer to get the full work experience, but that doesn't matter if it's negatively affecting your faith and your health (emotional, psychological, and physical)."

This thread exemplifies reflexivity, which according to Dahlberg (2001) is the "attempt to critically examine [one's] cultural values, assumptions and interests, as well as the larger social context."[126] The posters in this thread were courageous enough to openly share their weaknesses and to provide support and encouragement to each other, without any kind of judgment. Therefore, this thread helps to reinforce the sense of belonging to a "community of faith" and a "Muslim sisterhood" among these women. This thread wasn't just about acceptance. It allowed ordinary women to admit to their ordinariness and weaknesses, which actually made them stronger through their belongingness to this shared "community of faith," as well as through their sincere attempts to engage in self-evaluation and self-improvement.

Regardless of the approach taken by female posters in their self-assessment, or in their relationship with males, there is no question that the inclusion of females in these forums is a big departure from Habermas' bourgeois public sphere, where females were totally excluded, as we alluded to in chapter 1. "Habermas does indeed emphasize the extent to which the conceptual universality of the public sphere was still an ideological fiction for women, deriving as it did from an intimate domestic sphere in which they remained subjected to male authority."[127] According to Habermas, "the exclusion of women has been constitutive for the political public sphere not merely in that the latter has been dominated by men as a matter of contingency but also in that its structure and relation to the private sphere has been determined in a gender-specific fashion...The exclusion of women had structuring significance."[128]

As we mentioned in chapter 1, several scholars, such as Nancy Fraser (1992), called for the expansion of the discursive environment by creating multiple public spheres known as "subaltern counterpublics"[129] that would include marginalized groups, particularly women and people of color. It is obvious from analyzing the Islamic forums under study in this book (particularly Islamway English forum) that Muslim women actively express their views through these forums, and they play a critical role in shaping and exchanging opinions, within the framework of the "virtual *umma*." In this context, Tayyibah Taylor was cited in Karim (2005) as saying that "the contemporary Muslim woman…[is] someone who contributes actively to her community, has confidence in her faith, believes in the inherent pluralism of Islam, and does not apologize for being Muslim or for being a woman."[130]

Concluding Remarks on the Threads Dealing with Religio-Social Issues

The threads that were analyzed in this section revealed a number of important points. One of these points was the "nuanced consensus," which manifested itself through the participants' sophisticated discussions and discourses, especially in IslamWay English forum, which was characterized by the use of refined language, clear and elegant expressions, and the avoidance of any offensive or insulting words. Thus, it provided a healthy, "therapeutic" environment for addressing social issues and resolving marital problems and disputes.

Another important point was the emergence of several manifestations of "Islamic feminism," as previously mentioned, which empowers women through giving them a "voice" and enabling them to express their views, to seek solutions for their problems, and to freely express their individual and collective identities and resistances. This perfectly exemplifies the emergence of a new trend sanctioning and endorsing women's empowerment within a pluralistic, Islamic context, as discussed in chapter 3.

Moreover, one may discern in forums such as Islamway Sisters a degree of uniformity and collectivism made possible by the intertwining of gendered identities with their specific historical, cultural, political, and religious contexts, which reminds us that we can only study gendered identities "as intersecting with cultural and ethnic identity."[131] For the purpose of this study, we can certainly add "religious identity" as another important factor intersecting with gender, in light of the previously analyzed discourses.

Concluding Remarks on the Threads in General

In conclusion, the posters in the various threads in this chapter "expressed several intersecting collective identities…with intertwined social, political, cultural, and spiritual meaning dimensions."[132] This highlights the importance of studying intersecting and interrelated collective identities, encompassing "cultural, religious, and sociopolitical meaning dimensions,"[133] which allows for a more dynamic, comprehensive, and realistic view of the process of constructing and expressing collective identities, since "conceptualizing groups of people as exclusively ethnic, national, or cultural can impose static identities that might not be meaningful to people."[134]

The discussions between these posters clearly show "that people make choices with regard to their collective identifications. Expressing collective identities is an interactive process that depends on the settings, audiences, and purposes of an interaction *and* on speakers' beliefs about how interlocutors will respond to particular identifications."[135] Moreover, the high salience of the "Muslim" identity, which is shared by the participants in these forums, as members of the same *umma*, deserves special attention. It is clear from the discussions between the posters that they consider being a "Muslim" as the most important "identity-signifier" in their lives. Although in some cases, especially while discussing political issues of a pan-Arab nature, a parallel Arab identity also emerged, confirming the parallelism and interrelatedness of "Arab" and "Muslim" identities, as well as the interconnectedness of pan-Arab and pan-Islamic issues, greater emphasis was placed on the "Muslim" dimension, as evidenced throughout this chapter.

Here, it is important to highlight that "Two themes related to a Muslim identity were shared ways of living and the ability to transcend ethnic, national, and linguistic boundaries through these shared ways of living, faith, and knowledge of the Qur'an. Overall, being Muslim was defined as a philosophy that tells an individual and a community of believers how to live their lives."[136]

Moreover, the previous discussions reveal how "Islam becomes represented in new forms and via new media,"[137] a phenomenon that has special significance in the context of "the fragmentation of traditional sources of religious authority."[138] This means that "the traditional *ulama* are increasingly finding themselves bypassed in favour of, for instance, Muslim youth workers, in the search for religious knowledge."[139] This has special significance due to "the importance that Muslims today are laying on rereading and reassessing the textual sources of Islam in new contexts. Media technologies...are playing a key role in making these texts available to a wider constituency."[140]

This new wave of "mass interpretation" of religion by a wider group of people, due to the rapid expansion and spread of modern technology, especially the Internet, has a number of important implications. It enables members of the Muslim *umma* to engage in online discussions and deliberations, which can help in expressing, shaping, and negotiating Muslim identities. This reminds us of the previously discussed notion of "mediazation of tradition,"[141] especially the role of the Internet in this case, which can act as a possible bridge between "tradition" and "modernity," thus aiding the creation of "alternative voices online" and facilitating the spread of democratization, which is one of the major challenges confronting the *umma* today.

The various platforms for dialogue that are made possible online have given an opportunity to Muslims from all sides to present their opinions, and have opened the door for stronger competition across the religious spectrum.[142] However, the danger lies in the anonymous sources who can easily post their opinions online, without necessarily possessing the needed skills or the appropriate religious knowledge, since "traditional notions of religious authority can be circumnavigated in a computer-mediated environment."[143]

Another important implication of this new wave of "mass interpretation" is enabling members of the Muslim *umma*, that is, lay people, to engage in the processes of *shura, ijtihad,* and *ijma*, which were previously restricted to a selected group of religious scholars. Today, thanks to modern technology, particularly the Internet, *ijtihad* can be practiced by lay interpreters and "New intellectuals, university students and lay Muslims—men *and* women—can to some degree all be seen as sources of *ijtihad* and purveyors of authentic Islam. Their debates and critiques...constitute a dramatic widening of the *Muslim public sphere*."[144]

Interestingly, it can be argued that just like there was a process of overwhelming, uncritical consensus, which was not based on the Habermasian-styled, rational-critical debates and deliberations, there was also a general type of sweeping uniformity and collectivism, which gave birth to a general form of *ijma*, that did not emanate from the Islamic principles of *ijtihad* and *shura*.

Finally, as previously mentioned, the *umma* combines both aspects of similarity and difference between its members, and both aspects complement each other through the virtual *umma*, since "Computer-mediated communication provides a sense of commonality, associated with shared expressions and understandings, which might be described or associated with the concept of *umma*. The Internet also gives indications of the diversity associated with these Muslim expressions and understandings."[145]

Therefore, while the Internet technology helps to unify Muslims by compressing distance and time between them, it also serves as a mirror through which Muslims can realize how diverse they are.[146] This last point provides a smooth transition to the next chapter, which deals with divergent identities between Muslims and other Muslims, who are members of the same *umma*, on one hand, as well as divergent identities between Muslims and those who are outsiders to this community of faith, that is, non-Muslims, on the other hand.

CHAPTER 5

Islamic Websites:
Divergent Identities in Cyberspace

After exploring the theme of collective identities in the previous chapter, we shift our attention in this chapter to divergent identities, which exhibit clear-cut demarcations around highly divisive issues, a phenomenon that gives birth, in turn, to multiple resistances. This includes a discussion of divergent identities as they manifest themselves through some of the heated debates between members of the Muslim *umma* and those who do not belong to it, as in the case of some of the discourses between Muslims and non-Muslims, as well as some of the discourses between different Muslim sects, such as Sunnis and Shi'ites, in addition to some of the heated debates around gender discourses and political discourses.

Exploring Identity in the Realm of Divergence

In line with our understanding of the concept of identity as a nonessentialist, flexible, interrelated, and multifaceted concept, we argue that it is possible to find differences resulting from competing or even conflicting identities. This requires an understanding of the notion of identity as a dynamic concept that attempts to "differentiate in order to identify,"[1] as well as a complex concept that is "always partial and incomplete, multiple and mobile."[2] This means that "We have several identities, each one constituting us in a partial way"[3] and that "Power...is always inextricably linked to the relation between identity and the difference that supports that identity."[4] Therefore, defining identity on the basis of difference means analyzing how "we are what we are *not*."[5]

In the rest of this chapter, we will explore different shades of juxtaposing identities based on several factors, such as religious affiliation, gender, or political orientation. In exploring these diverse identities, we uphold the view that the identity positions inhabited by forum participants reflect distinct locations on the social, cultural, religious, and political map. In addition, we are equally sensitive to the fact that these identities are also "gendered" identities, which are prone to exhibit varying manifestations of masculinity and femininity.

The following section explores divergent identities that exist within the realm of the unified Muslim *umma*, or the same community of faith, yet they exhibit clear identity demarcations based on Sunni versus Shi'ite sectarian divisions.

DIVERGENT IDENTITIES AROUND "SUNNI VERSUS SHI'ITE DISCOURSES"

What Do You Think about Marriage between Sunni and Shi'ite Muslims?

In this thread from Islamonline Arabic forum, Safiyya, the original poster and a female Sunni Muslim, as indicated by both her posted name and the content of her posting, posed the following questions: "My honorable Sunni brother: If you fall in love with a Shi'ite woman, who meets all your required criteria, will you marry her? My honorable Sunni sister: If a Shi'ite man, who meets all your expectations in a spouse, were to propose to you, will you marry him despite the differences in religious orientation?"

> Abdelrahman: "Marriage between Sunni and Shi'ite Muslims is permissible by Islamic law since they both share the same religion."
>
> Sherif: "No, their religion is not the same. They (the Shi'ites) rejected the core of Islamic beliefs and deviated from our path. They are considered infidels and delinquents."

Sherif included verses from the Qur'an that talked about how Muslims are not allowed to marry "infidels."

> Mahmoud, addressing his words to Sherif: "You seem to be unnecessarily intolerant and narrow-minded in your opinion, which is not based on a strong Islamic foundation. Islam has allowed Muslim men to marry "People of the Book" (i.e., Christians and Jews), and so Muslim Sunnis are allowed to marry Shi'ites who hold the same beliefs. Moreover, in Islam, the processes of *ijtihad* [interpretation] and giving *fatwas* [religious edicts] are not open to everybody, but they are limited to the religious scholars who have studied Islamic schools of thought. In addition, nobody has the right to use the word 'infidel' to describe a Muslim who believes in God, His messenger Mohammed, and the five pillars of Islam. The Shi'ites do believe in all these pillars. All these points were agreed upon by more than fifty respectable 'ulama who attended the Islamic Organization summit held in Amman, Jordan in July 2006. I am including a link below, so that you can read the proceedings of this summit and the opinions of those 'ulama in this regard."

Salwa, addressing her words to Abdelrahman: "Please answer this question honestly and clearly: If a Shi'ite man, who is ready for marriage, proposes to marry your daughter, would you agree?"
Abdelrahman: "I don't give *fatwa*. This is discussion forum, not a *fatwa* forum. I would appreciate if you answer the following questions: Doesn't a Shi'ite Muslim acknowledge that there is no God but Allah and that Prophet Mohammed is His messenger? Doesn't a Shi'ite Muslim pray five times a day, fasts in the holy month of Ramadan, pays *Zakah* (elms) and performs *hajj* (pilgrimage to Mecca)? Doesn't a Shi'ite Muslim believe in God, his angels, his messengers, his books, and the afterlife?"
Salwa, again addressing her words to Abdelrahman: "My question to you is clear and direct. I am asking about your own belief: Would you give your daughter to a Shi'ite husband? I am also including a link below to a site that gives more information about the Shi'ites."

The link was to an op-ed piece that discussed how some Shi'ites today are using offensive language to describe some of the Prophet's companions.

Abdelrahman addressing his words to Salwa: "My reluctance to answer your question indicates that I have failed in convincing you; I am also not convinced by your evidence and your argument, and that puts an end to the futile dialogue between us."
Sherif, addressing his words to Abdelrahman: "I disagree with you on basic, rather than marginal, issues."
Safiyya, the original poster: "I agree that the Shi'ites perform all five pillars of Islam, and that they believe in God, his messengers, his angels, and the afterlife. However, they do not believe that the Qur'an we use today is totally valid and accurate. They accused some of the Prophet's companions of deleting some verses from the Qur'an and adding others to serve their own interests. They even insulted some of the Prophet's best companions, particularly Omar ibn Al Khattab and Abu Bakr Al Seddeeq. After all that, can a Sunni marry a Shi'ite or vice versa? And to be more specific, Can brother Abdelrahman agree to his daughter marrying a Shi'ite who insults the Prophet's companions?"

Safiyya included links to sites that included information supporting what she noted.

Abdelrahman: "I would not agree to having my daughter marry anybody who insults the Prophet's companions. But we should not accuse all the Shi'ites of doing so. We should not help those who want the Muslims today to be divided, rather than united. Look at Europe—a continent that was able to unite despite religious, ethnic and linguistic differences. We have to wake up as Muslims and create some unity among us."
Nareeman: "I am a Shi'ite woman. I have a Shi'ite friend who is married to a Sunni man, and they asked several religious scholars who said that it is permissible in Islam for Sunnis and Shi'ites to marry each other."

Sherif: "I have been trying over the past four years to reveal the lies and atrocities committed by the Shi'ites against Islam, such as their wrong interpretation of the Qur'an and their support for Muslims' enemies, particularly in Iraq."

Mahmoud, addressing his words to Sherif: "It seems that your intolerance has controlled your heart and mind. Do you think you are right and all the *ulama* are wrong? I advise you to get involved in something else and leave this issue to people who are qualified to talk about it."

This thread reflects sharp disagreements and divisions regarding the questions posed by Safiyya, the original poster. It also manifests a clear demarcation between Sunnis and Shi'ites, to the point that made one Sunni poster use words like "infidels" and "delinquents" to describe the Shi'ites. Although some posters showed a degree of willingness to present their opinions in a rational way, the overall tone in the thread did not reflect a true Habermasian public sphere, since many of the posters' claims were provided assertively, rather than reasonably.

Some posters, particularly Sherif, were very forceful and confrontational in presenting their opinions, and they did not exhibit any reflexivity, due to the absence of any willingness on their part to reassess their position on the issue, even when provided with convincing counterarguments. Other participants, particularly Abdelrahman, gave up on their "ideal role taking"[6] and their engagement in an ongoing dialogue after feeling that they reached a dead end with the other posters. And this might have prompted Abdelrahman to say that the door of dialogue was closed for him. Even the posters who showed some sincerity in providing information relevant to the issue at hand made sure that this additional information (e.g., links to websites dealing with the issue) was supportive of their own side of the argument only, rather than providing information to shed light on the issue as a whole.

We can safely conclude that this thread lacked most of Dahlberg's criteria for a rational-critical debate except for two that are reflected in all of the threads we came across: "Discursive inclusion and equality" and "autonomy from state and economic power."[7] This thread included Sunni and Shi'ite posters, and they were given an equal opportunity to participate away from political and economic pressures. This thread, as all the other threads in the three forums under study, "is not affiliated to any political party, interest group or private concern."[8] As we mentioned in chapter 2, the virtual environment allows for a "community of equals,"[9] where everybody is entitled to pose any question or comment without interference from outside factors or powers. This thread, however, as most other threads that exemplified somewhat antagonistic debates, was limited by what Dahlberg described as "inequalities within discourse, where some dominate discourse and others struggle to get their voices heard."[10] The confrontational attitude of some posters may discourage other more reasonable posters from voicing their opinions through these threads, as in the case of Abdelrahman.

A significant observation about this thread is the absence of traditional Muslim scholars, whose voice was mostly needed in the debate about Sunni-Shi'ite relationship to validate claims made by lay Muslims. Posters in this thread provided their opinions, but they were not qualified to issue religious edicts in any religious matter. In fact one of the posters (Abdelrahman) said that he was just expressing his personal point of view on the matter, not a *fatwa*. Lacking the '*ulamas*' voice in such a thread can increase lay people's confusion and disagreement around such a controversial issue, and can undermine their understanding of it. It can also lead to what Dawson and Cowan (2004) referred to as a "crisis of [religious] authenticity"[11] online, meaning that the information presented by the lay Muslims in these forums is not being authenticated by the religious scholars.

Unlike the previous thread that reflected a highly confrontational discourse, the next thread—taken from Amrkhaled forum and also dealing with the Sunni-Shi'ite dichotomy—reflects a discussion that is close to a rational-critical debate, as envisioned by Habermas.

Persian Hegemony

Ahmad, the original poster, discouraged Muslims from believing what the west, and particularly the United States, is trying to spread about Iran, which is that it is working against the interests of the Sunni Muslims in the area. Ahmad posed the following questions: "Is it logical to believe that a Muslim brother who believes in God and in the hereafter would do what Iran is accused of doing today? Is it possible that a country like Iran which supports the Islamic resistance movements in the area, including Hezbollah, would contribute to the bloodshed in Iraq as claimed by the Western media?" Ahmad warned against the spread of unrest (*Fitna*) in the Islamic world and called for uniting the Sunnis and Shi'ites under one umbrella. He used Qur'anic verses to support his argument. He also argued that the Sunni Muslims are in a weaker position compared to Shi'ites given that they lack a united front that would help strengthen and legitimize their cause. He wrote: "God created us as Muslims; why are we classifying ourselves as Sunnis and Shi'ites? The Iranians are extending a helping hand to you under the banner of Islam. Do not refuse this helping hand under the banner of Arabism. If you let down your Muslim brothers in Iran, the United States will get rid of the Islamic regime in Iran and will appoint its own leadership, which will be very dangerous to the future of the region."

Other posters had mixed feelings about Ahmad's posting.

> Seif: "I do not agree with you when it comes to the necessity of collective agreement among Sunni and Shi'ite groups. In fact, the Prophet himself

encouraged and approved disagreement in opinion, and he opened the door for personal interpretation *(ijtihad)*. The diversity of opinions allows for a healthy society."

Nabil, addressing his words to Ahmad: "What I sense from your words is the need to support Iran. My dear: Iran is in no need for support. It is spreading its hegemony in the area, and I do not believe that any power in the world can stop it. Iran is exploiting the current situation to its own benefits. Iran is helping Hezbollah just to win the sympathy of the Arabs and Muslims and to rise as a hero that is helping the weak factions...To tell you the truth, though, I admire the Iranian diplomacy and the Iranian leadership; however, I think that Iran is on its way to swallowing all Arabs, and the future will prove to you that my predictions are accurate. I still respect and appreciate your opinion."

Ahmad responded: "The main problem is that the voices of moderation and reason on both sides (Sunnis and Shi'ites), who call for unity under one banner, are weak and hardly heard. Unfortunately, the sweeping majority of lay Muslims fall prey to foreign attempts to divide the Muslims. We should not surrender to such attempts because if we do, that would lead to the eradication of Islam from the world. We have to understand that Sunnis and Shi'ites are like one body. It is strange that while we are proud of our history of liberating Jerusalem under the leadership of Saladin, we refuse to support Iran's calls for a united Muslim front to fight the Israelis."

Samer: "Please do not mix politics and religion. Most polls show that the Iranians hate the Egyptians."

Ahmad: "I am talking about what the Qur'an says and you're citing Western polls? Egypt and Iran together can form an unbeatable power. Our Prophet ordered us to support any Muslim country that becomes subject to attacks by foreign powers. We are like one body."

Akram: "Who are the beneficiaries from the spread of unrest between Sunnis and Shi'ites? The answer is strikingly clear: Israel and the United States. It is not my job to debate the Shi'ite line of thinking or their doctrine, which is different from that of the Sunni Muslims. Let us leave that matter to God to decide on the Day of Judgment. In the meantime, we should not frame Iran and the Shi'ites as a danger to the Islamic world. The true danger is coming from Israel and the United States. But Iran, Hezbollah, Hamas, and the Palestinian *Jihad* in Palestine are the last hope for restoring the dignity of this Muslim *umma*."

Nadia addressing her words to Akram: "My brother: We have to differentiate between the genuine *jihad* (holy war) in Palestine and the deceiving positions of Iran and Hezbollah."

Shawky addressing his words to Nadia: "May God guide you to the right path my sister. I don't see how you can describe Hezbollah as "deceiving," when even its own enemies had acknowledged its genuine intentions in Lebanon."

Ahmad: "I wish sister Nadia had listened to the lectures of Mr. Al'awwa (a renowned Sunni Muslim scholar), who called on the Sunnis to have

open-mindedness in dealing with our Shi'ite brothers...Our enemies are the only beneficiaries from a divide between Sunnis and Shi'ites."
Sawsan: "I call on Muslims—Sunnis and Shi'ites—to unite and face the United States and Israel as one front."

This thread exemplified a clear resistance to what the posters perceived as foreign domination and hegemony, particularly on the part of Israel and the United States. Some posters (clearly Sunni Muslims) also expressed their fear of Shi'ite hegemony, which they felt is represented by Iran and Hezbollah. So, the thread reflected a form of demarcation between Sunni and Shi'ite Islam. This demarcation was expressed in a reasoned, rather than an emotional or coercive manner, and there was a relatively rational-critical debate among the posters. Although this debate did not lead to a consensus *(ijma)*, or even to a revision of positions or reflexivity, in a way that would emulate Habermas' communicative action, still the posters expressed their willingness to listen to each others' opinions and to engage "in reciprocal critique of normative positions."[12] In this context, it is worth reiterating what we alluded to in chapter 1, which is that Habermas was criticized for overstating the deliberants' ability to reach consensus in rational-critical debate. According to McCarthy (1992), "This (reaching consensus) is a lot to ask of participants in a...(public debate)...For not only will the consequences differ among individuals and groups, the interpretation and assessment of those consequences will differ among them as well."[13]

The posters in this thread also adopted "ideal role taking" by showing respect to each others' opinions and "validity claims" and abstaining from personal attacks. For example, Nabil, who disagreed with Ahmad, the original poster, told him that he still respected his opinion. And even though he expressed his opposition to Iran, he admitted that he admired the Iranian diplomacy. Although we cannot conclude that this thread reflected a true Habermasian environment, still it was one of the rare threads that we came across where the posters' disagreement didn't stand in the way of expressing their perspectives in a civilized and reasoned manner.

Concluding Remarks on the "Sunni versus Shi'ite Discourses" Threads

The previous threads reveal one of the main dangers of Cyber Islamic Environments today, which is bringing about a "fragmentation" that "can impact on the real lives of individuals, at significant and at mundane levels."[14] This includes the introduction and discussion of variables that generate differences in diverse "Muslim contexts and cultural settings, both between and within the broad (and potentially interchangeable) categories of Sunni, Shi'a...Islam."[15] The heated discussions in the two previous threads highlight the existence of highly fragmenting variables between various Islamic sects within the domain of contemporary Cyber Islamic Environments.

Moreover, the previous discussions provide a clear example of the existence of "encounters with the 'Muslim other,' "[16] which, according to Mandaville (2001), can "relativise a Muslim's sense of identity and cause him or her to reassess the boundaries of inclusion/exclusion which determine who and what counts as 'authentic' Islam."[17] It is his argument that through Muslims' engagement in various global and translocal processes, "the process of reimagining the *umma* becomes one of *reconceptualising* the *umma*,"[18] because "Many Muslims do not see global processes simply as a means by which to bridge the differences and distances between them, but rather as an opportunity to critically engage with the question of who, what, and where Muslim…community can be."[19] Taking into account the fact that the discussion forums in cyberspace can offer an opportunity for such transnational and global interactions to take place, it can be argued that they can also offer a suitable opportunity to address the above-mentioned questions and to provide answers for them, through allowing Muslims from different backgrounds and orientations to revisit and requestion their own identities, as well as "other Muslims" identities simultaneously.

In addition to the clear-cut distinctions that manifest themselves between certain Islamic sects, such as Sunni and Shi'ite, through online discussion forums, it could also be argued that the mere "availability of Islamic sources on the Internet can be interpreted as one reflection of diversity in Islamic contexts, in terms of the breadth of material available."[20] In addition, "representations of diversity do emerge in discussions on 'legal' issues and interpretative matters."[21] In this context, Bunt (2000) reminds us that "Shi'a legal diversity, especially in relation to decision-making processes, is also reflected on several sites in cyberspace. In Shi'a Islam, the concept of *ijtihad* (striving for interpretation of primary sources in light of contemporary conditions) can possess a different emphasis from the definitions(s) of the term that can be found in Sunni' orthodoxy."[22] Thus, another major distinction between both sects lies in the fact that for Shi'ite Muslims "the concept of *fatwa* or rulings on specific issues has a particular significance, especially in relation to the opinions of specific contemporary *imams* and *ayatullahs*."[23] It can be argued that these differences could, in turn, contribute to increasing the severity of polemic online discourses between the followers of these two main Islamic sects, which can emphasize divisiveness and separation, rather than unity and solidarity, as witnessed in some of the threads in this section.

The threads in the following section deal with a different type of divisiveness, which is centered around the manifestation of divergent identities between Muslims and non-Muslims in cyberspace.

Divergent Identities around "Muslim versus Non-Muslim Discourses"

The first two threads in this section are selected from Islamonline English forum.

Marrying a Non-Muslim Man! Help!

Although this thread overlaps with some of the gender discourses, which will be discussed in the next section, we thought it fits best under this section, since it exemplifies divergent identities around the "Muslim versus non-Muslim" dichotomy. Mariana, the original poster, asked for advice regarding a personal problem facing one of her friends. She posted: "My Muslim female friend has fallen in love with a Christian man, and he treats her very well. They would like to get married, yet, she is unsure because it is prohibited in Islam for a woman to marry a non-Muslim man. What advice should I give her, and how does Islam deal with such cases?"

Mariana's question receives responses from both Muslim and non-Muslim posters.

> Hoda: "What your friend is doing is *haram* (religiously forbidden). She should ask God for forgiveness, and she should stop all contact with this Christian man. The other alternative is to ask him to convert to Islam, not for her sake, but out of sincere acceptance of Islam. Then she can marry him."
>
> Fatima: "It is not permissible for a Muslim woman to marry a non-Muslim from any other religion, whether from among the Jews or Christians, or any other *kaafir* [infidel] religion. It is not permissible for her to marry a Jew, a Christian, a Magian, a communist, an idol-worshipper, etc."

Fatima included two verses from the *Qur'an* that address this issue.

> Megan: "I am not a Muslim, but I am wondering why it is OK for a Muslim man to marry a non-Muslim woman and not a Muslim woman to do likewise. There are a lot of very unhappy people in this world. They wish they could find someone. People should never let religion or beliefs interfere with their future with someone."
>
> Jack: "It is definitely a double standard!! I think it might have something to do with making sure the children produced from the union are Muslim."
>
> Holmes, addressing his words to Megan: "But now you are questioning the book of hate just by asking that very sane question. This could get you in prison, lashed, or both in the land of the cult."
>
> Mahmoud: "A Muslim woman cannot marry a non-Muslim because the man/husband is the protector and overseer of his family and the children carry his name. Thus they will end up following the husband, their father, especially in matters of worship."

Holmes, addressing his words to Mahmoud: "I have never read a bigger
bunch of s*** than that which you just laid down for us. The hell with
Muslims. The whole Arab culture needs to be wiped out. Totally dis-
gusting in every facet!!"

Jill: "Lust guided the Muslim armies and allowed their men to have many
women as sexual partners, preventing deep bonding and love that God
created in the sexual union from being kept pure. So love isn't a factor
in marriage. This is the basic truth in Islam isn't it? Marriage is not for
love, but for the furthering of Islam. Jesus taught that the marriage
union is a sacred union between one man and one woman for the joining of their souls in a sexual bond that can never be undone by man."

Ameena, addressing her words to Jill: "You have no idea what you are
talking about when you mentioned the Muslim armies. This is a total
lie and an utter stupidity!. It just shows how biased and brainwashed
your mind is about Islam. Many Westerners, who are mostly Christian,
live in fornication, instead of blissful marriage. They are afraid to tie
themselves up in marriage, so they act irresponsibly by staying out of
marriage and having children out of wedlock. Is this what Jesus taught?
No. Jesus never taught this, but see how the Western lifestyle is so
immoral that if Jesus were to come to earth again, he would have cried
looking at the decay of most Christians' morality."

Jill addressing her words to Ameena: "I have no desire to tear you down,
but since your religion is positioned in opposition to jesus' word in
many ways, my pointing to these defects feels like a personal attack
upon you. Nobody is inventing things just to upset you. The word of
jesus is the word of god and it really is much more than what you have
been given to know."

Mahmoud, addressing his words to Jill: "We believe there is only one
God; whether or not you worship that God is up to you. What
Christians have done is deify Jesus (peace be upon him) and we certainly do not. So, a Christian cannot be a man of faith in the complete
sense, because he has not accepted all the articles of faith, which involve
accepting all the Prophets of God, and that includes Jesus and
Muhammad (peace be upon them both). Anyone who rejects
Muhammad (peace be upon him) is not a believer. As for the rest—you
have presented only more missionary talk—but that is, indeed, your
loss. As for Muhammad (peace be upon him)—you may spread lies—
yet Muhammad's name and legacy will forever remain and Jesus (peace
be upon him) will attest to it."

Jill, addressing her words to Mahmoud: "Muslims are deluded by their
belief that Jesus was not sent to be god's perfect word in the flesh, for
god's purpose; therefore Muslims can easily reject him for what God
created in Him, and say he is the same as Muhammad. Then they can
follow human will, reject God and not know they are rejecting what
god himself expressed in full perfection and truth through his created human Jesus, who was only sent for this one purpose and did
fulfill it."

Catholic Church No Longer Swears by Truth of the Bible

This thread revolves around an argument between two posters, one Muslim and the other Christian.

> Shamel, the original poster: "The hierarchy of the Roman Catholic Church has published a teaching document instructing the faithful that some parts of the Bible are not actually true. The Catholic bishops of England, Wales and Scotland are warning their five million worshippers, as well as any others drawn to the study of scripture, that they should not expect 'total accuracy' from the Bible."

> John: "What is important is to believe that Jesus is the Son of God, who died for our sins and rose from the dead for our salvation. Unless you believe in this, you will never inherit the kingdom of God."

> Shamel: "In a nice way they are telling us the Bible is a fabrication."

> John: "The Church is not built on the Bible, but on Jesus Christ, the Son of God. The same Holy Spirit that revealed unto Peter the true identity of Christ is the same Spirit that guides the Church unto all truth. The Bible was written by men just as the Quran was also written by men. The difference is that the men who wrote the Bible were inspired by God's Spirit, while those who fabricated the Quran were not."

> Shamel: "You are still talking about Peter? The Bible is based on lies and fabrication. This cannot be the book that Jesus preached."

> John: "Christians try to save those who have left Christ to follow Muhammed."

> Shamel: "Go and save your Bible man. The Muslims are monotheists and believe in one God. It is you who needs to be saved."

> John: "Being a monotheist won't save you from hell; even Satan knows and believes that there is one God. The only way to enter God's kingdom is by accepting Christ's sacrifice for your sins."

> Shamel: "And what evidence do you have since the bible is not a book of truth?"

> John: "The evidence of the Jews' survival despite centuries of exile and persecution and their return to the Land of Israel, and their victory over their enemies is proof enough that the Bible is the Word of God for this is as the Bible foretold."

> Shamel: "Is that the only evidence you have? All the religious books say that Jesus will come back to his people in the Middle East. That is no evidence."

The next thread is selected from Islamonline English forum.

Denmark and Muslims: Heading to Where?

> Samer: "Danish newspapers have reprinted one of several caricatures of the Prophet Muhammad which sparked violent protests across the

Muslim world two years ago. They say they wanted to show their commitment to freedom of speech after an alleged plot to kill one of the cartoonists behind the drawings. What's the point in this issue? Is it another attempt to annoy Muslims? What kind of freedom is involved in this issue? Is it really about freedom or spreading hatred? How should Muslims react to such action?"

Ahmad: "It's just another attack in a long line of attacks on Islam. I am all for freedom of speech and debate but within the bounds of respect and common courtesy, which should be applied by both Muslims and non-Muslims. I really hope Muslims don't overreact because that's what the West expects so as to show the world that all Muslims are violent and 'irrational.' I think it's a pity that the media feels that it needs to maintain a constant attack on Islam when they could put their time and resources to much better uses. There seems to be a real lack of common sense and people are too blood-thirsty."

John: "Some time ago, the Belgian magazine *Humo* published a cartoon of Jesus. It was a drawing of the last supper. It was accompanied by the words 'Jesus turns water into urine.' The cartoon depicted Jesus holding his genitals and peeing into a bottle. Nobody said a word."

Ali: "This clearly shows that you people have no respect for your prophets. Shame on you."

John: "By saying 'you people,' you imply that we are all Christians, which, of course, is wrong. I never said that priests liked the cartoon. They considered it blasphemy. But they didn't go out and call for the heads of the staff of *Humo*. They didn't throw molotov cocktails, they didn't burn cars. Instead, they just didn't buy the magazine. That's where the difference lies."

Ali: "You may not be a Christian, but why do you defend them? I agree the West is all about free speech, but freedom comes with responsibility. Is it right to hurt the sentiments of a certain faith which consist of billions of people? I would consider the priests to be silent devils. Just not buying the magazine is not going to have any effect on the abusers. Blasphemy is a serious offense and therefore Islam has severe punishment for it. This disease needs to be eradicated before it spreads. Just try to question the Holocaust in a Danish newspaper and see what happens."

John: "Freedom of speech ends when this speech calls for violent actions. Having fun of someone/something is not a call for violent action. Period."

Ali: "Let me put this straight. I am against all forms of violence like burning books or rioting, but I believe that those guilty of blasphemy and provoking should be severely punished. This cartoon case is a typical example of Western hypocrisy. This is the Danish version of freedom of speech where you ridicule others but should not be ridiculed. Question the Holocaust and you will end up in jail."

James: "The Danes are right to republish the cartoons in response to another murder being planned by the facist Islamic movement. Islam is not compatible with liberal Western democracy. Sadly, people are going to have to find this out the hard way."

The next thread is taken from the Social Club section of Islamonline English forum.

Can Female Muslims Date?

This thread also lends itself to gendered identity, but its postings mostly revolve around "Muslim versus non-Muslim" relationships. Jack, the original poster in this thread, is a Christian student in high school, who describes himself as religious. Jack said that he is in love with a Muslim girl in college. He is seeking Muslims' advice as to whether Muslim girls are allowed to date. Jack's question leads to a mix of responses—some are rational and reasonable, while others are emotional and aggressive.

Mona: "Unfortunately, Muslim girls cannot marry a man of another religion, unless he converts to Islam. If you feel you can sacrifice your religion to be with her, then do so. And if she's religious, I don't think dating her would be appropriate. You can talk to her and get to know her more, until you feel the time is right to get engaged."

Mahmoud, addressing his words to Mona: "How can you open your mouth and say it is 'unfortunate' that a Muslim woman can't marry a *Kaafir* man? On the contrary it is fortunately a blesssing from God not to marry one whom the Qur'an defines as *Naajis* [impure]."

Othman: "There is no such thing as dating in Islam. There is an engagement period. When engaged, time alone is permissible. This is the respectable, honorable way to approach the issue. If you sincerely like this Muslim girl, you can only approach her with the intent to marry. God Almighty did not create females to be girlfriends! They were created to be honored as mothers, sisters, daughters, aunts, grandmas...The only way you can seek a relationship is to become a Muslim. There is a wisdom behind this because the husband must lead and guide the wife and children on a path purely for God. A Christian husband with a Muslim wife will not do this with the complete respect of Prophet Muhammad. Denial of any of the prophets lowers the status of the believer."

Ayman, addressing his words to Jack, the original poster: "Sorry bruh, go date one of those nasty, Christian/Jewish fornicators—the Muslim women are not for you."

Ramzi, addressing his words to Ayman: "If your analogy is correct, then it should also apply to those hundreds of 'Muslim' brothers who are non-practicing and are worse than some Christian brothers. Those 'so-called Muslims' shouldn't marry our sisters either, because they also do not know their religion."

Ayman responded: "There is no such thing as a 'pious' Christian because they commit *shirk* [worshipping someone else besides God)...This, and a host of other reasons, excludes disbelievers from marrying Muslim women. Learn your religion before you try to talk smack."

Omar: "Unfortunately, the forum administrators are not fully moderating this board and even when they do they do not understand the emotional impact of the discussions on online users. Although the comments are only a perspective, the idea that some users have here is to flame the board and to argue through each post, without thinking. These discussions have not taken place only once, but on various occasions and unfortunately some users still stick to their old disbelief, verbal abuse and manipulating the forum following their egos—instead of using the guidelines set by Islam and that of common courtesy. This is why I feel that these forums are not really empowering us Muslims, but more so attending to the reactions and egos of those who wish to manipulate or spam the board with disinformation and hatred. There is a lot of improvement needed here, if only our moderators would realize the extent of the abuse on this site."

It is hard to discuss a true Habermasian public sphere in the four previous threads given the sharp confrontation and aggressive approach exhibited through their discourse. Rather than having a true deliberation, where posters would present their validity claims and positions with reason, their arguments were expressed in an assertive, combative, and defensive manner. Posters from each side interacted with the "Other" not to inform, but to justify and defend their own beliefs; and in doing so they bashed the "Other." There were hardly any attempts, on the posters' end, to engage in reflexivity or exhibit signs of respect. Some posters were not particularly well-versed in presenting their counterarguments. They did not show any level of civility, and even used derogatory terms in describing people of the other faith, such as "The hell with Muslims," "the book of hate," "utter stupidity," "infidel," and "Facist Islamic movement." This was a clear violation of one of the forum's rules, which calls on participants to "Refrain from offending institutions, individuals, countries, nations and religions."[24]

The disintegrating level of debate and the declining general taste in these threads were among the factors that Habermas lamented in his assessment of the contemporary public sphere, referring to it as the process of "commodification of culture,"[25] as we mentioned in chapter 1.

The highly polemic discourse reflected in these threads could have been better regulated by the moderators had they urged both sides to try to focus on the similarities between Islam and Christianity rather than engage in a futile debate that reached a dead end. In fact, the posting by Omar, the last participant in the last thread, was very eloquent in that it captured the essence of the problem, which is the absence of the moderators' role in many threads on this forum.

Overall, the discourse in these four threads reflected a highly polarized clash between Islam and Christianity, and a deep divide between the Islamic and the non-Islamic, particularly western identities, to the point that made one of the posters say that "Islam is not compatible with liberal Western democracy."

As we mentioned in chapter 3, initiating a constructive dialogue between Islam and the west can be described as one of the main challenges facing the Muslim *umma* today. This dialogue requires genuine attempts on the part of Muslims and non-Muslims to explain their positions reasonably, rather than assertively, while tolerantly listening to the other side, and, more importantly, to use John Esposito's words, to have "the ability to agree to disagree."[26] Most participants in the four threads included under this section did not know how to disagree. Moreover, they did not show any willingness to engage in what Habermas called "communicative action" by failing to explain their points of view in a rational way. However, participants in these threads were engaged in what Habermas described as "strategic action"—a concept that we explained in chapter 3—which means maneuvering their way in the argument and trying to forcefully change the positions or the beliefs of the other side. In this context, Habermas (1990) argued that

> Whereas in strategic action one actor seeks to influence the behavior of another by means of the threat of sanctions or the prospect of gratification in order to cause the interaction to continue as the first actor desires, in communicative action one actor seeks rationally to motivate another by relying on the illocutionary binding/bonding effect...of the offer contained in his speech act.[27]

Likewise, in explaining this phenomenon, Lynch (2006) refers to the clear absence of "the conditions widely assumed to be necessary for genuine communicative action"[28] in the dialogue between Muslims and westerners in the post-9/11 era, as previously mentioned in chapter 3. He attributes this to the fact that the predominant approach in most attempts to hold a dialogue between Islam and the west today "retains a strategic orientation, for all of its communicative overlay."[29] In other words, the emphasis is largely on "persuasion" and the attempt to change the other party's convictions, ideas, and beliefs, as the main "strategic" goal of this type of communication activity, rather than an authentic engagement in a liberal "exchange" of ideas between two parties that are equally interested in listening to each other and respecting each other's divergent opinions. This leaves us with a situation where "while all free to choose, there is only one correct choice."[30] This attitude, of course, is markedly in contrast with the notion of "communicative action" as envisioned by Habermas.

It is important to highlight the fact that we are not generalizing the confrontational discourse in the four previous threads to the overall relationship between Muslims and non-Muslims today. However, we can learn from these threads that adopting a strategic, rather than a communicative, action can hamper any attempts to initiate a constructive and enlightened dialogue between Islam and the west. This comes at a time when there is a great need for such a dialogue, especially in the post-9/11 era that marks the prevalence of many stereotypes and misperceptions about Islam in the west.

Unlike the four previous threads that reflected antagonistic confrontations between Muslims and non-Muslims, the following thread, taken from Islamonline English forum, has a more reasoned and rational debate among the posters.

A New Private Forum for Muslims Only

Mariam, the original poster: "I have seen too much hatred for Muslims in this forum. There is also disinformation, misinformation and Islamophobia. I have even seen Muslims going against one another. I suggest that this forum be only for Muslims to strengthen their morals rather than make them more confused because of the hate postings that is propagated here. Take note moderators that very few Muslims are actually posting and it is not fair that they have to deal with some abusive personalities. Many give up and leave gaining nothing from this except wasting time. The non-Muslims users have set themselves here against us. We have no time to spend arguing with those who do not respect our faith or who intimidate, ridicule, abuse, swear, slander and stereotype us just because this board is not effectively moderated. Even when the current wars on terror are evidently caused by the West, those people want us to provide them with sources while defending the atrocities and horror of war crimes."

Kaspar, addressing his words to Mariam: "Have some faith in your beliefs; discuss issues with those that are courteous and ignore those who feel the need to regurgitate hate and personal insults. Try not to judge all Westerners in the same manner, just as some of us do not consider all those that follow Islam to be terrorists. A little balance may be in order."

Taha: "Both Muslims and others are guilty of spreading many lies and distortions here. To me though, the idea of running away to hide in our own little corner and ignore those out there who spread these lies without a Muslim reply is unacceptable. It is our responsibility as Muslims to deal with these stories with words of wisdom and truth, and allow other readers to discern whom it is they believe to be telling them the truth. I myself have been attacked and threatened by "so called" Muslims here before. You'll find that some of our most close-minded posters in this forum are Muslims. We must reach the hearts and minds of both sides and do so with wisdom, truth and dignity. Running away solves nothing."

Jim: "I fully agree with Taha. We should always keep in mind that fear dies with knowledge, and that it is knowledge about each other that has the power to open the closed minds on all fronts, particularly religion and ideology."

Hassan, addressing his words to Mariam: "Your idea is good, but how would you guarantee that the forum you are calling for will be exclusively limited to Muslims? There are posters on this forum who may take up an Islamic username. Initially they may post things which are supportive of Islam so that they can win Muslim support. Then gradually they start their lies, manipulations and distortions against the Muslims."

Ismail: "My reasoning is that if you live in a land where English is generally spoken, you are going to be confronted with those kinds of people who assault Islam anyway. So it's just best to accustom to it and orient yourself to it. And if you want to spread the word about Islam among non-Muslims, just let them read what you have to say and let them all say whatever they want to say, even when they attack Islam."

Mostafa, addressing his words to Ismail: "Are you suggesting that we should accept bigots and abusers in this forum? Don't make accepting abuse appear as if it is 'normal' and 'acceptable.' "

Safwat: "Why can't we all just get along?"

Amgad: "The lies of the Western puppets will be exposed and that's why they are desperate and sent to this forum."

Ali: "Although I agree with Mariam, this does not mean that I am calling for preventing all non-Muslims from having their say. The abuse of the Islamonline forum by some non-Muslim posters should not make us forget all the decent discussions by other non-Muslims. We should use moderation, justice and unity to moderate the forum. Most of all, we should run an Islamic site according to the teachings of the Quran and our religion Islam. Unless moderators keep an eye on the users who abuse this forum, they might as well shut it down. Abuse, swearing and demonizing of Muslims are all the reasons why moderators must ban these users. There is nothing to enjoy reading and answering posts of abuse, threats and jeering. We can find such comments all over the Internet. But this is an Islamic forum, not an 'Abuse the Muslims on Islamonline forum.' "

Tom: "I have said a hundred times before: If I were a moderator, I would ban those who try to insult and threaten Muslims and Islam on this board. I am not a Muslim. However, after all, this is an Islamic board, and I have found Muslims on here and elsewhere far more tolerant than I would be had I been in their situation. Picture if Muslims came on a Christian website and posted insults against Christians and threatened them. They would be banned immediately."

The discourse in this thread comes close to a rational-critical debate. Although the posters had not reached a consensus on the issue, most of them were engaged "in reciprocal critique of normative positions that...[were] provided with reason rather than simply asserted."[31]

The original poster, Mariam, called for a forum that is defined and confined to Muslims and that excludes all non-Muslims. This is a form of discursive inequality, to use Dahlberg's terms, and a resistance to what she perceived as an unjustified and unfair attack on Muslims through this forum. Some posters disagreed with Mariam, and they encouraged her to think about the importance of dialogue between Muslims and non-Muslims.

Reflexivity was manifested in the postings of some Muslim as well as non-Muslim posters. Taha, for example, who is a Muslim, noted that even Muslim posters on Islamonline can be aggressive and close-minded, while Tom, a non-Muslim, acknowledged that many Muslims are tolerant, and he called for banning non-Muslim posters who attack Islam through this forum. Even the posters who disagreed with these opinions expressed their validity claims in a way that showed their "commitment to an ongoing dialogue"[32] and their respect to the opposite opinions.

This thread, unlike the four threads that preceded it, did not reflect what Habermas described as "strategic action" among its posters. We did not feel that the posters in this thread were trying to manipulate each other as much as they were making an effort to get their points across in a civilized and rational manner. This thread provides a ray of hope that dialogue between Muslims and non-Muslims is possible, if people from both sides are sincerely committed to it.

Concluding Remarks on
"Muslim Versus Non-Muslim Discourses" Threads

The highly polemic and divisive discussions in some of the previous threads reflect a "polarized scenario,"[33] which widens the gap and magnifies the distance between the "self" and the "Other," and which has been referred to by some western scholars as the discourse of "clash of civilizations" or "Jihad versus McWorld,"[34] in which "the tension between differentiation and uniformity (the local and the global) is ubiquitous, identities are perpetually contested."[35]

However, as we mentioned earlier, we are careful not to generalize this trend, which emphasizes divisiveness and separation between Muslims and non-Muslims, since it is certainly not representative of all the ongoing discourses between both parties, as evidenced in some of the more balanced threads, which reflected a reasonable degree of rationality and tolerance, and a willingness to listen to the "other."

The heated discussions and debates in some of the previous threads also draw our attention to the fact that "the common point between all fundamentalist and Islamist movements is that they draw a line inside the Muslim world between what is Islamic and what is not."[36] In the case of these online controversies, although we cannot be sure of the forums' participant identities or their affiliation with any particular religious group or movement, we have certainly witnessed what Roy (2004) describes as "reinventing mental borders," which is a process through which individuals attempt "to draw new borders between groups whose identity relies on a performative definition: we are what we say we are, or what others say we are."[37] In other words, the creation of "self-identity," in this case, is a process that is largely linked to "self-definitions," as well as to definitions ascribed by "Others." Therefore, "These new ethnic and religious borders…work in minds, attitudes and discourses. They are more vocal than territorial, but all the more eagerly endorsed and defended because they have to be invented, and because they remain fragile and transitory."[38]

Likewise, it is important to bear in mind that as "Islam becomes represented in new forms and via new media"[39] there is a significantly increasing emphasis now on "wider questions concerning Muslim identity and relations between Muslims and non-Muslims."[40] However, the fact that most of the previous discussions between Muslims and non-Muslims in this section were highly polemic, and sometimes even hostile and verbally aggressive, to the extent that they feature individuals who are "shouting, but not being heard,"[41] reminds us of the prevalence of "strategic action" over "communicative action" in the dialogue between Islam and the west, especially in the post-9/11 era, as previously discussed.

The next section deals with a different type of discourse, which offers another avenue for divergent identities to manifest themselves online, namely gender discourses.

DIVERGENT IDENTITIES AROUND "GENDER DISCOURSES"

The following thread is selected from Islamonline English forum.

Mr. Right but Married…Marry Him?

This thread deals with the issue of polygamy in Islam, and whether Muslim women would be happy as second, third, or fourth wives. Of all the participants in this thread, only two are Muslim males, and the rest except for two seem to be Muslim females (as clear from their usernames and the content of their postings).

> Samia, the original poster in this thread, poses the following question: "To the females in this forum: If a man proposes to you, and he seems to be the right person for you, but he's already married, will you still accept him?"
>
> Ameena: "The problem for me is not that this man is married! The problem is to be sure 100 percent that he is Mr. Right. Islam allows men to marry more than one wife, but it puts conditions for this case. If he is a real Mr. Right who can take care of two wives and be fair to both of them and to his kids, there is no problem."

Gameela: "This posting is relevant to my situation right now. I'm in love with a man, but he is married with one child. He is also in love with me. For me he is the right one"

Holy: "I can't believe what I am reading! Three intelligent young women think it is okay to fall in love with and marry a man who is already married to someone else! Before you take this step, stop and think. This guy was supposed to love the woman he is already married to, but he has set her aside in order to pursue you. What will happen when he meets cute little Prospect #3? Will you still think he loves you, or will you realize that he is simply continuing in the same mode of behavior he exhibited when he met you and wanted another sex partner? Don't settle for a part-time husband...Find a guy who wants to marry you and remain only with you for the rest of his life. One more thing...check out the blogs of women who are already in polygamous marriages. They are really sad, and of course they would be. Think, before you join the ranks of these women who cry themselves to sleep while their husbands are enjoying the company of another woman."

Khadeeja: "My answer is of course I will marry a man who is already married if he is a good practicing Muslim and can promise to do justice among his wives. I am talking based on personal experience. I was married to a man who was single, but that marriage caused frustration, since he had no understanding of Islam. We got divorced and after a couple of years I married this man who has two wives, but I can say for sure that in this polygamous marriage I am much happier both spiritually and with worldly things."

Holy, addressing her words to Khadeeja: "You have just proven my point...that the guy who is thinking of marrying wife # 2, will not stop there and will soon need wife # 3 in order to get his jollies. All of the women above are looking into marrying a man who is already attached to another woman. you women (the later wives) get to make the choice of whether or not to be part of a *harem*, but the women who are with these men right now (the first wives), have no say in this matter. They can express their feelings, but in the end they are told that if they do not wish to divorce, they should endure it because it is the will of God. hah! It is the will of a man who sees a pretty face and wants a piece of her action."

Hamid, a male poster, addressing his words to Holy: "You seem to be quite assertive in trying to impose your viewpoint on others whom you even don't know. In fact, this forum is an open forum. You can discuss, guide others and seek help from others without trying to impose your opinion on them. You are right in justifying monogamy. Islam prefers monogamy as a standard practice... but also allows polygamy in some situations (I don't want to go into details) one of them is where a married man and a single (unmarried/widowed/divorced) woman like each other. They are allowed to get married rather than falling into adultery. By the way, I am a 39-year old married man (still) having one wife and two children; and have found a (Ms Right) divorcee having one child. We will be getting married to save and protect our faith."

Holy, addressing her words to Hamid: "So you are taking a second wife
in order to protect yourself from committing adultery. Tell me, what
should your wife do when she meets a lonely divorced man and they
like each other? What should she do in order to save and protect her
faith?"

Hamid, addressing his words to Holy: "If a wife is in love with someone,
Islam gives her the opportunity to save her faith. She can ask for a
divorce and marry someone else, rather than deciding for adultery. But
polygamy is allowed for the husband not for the wife for several reasons. One of them, for example, is the child born to a polygamous
female will belong to which husband (no one can tell)?? That is not the
case with a polygamous husband who has his children born to their
respective mothers. So God has allowed polygamy for husbands only;
and only God knows why He has allowed it for that matter. I once
again repeat my words that Islam prefers monogamy as a standard practice.... but also allows polygamy in some situations. It is not for everyone as a standard practice."

Holy, addressing her words to Hamid: "Self-control, not polygamy is the
real answer when someone feels compelled to look at a person other
than their spouse."

Wafa'a: "A man cannot equally love two women, but he can have four
wives on condition that he has to be righteous to all of them."

Nagwa: "I know polygamy is allowed in Islam, but I would think very
carefully before entering such a marriage. Personally, I don't think I
would be able to cope with it, as I've had some negative experience in
a polygamous marriage. But that's not to say it will never work out,
because I'm sure there are women out there who would be happy in a
polygamous marriage."

Megan: "If both partners have thought the consequences through, and
maybe even discussed with their current partners what might lie ahead,
I think yes get married. But may be try to live together first before you
marry. Why the rush? What if you feel it is wrong after all. In that case,
it is better to just have had a pleasant time without being stuck in
another marriage."

Omneya, addressing her words to Mega: "It is very offensive and disre-
spectful to expect pious Muslim couples to 'live with one another' prior
to marriage as you expect licentious boyfriends or girlfriends to do in
the West nowadays, through several heart-breaking relationships.
Fornication, prostitution, homosexuality and adultery are huge sins in
Islam."

Alia'a: "We should remember that it is *haram* to criticize something which
God has made permissible. I am the third wife and I would have no
problem if my husband decides to marry a fourth wife. God has permitted this so who am I to stop my husband as long as he continues to do
justice among his wives? I do not know other people's experiences, but
all the three of us are very happy in this marriage. So, for me it does not
matter if the man wants to marry a third or a fourth wife, or if he just
wants to marry one wife, as long as he is a pious Muslim. This world is

temporary and if the husband is the means for us to get to paradise, then that's the best husband."

Holy, addressing her words to Alia'a: "Of course you can question the wisdom of a man who is about to take a second, third or fourth wife! any woman should have a say in a matter that will affect her life so greatly! Even if a man was required to take more than one wife, the existing wife should be allowed to have veto power in whether or not a certain woman should share her husband, her way of life, and eventually her inheritance. But men aren't required to take multiple wives, in fact, nowadays a man does so for only one reason...lust!"

Basmallah, addressing her words to Holy: "It appears that you are not very in tune with some of the Islamic teachings about marriage and polygamy. I'll try to educate you by providing you with one Muslim perspective based on the two sources of Islam, the Qur'an and example of the Prophet Muhammad (peace be upon him). First of all, the laws of God can never be wrong or immoral. That is a rule, from the Muslim perspective. Second of all, it is unfortunate that you continue to adopt an orientalist approach—telling people, who are different from you, what is good for them. This approach has been largely abandoned in anthropological circles, because it is recognized as culturally biased and flawed. It has been replaced by some degree of moral relativism, the idea that what is right for one person or group may not be so for others. Is it not quite arrogant to suggest to non-Muslim polygamists (African tribes, or Mormons in the United States, for example) that they are wrong, especially when many of the women say they prefer polygamy?

Finally, it might be deeply offensive to people, who come from different cultural/religious backgrounds than you, to suggest that their way of viewing marriage is wrong or stupid. For example, it is not a requirement that love precedes marriage in many (even non-Muslim) cultural traditions. It is my belief that this view should be respected. Many marriages that start with love end in divorce. And many marriages that start with compatibility, but without love, continue in bliss. Let us respect the ways in which different cultures marry. Perhaps it is time to recognize that some of the dominant assumptions about marriage in the contemporary West, one of the most adulterous and licentious civilizations in the history of humankind, might not be universally applicable.

Having said all of this, there are clearly many men in the Muslim and non-Muslim world who are not good husbands in these most terrible times. Many men abuse their right to polygamy and oppress innocent women in the process. I advise my Muslim sisters to be careful about any marriage contract they enter into, polygamous or not. It is possible that, given present circumstances, more care should be taken in entering into relationships with men who are already married."

Asma'a: "Most Muslims who make wrong critical comments about polygamy, do not know that they are making comments against the Qur'an. If Qur'an says something and we contradict it, then we are contradicting the Quran, and that is not acceptable."

Olfat: "My understanding of Mr. Right is that he is the one who is a good Muslim, and it has nothing to do with whether he has no wife, one wife or three wives. In any case Mr. Right should be the one who understands Islam, who practices Islam and the one who has *Taqwa* [piety]."

Mouneera: "No woman can be forced into polygamy. I think couples who are happy together should stay together without having another marriage. But if the husband feels the need to have another wife as the first cannot give him her undivided attention (as she too has her own responsibilities, such as her health problems, her kids, and her ambitions) and if they both mutually decide that another marriage to a second wife would be far more better for the success of their first marriage, then no one should impose their opinions on them. Instead of wallowing in anxiety, self pity, depression or worse, infidelity, it is better in this case for a man to remarry."

Mahmoud (another male poster): "There are more women in the world than men in nearly every country. What are the extra women going to do? They have three options: a) Remain single; b) Become "public property" (mistress, or worse); c) Marry a man who is already married. Islam allows for options a and c."

Hamid: "Islam has some basic beliefs one of which is that when we accept Islam we have to accept what God has said in the holy Quran and what Prophet Muhammad has done and said. If someone does not accept something out of The holy Quran, I am afraid he/she has to revise his/her basic beliefs to be a good Muslim. Quran has very clearly mentioned that a Muslim man is allowed to have upto four wives at a time."

Even though most of the posters in this thread expressed their validity claims about polygamy in Islam in a civilized and rational manner, we cannot conclude that the thread reflected a Habermasian public sphere or that it met most of Dahlberg's criteria for two reasons: First of all, most posters in this thread seemed to have been on the same page with regard to polygamy in Islam before they joined the thread, and so the discussion was more an expression of their opinions and a sharing of their experience rather than an engagement in a rational-critical debate with the aim of reaching a consensus. Moreover, the poster who seemed to be opposed to polygamy (Holy) had not changed her somewhat assertive position, even after her back-and-forth argument with Hamid. There was no attempt on Holy's part to express reflexivity or to acknowledge the opinions of the other participants.

Despite the fact that this thread did not reflect a true rational-critical debate, still some posters adopted an ideal role-taking by expressing a commitment to the discussion and by being respectful to the other opinions. For example, Nagwa expressed her reservations about polygamy, but she still acknowledged the possibility that many women out there maybe happy in a polygamous marriage. She did not try to impose her opinion on the other participants, and she made it clear that her opinion on that matter may not be representative of all Muslim women and, therefore, should not be generalized.

The discussion of an issue like polygamy in Islam in this thread is a good example of a situation where lay Muslims are inquisitive about their religion and are curious to interpret the meaning and logic of various aspects of this religion. As we mentioned in chapter 2, the anonymity that is guaranteed through these online discussion forums has encouraged many young Muslims to ask questions about their religion that they would not dare ask in face-to-face encounters with traditional Islamic scholars.[42]

This curiosity on the part of many lay Muslims to know more about their religion and to ask specific questions embodies the concept of "objectification of Islam," which we discussed in chapter 1, and which was defined by Eickelman and Piscatori (2004) as "the process by which basic questions come to the fore in the consciousness of large numbers of believers: 'What is my religion?' 'Why is it important in my life?' and 'How do my beliefs guide my conduct?' "[43] The importance of objectifying Islam has increased in the postmodern era where " 'true believers' are confronted with ways of life, images, films, cultural models, educational systems, consumer habits and economic practices that are heavily influenced by a secular and Western world."[44] This has required "a move towards rethinking what should be seen as 'true' Islam."[45]

Online discussion forums, such as the ones under study in this book, have facilitated the process of objectification of Islam by allowing Muslims from all walks of life to discuss critical matters that go to the heart of their religion. Those lay Muslims are engaged in what Gary Bunt (2003) described as "e-*ijtihad*"[46] or electronic *ijtihad*—a concept that we discussed in chapter 2. According to Bunt, "The debate on Islamic decision-making issues has now transcended traditional contexts, to emerge within cyberspace, acquiring a global dimension in the process."[47] Of course, several scholars expressed their reservations about leaving the process of objectifying Islam and *ijtihad* exclusively to the lay Muslims involved in these discussion forums without the supervision of the *'ulama*,[48] as we discussed before.

Having mentioned that, it is important to highlight the fact that the concepts of *shura*, *ijtihad*, and *ijma'* are only limited to Muslims. In this context, Sheikh Samy Al-Sersawy, the Al-Azhar-certified Muslim preacher, to whom we referred in chapter 2 said: "The processes of *shura*, *ijtihad* and *ijma'* are ingrained in Islam. Only Muslims are entitled to carry out these processes since they are the ones who are familiar with their religion and are able to discuss both spiritual and mundane issues in light of the Qur'an, *hadith* (Prophet's sayings) and the *Shari'a* [Islamic canonical law]."[49] This means that the exemplification of these concepts in the virtual public sphere would be limited to the threads that have only Muslim participants. It is for this reason that we cannot examine the suitability and applicability of these concepts to many threads in this chapter.

Most posters in this thread discussed polygamy in Islam reflexively and reasonably. Interestingly, most Muslim females who participated in the thread were not critical of polygamy. On the contrary, they seemed to be totally receptive to polygamy on the grounds that it was permitted by God, as mentioned in the *Qur'an*. In fact, one female poster (Alia'a) said in that regard: "God has permitted this so who am I to stop my husband as long as he continues to do justice among his wives?" Also, Basmallah mentioned, in her reference to polygamy: "The laws of God can never be wrong or immoral. That is a rule, from the Muslim perspective." This approach is an exemplification of the concept of "Islamic feminism," which we referred to in chapter 4. Muslim feminists are empowered, not by mundane things, but by their religion. They gain their power from abiding by what he *Qur'an* and *Sunna* (Prophet Muhammad's sayings and deeds) call for. For them, polygamy is not a cause for sorrow or pity as much as it is an option allowed by God to make some marriages happier. Those women are willing to do everything in their capacity to please their husbands because by doing so, they would be pleasing God. In this context, Alia'a said: "This world is temporary and if the husband is the means for us to get to paradise, then that's the best husband." That is why, most female posters in this thread noted that "Mr. Right" for them is a pious husband, regardless of whether or not he is married to more than one wife.

Like the previous thread, the following thread is also selected from Islamonline English forum.

Intercultural/Interracial Marriage: Barrier or Bridge?

Ameera, the original poster in this thread, poses the following question: "Do intercultural/racial marriages work? Do they pose more problems than a marriage wherein the couple share the same background? I have friends who are married interracially and are happy. But then I know people who are married to spouses from the same race and are unhappy. What do you think?"

> Amal: "Assalamu alaikum [Peace be upon everyone]. There is no guarantee in marriage. It's something of a risk and something we have to prepare ourselves for. Maybe the problem of marriages not succeeding is because the people involved do not know themselves and the other per-

son's background enough. I mean, isn't it important to have someone who suits you and your ways? And that person might be from your culture or another one. At the same time, cultures do have dominant characteristics, like some cultures are quiet and gentle, while others are a bit tough (in their ways), so if, for example, you're a sensitive person, then you'd have to go for the person and the 'culture' that suits you."

Azza: "I think that it's a great thing to marry a person from another culture. It makes you have a lot of information about different cultures. I heard something which is really weird: Some people claim that it might be forbidden in Islam to marry someone from another race. I was really shocked to hear that because I know that God did not forbid marraying interracially. In addition, Prophet Muhammed married a Coptic woman from Egypt. So, that is the best example of intercultural marriage in Islam. Another point which illustrates that is a verse in the Qur'an in chapter 49 Al-Hujurat verse 13: 'O mankind! We have created you from a male and a female, and made you into nations and tribes, that you may know one another. The most honorable of you in the sight of Allah [God] is that—believer—who has At-Taqwa [piety].'Finally, I think that it's a bridge, not a barrier, but this is my own point of view."

Salma: "I am against intercultural marriage. Of course this is only for me. I think it is really nice to marry someone of the same culture and race, to have many things in common and to have mutual interests. Also, to have strong bonded families and children know very well to which culture they belong."

Omneya: "The Prophet said, 'A woman is married for four things, i.e., her wealth, her family status, her beauty and her religion. So you should marry the religious woman (otherwise) you will be a loser.'

Following the teachings of our Prophet peace be upon him, I think we should choose our life partner based on his/her religion and the other aspects such as, in this discussion, culture and race, are secondary. There is no doubt that when one decides to marry from another race or culture, which could possibly imply from another country, other issues arise. For instance, where the couple chooses to reside, how much one partner is willing to learn or adapt to his/her partner's culture or language. These issues might not seem to be a big deal during the earlier stages of marriage, but could be a potential reason for disagreement in a marriage or worse, a divorce. So I think, it is best for couples to talk and be clear about such issues early in the engagement period as long as it is before marriage just so that they can avoid any disappointment as a result of false expectations."

Mervat: "I believe that intercultural marriage is not a barrier but it is an amazing bridge between different cultures and traditions. It is a wonderful world where various cultures live together in love, tolerance and mutual respect. If we love each other, I think that life would be very successful, even if we belong to different races, countries or even cultures. If we are good Muslims, our marital journey will be happy and wonderful. For me as a Muslim girl, I wish to have a husband from a different culture."

Soad: "Well, I think the success of intercultural/racial marriages depends on the couple. If both of them are aware of the differences that they will face, and can adjust to these differences, I am sure they will be alright."

Gameela: "Yes, I agree with this. As an Australian woman married to an Arab man, I can say that intercultural marriages can definitely work but it is very important that both parties understand that there will be cultural differences and that they are willing to work through issues if they arise."

Yasser: "I am the product of an intercultural marriage (Muslim from the Middle East and Christian from Belgium). My entire family comes from all over the place. Russia, Albania, Morocco, Kosovo, Belgium...I have some family in Britain and the U.S. as well. My parents have more than succeeded. Yes. Multicultural marriages do work beyond a doubt. In the end, it all depends on your state of mind."

Kamilia: "What is important in marriage is two people that love each other and work together on all their challenges. Cross-cultural religious marriages do work but it takes two people with an open mind and heart to know and love one another."

This thread is clearly similar to the one that preceded it in that there was more agreement than disagreement among the posters. In this thread, all participants, except for one, agreed that intercultural and interracial marriages can be successful. Posters expressed their opinions in a reasoned, nondogmatic manner, and some of them made a sincere effort to provide information from the *Qur'an* and the Prophet's *hadith* to substantiate their opinions. However, there was no Habermasian-styled rational-critical debate since most participants were on the same page. The gender homogeneity in this thread, where all posters, except for one, were Muslim females (as indicated by their posted names and the contents of their postings) might have contributed to the general agreement among them in this matter.

The issue of intercultural and interracial marriages that was discussed in this thread raises the bigger issue of pluralism in Islam. According to Esposito (2003), "pluralism is a critical concern both for Muslim majority countries and for Muslim minority communities."[50] Pluralism is directly related to tolerance, which is "based more genuinely on mutual understanding and respect..."[51] The fact that all posters in this thread, except for one, were tolerant of interracial/intercultural marriages is an encouraging sign in the sense that they had no problems reaching out to people from different cultural and ethnic backgrounds. In fact, some posters used the terms "mutual respect," "tolerance," and "cultural bridge" in the course of explaining their points of view.

An integral aspect of pluralism in Islam is the empowerment of Muslim women, whose role in shaping the contemporary Islamic discourse in both the traditional and virtual *umma* has been gaining more momentum. In this context, Esposito (2003) argued that "In areas as diverse as the Arab world, Iran, South and Southeast Asia, [Muslim] women have formed their own women's organizations, created their own magazines, and contributed to newspapers in which they set forth new religious and social interpretations and visions of gender relations."[52] This thread is a strong exemplification of Muslim women's empowerment since all the posters, except for one, were Muslim females, who were able to eloquently and vividly express their opinions on such a critical issue as interracial/intercultural marriages.

Concluding Remarks on the "Gender Discourses" Threads

In the previous threads in this section, we explored "gender" as an "interrelated identity,"[53] that intersects cultural, ethnic, and religious identities. This complexity and interrelatedness clearly manifested itself in the way the participants in these threads debated, contested, accepted, or rejected various notions in the previously discussed threads, ranging from polygamy to intercultural marriage, based on the intersecting variables of gendered identity, religious affiliation, cultural background, and ethnicity.

The previous discussions in these threads were not "gender-neutral or gender-impartial";[54] rather, they exemplified gendered discourses, which offered a platform for the manifestation and negotiation of both femininity and masculinity in different contexts and across a wide array of topics. Therefore, "Taking into account the fact that identities are gender-specific,"[55] these threads reveal a number of important findings regarding the constructions of femininity and masculinity in cyberspace, which reminds us that "we can...explore the constitution of femininity and masculinity as not fixed or appropriated, but struggled over in a complex relational dynamic."[56]

In other words, gender constitutes one factor, among many other factors, which contribute to the creation of our own identities, through a process of "self-definition." Therefore, it can be argued that

> To negotiate identity is to enact a process whereby one attempts to maintain, retain or retrieve custody and authority over defining the self despite knowing that one cannot control how one's self is socially understood. When adding the prefix of race, culture, or gender to identity, there are values, norms and worldviews at stake in the identity negotiation process.[57]

Furthermore, the various manifestations of women's empowerment through their engagement in the above-mentioned online discourses provide another evidence of the existence of "Islamic feminism," as discussed earlier, which acknowledges women's rights within an Islamic framework that attempts to strike a balance between tradition and modernity, through the practical application of Islamic teachings in all aspects of everyday life, including marital relations.

Here, it is also important to remember some of the criticisms against the restrictive nature of the elitist, bourgeois, and exclusively masculine Habermasian public sphere by a number of authors, including Nancy Fraser, who preferred "arrangements that permit contestation among a plurality of competing publics than by a single, comprehensive public sphere,"[58] in the hope that such pluralistic arrangements can allow for a greater balance between "private" and "public" domains and can permit a higher degree of gender equality. It is Fraser's argument that such a pluralistic public sphere, which allows for deliberations between several "counterpublics," will render visible the ways in which social inequality taints deliberation between and within several publics; it should show how inequality affects relations among publics; how publics are differentially empowered or segmented; and how some are involuntarily enclaved and subordinated to others. Most importantly, it should expose ways in which the labeling of some issues and interests as "private" limits the range of problems, and of approaches to problems, that can be widely contested in contemporary societies.[59]

Moreover, the previous discussions in this section revealed varying forms and degrees of resistance, which were sometimes voiced against male figures, especially husbands; against social, cultural, or religious forces that were perceived as repressive to women; or against "other" women, who were criticized for accepting such repressive forces. In every case, we witnessed a "tension" resulting from competing identities and subjectivities, an assertion of conflicting worldviews, and a resistance to "other" views.

The next section sheds light on a different type of discourses, namely discourses revolving around highly politicized issues.

DIVERGENT IDENTITIES AROUND POLITICAL DISCOURSES

The following two threads from Islamonline English forum deal with the Palestinian-Israeli conflict and include pro-Palestinian, as well as pro-Israeli posters.

Illegal Occupation

Kareema, the original participant, whose posting indicated she is either Palestinian or pro-Palestinians, posted a timeline, accompanied by maps, showing what she referred to as the "illegal occupation" of Israel in Palestine. She also included a copy of the Balfour Declaration, which called for "the establishment in Palestine of a national home for the Jewish people." At the end of her long posting, Kareema wrote: "[The British government] wanted, along with Europe, to get rid of the Jews. Were they afraid of their retaliation after WWII, or just sick of them, God knows!! So, they decided to send them all away and gave them Palestine. A promise from the British occupiers who did not own the land to those who did not deserve it as it already had its rightful owners."

> Gaber: "If England was so anxious to give the Jews a home, they should have taken them to England. Not steal land from the rightful owners: The Palestinians."
>
> Ameera, addressing her words to Kareema: "Very good work. Never be in doubt as to the legitimate right of the Palestinians. You must not despair and rest assured that the credit the Zionist Jews accumulated with Christendom will eventually run out. Everybody can see this except the worst pupils in history, the Zionfascist Jews."
>
> James, addressing his words to Ameera: "[You are] a run of the mill racist and Jew hater; that is all you are."
>
> Sam, addressing his words to James: "It maybe true that Ameera doesn't like Jews very much due to their criminal activities that not only drove millions of Palestinians out of their homes and lands, but also caused millions to die and thousands to get tortured. Now, can you explain to us what the thieves among the Jews had done since they came to occupy Palestine that would deserve our love and respect?"
>
> James: "The state is called Israel. There has never been a Palestinian state."
>
> Sam: "It is not surprise that thieves are claiming this to be true, which is the root cause of the whole problem in the Middle East. If you have some thieves who came to another house and put a claim on the house and than claim that it is their home all along, then of course there is going to be a problem."
>
> Sylvia from Israel, addressing her words to Kareema, the original poster: "After taking all this trouble to type a post of hatred... you could have thought one second more before pressing the "post" button. Your post is meaningless anyway because it is full of distortions and hate and really serves no purpose at all—particularly because all it shows is your hatred for my country, and hate is a waste of energy—especially when it's directed at something you can't change—namely the existence of the state of Israel....yes...israel (not Palestine)."
>
> Kareema, addressing her words to Sylvia: "What was 'hateful' about my message? Is it hateful because you know it's true but you can't answer? Is it hateful because you know you took my house by force when you occupied Palestine? Is it hateful because you know you've been committing genocide and ethnically cleansing more than 418 villages and driven away more than 700,000 Arabs from their homes in palestine?"
>
> Cory: "Israel isn't going any where and there's nothing anyone can do about that. The Muslims have tried and tried and failed and failed. So, learn to live with it or not. It doesn't change the facts."

Ameera, addressing her words to Cory: "Neither are the Palestinians going anywhere. The West may pamper and entertain your claim, because you control and manipulate the politicians and media powers, but we shall not budge in our quest for justice, neither shall we be denied it eternally."

James, addressing his words to Ameera: "Then you will continue to die...plain and simple."

Sa'ad, addressing her words to Kareema: "Excellent post substantiated by excellent proof. I hope those spamming the board with senseless posts would reply by using evidence and facts rather than reply for the sake of spoiling facts."

Israel Kills Five-Month-Old Mohammed Nasser

Kamal, a Palestinian, and the original poster in this thread, pointed to the killing of Mohammed Nasser, a five-month-old Palestinian baby as a result of an Israeli raid over Gaza. He also included photos of other Palestinian children, whom he said are victims of the Israeli raids against the Palestinians. Among the photos included was the now famous picture of the Palestinian child Mohammed Aldurra, who was killed in his father's arms a few years ago by what many witnesses claimed was an Israeli bullet. Kamal wrote: "Isn't it high time for the world to react justly and fairly? Or is Israel superior to anyone?"

> Raul (from Israel): "The pictures, of course, are awful. But the question is: are they true or hoax? To tell you the truth, I do not give a damn if [those children were] killed—or not. I am not going to cry over their children, while they are trying to kill mine."
>
> Sylvia (from Israel): "The blood of each and every dead Palestinian child is on Hamas' hands—not ours! I can find pictures of the three Sederot children who were killed by [Palestinian] rockets over the past few months plus the nine [Israeli] civilians who were killed since 2000 plus the little eight-year old boy whose leg was amputated last week after a shell fell right next to him...but I won't. Unlike the Hamas evil PR machinery—we don't make a mockery of our dead and wounded by parading them for the world to see. We hold life to be sacred and we leave the families alone in their time of grief. It is Hamas and Hamas alone who is responsible for the carnage going on in Gaza and they will be accountable in the end...and believe me the end will be here soon enough. Gaza will not be another Lebanon!"
>
> Kamal, addressing his words to Sylvia: "Shame on you Sylvia! Instead of denouncing the action, you try to justify it! May you tell us how many Palestinian children were murdered by Israel since September 2000?"
>
> Sylvia, addressing her words to Kamal: "Shame on me???...For what?...I do not denounce the Israeli action in Gaza and, yes, I do justify it!...Why would I deny my country's right to defend itself against murderous terrorists who constantly use our citizens in [the Israeli cities

of] Sederot (and now Ashkelon) as cannon fodder? Now let me ask you a question...how many Palestinian children has Israel targeted since 2000?,...the answer?...none! How many Israeli children has Hamas targeted?...the answer: hundreds!...Now before you call me cold and heartless I'd like you to think about what brought on this terrible situation—and don't give me the usual garbage about 60 years of occupation. The Palestinian problem could have been solved the day Israel was established if the Arab states had not decided to go to war with us (a situation that has never stopped since). I've said in countless posts that we've tried so many times to make peace with our neighbors only to have the doors slammed in our face time and again. The Palestinians created their own problem by constantly looking for new ways to destroy us and demoralize us—to no avail. When the Palestinian people were forced to vote Hamas into power (that's right...forced) that was the nail in the coffin of any chance for peace. We knew (and the world knew also) that there was no negotiating with Hamas because they are a terrorist organization with only one purpose—to wipe Israel off the map (hahahaha...). If I were a Palestinian living in Gaza, I would stand in the city square and demand the resignation of the Hamas government and call for people to rise up and elect another government that puts my basic needs as a human being before any futile attempts to wipe out my enemy (which isn't going to happen anyway). So, in short, do I justify my country's defensive strikes? yes"

Seif, addressing his words to Sylvia: "Hamas was elected fair and square by the Palestinian people. That is democracy, but just because they will not cater to Israel, they are labeled terrorists. The last thing Israel wants is peace. They want to keep problems going and stall for a long time to steal more Palestinian land. They want to expand settlements under the disguise of security. Can you tell me what expanding settlements have to do with Israel's security? How can you put Israeli civilian people in settlements on Palestinian land, in most cases surrounded by Palestinians.

Nada: "Israel needs innocent blood to survive. If there is no blood, there is no help from the *shaytan* [Satan]."

Haleema: "To the Israeli that wants to stick up for Israel, good luck with that. Can I just remind everyone that you should not fight with an Israeli who thinks that Palestinians and all Muslims are wrong. Israel did not even have a country until after WWII. The Jews were spread all throughout the world then they decided that they needed their own place. Well, as Muslims let's all remember that we do not need our own country, that we can worship anywhere in the world. God is always with us and in his hands we will return. Let's just pray for our brothers and sisters in Palestine and in the rest of the world facing terrible adversity. We all know and read of what is to come. Let's get back to where we should be, so that in the end we can say that we are better than them."

Gasser included a link to a website where a group of Palestinian children in Gaza are talking about what they witnessed during Israeli raids on their homes.

Unlike the threads dealing with the Palestinian-Israeli conflict on the Arabic version of Islamonline forum, which we analyzed in chapter 4, and which generally reflected a collective consciousness created by a homogeneous, pan-Arab and pan-Islamic identity, these two threads included a highly polemic discourse. The lack of ability to counterargue was evident in postings by the pro-Palestinian as well as the pro-Israeli posters. Needless to say, these threads did not reflect any characteristic of a true Habermasian rational-critical debate. The posters showed no sincerity or reflexivity in presenting their arguments, and they did not seem committed to an ongoing dialogue. In fact, this particular exchange of claims hardly passes for civil discourse, and it reflects highly antagonistic feelings on both sides. Some posters' use of terms such as "Jew hater," "run of the mill racist," and "Zionfascist" reflected the level of aggressive discourse in these two threads.

These two threads are highly emotional, with extremely polarized viewpoints between the pro-Palestinian posters on one side and the pro-Israeli posters on the other. The threads also reflect a strong political resistance on the part of the Arabs to the Israeli occupation of Palestinian territories and strong feelings on the part of the Israeli posters (particularly Raul and Sylvia in the second thread) against the rockets fired by the Palestinians on Israeli cities. The Palestinian posters could not convince the Israeli posters of the validity of their claims and the opposite was true. In this context, McCarthy (1992) argued that

"if we were...to drop the pragmatic presupposition that we could convince others of the validity of claims by offering good reasons in support of them, most of our rational practices would lose their sense, and this, it goes without saying, would entail far-reaching changes in our form of life. In Habermas's view, it would mean the elimination of our main alternative to violence, coercion, and manipulation as a means of conflict resolution and social coordination."[60]

The Palestinian-Israeli conflict is a highly sensitive issue for Arabs and Muslims in general, and Palestinians in particular. "The coverage [by Arab satellite channels] of the suffering of the Palestinians under the weight of the Israeli war machine has, in more than one way, intensified the feeling of solidarity among the Palestinian people."[61]

The sensitivity surrounding this conflict and the "emotional baggage" that is often associated with it on the part of the Palestinians as well as the Israelis might have led to the absence of a Habermasian rational-critical debate in these threads. "Under ideal conditions...[engaging in a rational-critical debate to reach a consensus] would be backed by the requirement that each [participant] have the opportunity to present his or her point of view and to seek to make it comprehensible and plausible to others."[62] However, this may not be pragmatic when it comes to a highly loaded issue like the Palestinian-Israeli conflict where participants' emotional proximity and involvement in the issue stand in the way of their reaching a consensus through public deliberations. Even compromise seemed to be extremely distant among Palestinian and Israeli posters, who had "fundamental divergences in value orientations."[63]

The next thread from Islamonline Arabic forum also deals with the Palestinian-Israeli conflict, but from a different perspective.

I Smell a Jewish Lobby in the Forum

Abdullah, the original poster, said that he had a feeling some participants in the forum are siding with what he referred to as the "Jewish lobby." He did not specify the reason for his feeling, but he asked the other posters to share their views on what he noted.

> Manal: "I agree with you. My suspicions revolve around a poster in the political forum."
>
> Ahmad: "I agree with you too, particularly with regard to those posters' opinions about the heroic Palestinian resistance."
>
> Arwa: "Everybody is entitled to express their opinion; this is supposed to be a forum for free debate, where we have to respect others' opinions, even if we do not agree with it. Does it make sense that if a Muslim disagrees with another Muslim that he would accuse him of being a traitor?"
>
> Abdullah: "If freedom of opinion harms others, it should not be justified, as it steps on others' toes. Since we are in an Islamic forum, our dialogue and debate should be within the limits of what our Islamic religion has set for us; there are other non-Islamic forums which are open for those who are not comfortable with the limits of this forum. My intention here is not to suppress opinions or to unfairly accuse others of being traitors, but we still have to be cautious."
>
> Mahmoud: "I think that Abdullah [the original poster] was referring to me when he mentioned that he felt there were Jews in the forum. This is because I made another posting saying that Palestinians should not bomb Israeli restaurants that have Arab residents, particularly women and children. And I was wondering if this was against Islam. And now I ask Abdullah: If my opinion does not appeal to you, does that give you the right to imply that I am a Jew and a traitor?"
>
> Abdullah, responding to Mahmoud: "I did not say that you were Jewish. Islam forbids us from accusations that are not based on evidence. Since the launching of this forum, we have been engaging in deliberations with Jews and non-Muslims, who could have deceived us had it not been for our attentiveness. Some of those folks might have attempted to divide us Muslims and to spread *Fitna* [trial] among us. I hope that my words have not hurt you, and I apologize for any harm this might have caused to you."

Manal: "I do not believe in the opinion and the other opinion if this other opinion is opposed to the Islamic jurisdiction."

Ahmad, addressing his words to Mahmoud: "The opinion and the other opinion is the banner that is raised by those who want to cunningly invade our *umma*. I am opposed to what you wrote about the Palestinian people and to anything that harms the Muslim *umma*."

Kareem, addressing his words to Manal: "I call on you to revise your position with regard to those whose opinions you disagree with."

Arwa, addressing her words to Manal and Ahmad: "Even if you disagree with brother Mahmoud, that should not give you the right to insult him. If we follow what you believe, then we should carry knives and slaughter those whose opinions are not in agreement with the Islamic jurisdiction. If you are not able to engage in a dialogue or to convince a fellow Muslim, how do you expect to convince a Christian, a Jew, or an atheist of our Islamic principles?"

Fareed, addressing his words to Mahmoud: "Myself and others accuse you of attempting to harm the reputation of the Palestinian resistance. I will keep an eye on your postings; so be careful not to criticize Muslims or those who fight for their freedom."

Mahmoud: "I have the right to address any issue as long as it does not oppose Islam. I am not against the [Palestinian] resistance. I am supportive of it. And I believe that every martyr is a hero. But my question addresses a different issue: If the victims [of the suicide bombings] are Muslims, is this still right? Who is to blame?"

Abdullah, addressing his words to the posters in general: "Make sure not to accuse anybody without a clear evidence."

Sunny: "Many people are obsessed with conspiracy theories. Since this forum is supposed to be open to everybody, we have to be open to listening to those with whom we disagree. And we should not accuse people of something that they did not say about themselves."

This thread exemplifies a situation where participants who post viewpoints that are not in agreement with the majority opinion are sometimes harshly criticized. Habermas (1992) referred to such situation as the "tyranny of the majority."[64] This is especially the case when it comes to discussing highly sensitive issues, such as the Palestinian-Israeli conflict. This whole situation detracts away from the potential of creating true deliberations since it discourages participants who feel that their opinions may not be well-received (such as Mahmoud in this thread) from sharing those opinions in the forum. This has serious consequences on the general deliberatory environment that is to be expected in these forums.

In this thread, there were irreconcilable differences among the posters. This is despite the fact that the discussions dealing with the Palestinian-Israeli conflict on Islamonline Arabic forum are generally consensual because of the homogeneous ethnicity of the posters on this forum. Some posters in this thread did present their opinions in a reasoned manner, while others took a more emotional and dogmatic approach. The accusatory tone used by some posters against others in this thread demonstrated Habermas' depiction of the deterioration of the postbourgeois public sphere "from a 'reasoning' to a 'consuming' one."[65]

The next two threads, taken from Islamonline English forum, deal with another significant political issue, and that is the perception of the United States in the international community and the hegemony of the U.S. military.

How Much U.S. Owes International Community

Samy: "Every robbery ideologist will tell you that the United States had given billions to their victims around the world. Is this given out of generosity or as part of robbery operations declared war? To me as anti-robbery speculator, I have to say that if you count all the destruction Bush and other criminal elements in the American government, all the death, all the slavery, all the worldwide tortures, all the human degrading, all the mass bombings, and all the other evil acts against the international community, including Iraq, the U.S. would owe the world billions of dollars or more. Please respond in a positive manner."

Smith, addressing his words to Sam: "I believe that you, as a Muslim, may have a right to resent Bush and the American people. But for all their faults the American people mean well. The fact that you view the entire American government as a murdering raping war beast can only testify to your ignorance on the matter.

The United States is the largest foreign aid provider in the world. Funny, last time I checked I don't really recall how much the Middle East helps the rest of the world. It may be true that at this time that section of the world may not be in a position to help others, but it doesn't make the help the American people provide any less meaningful. They are providing help that is saving hundreds of millions of lives. America is not stealing anything from the people of the Middle East, and is giving much in return. Let's face it, America might have gone to war for the wrong reasons, but they are staying for the right ones. They are staying so those people won't have to suffer under totalitarian leaders, they are staying so your people, innocent Muslims may enjoy basic civil liberties.

Do you not realize how bad the Middle East was even before the war? Something had to be done, and you weren't doing it. Your people were suffering and you were doing nothing!! all you were doing was killing each other like ******* primitives!!"

Samy, addressing his words to Smith: "You claimed that the U.S. is the largest foreign aid donor. While that may be true in dollar sense, if you count all the past and ongoing robbery, the exploitation, the slavery, the mass killings, the mass torturing, and the mass destructions that the U.S. has committed on a regular basis in the past and today, you would realize that the U.S. had not given anything. You murdered and robbed most of the people in a country and you gave a few people some small cash as a form of propaganda. This does not count as a donation."

Anees: "We tend to forget something: that the Americans booted the British out of the U.S. And today, the Americans are doing the exact same thing in places like Iraq. If the Iraqis fight back, (as they should) they are called terrorists. Let's hope eventually the Iraqis will succeed in driving the illegal occupation from their lands."

Jack, addressing his words to Anees: "You are a fool."

Samy, addressing his words to Jack: "Just because you are telling someone that they are a fool, that does not make them a fool. You still have to engage in debates and pay attention to what others said so that you can learn to effectively respond to their argument. If we all agree with each other, there would be no point on a discussion forum. Have you ever noticed that I tend to write to those who disagree with me more than to those who agree? That is what smart people often do. You tend to write a lot, but you call people all kinds of names without any backup and logical points that can lead to a useful conclusion."

Jack, addressing his words to Samy: "You are too ignorant to even hold a conversation, let alone debate."

Mouneera, addressing her words to Samy: "Don't pay attention to Jack. You're doing a great job here, keep it up."

Safwan: "To hate does not solve any problem; to have a grudge against a nation does not solve any problem; we have to gather around what we as humans have in common. Humans are essentially, the same. Where you're born, and the family that you're born into determines a lot. Hating will eat your soul from within."

Samy, addressing his words to Safwan: "Thanks for dropping by and giving this very good advice that all humanity can accept. We should not hate one another and we should not hold a grudge against a nations, because like you said it won't solve anything or cure the thieves in the U.S. and their addiction to robbery, torture, and mass murders."

Jack, addressing his words to Samy: "Hey fraud, what thieves are you talking about in this post. Name some of these thieves?"

Samy: "On this particular post, I was talking about the oil thieves, including Bush and his gang; all the killers who came from the U.S. to kill Iraqis. I think you can find some of the high-ranking thieves in places like Halliburton, Exxon Mobile, and other oil powerhouses."

Why is the Suicidal Rate in the U.S. Army Rising?

Mahmoud: "About 2,100 U.S. army members have tried to commit suicide in 2007, 89 suicide deaths were confirmed and 32 cases are still pending among active-duty and activated reserve-component soldiers. Why?"

Akram: "Yes, when you murder, rape, torture, and try to rob someone and God is punishing you in a form of nightmare, it must be pretty hard to live. Whatever the situation is, the soldiers who took their own lives must have understood the degree of their crimes."

Samar: "I hear of people shooting people at malls and schools more often. We are bringing a curse on ourselves. The time of destruction is coming upon us here. We have the power to stop Bush; however not many people really care to sacrifice their lives."

Safwat: "There are possible reasons that could have motivated the GIs to commit suicide: Their mission was based on lies and so they found it immoral on their part to accede to orders to kill innocent humans. They cannot contain the international repercussion and condemnation at the way their leaders have dragged their once proud and noble national legacy to that of being a scourge of war mongering and blatant lying without feeling any remorse in the way of international legitimacy and human decency."

Amgad: "Actually I did not find this report surprising since this is what happens when you fight illegal wars and kill innocent people. The guilt will haunt you till you're dead and some cannot bear it, and they end their own life."

Kyle: "You don't know what you're talking about. It doesn't matter what the cause is when you go into combat and see people being torn apart. It affects people and some people can't deal with it. There were suicides in WW2 when we were fighting the Nazi in a just cause. This proves that what you said is false."

Tom, addressing his words to Mahmoud: "Our soldiers are just fine and will complete the job of ridding the world of you pukes."

Amgad: "Sorry pals, this Todd is just trying to take you out for a ride into nowhere. Apparently, he's been hurt and can't find anything sane and humanly enough to say. You must understand his predicament too."

Michael, addressing his words to Amgad: "The American soldiers will be rewarded for killing the terrorist pukes. Take off your fuzzy Muslim glasses...nobody looks at the world the way you pukes do."

Simon: "It's really a pity for the great American people to be unduly thrust into the world stage of controversy and condemnation for no fault of their own. This demonization of the American psyche started only when the 'Neocons' took full control of the U.S. government with most of its foreign policy being made in Israel. However, the American people are learning the lessons of the past and must be exerting efforts to regain control of the government after having identified who the 'American *****' who are tarnishing their image are."

Salma: "Suicide is bound to happen if you leave your country being proud of it, thinking it was some sort of heaven where justice and integrity flourish only to find out that it's nothing but a decaying mound of hypocrisy. Hypocrisy in the mouths of the big folks at the top; hypocrisy in the mouths of your mates as they slit the throat of some poor Iraqi for the hell of it; hypocrisy and murder glaring from the insane eyes of the officers; hypocrisy from the proud American media, and there is no aim, no achievement, and think about it: the poor souls are going to have to live with themselves for the rest of their lives, live the lie, their wives and kids are going to be so proud of them and their smiles and jokes will be lies upon lies upon lies."

Despite some posters' attempts to engage in a rational-critical debate, the discourse in the two above threads was hijacked by the use of profanities and by the sharp confrontations and aggressive—even uncivilized expressions of opinions by several posters. Similar to the Palestinian-Israeli conflict, the issue of the role played by the United States in the international community and how that role is perceived, particularly in the Arab and Islamic world, is highly sensitive. Today, the U.S. image in the Middle East is very negative due to a variety of reasons. In this context, Roberson (2003) argued that

> While colonialism has long since been relegated to the past, Middle Eastern peoples increasingly have begun to regard the West, particularly the U.S., in large part, as standing in the way of the success of their futures…[The] U.S. gradually has become regarded as responsible for the continued poor performance of their governments. Regardless of the accuracy of the public view, the U.S. is seen as responsible for the effects of globalization which has a growing impact on the society and the economy. The anti-terrorism pursued by the U.S. so avidly is seen as an attempt by it to contrive a crisis situation in order to interfere in the region, a view held not only by Middle Easterners.[66]

In addition to the reasons that Roberson mentioned, the United States is perceived by many Arab Middle Easterners as an unfair broker in the Palestinian-Israeli conflict by being biased to the Israeli interests at the expense of the Palestinian interests. Addressing this issue, Zayani (2005) argued that "the Palestinian *intifada* [uprising] preceding the American War on Terrorism had shaped Arab public opinion in relation to Washington. The position of the U.S. government on this issue promoted anger towards U.S. policy in the Middle East."[67]

The above-mentioned factors might have played a role in the absence of a rational-critical debate in these threads. Several posters, even the ones who were more on the reasonable side, still used negative epithets that were not substantiated by evidence. Most posters were not self-critical or reflexive and they did not exhibit any sign of committing to an ongoing, civilized dialogue. They lacked the ability to counterargue or to attempt to rationally convince each other of what they were saying. In the context, Habermas (1990) argued that "The fact that a speaker can rationally motivate the hearer to accept…[his] offer is due not to the validity of what he says but to the speaker's guarantee that he will, if necessary, make efforts to redeem the claim that the hearer has accepted. It is this guarantee that effects the coordination between the speaker and hearer."[68] Regardless of the validity of those posters' claims, they failed to rationally motivate each other to engage in a meaningful dialogue. The posters who showed strong antihegemonic approach to the U.S. policies were on a collision course with the ones on the other side of the camp, and this contributed to a dogmatic, assertive and polarized discourse in these two threads.

The next thread from Islamonline English forum deals with the issue of democracy in the context of the political situation in Lebanon.

Violence in Lebanon Escalates

Sameer: "Lebanon's Hezbollah-led opposition supporters have clashed with those backing the government for a second day in Beirut as the confrontation spilled over to other parts of the country. Tensions have been rising after a strike called by the main labor union to press the government for a salary increase got under way."

Mona: "Let's hope that the escalation by the supporters of each group STOPS for the sake of Lebanon. Don't ever forget that such acts are against the stability of Lebanon and the parties that win actually will be Israel and the USA."

Omar: "The violence comes from the concept of Majority rule and man-made law i.e. democracy. The solution is to follow Islamic (accountably elected) Governance and reject democracy, which only brings sectarian division. It is the failure of Islamic Scholars and political activists to make a strong enough stance against democracy against man-made law that is diverting the *Umma* from islamic unity."

Ashraf, addressing his words to Omar: "You are talking about sectarian division? Who is more divided than Islam and which sect should rule? No religion in the present day is more divided than Islam. Muslim against Muslim all over the world. How can you ever hope for peace until you can reconcile Sunnis, Shi'ites etc? As the old saying goes— United, we stand—Divided we fall. You keep blaming the scholars for bad leadership because even they cannot agree. Strangely enough, it is the democratic countries that have outperformed Islam in every sphere—Doesn't that tell you something?"

Ameena, addressing her words to Omar: "Democracy is *Shirk* [infidelity]? Is that what you've concluded? I find this very distinctive but a conclusion that should only be based on some proof of the Qur'an or *Hadith* [Prophet's sayings]. It is misleading to use the mathematical sequence of "since" and therefore" to reach such a conclusion that you should only base upon direct proof. May God have mercy upon us all!"

Gamal: "Can anyone seriously believe that the Lebanese government is working in the interests of Lebanon?

How does dismantling the security apparatus of the state, a state at war with an intractable enemy for the past sixty years, serve the interests of Lebanon?"

Hope: "Lebanon is in a very tense and dangerous situation. Many say that this is the beginning of the civil war that has been feared for the past three years. May God save Lebanon and return those to their minds soon before the destruction."

This short thread is significant in that it touches on the issue of democracy, which is one of the challenges facing the contemporary Muslim *umma* in the international public sphere. Posters in this thread presented their opinions rationally, but they could not agree on what constitutes democracy in an Islamic context. Omar, obviously, was opposed to what he referred to as "man-made democracy," since he saw it as a divisive, rather than a unifying force, for the Muslim *umma*. According to the classifications, which we presented earlier in chapter 3, Omar would belong to the radical Islamists' school of thought in that regard. Radical Islamists regard democracy as a western product that is not suitable for implementation in an Islamic environment. Ashraf and Ameena encouraged Omar to use some reflexivity in approaching the issue. Ameena, in particular, sounded surprised by Omar's conclusion that democracy is incompatible with Islam, and she alluded to the importance of using credible evidence from Islam's two main sources: The *Qur'an* and the Prophet's sayings to substantiate that conclusion.

Addressing the issue of democracy in an Islamic context, Esposito (2003) argued that "The political realities of the Muslim world have not been conducive to the development of democratic traditions and institutions...Few rulers in the region have been democratically elected and...many who speak of democracy only believe in 'risk free democracy.' They permit political participation and liberalization as long as there is no risk of a strong opposition."[69] According to Esposito, the concepts of *ijtihad* and *shura* can serve as catalysts for democratization in an Islamic context,[70] as we mentioned in chapters 1 and 3. Of course, the lay Muslims' engagement in discussions and debates that is made possible by online forums such as the ones under study in this book can contribute to the democratization of the Islamic public sphere. However, they are not solely sufficient to give birth to democracy, or to ensure the existence of the conditions necessary for giving birth to democratic practice, as previously mentioned.

Concluding Remarks on the "Political Discourses" Threads

The previously discussed threads in this section reveal that "identity expression became more of a political than social communicative act,"[71] which reminds us of the significance of studying identities within their specific sociopolitical and historical contexts, as mentioned in chapter 4. This is especially true since the politicization of expressed identities, which clearly manifested itself in these threads, could be seen as the nat-ural outcome of the political tensions that imposed themselves on the relationship between Arabs and Muslims, on one hand, and the West, especially the United States, on the other hand, after 9/11, as previously discussed in the introduction.

The significant impact of September 11 was clearly evidenced in the Arab-Muslims attempts not only to explain themselves as Arabs and Muslims, but also to justify their own ethnic, religious, and political identities, and even to defend themselves and their identities against actual or potential attacks by others[72]. These complex processes were, in turn, reflected in the heightened politicization of Arab-Muslim identities in the post-9/11 era, which manifested itself in the previously discussed threads in this section, through some of the postings, which were either too defensive or too hostile.

The highly polemic discourses and controversial debates that mani-fested themselves in the various threads in this section necessitate an important distinction between, what Peter Mandaville (2001) refers to as, "political identity" and "politicized identity." In explaining the dis-tinction between these two terms, Mandaville argues that "a political identity refers to a particular normative vision, a set of beliefs about the nature of 'the good' and how one should go about achieving it. A polit-icized identity, on the other hand, is a political identity which has been placed in a situation of antagonism such that its ethical claims are chal-lenged by counter-claims from other political identities."[73] In explaining the "dialectical relationship between political identity and the politiciza-tion of identity,"[74] Mandaville points out that "The politicization of identity is very often the process which constructs (new) political identi-ties. In other words, it is often the encounter with 'the other' that engen-ders the shifts, negotiations and debates which produce new ethical claims and hence new political identities."[75] In this context, "Translocal political space emerges as a particularly rich site of both political identi-ties (i.e. different conceptions of 'the good') and politicized identities (i.e. dialogue between these differing conceptions)."[76]

Furthermore, Mandaville argues that "social *antagonism* is one possi-ble root of the political. Antagonism refers to a condition in which the differentiation of identity—the split between us and them—begins to appear as something more than just difference. In an antagonistic situa-tion, one identity (the 'self') comes to see the other as a force seeking to negate its identity."[77] In light of this understanding "Antagonism is therefore the product of a politics of identity. In this sense 'the political' is not a sharply demarcated sphere of activity unto itself, but rather it describes a mode of interaction—one characterized by the negotiation of identity."[78]

Within this conceptual framework, we can argue that the conflicting identities that manifested themselves in this section, through highly polemic discourses between "the self" and "the other," could fall under the category of politicized identities, due to the sharp demarcations, highly divisive discourses, and large degree of antagonism, which they exhibited. In contrast, it can be argued that the collective identities, through highly consensual discourses among members of the same *umma*, or community of faith, could be categorized as "political identities," due to the uniform ethical claims, political views, and moral conceptions which they shared around religio-political topics.

General Concluding Remarks

Throughout this chapter, we explored the various factors which contributed to the manifestation of divergent identities in the discussion forums of various Islamic websites by investigating "the interrelationship between identity and communication."[79] One of the explored variables was "the role of communicative means, specifically identity labels, in constituting personal and communal relationships,"[80] and how these various "identity signifiers"[81] and labels, which were often "imbued with meanings from public discourse,"[82] were utilized as "divisive strategies" and "markers of difference" to identify and demarcate the "self" and the "other," such as the terms "Muslim," "Arab," "infidels," "Westerners," and "nonbelievers," to mention only a few.

Likewise, we also explored the "refutation of identity signifiers,"[83] which is a "communicative act that is central to identification processes as people align themselves with a particular image or group of people and distance themselves from others."[84] This process could be interpreted as a form of resistance to the identity labels assigned by "others," which were not always perceived as an accurate or valid representation of the "self," such as the attempts by non-Muslims to refute labels, such as "infidels" or "impure," which were occasionally assigned to them in some threads by some Muslim participants, as well as the attempts by some Muslims to resist labels, such as "ignorant" or "primitive," which were sometimes assigned to them by non-Muslim participants.

It could be said that the "identity-less" nature of the virtual *umma*, which we previously referred to, meant that some participants in Internet discourses can hide behind the curtain of anonymity and obscurity and allow themselves to use the worst possible language, as evidenced in some of these threads. The strong language and profanities, which were freely exchanged between some of the participants in these threads, expressed feelings of hatred, ridicule, and contempt toward "the Other," on the basis of religious and/or cultural and ethnic differences. It could be said that the anonymity in these Internet discourses allowed such participants to say things which would be otherwise "unsayable" in interpersonal communication, or in any other form of communication where real identities are revealed.

In addition to the resistances which were expressed against the different identity labels and "identity-signifiers," which were assigned by "the Other," multiple other resistances were also manifested in different forms and on many levels, throughout this chapter. Some of these resistances were expressed against those who inhabited different identity positions on the basis of religious affiliation, whether within the boundaries of the same *umma*, or community of faith, as in the case of the heated debates around "Sunni versus Shi'ite" discourses, or outside the boundaries of this unified community of faith, as in the case of some of the heated discussions around "Muslim versus non-Muslim" discourses. In addition, resistances were also manifested between those who expressed conflicting views, reflecting their divergent identities and subjectivities, around different topics in the realm of gendered discourses and political discourses.

To sum up, it can be argued that the cyberspace environment is one that Prophet Muhammad might recognize, in some aspects, "but if he were to return, the Prophet would also identify some of the schismatic behavior that he predicted, and that the Qur'an reflected upon: 'And verily this Brotherhood of yours is a single Brotherhood and I am your Lord and Cherisher: therefore fear Me (and no other). But people have cut off their affair (of unity) between them into sects: each party rejoices in that which is with itself' " (Surat al-Mu'minun, 23:52–3).[85]

The next and last chapter provides general concluding remarks summing up the major themes and arguments of this book.

CHAPTER 6

Virtual Islamic Discourses: Platforms for Consensus or Sites of Contention?

As we mentioned in the introduction, there is a striking shortage in the scholarly literature that focuses on analyzing the content and discourses of mainstream Islamic websites. This has led to lack of knowledge about the nature, underlying tone and style of the deliberations, and discussions going on through these sites. This comes at a time when many people, particularly Westerners, are hungry for information about how Muslims define their identities and how they perceive themselves in relation to others in both the online and offline communities.

In this book, we tried to fill this void in the literature, particularly in the area of communication studies, through analyzing some of the contemporary discourses and mainstream currents in the discussion forums of three of the most popular mainstream Islamic websites with all their complexities, intricacies, and multiplicities. We hope that our in-depth analysis of these discourses that reflect the plurality and diversity of Muslim voices, identities, and subjectivities can help in countering the somewhat simplistic and negativistic approach that obscures the multiple realities and complex identities of Muslims today. This is especially important in the context of the international, political changes in the post-9/11 era that drew the world's attention to Muslims and Arabs more than ever before, though not always for the best reasons or with the right understanding.

This last point explains our decision to conceptualize identity as a complex, dynamic, interrelated, and multifaceted concept that manifests itself on different individual, communal, and global levels. We believe that adopting such a comprehensive and flexible approach in examining the concept of identity that does not exclusively define people on the basis of already existing categories, such as religious affiliation, ethnicity, nationality, and race, avoids the potential danger of projecting "static identities that might not be meaningful to people,"[1] and that can prove to be counterproductive since they "mark people as being different and can exoticize and vilify them."[2]

Therefore, we were keen to employ a culturally sensitive, context conscious, and participant-centered approach throughout this book to elicit the multiple realities, subjectivities, and identities that revealed themselves through the heated discussions and debates in the various Islamic websites under study, as well as the diverse, competing, and even conflicting, views and voices, which emerged online through them.

In doing so, one of the key angles we focused on in this book was the manifestation of diverse identities online through the acceptance or refutation of "identity signifiers,"[3] which were either formulated by the "self" or the "Other". We argued that sharing and exchanging these identity labels played a simultaneous dual role. On one hand, it increased the uniformity, solidarity, and cohesion between those who shared a "collective identity," as in the case of some online discourses involving Muslims who belonged to the same *umma*. On the other hand, it widened the gap and demarcated the boundaries between "divergent identities," as in the case of some online discourses between Muslims and non-Muslims, as well as between different categories of Muslims, such as Sunnis and Shi'ites.

In other words, in examining these online identities special attention was paid to how the participation in such discussion boards helped to promote a sense of religious communalism and collectivism that allowed members of the Muslim *umma* to (re)construct their identities as members of the same community of faith, on one hand, as well as discovering the differences among themselves and demarcating themselves from non-Islamic practices and lifestyles, on the other hand.

In our analysis of the three Islamic forums under study, we tested the extent to which participants in these forums adopted the concepts of "rational-critical debate," "communicative action," and "collective consensus" in the context of a Habermasian public sphere, as well as what we believe are their somewhat equivalent concepts of *shura* (consultation), *ijtihad* (independent interpretation), and *ijma'* (consensus) in the Islamic context.

We can safely conclude—based on our textual analysis of numerous threads from the discussion forums of Islamonline.net, Islamway.com, and Amrkhaled.net—that neither the Habermasian public sphere nor the Islamic concepts of *shura, ijtihad,* and *ijma'* were fully reflected through these forums.

The emergence of the new online public sphere and the reconfiguration of the virtual *umma* have led to the creation of multiple identities and multiple resistances, which clearly manifested themselves through various Islamic websites, producing varying degrees of consensus, divergence, and negotiation. Therefore, one of the main objectives of this book was to investigate the degree to which these competing and contesting identities overlapped, diverged, or created an in-between position of negotiation and compromise, as well as the reasons behind these multiple positions.

In conducting this investigation we found abundant evidence showing the existence of two diametrically opposed poles as exhibited through the analyzed online threads in chapters 4 and 5, namely the poles of consensus and divergence. However, the middle ground of negotiation, which captures the essence of both rational-critical debates and *shura*, seemed largely missing in most of these threads. This clearly restrains the potential for having authentic mutual consultation and interpretation, as defined in an Islamic context, or true rational-critical deliberations, as defined within the context of the theoretical frameworks proposed by both Jürgen Habermas[4] and Lincoln Dahlberg[5].

THE ABSENCE OF A
HABERMASIAN PUBLIC SPHERE

The Habermasian public sphere and the requirements set by Dahlberg "to determine the extent to which online deliberations are facilitating rational-critical discourse"[6] have proven to be too idealistic to be fully applied to the discussion forums that we analyzed.

In the threads where participants were in total agreement, the consensus was not reached through rational-critical debates or, to use Dahlberg's words, "the exchange and critique of reasoned moral-practical validity claims"[7] among the participants. Rather, it was the result of gender, political, or religious homogeneity and the participants' emotional involvement in the issues at hand. In other words, it was the nature of the issues under discussion and the participants' backgrounds, ideologies, and interest in these issues, rather than their willingness to engage in a Habermasian-style debate that determined their consensual approach and their level of collective identity. This was particularly the case in the Arabic threads that dealt with "pan-Arab" and "pan-Islamic" issues, such as the Palestinian-Israeli conflict and the Danish cartoons about the Muslim Prophet, as we explained in chapter 4. Consensus on these issues emanated mostly from the participants' emotional uniformity and common subjectivity, rather than their objective, rational thinking.

Such issues tended to lend themselves to the theme of a "unified *umma*." They helped create a sense of "Islamic consciousness" or "*umma* consciousness,"[8] which unites Muslims under the banner of common faith and shared belief, stressing the moral unity of the *umma*, in the face of its external enemies and opposing forces, and suppressing its political conflicts and sectarian fragmentation. All these factors led to an emotional consensus among participants in the threads that discussed such

"pan-Islamic" issues. We noticed that the consensual spirit that dominated many threads led to simplistic and superficial postings that
expressed agreement with the original poster along the lines of "I agree
with you," "God bless you for posting this," or "I admire your posting,"
without, in most cases, providing any in-depth, sophisticated discussion
of the issue at hand, or any serious, analytical engagement with its various aspects.

Islamway English was the only forum where consensus went beyond
gender and religious homogeneity. This forum exemplified what we can
describe as a "nuanced consensus" that resulted from the sense of "Islamic
sisterhood" among its female participants. Those participants showed a
genuine interest in listening to each other and a strong deference to the
members who seemed to have extensive life experiences. In addition, they
utilized their religious knowledge to provide solutions to each others'
problems and to offer genuine religious advice to the other members of
their "Islamic online family."

In this sense, they represented an ideal example of a "knowledge
community,"[9] whose members sincerely utilized their "collective
intelligence"[10] to offer help, support, and advice to the other members of
their community. However, this consensus was still not based on rational-
critical debates, since all participants in this forum seemed to be often on
the same page and in total agreement around the discussed topics throughout the examined threads. These overwhelmingly consensual discourses,
where agreement was not the outcome of deliberation or negotiation, are
in remarkable contrast with the rational, critical Habermasian public
sphere, since they clearly show that "rhetorically salient meanings are
unstable, and their production is an arational process,"[11] which is often
dependent on "the formation of shared judgments."[12]

The threads that reflected divergent identities were more complex.
Divergence in these threads, particularly Islamonline English forum, was
the result mostly of different ethnic, racial, religious, and political ideologies. This is clearly a stark contrast with Habermas' vision of a homogeneous public sphere, where participants forget their differences[13] and try
to focus on the issues at hand with the objective of reaching a consensus,
resulting from rational-critical deliberations. Habermas' perception of an
elitist, "bourgeois public sphere," which works best when limited to "educated white males"[14] did not fit the gender, ethnic, ideological, and religious diversity that we came across in our analysis of the discussion
forums, the contrasting views and positions among these forums' participants, and the polemic discourses that were exchanged between them.

Interestingly, instead of finding participants who leave their differences behind before engaging in deliberations, as envisioned by Habermas
as a requirement for the creation of an ideal public sphere, we actually
witnessed participants bringing their differences and disagreements to

the discussion forums. This diversity illustrated what Nancy Fraser referred to as "competing public spheres"[15] or "subaltern counterpublics,"[16] which can expand and enrich any discursive environment.

Unfortunately, however, most participants in these forums did not utilize their diversity and differences to enrich the discussions or to reach a middle ground based on enlightened debates. Rather, they engaged in sharp disagreements and emotional confrontations, allowing their differences to stand in the way of creating a Habermasian rational-critical debate. There were some participants who seemed committed "to ongoing deliberations with difference"[17] and "to rethink their positions"[18] in a reflexive manner. There were also a few participants who made "a sincere effort to provide all information relevant to the particular problem under consideration."[19] However, these efforts were overshadowed by the assertiveness, dogmatism, and defensiveness expressed by many participants, who seemed unable to even engage in a civilized debate with other participants with whom they disagreed. Some participants even reverted to the use of profanities to aggressively attack other participants simply for being on the other side of the argument. The participants' inability to express their disagreement or to settle their differences in a rational manner seemed to be a pattern in many of the threads that we analyzed.

This led to the emergence of clearly demarcated, and even antagonistic identities along the lines of Sunnis versus Shi'ites, Muslims versus non-Muslims, and males versus females. Some participants even expressed these demarcations through the use of such terms as "infidels" and "impure" to refer to people from the other side in a manner that exemplified and strengthened the concept of "clash of civilizations."

Islamonline English forum in particular stood out in this regard due to its heated debates between Muslims and non-Muslims. In several threads, Muslim participants were forced to adopt a defensive position, which, in some cases, escalated into an offensive tone. To further explain this point, some Muslim participants felt that they should either "defend" themselves against false claims, or that they should "attack" others who opposed them and disagreed with them, as a means of taking a "proactive" position in the hope of preventing possible attacks. This whole situation detracted away from the potential of creating true deliberations.

But even in forums where religious differences seemed to be absent, such as Islamonline Arabic, Muslim participants who tried to be somewhat reflexive in their discussion of highly sensitive issues, such as the Palestinian-Israeli conflict, were sometimes shunned by other Muslim participants, and even attacked and accused of being "traitors." Of course, this suppresses any potential for a rational-critical debate, and, more importantly, it discourages participants who are willing to present a somewhat different opinion from doing so out of fear that they would be framed as "outliers" by the dominant majority.

The aggressive tone and the emotional confrontations that character-ized many of the threads we analyzed make us agree with Habermas' argument that the quality of the public sphere, and consequently the level of discussions and debates taking place within its boundaries, has deteriorated. This was certainly manifested in the way participants in the forums we analyzed tried to propagate and promote their own view-points and positions in a very aggressive, or even offensive way, at the expense of a true rational-critical debate.

Most of the threads we analyzed reflected a "nondeliberative" public sphere, where participants were keen on establishing and reinforcing their religious and ideological beliefs, but they were less apt to support civil discourse on topics that did not easily lend themselves to opinion change and consensus. We believe that the anonymity and easy accessi-bility that were made possible through these forums have contributed to creating a nondeliberatory environment, rather than improving the quality of a truly rational-critical Habermasian discourse. This high-lights the limitations of using the Internet to enhance civic participation and actual democratic practices. As we mentioned in chapter 2, the Internet is what its users make of it. It can be either a dynamic public sphere that allows for democratic discussions or simply a public space that does not contribute to any open exchange of ideas.[20] Most partici-pants in the forums under study in this book did not utilize these forums to engage in truly democratic discourse and open deliberations. Rather, they used their participation to release emotions, express anger, propa-gate an already existing viewpoint, or preach to others to adopt their views.

Moreover, the two extreme, diametrically opposed poles of divergence and consensus, which revealed themselves through the analyzed discus-sion forums in this book, reflect the distinction between "warm" and "cold" circles,[21] which are both currently coexisting in cyberspace. On one hand, "warm" circles, such as Islamway.net English discussion forum, are characterized by a high degree of loyalty, reciprocity, warmth, familiarity, and a sense of collectivism. On the other hand, "cold" circles, such as Islamonline.net English discussion forum, are usually more "for-mal, distant, and single-stranded."[22] The parallel coexistence of these cold and warm currents side-by-side through modern interactive media, such as the Internet, offers the potential for "two equally likely alterna-tives, a stable climate or destructive tempest."[23]

The lively discussions and heated debates that revealed themselves throughout this book are a clear indication of the possible coexistence of both alternatives within the realm of "Cyber Islamic Environments"[24] today. However, the absence of actual interaction or overlap between these two alternatives resulted in the lack of energy that can only be pro-duced through mixing both "warm" and "cold" currents, and, therefore, it contributed to the nonexistence of the middle ground of negotiation in these online discourses.

In every case, whether within the realm of the warm, stable climate of consensus, or the cold, destructive tempest of divergence, the elitist, idealistic, and unitary public sphere envisioned by Habermas was not found to be applicable. The findings of our textual analysis of the threads in the three discussion forums clearly revealed the existence of multiple public spheres, which exemplified "a conversational model of society,"[25] whose participants exchange shared and contested "intersubjective meanings,"[26] based on their attitudes, beliefs, values, and opinions.

Therefore, we can conclude that the Habermasian model of the idealized, universal public sphere neglects, or even excludes, the richness and diversity of already existing, multiple public spheres, since it "conceals the ways in which particular, often marginalized public arenas form and function."[27] Moreover, its "criterion of communicative rationality"[28] contributes to its exclusionary and restrictive nature, which constraints open access and ignores "the conditions of diversity that define civil society."[29]

Lay Muslims' *Ijtihad* and the Absence of the *'Ulama's* Role

As we explained in chapter 3, the Muslim *umma* is about creating unity among Muslims, but it also welcomes pluralism and dialogue, whether among Muslims or between Muslims and non-Muslims. In fact, Muslims are encouraged to reach out to the "Other" in a way that creates an informed middle ground.

Our analysis of the three discussion forums showed how some Muslim participants were mostly united around certain pan-Islamic themes, and how they showed a strong sense of collective consciousness that emanated from their Islamic identity. This was particularly clear in the Arabic discussion forums, in which participants seemed to be Arab-Muslims, as inferred from their posted names and the content of their postings. The threads that exemplified uniformity and unanimity of opinion had a sense of *ijma'* (consensus) among the participants. However, this *ijma'* was not the result of *shura* (consultation). In fact, many posters seemed to be already in agreement, even before participating in the forums. In many of these threads, there was hardly any debate or disagreement; however, there was a collective attempt on the participants' part to reaffirm their Muslim faith and their sense of belongingness to the *umma* at large through their participation in the virtual *umma*.

Most participants provided their personal interpretations (a form of *ijtihad*) on issues as serious as advancing the Islamic *umma*, and as simple as a wife's complaint about her husband's ignorance about the number of birthmarks she has. In discussing all these matters, very few participants made an effort to seek the *ʿulama's* advice. In fact, it was only one thread that we analyzed in chapter 4 where one of the participants tried to answer another participant's question by seeking a Muslim scholar's advice on the issue at hand.

The concept of *ijtihad*, in its classic form, as we mentioned in chapters 1 and 3, is limited to the *ʿulama* (religious scholars).[30] "*Ijtihad* has its specific guidelines and conditions, and the lay Muslims are not qualified to get engaged in this process,"[31] said Sheikh Samy Al- Sersawy, Al-Azhar educated *alim* (religious scholar), in a telephone interview. However, there are some young diasporic Muslims who believe that *ijtihad* is a form of "free thinking…[and is] a competence possessed by all Muslims and not simply an elite (albeit socially detached) group of *ʿulama*. For many young Muslims today, a legitimate promulgator of *ijtihad* is anyone who speaks to a particular question or cause with morality, perspicacity and insight."[32]According to Mandaville (2001), "The implication here is that an opinion is not somehow inherently 'true' simply by virtue of having emanated from the *ʿulama*; rather, these opinions simply enter the 'public sphere'—that is to say, they become contestable and open to re-interpretation."[33]

This trend toward the lay Muslims' interpretation of Islamic issues is accompanied by marginalization and fragmentation of the *ʿulama's* authority in postmodern Islam[34] and a lack of trust on the part of some Muslims in the institutional authority of the *ʿulama*, as we alluded to throughout this book. In fact, we came across a thread in Islamonline Arabic forum, which was titled: "Did we lose trust in the official *da'wa* (propagation of faith)?"[35] Several posters in this short thread expressed their lack of trust in the *ʿulama*, because they felt they were "too close to the governments".

Theoretically, the Internet technology has provided the means to engage in *ijtihad*, to create a new consensus on a number of critical issues and to stimulate discussion within the *umma*. Theoretically also, the Islamic websites' discussion forums can present a further opportunity in this regard by allowing an informed Muslim community to reach out across international boundaries. Thus, they can combine the processes of *ijtihad* and the establishment of *ijma'* on major points of law set by the *ʿulama*, along with permitting a limited process of consultation among lay citizens of the international Muslim community.

Reality, however, is different from theory in this regard. What we found goes against the above-mentioned expectations of the Islamic sites' discussion forums. The nature of the debate in many of these forums is either overwhelmingly consensual in a way that does not allow for *ijtihad*, or overwhelmingly dogmatic, assertive, and opinionated in a way that does not allow for any form of insightful consultation that can possibly lead to *ijma'*. Moreover, the absence of the *ʿulama's* voice in these forums creates a knowledge void that cannot be filled by lay Muslims. It is worth mentioning here that the *ulama* are not totally absent from the Islamic websites under study in this book. They post their lectures on some of these sites, and they participate in the *fatwa* (religious edict) section, but they don't participate in the discussion forums. Sheikh Al-Sersawy, the Al-Azhar scholar, who posts his lectures on Islamway Arabic website, blamed these forums' moderators for the absence of the *ulama's* voice. "The *ulama* don't have the time to check out all kinds of discussion forums on these Islamic sites. That is why it is the moderators' responsibility to go out of their way to invite credible *ulama* to participate, in case their opinions are needed, rather than leave the forums exclusively for lay Muslims to provide *fatwas*."[36]

The Islamic forums that we analyzed exemplified a form of *ijtihad* that is quite different from what *ijtihad* originally meant in an Islamic context. *Ijtihad* in the context of these forums has opened the door for lay people, with hardly any religious qualifications, to express their views, and, in some cases, even frame the agenda on issues related to Islam.

Ironically, despite the antagonistic, dogmatic, and assertive environment that dominated several threads on these Islamic public forums, there is a new manifestation of a Muslim *umma* that is not based on authority, but on public participation. In other words, there is an independence from traditional religious authority and institutional hegemony, where the "discourse...[is] driven by the concerns of publicly-oriented citizens rather than by...[institutional] power[s]."[37] This is supported by the fact that it is the participants, not the moderators, who set the agenda for the issues to be discussed in most of the forums that we analyzed. However, we strongly believe that this communal authority of the average people, which seems to have replaced the religious authority of the traditional *ulama*, is close to anarchy. And mainstream religions, including Islam, are opposed to an anarchic environment, where assertive, and even irrational, personal whims are the norm, rather than the exception. The fact that the role of the religious *ulama*, and even the moderators, is totally absent in some of these forums opens the door for spreading false and inaccurate religious information about Islam. The absence of the *ulama's* voice in these forums also opens the door for strengthening, rather than eradicating, conspiracy theories against Islam, as well as dogmatic perspectives, which are not validated by credible and qualified religious authorities. Although there is a new configuration of the public sphere through these discussion forums in a way that allows average people to engage in, what they perceive as, "free debates" on religious issues, outside the realm of the traditional religious authorities, this newly configured public sphere does not seem to embody many of the criteria required for productive deliberation.

A Last Word ...

While this book is not meant to explain or interpret radical and marginal currents in Islam, its theoretical and methodological foundations may be relevant to future studies of online religious communities on the fringe of the Islamic establishment.

We hope that we were able to provide our readers with a realistic and comprehensive insight into one major slice of the discussion forums on three popular, mainstream Islamic websites. We would also like to reiterate that we do not claim that these discussion forums are generalizable to, or representative of, all Islamic online discourses. Our analysis just aims to provide you with an idea of a particular discourse, taken from particular discussion forums, at a particular point in time. Finally, bearing in mind the multiple challenges confronting the Muslim *umma* in the international public sphere today, we sincerely hope that both Muslims and non-Muslims can work harder to utilize the online discussion forums made available through Islamic websites in a manner that would help enhance the values of democratization, pluralism, and dialogue of civilizations.

Epilogue

The role of political Islam has been on the rise in the Middle East over the past three decades. In Egypt, for example, the Muslim Brotherhood, which is considered to be the largest and most organized opposition party in the country, won almost 20 percent of the parliamentary seats in the November 2005 elections despite the restrictions of the state security apparatus on the group. Islamist groups like the Brotherhood present themselves as a better alternative to corrupt and repressive regimes. "The 'Islamic state' is seen as a kind of social-democratic welfare structure that will provide justice and dignity to the workers; at the same time it is an ultra-conservative and reactionary utopia in which women, workers, minorities and others are taught to listen and obey. Such flexibility allows... [these groups] to carry both counter-hegemonic and hegemonic impulses and tendencies" (Naguib, 2009, 119).

The counter-hegemonic aspect of the Islamist groups has been exemplified in their use of the Internet and social media to project their views and disseminate their ideologies. In this context, some political observers argued that there is "a new generation of Islamic-oriented bloggers in the Middle East whose willingness to air internal matters online has created as much of a stir as their opinions" (Williams, 2008).

Again, Egypt is a case in point, where members of the Muslim Brotherhood have started their own blogs to express their resentment of the torture and brutal tactics practiced by the now ousted Mubarak regime. "Often constrained in their own organization, Brotherhood bloggers have begun to savor the freer outlet of the Internet. Now they are writing unprecedented, blunt public criticism of certain aspects of the Brotherhood... They resent their political and social situation, and disagree with their organization's rhetoric and jurisprudential stances. These bloggers comprise a vanguard searching for new frameworks that will exploit its abilities and fulfill its ambitions... Some of these bloggers have sacrificed their future within the movement to lay bare the group's organizational legacy, revealing many secrets about the hierarchy of Islamist organizations" (Al-Anani, 2008, 29). This has serious, long-term implications for the group. "Until recently, no one could have imagined that some of the Brotherhood's youngest members would criticize their leaders so openly. These blogs crossed many of the Brotherhood's accepted boundaries on members' behavior . . . The blogs have also altered the image of the Muslim Brotherhood, since they gave many Internet-savvy Egyptians first-hand exposure to the ideas floating around in the organization" (Al-Anani, 2008, 38).

So in a way, it can be argued that the virtual world has freed several members of Islamist movements, such as the Brotherhood, of the restrictions and limitations that they are facing in the real world within their organizations and their society at large. Their newly gained freedoms online have empowered them politically and redefined their identities in the offline world.

"This fast-shifting reality due to the new empowering nature of media technologies 'for all' has changed beyond recognition the prism of how the new real-time information flows impact on institutional power, governance and therefore policy making or responses. This is especially the case in those unexpected shock moments of acute crisis or tension" (Gowing, 2011, 15).

"If you want to free a society, just give them Internet access." These were the words of 30-year-old Egyptian activist Wael Ghonim in a CNN interview on February 9th, 2011, just two days before long-time dictator Hosni Mubarak was forced to step down under pressure from a popular and peaceful revolution that started on January 25 and lasted for 18 days in Egypt. This signifies the prominent role that new media, especially the Internet, played, and is still playing, in triggering the popular uprisings that are shaking up the Arab world. These uprisings were largely characterized by the instrumental use of online social media, especially Facebook, Twitter, and YouTube by protesters, to bring about political change and democratic transformation. These Internet-based communication tools acted as effective weapons for promoting civic engagement, through supporting the capabilities of the democratic activists by allowing forums for free speech and political networking opportunities; providing a virtual space for assembly; and supporting the capability of the protestors to plan, organize, and execute peaceful protests. Additionally, these new media avenues enabled an effective form of citizen journalism, through providing forums for ordinary citizens to document the protests; to spread the word about ongoing activities; to provide evidence of governmental brutality; and to disseminate their own words and images to each other, and, most importantly, to the outside world through both regional and transnational media.

Although the Brotherhood leadership did not publicly endorse the Egyptian revolution from the beginning, the group's members were part and parcel of the online and offline activities throughout the course of the revolution. In this context, Ahmed Abdel Gawad, the coordinator of the students' media committee for the Muslim Brotherhood in Egypt said in a personal interview with this book's authors that the Brotherhood launched a Facebook page at the beginning of the revolution that was restricted to its members and that helped coordinate efforts among its youth. This page was functioning for only three days after which the group's online activists took their activities to the streets.

The Internet played a number of important roles before and during the uprisings that are part of what is referred to as the "Arab Spring Revolutions." It provided forums for self expression, channels for public mobilization, avenues for mass organization, and acted as a catalyst for change. Through magnifying and amplifying the voices of protest in the Arab world and enabling the creation of effective political and communication networks, the Internet enabled the snowballing of these uprisings, both inside and across several countries.

Social media were also effective in the course of the Tunisian revolution, which preceded and might have instigated the Egyptian revolution. In this context, Rashed Al-Gannushi, the leader of the Tunisian Islamist Renaissance Party, said in a personal interview with this book's authors: "Social media played a big role in the Tunisian revolution. I consider them to be a partner in this revolution because they have led to the failure of the former Tunisian regime in the news blackout that it was imposing on the uprisings inside the country. The regime succeeded in isolating the country by controlling all the mainstream official media, but the social media broke that isolation and provided an insight and a true picture of what was happening inside Tunisia" (Al-Gannoushi, 2011). Members of Al-Gannoushi's Islamist party use social media to organize their activities. "While I was living in exile in Britain [during the ruling of the ousted Tunisian President Zein Al Abedeen bin Ali], social media were my main source of communication with my followers back home in Tunisia," said Al-Gannoushi.

This new wave of political upheavals compels us to consider not just the political struggle, but also the communication struggle which erupted between the people and their governments, leading to the creation of heated "cyberwars", alongside equally heated political wars. In brief, it became equally important to analyze how people engaged in both a political struggle to impose their own agendas and ensure the fulfillment of their demands, while at the same time engaging in a communication struggle to ensure that their authentic voices were heard and that their side of the story was told, thus, asserting their will, exercising their agency, and empowering themselves. These aggregate efforts ultimately resulted in tilting the political and communication balance in favor of freedom-fighters and political activists.

Another major feature of this new wave of popular uprisings is the leaderless, horizontal, bottom-up, across the board nature of these grassroots movements, which made them very difficult to break. That's mainly because they were more about "processes" not "persons", and "networks" not "organizations". In other words, they were characterized by collective and effective processes of group mobilization, both online and offline, rather than individual acts of leadership by one or more charismatic persons or structured actions by one or more parties or groups.

The largely "leaderless" nature of these revolutions signals the importance of closely analyzing the role of "opinion leaders" or authoritative figures in both the political, as well as the religious, domains, within both the Arab and the Muslim world, and their potential influence on reshaping public opinion trends locally, regionally, and globally in the highly intertwined areas of politics and religion.

Therefore, many of the issues discussed in this book pertaining to the role of the Internet and the formation of discourses in cyberspace help us to better understand how and why these new online-based communication venues played such important and distinct roles before and during the current wave of revolutions that are transforming the political and communication landscapes in a number of Arab and Muslim countries.

After all, it was through these innovative and creative means of communication in cyberspace that political activists were able to tilt the balance of power in a number of Arab and Muslim countries; to reconstruct the main features of political, social, and religious discourses in cyberspace; to reshape the structure of virtual public spheres; and to redefine the concepts of leadership and moral authority. All of these aspects add relevance and significance to the discussions in this book around the notion of contemporary discourses in cyberspace, their current impacts, and their future implications.

NOTES

INTRODUCTION

1. Philip Seib, "New Media and Prospects for Democratization," in *New Media and the New Middle East*, ed. Philip Seib (New York: Palgrave Macmillan, 2007), 1–17, 12.
2. Ibid.
3. Ibid.
4. Ibid., 13.
5. Gary Bunt, "The Islamic Internet Souq," *Q-News*, 325 (November, 2000), http://www.lamp.ac.uk/cis/liminal/virtuallyislamic/souqnov2000.html (accessed September 14, 2008).
6. Peter Mandaville, "Digital Islam: Changing the Boundaries of Religious Knowledge?" *International Institute for the Study of Islam in the Modern World* (March, 1999): 1–23.
7. Peter Mandaville, "Reimagining the Umma? Information Technology and the Changing Boundaries of Political Islam," in *Islam Encountering Globalization*, ed. Ali Mohammadi (London: Routledge Curzon, 2002), 61–90, 79.
8. See Mandaville, "Digital Islam: Changing the Boundaries of Religious Knowledge."
9. Dale Eickelman and Jon W. Anderson, "Redefining Muslim Publics," in *New Media in the Muslim World: The Emerging Public Sphere*, ed. Dale Eickelman and Jon Anderson (Bloomington: Indiana University Press, 1999), 1–18, 14.
10. Gary R. Bunt, *Virtually Islamic: Computer-Mediated Communication and Cyber Islamic Environments* (Cardiff: University of Wales Press, 2000), 1–186.
11. See Mandaville, "Digital Islam: Changing the Boundaries of Religious Knowledge."
12. Bonnie J. Dow and Celeste M. Condit, "The State of the Art in Feminist Scholarship in Communication," *Journal of Communication* 55, no. 3 (2005): 448–78, 467.
13. Sahar Khamis, "The Role of New Arab Satellite Channels in Fostering Intercultural Dialogue: Can Al Jazeera English Bridge the Gap?" in *New Media and the New Middle East*, ed. Philip Seib (New York: Palgrave Macmillan, 2007), 39–51, 41.
14. Lina Khatib, "Communicating Islamic Fundamentalism as Global Citizenship," *Journal of Communication Inquiry* 27, no. 4 (2003): 389–409, 390.
15. See Khamis, "The Role of New Arab Satellite Channels in Fostering Intercultural Dialogue," 39.

16. Saskia Witteborn, "The Situated Expression of Arab Collective Identities in the United States," *Journal of Communication* 57 (2007): 556–75, 572.

17. Ibid.

18. M. Karen Walker, "Proposing a Joint Enterprise for Communication and Terrorism Studies: An Essay on Identity Formation and Expression within the Arab Public Sphere," *The Review of Communication* 7, no. 1 (2007): 21–36, 21.

19. Ibid.

20. Ibid., 22.

21. See Witteborn, "The Situated Expression of Arab Collective Identities," 573.

22. Olivier Roy, *Globalized Islam: The Search for a New Ummah* (New York: Columbia University Press, 2004), 38.

23. M. Karen Walker, "The Search for Community as Described in the Literature Addressing Identity Discourses in the Arab Public Sphere," http://www.rhetoricalens.info/index.cfm?fuseaction=feature.display&feature_id=24 (accessed September 14, 2008).

24. Jon W. Anderson, "New Media, New Publics: Reconfiguring the Public Sphere of Islam," *Social Research* 70, no. 3 (2003): 887–906, 892.

25. Jürgen Habermas, *The Structural Transformation of the Public Sphere: An Inquiry into a Category of Bourgeois Society* (Cambridge, MA: MIT Press, 1989), xi.

26. Lincoln Dahlberg, "The Internet and Democratic Discourse: Exploring the Prospects of Online Deliberative Forums Extending the Public Sphere," *Information, Communication & Society* 4, no. 4 (2001): 615–33, 615.

27. Peter Mandaville, "Communication and Diasporic Islam: A Virtual Ummah?" in *The Media of Diaspora*, ed. Karim H. Karim (London: Routledge, 2003), 135–47, 137.

28. See Dahlberg, "The Internet and Democratic Discourse," 623.

29. Ibid.

30. Ibid.

31. Ibid.

32. Ibid.

33. Ibid.

34. Ibid.

35. Marc Lynch, *Voices of the New Arab Public Sphere: Iraq, Al-Jazeera, and Middle East Politics Today* (New York: Columbia University Press, 2006), 32.

36. See Walker, "Proposing a Joint Enterprise for Communication and Terrorism Studies," 27.

37. R. K. Polat, "The Internet and Political Participation: Exploring the Explanatory Links," *European Journal of Communication* 20, no. 4 (2005): 435–59, 452.

38. See Walker, "The Search for Community," 1.

39. Ibid., 2.

40. See Witteborn, "The Situated Expression of Arab Collective Identities," 573.

41. See Mandaville, "Communication and Diasporic Islam: A Virtual Ummah?" 136.

42. Ibid.

43. Ibid.

44. See Lynch, *Voices of the New Arab Public Sphere*.

45. See Walker, "Proposing a Joint Enterprise for Communication and Terrorism Studies," 23.

46. Ibid.

47. Jocelyne Cesari, *When Islam and Democracy Meet: Muslims in Europe and in the United States* (New York: Palgrave Macmillan, 2004), 92.
48. Ibid., 91.
49. See Bunt, *Virtually Islamic*, 4.
50. See Walker, "Proposing a Joint Enterprise for Communication and Terrorism Studies," 23.
51. Henry Jenkins, *Convergence Culture: Where Old and New Media Collide* (New York: New York University Press, 2006), 2.
52. Ibid.
53. Ibid., 3.
54. Ibid., 2.
55. Albercht Hofheinz, "The Internet in the Arab World: Playground for Political Liberalization" (March, 2005), 78–96, www.library.tes.de/pdf-files/id/ipg/02941.pdf (accessed September 14, 2008).
56. Islamonline.net, http://www.islamonline.net/English/AboutUs.shtml
57. Ibid.
58. Ibid.
59. See Hofheinz, "The Internet in the Arab World."
60. Peter Mandaville, *Global Political Islam* (London: Routledge, 2007), 326.
61. Jon W. Anderson, "New Media, New Publics: Reconfiguring the Public Sphere of Islam," *Social Research* 70, no. 3 (Fall 2003): 887–906, 892.
62. Jon W. Anderson, "Muslim Networks, Muslim Selves in Cyberspace: Islam in the Post-Modern Public Sphere" (October, 2001), http://www.mafhoum.com/press3/102S22.htm (accessed September 14, 2008).
63. Hugh Miles, *Al-Jazeera: The Inside Story of the Arab News Channel That Is Challenging the West* (New York: Grove Press, 2005), 43.
64. Ibid.
65. Leif Stenberg, "Islam, Knowledge, and the West: The Making of a Global Islam," in *Globalization and the Muslim World: Culture, Religion and Modernity*, ed. Birgit Schaebler and Leif Stenberg (Syracuse, NY: Syracuse University Press, 2004), 93–110, 108.
66. See Miles, *Al-Jazeera*, 42.
67. Gary R. Bunt, "Towards an Islamic Information Revolution," *Global Dialogue* 6, no. 1–2 (2004): 107–17.
68. Jakob Skovgaard-Peterson, "The Global Mufti," in *Globalization and the Muslim World: Culture, Religion and Modernity*, ed. Birgit Schaebler and Leif Stenberg (Syracuse, NY: Syracuse University Press, 2004), 153–65, 156.
69. Ibid.
70. Islamonline webmaster, interviewed by authors, February 2007.
71. Ibid.
72. Ibid.
73. Jon W. Anderson, "Wiring Up: The Internet Difference for Muslim Networks," in *Muslim Networks: From Hajj to Hip Hop*, ed. Miriam Cooke and Bruce Lawrence (Chapel Hill: University of North Carolina Press, 2005), 252–63.
74. See Anderson, "Muslim Networks, Muslim Selves in Cyberspace."
75. Jon W. Anderson and Yves Gonzalez-Quijano, "Technological Mediation and the Emergence of Transnational Muslims Publics," in *Public Islam and the Common Good*, ed. Armando Salvatore and Dale Eickelman (Boston: Brill, 2006), 53–71, 63.
76. See Hofheinz, "The Internet in the Arab World."

77. Muhammad Qasim Zaman, *The 'Ulama in Contemporary Islam: Custodians of Change* (Princeton, NJ: Princeton University Press, 2002), 1.
78. Lindsay Wise, "Words from the Heart: New Forms of Islamic Preaching in Egypt" (Unpublished Masters Thesis, St. Anthony's College, Oxford University, 2003)
79. See Mandaville, *Global Political Islam*, 329.
80. Ibid.
81. See Hofheinz, "The Internet in the Arab World," 91.
82. See Mandaville, *Global Political Islam*, 329.
83. Ibid.
84. Ibid., 330.
85. See Hofheinz, "The Internet in the Arab World," 91.
86. Ibid., 92.
87. Asra Nomani, "Amr Khaled," *Time*, April 30, 2007, http://www.time.com/time/specials/2007/time100/article/0,28804,1595326_1615754_1616173,00.html (accessed September 14, 2008).
88. See the July/August 2008 issue of *Foreign Policy* magazine, 54–7, http://ForeignPolicy.com/extras/intellectuals (accessed September 14, 2008).
89. Ne'mat Awadallah, interviewed by authors, Cairo, Egypt, 2007.
90. Islamway.com, http://english.islamway.com/bindex.php?section=aboutus
91. Ibid.
92. Charles Hirschkind, "Civic Virtue and Religious Reason: An Islamic Counterpublic," *Cultural Anthropology* 16, no. 1 (2001): 3–34, 5.
93. See Bunt, *Virtually Islamic*, 17.
94. Ibid.
95. Ibid., 18.
96. Mohammed Ayoob, "Deciphering Islam's Multiple Voices: Intellectual Luxury or Strategic Necessity?" *Middle East Policy* 12, no. 3 (2005): 79–90, 80.
97. Ibid., 81.
98. All Participants in Islamway Arabic forum were also Muslim women
99. See Zaman, *The 'Ulama in Contemporary Islam*, 1.
100. See Bunt, *Virtually Islamic*, 37.
101. Norman Fairclough, *Analyzing Discourse: Textual Analysis for Social Research* (London: Routledge, 2003), 3.
102. Ibid., 10–11.
103. Ibid., 11.
104. Alan McKee, *Textual Analysis: A Beginner's Guide* (London: Sage, 2006), 1–156.
105. Ibid.
106. Ibid., 52.
107. Carolina Acosta-Alzuru and Peggy J. Kreshel, "I'm an American Girl…Whatever That Means: Girls Consuming Pleasant Company's American Girl Identity," *Journal of Communication* 52, no. 1 (2002):139–61, 146–7.
108. Stuart Hall, "Introduction," in *Paper Voices: The Popular Press and Social Change, 1935–1965*, ed. A.C.H. Smith (London: Chatto and Windus, 1975), 11–24, 15.
109. See Dahlberg, "The Internet and Democratic Discourse."
110. See Walker, "Proposing a Joint Enterprise for Communication and Terrorism Studies," 23–4.
111. See Bunt, *Virtually Islamic*, 12.

112. See Zaman, *The 'Ulama in Contemporary Islam*, 1.
113. John L. Esposito, "Introduction: Modernizing Islam and Re-Islamization in Global Perspective," in *Modernizing Islam: Religion in the Public Sphere in Europe and the Middle East*, ed. John L. Esposito and Francois Burgat (New Brunswick, NJ: Rutgers University Press, 2003), 1–14, 4.

1 THE PUBLIC SPHERE IN AN ISLAMIC CONTEXT

1. Robert C. Holub, *Jürgen Habermas: Critic in the Public Sphere* (London: Routledge, 1991), 1–205.
2. Alan McKee, *The Public Sphere: An Introduction* (London: Cambridge University Press, 2005), 6.
3. Dale Eickelman, "The Coming Transformation of the Muslim World," *Middle East Review of International Affairs* 3, no. 3 (September 1999), http://www.biu.ac.il/SOC/besa/meria/journal/1999/issue3/jb3n3a8.html (accessed September 14, 2008).
4. Armando Salvatore and Dale Eickelman, "Muslim Publics," in *Public Islam and the Common Good*, ed. Armando Salvatore and Dale Eickelman (Boston: Brill, 2006), 3–27, 7–8.
5. Peter Dahlgren, "Introduction," in *Communication and Citizenship: Journalism and Public Sphere*, ed. Peter Dahlgren and Colin Sparks (London: Routledge, 1997), 1–24, 7.
6. Shelton A. Gunaratne, "Public Sphere and Communicative Rationality: Interrogating Habermas's Eurocentrism," *Journalism Communication Monographs* 8, no. 2 (Summer 2006): 96.
7. Jürgen Habermas, *The Structural Transformation of the Public Sphere: An Inquiry into a Category of Bourgeois Society* (Cambridge, MA: MIT Press, 1989), 27.
8. Ibid., 175–6.
9. See McKee, *The Public Sphere: An Introduction*, 51.
10. See Habermas, *The Structural Transformation of the Public Sphere*.
11. See Dahlgren, "Introduction."
12. See Habermas, *The Structural Transformation of the Public Sphere*, 36.
13. See McKee, *The Public Sphere: An Introduction*.
14. Jürgen Habermas, *The Theory of Communicative Action*. Vol. 1, *Reason and the Rationalization of Society* (Boston: Beacon Press, 1984), 10.
15. Jürgen Habermas, *Moral Consciousness and Communicative Action* (Cambridge, MA: MIT Press, 1990).
16. Thomas McCarthy, "Practical Discourse: On the Relation of Morality to Politics," in *Habermas and the Public Sphere*, ed. Craig Calhoun (Cambridge, MA: MIT Press, 1992), 51–72, 60.
17. See Gunaratne, "Public Sphere and Communicative Rationality," 118.
18. See Holub, *Jürgen Habermas: Critic in the Public Sphere*, 15.
19. James Curran, "Rethinking the Media as a Public Sphere," in *Communication and Citizenship: Journalism and Public Sphere*, ed. Peter Dahlgren and Colin Sparks (London: Routledge, 1997), 27–57, 29.
20. Shmuel N. Eisenstadt, "Concluding Remarks: Public Sphere, Civil Society, and Political Dynamics in Islamic Societies," in *The Public Sphere in Muslim Societies*, ed. Miriam Hoester, Shmuel Eisenstadt, and Nehemia Levitzion (New York: State University of New York Press, 2002), 139–61, 141.

21. Craig Calhoun, "Introduction," in *Habermas and the Public Sphere,* ed. Craig Calhoun (Cambridge, MA: MIT Press, 1992), 1–48, 8–9.
22. See Holub, *Jürgen Habermas: Critic in the Public Sphere,* 3–4.
23. Luke Goode, *Jürgen Habermas: Democracy and the Public Sphere* (London: Pluto Press, 2005), 1–174.
24. John Michael Roberts and Nick Crossley, "Introduction," in *After Habermas: News Perspectives on the Public Sphere,* ed. Nick Crossley and John Michael Roberts (New York: Blackwell, 2004), 1–27.
25. Michael Warner, *Publics and Counterpublics* (New York: Zone Books, 2002), 47.
26. Colin Sparks, "Is There a Global Public Sphere?" in *Electronic Empires: Global Media and Local Resistance,* ed. Daya Thussu (London: Arnold, 1998), 108–24, 112.
27. See McKee, *The Public Sphere: An Introduction,* 145.
28. Ibid.
29. Ibid., 4.
30. Tanni Haas, "The Public Sphere as a Sphere of Publics," *Journal of Communication* 54, no. 1 (March 2004), 178–84, 180.
31. Ibid., 180.
32. See Habermas, *The Structural Transformation of the Public Sphere.*
33. Ibid., 161.
34. See Hass, "The Public Sphere as a Sphere of Publics."
35. Ibid., 179.
36. See Sparks, "Is There a Global Public Sphere?" 111.
37. See Gunaratne, "Public Sphere and Communicative Rationality."
38. Ibid., 105.
39. John Thompson, *Ideology and Modern Culture: Critical Social Theory in the Era of Mass Communication* (Palo Alto, CA: Stanford University Press, 1990), 113.
40. See Warner, *Publics and Counterpublics,* 49–50.
41. See Roberts and Crossley, "Introduction," 5–6.
42. Ibid.
43. See Goode, *Jürgen Habermas: Democracy and the Public Sphere.*
44. See Sparks, "Is There a Global Public Sphere?"
45. See Habermas, *The Structural Transformation of the Public Sphere,* 166.
46. See Calhoun, "Introduction," 23.
47. See Habermas, *The Structural Transformation of the Public Sphere,* 162.
48. See Goode, *Jürgen Habermas: Democracy and the Public Sphere,* 24.
49. See Gunaratne, "Public Sphere and Communicative Rationality," 151.
50. See McCarthy, "Practical Discourse: On the Relation of Morality to Politics," 60.
51. See Calhoun, "Introduction," 13.
52. See Goode, *Jürgen Habermas: Democracy and the Public Sphere,* 8.
53. See Calhoun, "Introduction," 3.
54. Ibid., 7.
55. Michael Schudson, "Why Conversation Is Not the Soul of Democracy," *Critical Studies in Mass Communication* 14 (1997): 297–309, 298.
56. Nancy Fraser, "Rethinking the Public Sphere," in *Habermas and the Public Sphere,* ed. Craig Calhoun (Cambridge, MA: MIT Press, 1992), 109–42, 119.
57. See Roberts and Crossley, "Introduction," 12.
58. See Fraser, "Rethinking the Public Sphere," 115.
59. Ibid., 125.
60. Ibid., 123.
61. Ibid., 136.

62. See Goode, *Jürgen Habermas: Democracy and the Public Sphere*, 20.
63. See Habermas, *The Structural Transformation of the Public Sphere*, 170–71.
64. See Goode, *Jürgen Habermas: Democracy and the Public Sphere*, 20.
65. See Thompson, *Ideology and Modern Culture*, 115.
66. Ibid., 227.
67. See Gunaratne, "Public Sphere and Communicative Rationality."
68. See McKee, *The Public Sphere: An Introduction*, 7.
69. Seyla Benhabib, "Models of Public Space: Hannah Arendt, the Liberal Tradition, and Jürgen Habermas," in *Habermas and the Public Sphere*, ed. Craig Calhoun (Cambridge, MA: MIT Press, 1992), 73–98, 89–90.
70. See Fraser, "Rethinking the Public Sphere," 129.
71. See Gunaratne, "Public Sphere and Communicative Rationality."
72. See Calhoun, "Introduction."
73. See Gunaratne, "Public Sphere and Communicative Rationality," 102.
74. See Salvatore and Eickelman, "Preface," in *Public Islam and the Common Good*, ed. Armando Salvatore and Dale Eickelman (Boston: Brill, 2006), xiv.
75. See Eickelman, "The Coming Transformation of the Muslim World."
76. See Salvatore and Eickelman, *Public Islam and the Common Good*.
77. Ibid., xii.
78. Ibid.
79. Ibid., xii.
80. Ibid.
81. Muhammad Qasim Zaman, "The 'Ulama of Contemporary Islam and Their Conceptions of the Common Good," in *Public Islam and the Common Good*, ed. Armando Salvatore and Dale Eickelman (Boston: Brill, 2006), 129–56, 130.
82. See Salvatore and Eickelman, *Public Islam and the Common Good*.
83. Mohammed Abu-Nimer, "Framework for Nonviolence and Peacebuilding in Islam," in *Contemporary Islam: Dynamic, Not Static*, ed. Abdul Aziz Said, Mohammed Abu-Nimer, and Meena Sharify-Funk (London: Routledge, 2006), 132–72, 159.
84. Ibid., 160.
85. Björn Olav Utvik, "The Modernizing Face of Islamism," in *Modernizing Islam: Religion in the Public Sphere in Europe and the Middle East*, ed. John L. Esposito and Francois Burgat (Piscataway, NJ: Rutgers University Press, 2003), 43–68, 65.
86. See Abu Nimer, "Framework for Nonviolence and Peacebuilding in Islam," 160.
87. Ibid.
88. Armando Salvatore, "Public Religion, Ethics of Participation, and Cultural Dialogue," in *Contemporary Islam: Dynamic, Not Static* (London: Routledge, 2006), 83–100, 98.
89. Stewart Hoover and Knut Lundby, *Rethinking Media, Religion, and Culture* (London: Sage, 1997), 41.
90. Gudrun Krämer and Sabine Schmidtke, "Introduction: Religious Authority and Religious Authorities in Muslim Societies: A Critical Overview," in *Speaking for Islam: Religious Authorities in Muslim Societies*, ed. Gudrun Krämer and Sabine Schmidtke (Boston: Brill, 2006), 1–14, 1.
91. Ibid.
92. Ibid., 3.
93. Albert Hourani, *Arabic Thought in the Liberal Age, 1798–1939* (London: Cambridge University Press, 1993), 2.
94. Ibid.

95. Ibid.
96. Ibid.
97. Ibid.
98. Mansoor Moaddel, *Islamic Modernism, Nationalism, and Fundamentalism: Episode and Discourse* (Chicago: University of Chicago Press, 2005), 32.
99. Ibid.
100. Ibid.
101. Ibid.
102. Ibid.
103. See Hourani, *Arabic Thought in the Liberal Age*, 8.
104. Ibid.
105. Ibid.
106. Ibid.
107. Tareq Y. Ismael and Jacqueline S. Ismael, *Government and Politics in Islam* (New York: St. Martin's Press, 1985), 8.
108. Ibid.
109. Mona Abul-Fadl, *Islam and the Middle East: The Aesthetics of a Political Inquiry* (Hendon, VA: International Institute of Islamic Thought, 1990), 22–3.
110. Ibid., 23–4.
111. See Hourani, *Arabic Thought in the Liberal Age*, 5.
112. Ibid., 6.
113. Ibid.
114. Abelwahab El-Affendi, "Democracy and Its (Muslim) Critics: An Islamic Alternative to Democracy?" in *Islamic Democratic Discourse: Theory, Debates, and Philosophical Perspectives*, ed. M.A. Muqtader Khan (Lanham, MD: Lexington Books, 2006), 227–56, 235.
115. Ibid.
116. See Ismael and Ismael, *Government and Politics in Islam*, 11.
117. Ibid., 11–12.
118. Ibid., 12.
119. Ibid.
120. Ibid.
121. See El-Affendi, "Democracy and Its (Muslim) Critics," 245.
122. Ibid., 246.
123. Ibid., 244–5.
124. Ibid., 245.
125. Ismael and Ismael, *Government and Politics in Islam*, 12.
126. Cengiz Kirli, "Coffeehouses: Public Opinion in the Nineteenth-Century Ottoman Empire," in *Public Islam and the Common Good*, ed. Armando Salvatore and Dale Eickelman (Boston: Brill, 2006), 75–97, 76.
127. Ibid.
128. Peter Van Der Veer, "Secrecy and Publicity in the South Asian Public Arena," in *Public Islam and the Common Good*, ed. Armando Salvatore and Dale Eickelman (Boston: Brill, 2006), 29–51.
129. Peter Mandaville, "Reimagining the Ummah? Information Technology and the Changing Boundaries of Political Islam," in *Islam Encountering Globalization*, ed. Ali Mohammadi (London: Routledge, 2002), 61–90, 70.
130. See Kirli, "Coffeehouses: Public Opinion in the Nineteenth-Century Ottoman Empire," 96.
131. Patrick D. Gaffney, *The Prophet's Pulpit: Islamic Preaching in Contemporary Egypt* (Berkeley: California University Press, 1994), 25.

132. Annabelle Böttcher, "Sunni and Shi'i Networking in the Middle East," in *Shaping the Current Islamic Reformation*, ed. B.A. Roberson (London: Frank Cass, 2004), 42–63, 43.
133. Ibid.
134. See Abul-Fadil, *Islam and the Middle East*, 23.
135. Hamid Mowlana, *Global Communication in Transition: The End of Diversity?* (London: Sage, 1996), 140.
136. See Gaffney, *The Prophet's Pulpit*.
137. Olivier Roy, *Globalized Islam: The Search for a New Ummah* (New York: Columbia University Press, 2004), 158.
138. Ira M. Lapidus, *A History of Islamic Societies*, 2nd ed. (London: Cambridge University Press, 2002), 206–7.
139. See Hourani, *Arabic Thought in the Liberal Age*, 11.
140. Ibid., 11–12.
141. See Lapidus, *A History of Islamic Societies*, 206.
142. Ibid., 207.
143. See Zaman, "The 'Ulama of Contemporary Islam and Their Conceptions of the Common Good," 131.
144. See Mandaville, "Reimagining the Ummah?"
145. Miriam Cooke and Bruce Lawrence, "Introduction," in *Muslim Networks: From Hajj to Hip Hop*, ed. Miriam Cooke and Bruce Lawrence (Chapel Hill: University of North Carolina Press, 2005), 1–30, 6.
146. Ibid., 6–7.
147. Muhammad Qasim Zaman, *The 'Ulama in Contemporary Islam: Custodians of Change* (Princeton, NJ: Princeton University Press, 2002), 180.
148. Dale Eickelman and James Piscatori, *Muslim Politics* (Princeton, NJ: Princeton University Press, 2004), 70.
149. Ibid.
150. See Zaman, "The 'Ulama of Contemporary Islam and Their Conceptions of the Common Good."
151. See Moaddel, *Islamic Modernism, Nationalism, and Fundamentalism*, 33.
152. Ibid.
153. Marshall G.S. Hodgson, *The Venture of Islam: Conscience and History in a World Civilization*. Vol. 1, *The Classical Age of Islam* (Chicago: University of Chicago Press, 1974), 248.
154. Ibid.
155. Ibid., 250.
156. Ibid.
157. See Ismael and Ismael, *Government and Politics in Islam*, 6.
158. Ibid., 6–7.
159. Ibid., 7.
160. See Moaddel, *Islamic Modernism, Nationalism, and Fundamentalism*, 33.
161. See Hourani, *Arabic Thought in the Liberal Age*, 15.
162. Ibid., 19.
163. Ibid., 10.
164. Ibid., 6.
165. M. Raquibuz Zaman, "Islamic Perspectives on Territorial Boundaries and Autonomy," in *Islamic Political Ethics: Civil Society, Pluralism, and Conflict*, ed. Sohail H. Hashmi (Princeton, NJ: Princeton University Press, 2002), 79–101, 88.
166. Ibid.
167. Ibid., 88–9.

168. Ibid., 88.
169. See Lapidus, *A History of Islamic Societies*, 207.
170. See Moaddel, *Islamic Modernism, Nationalism, and Fundamentalism*, 34.
171. See Mandaville, "Reimagining the Ummah?"
172. Ibid., 70.
173. See Gaffney, *The Prophet's Pulpit*.
174. Ibid., 35.
175. Malika Zeghal, "Religion and Politics in Egypt: The Ulema of Al-Azhar, Radical Islam, and the State," *International Journal of Middle East Studies* 31, no. 3 (August 1999), 371–99.
176. Jocelyne Cesari, *When Islam and Democracy Meet: Muslims in Europe and in the United States* (New York: Palgrave Macmillan, 2004), 44.
177. See Lapidus, *A History of Islamic Societies*, 207.
178. Ibid.
179. Ibid.
180. See Zeghal, "Religion and Politics in Egypt."
181. See El-Affendi, "Democracy and Its (Muslim) Critics," 247.
182. See Salvatore and Eickelman, *Public Islam and the Common Good*, xii.
183. Ibid., 147.
184. See Eickelman, "The Coming Transformation of the Muslim World."
185. Jon Anderson, "New Media, New Publics: Reconfiguring the Public Sphere of Islam," *Social Research* 70, no. 3 (Fall 2003): 887–906, 892.
186. See Eickelman, "The Coming Transformation of the Muslim World."
187. John Thompson, *The Media and Modernity: A Social Theory of the Media* (Palo Alto, CA: Stanford University Press, 1995), 180.
188. See Hoover and Lundby, *Rethinking Media, Religion, and Culture*, 6.
189. See Eickelman and Piscatori, *Muslim Politics*, 43.
190. Ibid., 43.
191. Dale Eickelman and Jon Anderson, "Preface," in *New Media in the Muslim World: The Emerging Public Sphere* (Bloomington: Indian University Press, 1999), vii–ix, viii.
192. See Zaman, *The 'Ulama in Contemporary Islam: Custodians of Change*, 179.
193. See Eickelman and Piscatori, *Muslim Politics*.
194. See Mandaville, "Reimagining the Ummah?" 70.
195. A. Reza Sheikholeslami, "From Individual Sacrament to Collective Salvation," in *Contemporary Islam: Dynamic, Not Static*, ed. Abdul Aziz Said, Mohammed Abu-Nimer, and Meena Sharify-Funk (London: Routledge, 2006), 49–63, 55.
196. B.A. Roberson, "The Shaping of the Current Islamic Reformation," in *Shaping the Current Islamic Reformation*, ed. B.A. Roberson (London: Frank Cass, 2004), 1–19, 15.
197. Thomas Luckman, *The Invisible Religion: The Problem of Religion in Modern Society* (New York: Macmillan, 1967).
198. Armando Salvatore and Mark LeVine, "Introduction," in *Religion, Social Practice and Contested Hegemonies: Reconstructing the Public Sphere in Muslim Majority Societies*, ed. Armando Salvatore and Mark LeVine (New York: Palgrave Macmillan, 2005), 1–25, 15.
199. José Casanova, *Public Religions in the Modern World* (Chicago: University of Chicago Press, 1994), 65–6.
200. Ibid., 230.
201. Ibid., 3.

202. Ibid., 234.
203. See Thompson, *The Media and Modernity: A Social Theory of the Media*, 194.
204. See Eickelman and Piscatori, *Muslim Politics*, 23.
205. Ibid., 25.
206. Daniel Lerner, *The Passing of Traditional Society: Modernizing the Middle East* (Glencoe, IL: Free Press, 1963), 405.
207. See Eickelman and Piscatori, *Muslim Politics*, 24.
208. See Thompson, *The Media and Modernity: A Social Theory of the Media*.
209. Ibid., 193.
210. Karin Wilkins, "Communication and Transition in the Middle East," *Gazette, the International Journal for Communication Studies* 66, no. 6 (December 2004), 483–96, 486.
211. Ibid.
212. See Thompson, *The Media and Modernity: A Social Theory of the Media*, 184.
213. Peter Mandaville, *Transnational Muslim Politics: Reimagining the Umma* (London: Routledge, 2001), 65.
214. Pernilla Ouis, "Islamization as a Strategy for Reconciliation between Modernity and Tradition: Examples from Contemporary Arab Gulf States," *Islam and Christian-Muslim Relations* 13, no. 3 (2002): 315–34, 317.
215. Ibid., 315.
216. Ibid., 331.
217. Ibid., 317.
218. See Eickelman and Piscatori, *Muslim Politics*.
219. Ibid., 33.
220. Ibid.
221. Ibid., 34.
222. See Salvatore and Eickelman, "Muslim Publics," 16.
223. See Eickelman and Piscatori, *Muslim Politics*.
224. Jakob Skovgaard-Peterson, "The Global Mufti," in *Globalization and the Muslim World: Culture, Religion and Modernity*, ed. Birgit Schaebler and Leif Stenberg (New York: Syracuse University Press, 2004), 153–65, 164.
225. Hamid Mowlana and Laurie Wilson, *The Passing of Modernity: Communication and the Transformation of Society* (New York: Longman, 1990).
226. Akbar Ahmed and Hastings Donnan, "Islam in the Age of Postmodernity," in *Islam, Globalization and Postmodernity*, ed. Akbar Ahmed and Hastings Donna (London: Routledge, 2002), 1–20, 12.
227. Tomas Gerholm, "Two Muslim Intellectuals in the Postmodern West: Akbar Ahmed and Ziauddin Sardar," in *Islam, Globalization and Postmodernity*, ed. Akbar Ahmed and Hastings Donna (London: Routledge, 2002), 190–212, 209.
228. See Eickelman and Piscatori, *Muslim Politics*, 38.
229. Ibid., xi.
230. Ibid., 69.
231. Dale Eickelman, "Clash of Cultures? Intellectuals, Their Publics, and Islam," in *Intellectuals in the Modern Islamic World: Transmission, Transformation, Communication*, ed. Stéphan Dudoigan, Komatsu Hisao, and Kosugi Yasushi (London: Routledge, 2006), 289–304, 300.
232. Ibid., 301.
233. See Roy, *Globalized Islam*, 20.
234. Ibid., 151.
235. Ibid., 34.

2 RELIGION IN THE VIRTUAL
PUBLIC SPHERE: THE CASE OF ISLAM

1. Howard Rheingold, *The Virtual Community: Homesteading on the Electronic Frontier* (Cambridge, MA: MIT Press, 2000), xx.

2. Jan Fernback, "The Individual with the Collective: Virtual Ideology and the Realization of Collective Principles," in *Virtual Culture: Identity & Communication in Cybersociety,* ed. Steven G. Jones (London: Sage, 2002), 36–54.

3. Jan Fernback, "There Is a There There: Notes toward a Definition of Cybercommunity," in *Doing Internet Research: Critical Issues and Methods for Examining the Net,* ed. Steve Jones (London: Sage, 1999), 203–20.

4. Heidi Campbell, *Exploring Religious Community Online: We Are One in the Network* (New York: Peterlang, 2005), xvi.

5. Ibid., 44.

6. Ibid., 48.

7. Ibid., 48–9.

8. James Bohman, "Expanding Dialogue: The Internet, the Public Sphere and Prospects for Transnational Democracy," in *After Habermas: New Perspectives on the Public Sphere,* ed. Nick Crossley and John Michael Roberts (Oxford: Blackwell, 2004), 131–55.

9. Deborah L. Wheeler, *The Internet in the Middle East: Global Expectations and Local Imaginations in Kuwait* (New York: State University of New York Press, 2006), 27.

10. Ibid.

11. James Slevin, *The Internet and Society* (London: Polity, 2000), 79–80.

12. See Bohman, "Expanding Dialogue."

13. See Campbell, *Exploring Religious Community Online,* xvii.

14. Mark Poster, "Cyberdemocracy: The Internet and the Public Sphere," in *Virtual Politics: Identity and Community in Cyberspace,* ed. David Holmes (London: Sage, 1997), 212–28.

15. See Slevin, *The Internet and Society.*

16. Jon Anderson, "Cybarites,' Knowledge Workers and New Creoles on the Superhighway," *Anthropology Today* 11, no. 4 (August 1995): 13–15, 13.

17. Lorne Dawson and Douglas Cowan, "Introduction," in *Religion Online: Finding Faith on the Internet,* ed. Lorne Dawson and Douglas Cowan (London: Routledge, 2004), 1–16, 8.

18. Ibid.

19. Peter Dahlgren, "The Public Sphere and the Net: Structure, Space, and Communication," in *Mediated Politics: Communication in the Future of Democracy,* ed. W. Lance Bennett and Robert M. Entman (London: Cambridge University Press, 2001), 33–55, 51–2.

20. See Rheingold, *The Virtual Community,* xxx.

21. Ibid.

22. See Fernback, "The Individual with the Collective: Virtual Ideology and the Realization of Collective Principles," 37.

23. Ibid., 39.

24. Teresa M. Harrison and Timothy Stephen, "Researching and Creating Community Networks," in *Doing Internet Research: Critical Issues and Methods for Examining the Net,* ed. Steve Jones (London: Sage, 1999), 221–42.

25. See Dawson and Cowan, "Introduction."

26. See Dahlgren, "The Public Sphere and the Net: Structure, Space, and Communication," 50.

27. See Rheingold, *The Virtual Community*.

28. Zizi Papacharissi, "The Virtual Sphere: The Internet as a Public Sphere," *New Media & Society* 1, no. 9 (2002): 9–27.

29. Ibid., 14.

30. Beth Kolko and Elizabeth Reid, "Dissolution and Fragmentation: Problems in On-Line Communities," in *Cybersociety: Revisiting Computer-Mediated Communication and Community*, ed. Steven G. Jones (London: Sage, 1998), 212–30, 221–2.

31. Hamid Mowlana and Laurie Wilson, *The Passing of Modernity: Communication and the Transformation of Society* (New York: Longman, 1990), 85.

32. George Rodman, *Mass Media in a Changing World* (Boston: McGraw Hill, 2007), 40.

33. Neil Postman, *Technopoly: The Surrender of Culture to Technology* (New York: Vintage Books, 1993), 71.

34. See Rheingold, *The Virtual Community*, xix.

35. See Bohman, "Expanding Dialogue: The Internet, the Public Sphere and Prospects for Transnational Democracy," 140.

36. Ibid.

37. See Wheeler, *The Internet in the Middle East*, 21–2.

38. Ibid.

39. Barry Wellman and Milena Gulia, "Virtual Communities as Communities: Net Surfers Don't Ride Alone," in *Communities in Cyberspace*, ed. Marc A. Smith and Peter Kollock (London: Routledge, 2003), 167–94, 187.

40. Oliver Krüger, "Methods and Theory for Studying Religion on the Internet: Introduction to the Special Issue on Theory and Methodology," *Online Heidelberg Journal of Religions on the Internet* 1, no. 1 (2005).

41. Stewart M. Hoover, "Religion, Media and Identity: Theory and Method in Audience Research on Religion and Media," in *Mediating Religion: Conversations in Media, Religion and Culture*, ed. Jolyon Mitchell and Sophia Marriage (New York: T&T Clark, 2003), 9–19.

42. Christopher Helland, "Popular Religion and the World Wide Web: A Match Made in (Cyber) Heaven," in *Religion Online: Finding Faith on the Internet*, ed. Lorne Dawson and Douglas Cowan (London: Routledge, 2004), 23–36.

43. Oliver Krüger, "The Internet as Distributor and Mirror of Religious and Ritual Knowledge," *Asian Journal of Social Sciences* 32, no. 2 (2004): 183–97.

44. Karine Barzilai-Nohan and Gad Barzilai, "Cultured Technology: The Internet and Religious Fundamentalism," *Information Society* 21 (2005): 25–40, 29.

45. Ibid., 27.

46. Eileen Barker, "Crossing the Boundary: New Challenges to Religious Authority and Control as a Consequence of Access to the Internet," in *Religion and Cyberspace*, ed. Morten T. Højsgaard and Margit Warburg (London: Routledge, 2005), 67–85, 76.

47. See Krüger, "The Internet as Distributor and Mirror of Religious and Ritual Knowledge."

48. Anthony Giddens, *The Consequences of Modernity* (Palo Alto, CA: Stanford University Press, 1990), 21.

49. See Krüger, "The Internet as Distributor and Mirror of Religious and Ritual Knowledge."

50. Morten T. Hójsgaard and Margit Warburg, "Introduction," in *Religion and Cyberspace*, ed. Morten T. Hójsgaard and Margit Warburg (London: Routledge, 2005), 1–12, 2.

51. Heidi Campbell, "Spiritualizing the Internet: Uncovering Discourses and Narratives of Religious Internet Usage," *Online Heidelberg Journal of Religions on the Internet* 1, no. 1 (September 2005): 2.

52. Heidi Campbell, "Considering Spiritual Dimensions within Computer-Mediated Communication Studies," *New Media & Society* 7, no. 1 (February 2005): 110–34, 111.

53. See Campbell, "Spiritualizing the Internet," 3.

54. See Barzilai-Nohan and Barzilai, "Cultured Technology: The Internet and Religious Fundamentalism," 26.

55. Christopher Helland, "Online Religion as Lived Religion: Methodological Issues in the Study of Religious Participation on the Internet," *Online Heidelberg Journal of Religions on the Internet*, 1, no. 1 (2005): 1.

56. Sara Johnson, "Religion and the Internet: The Techno-Spiritual in Cyberspace" (December 9, 2001), http://www.umanitoba.ca/faculties/arts/anthropology/courses/478/religion.html (accessed September 14, 2008).

57. See Campbell, "Considering Spiritual Dimensions within Computer-Mediated Communication Studies."

58. Ibid., 5.

59. Ibid., 12.

60. Mia Lövheim, "Young People and the Use of the Internet as Transitional Space," *Online Heidelberg Journal of Religions on the Internet* 1, no. 1 (September 2005): 16.

61. Oliver Krüger, "Discovering the Invisible Internet: Methodological Aspects of Searching Religion on the Internet," *Online Heidelberg Journal of Religions on the Internet*, 1, no. 1 (September 2005): 1–27.

62. See Krüger, "The Internet as Distributor and Mirror of Religious and Ritual Knowledge," 185.

63. Gary R. Bunt, "The Islamic Internet Souq," *Q-News* 325 (November 2000), http://www.lamp.ac.uk/cis/liminal/virtuallyislamic/souqnov2000.html, (accessed September 14, 2008).

64. Gary R. Bunt, *Virtually Islamic: Computer-Mediated Communication and Cyber Islamic Environments* (Cardiff: University of Wales Press, 2000), 6.

65. Gary R. Bunt, *Islam in the Digital Age: E-Jihad, Online Fatwas and Cyber Islamic Environments* (London: Pluto Press, 2003).

66. Peter Van Der Veer, "Secrecy and Publicity in the South Asian Public Arena," in *Public Islam and the Common Good*, ed. Armando Salvatore and Dale Eickelman (Boston: Brill, 2006), 29–51, 49.

67. See Bunt, *Islam in the Digital Age*.

68. Jocelyne Cesari, *When Islam and Democracy Meet: Muslims in Europe and in the United States* (New York: Palgrave Macmillan, 2004).

69. Ibid., 119.

70. See Bunt, *Virtually Islamic*.

71. See Bunt, *Islam in the Digital Age*, 27.

72. Ibid.

73. Ibid.

74. Ibid., 29.

75. Jon Anderson, "Muslim Networks, Muslim Selves in Cyberspace: Islam in the Post-Modern Public Sphere" (October 2001), http://www.mafhoum.com/press3/102S22.htm (accessed September 14, 2008).

76. Ibid.

77. Jon Anderson, "Wiring Up: The Internet Difference for Muslim Networks," in *Muslim Networks: From Hajj to Hip Hop*, ed. Miriam Cooke and Bruce Lawrence (Chapel Hill: University of North Carolina Press, 2005), 252–63.

78. Albercht Hofheinz, "The Internet in the Arab World: Playground for Political Liberalization" (March 2005), 78–96, 85, www.library.tes.de/pdf-files/id/ipg/02941.pdf (accessed September 14, 2008).

79. Jon Anderson, "Internet Islam: New Media of the Islamic Reformation," in *Everyday Life in the Muslim Middle East*, ed. Donna Lee Bowen and Evelyn A. Early (Bloomington: Indiana University Press, 2002), 300–305.

80. See Anderson, "Muslim Networks, Muslim Selves in Cyberspace."

81. Pierre Bourdieu, *Outline of a Theory of Practice* (London: Cambridge University Press, 2007), 40.

82. See Anderson, "Muslim Networks, Muslim Selves in Cyberspace," and Anderson, "Wiring Up."

83. See Anderson, "Wiring Up."

84. See Anderson, "Muslim Networks, Muslim Selves in Cyberspace."

85. Ibid.

86. See Bunt, *Virtually Islamic*.

87. Gary R. Bunt, "Towards an Islamic Information Revolution," *Global Dialogue* 6, no. 1–2 (2004): 107–17.

88. See Bunt, *Virtually Islamic*.

89. See Hofheinz, "The Internet in the Arab World," 91.

90. Musa Maguire, "The Islamic Internet: Authority, Authenticity and Reform," in *Media on the Move: Global Flow and Contra-Flow*, ed. Daya Thussu (London: Routledge, 2006), 237–50.

91. See Bunt, *Virtually Islamic*, 12.

92. See Hofheinz, "The Internet in the Arab World," 78.

93. See Anderson, "Internet Islam."

94. Muhammad Qasim Zaman, *The 'Ulama in Contemporary Islam: Custodians of Change* (Princeton, NJ: Princeton University Press, 2002), 1.

95. Dale Eickelman and Jon Anderson, "Redefining Muslim Publics," in *New Media in the Muslim World: The Emerging Public Sphere*, ed. Dale Eickelman and Jon Anderson (Bloomington: Indiana University Press, 1999),1–18, 10.

96. Omar El-Deeb, interviewed by authors, Cairo, Egypt, December 2006.

97. Mahdy Shaltout, interviewed by authors, Cairo, Egypt, March 2007.

98. Samy Al-Sersawy, interviewed by authors, Cairo, Egypt, January 2007.

99. Ibid.

100. Jon Anderson, "Is the Internet Islam's 'Third Wave' or the End of Civilization?" *United States Institute of Peace* (April 1997), http:www.usip.org/virtualdiplomacy/publications/papers/polrelander.html (accessed September 14, 2008).

101. Ibid.

102. Jon Anderson, "Technology, Media, and the Next Generation in the Middle East," *Middle East Institute* (September 28, 1999), http://www.mafhoum.com/press3/104T45.htm (accessed September 14, 2008).

103. See Eickelman and Anderson, "Redefining Muslim Publics," 12.
104. Jon Alterman, "Transnational Media and Social Change in the Arab World," *Transnational Broadcasting Studies Journal* 2 (Spring 1999): 1–2.
105. See Bunt, *Virtually Islamic.*
106. Peter Mandaville, "Digital Islam: Changing the Boundaries of Religious Knowledge?" *Newsletter of the International Institute for the Study of Islam in the Modern World* (March 1999): 1–23.
107. Ibid.
108. See Cesari, *When Islam and Democracy Meet*," 120.
109. See Papacharissi, "The Virtual Sphere."
110. Nancy Fraser, "Rethinking the Public Sphere," in *Habermas and the Public Sphere*, ed. Craig Calhoun (Cambridge, MA: MIT Press, 1992): 109–42, 123.
111. Todd Gitlin, "Public Sphere or Public Sphericules?" in *Media, Ritual and Identity*, ed. Tamar Liebes and James Curran (London: Routledge, 1998), 168–74, 170.
112. Peter Dahlgren, "The Internet, Public Spheres, and Political Communication: Dispersion and Deliberation," *Political Communication* 22 (April–June 2005): 147–62, 152.
113. Bruce B. Lawrence, "Allah On-Line: The Practice of Global Islam in the Information Age," in *Practicing Religion in the Age of the Media: Explorations of Media, Religion, and Culture*, ed. Stewart M. Hoover and Lynn Schofield Clark (New York: Columbia University Press, 2002), 237–53.
114. Ibid., 240.
115. Augustus Richard Norton, "The New Media, Civic Pluralism and the Slowly Retreating State," in *New Media in the Muslim World: The Emerging Public Sphere*, ed. Dale Eickelman and Jon Anderson (Bloomington: Indiana University Press, 1999), 19–28.
116. See Bunt, *Virtually Islamic.*
117. See Bunt, *Virtually Islamic*, 104–5.
118. See Bunt, *Islam in the Digital Age*, 127.
119. Ibid., 135.
120. Annabelle Sreberny, "Media, Muslims, and the Middle East: A Critical Review Essay," *Political Communication* 19, no. 2 (April 2002), 273–280.
121. See Bunt, *Islam in the Digital Age.*
122. Deborah Wheeler, "The Internet and Youth Subculture in Kuwait," *Journal of Computer Mediated Communication* 8, no. 2 (January 2003): 133–62.
123. See Dawson and Cowan, "Introduction," 2.
124. Göran Larsson, "The Death of a Virtual Muslim Discussion Group: Issues and Methods in Analyzing Religion on the Net," *Online Heidelberg Journal of Religions on the Internet* 1, no. 1 (September 2005).
125. See Lövheim, "Young People and the Use of the Internet as Transitional Space," 2.
126. See Giddens, *The Consequences of Modernity*, 2.
127. Ibid., 3.
128. Mia Lövheim, "Young People, Religious Identity, and the Internet," in *Religion Online: Finding Faith on the Internet*, ed. Lorne Dawson and Douglas Cowan (London: Routledge, 2004), 59–73.
129. See Giddens, *The Consequences of Modernity.*
130. Ibid., 92.
131. See Lövheim, "Young People and the Use of the Internet as Transitional Space."
132. Ibid., 5.

133. Morten T. Hójsgaard, "Cyber-Religion: On the Cutting Edge between the Virtual and the Real," in *Religion and Cyberspace,* ed. Morten T. Hójsgaard and Margit Warburg (London: Routledge, 2005), 50–63, 61.

134. See Slevin, *The Internet and Society,* 175.

135. Ibid.

136. See Lövheim, "Young People and the Use of the Internet as Transitional Space," 17.

137. Alf Linderman and Mia Lövheim, "Internet, Religion and the Attribution of social trust," in *Mediating Religion: Conversations in Media, Religion and Culture,* ed. Jolyon Mitchell and Sophia Marriage (New York: T&T Clark, 2003), 229–40.

138. See Bunt, *Virtually Islamic,* 18–19.

139. Ibid.

140. Mamoun Fandy, "Information Technology, Trust, and Social Change in the Arab World," *Middle East Journal* 54, no. 3 (July 1, 2000): 378–94.

141. Ibid.

142. See Bunt, *Virtually Islamic.*

143. See Fandy, "Information Technology, Trust, and Social Change."

144. Jenny B. White, "Amplifying Trust: Community and Communication in Turkey," in *New Media in the Muslim World: The Emerging Public Sphere,* ed. Dale Eickelman and Jon Anderson (Bloomington: Indiana University Press, 1999), 162–79, 176.

145. John Thompson, *The Media and Modernity: A Social Theory of the Media* (Palo Alto, CA: Stanford University Press, 1995), 196.

146. See Cesari, *When Islam and Democracy Meet,* 119.

147. Jon Anderson and Yves Gonzalez-Quijano, "Technological Mediation and the Emergence of Transnational Muslims Publics," in *Public Islam and the Common Good,* ed. Armando Salvatore and Dale Eickelman (Boston: Brill, 2006), 53–71, 61.

148. Ibid.

149. Pippa Norris, *Digital Divide: Civic Engagement, Information Poverty, and the Internet Worldwide* (London: Cambridge University Press, 2006), 4.

150. Ibid., 66.

151. The Arab Human Development Report: Building a Knowledge Society, *United Nations,* 2003, http://hdr.undp.org/en/reports/regionalreports/arabstates/Arab_States_2003_en.pdf (accessed September 14, 2008).

152. See Hofheinz, "The Internet in the Arab World."

153. See Bunt, *Virtually Islamic,* 132.

154. Cees Hamelink, "The Decent Society and Cyberspace," in *Mediating Religion: Conversations in Media, Religion and Culture,* ed. Jolyon Mitchell and Sophia Marriage (New York: T&T Clark, 2003), 241–56, 243.

3   Is the *Umma* a Public Sphere?

1. Fred Halliday, "The Politics of the *Umma*: States and Community in Islamic Movements," in *Shaping the Current Islamic Reformation,* ed. B.A. Roberson (London: Frank Cass, 2003), 20–41.

2. John L. Esposito, *Islam and Politics,* 2nd ed. (New York: Syracuse University Press, 1987), 4.

3. Tariq Ramadan, *In the Footsteps of the Prophet: Lessons from the Life of Muhammad* (New York: Oxford University Press, 2007), 25.

4. Ibid., 26.
5. Marshall G.S. Hodgson, *The Venture of Islam: Conscience and History in a World Civilization.* Vol. 1, *The Classical Age of Islam* (Chicago: University of Chicago Press, 1974), 248.
6. Jocelyne Cesari, *When Islam and Democracy Meet: Muslims in Europe and in the United States* (New York: Palgrave Macmillan, 2004), 91.
7. Michael Gilsenan, *Recognizing Islam: Religion and Society in the Modern Middle East* (London: I.B. Tauris, 2000), 15–16.
8. Richard Hooker, "Ummah Community," *World Civilizations*, 1996, http://www.wsu.edu/~dee/GLOSSARY/UMMAH.HTM (accessed September 14, 2008).
9. Martin Kramer, "Political Islam," *Washington Papers* 3, no. 73 (Washington, DC: Georgetown University Center for Strategic and International Studies, 1980), 10.
10. See Cesari, *When Islam and Democracy Meet*, 91–92.
11. A. Reza Sheikholeslami, "From Individual Sacrament to Collective Salvation," in *Contemporary Islam: Dynamic, Not Static*, ed. Abdul Aziz Said, Mohammed Abu-Nimer and Meena Sharify-Funk (London: Routledge, 2006), 49–63, 59.
12. Miriam Cooke and Bruce B. Lawrence, "Introduction," in *Muslim Networks: From Hajj to Hip Hop*, ed. Miriam Cooke and Bruce Lawrence (Chapel Hill: University of North Carolina Press, 2005), 1–28, 2.
13. Albert Hourani, *Arabic Thought in the Liberal Age, 1798–1939* (London: Cambridge University Press, 1993), 2.
14. Ibid.
15. Ibid., 19.
16. See Cesari, *When Islam and Democracy Meet*, 91–2.
17. Olivier Roy, *Globalized Islam: The Search for a New Ummah* (New York: Columbia University Press, 2004), 30.
18. John R. Bowen, "Beyond Migration: Islam as a Transnational Public Space," *Journal of Ethnic and Migration Studies* 30, no. 5 (September 2004): 879–94, 882.
19. See Halliday, "The Politics of the *Umma*," 24.
20. "What Is the Muslim Understanding of "Ummah?" *The Christian Broadcasting Network,* http://www.cbn.com/spirituallife/onlinedisciple-ship/understandingislam/What_is_the_Muslim_understanding_of_Ummah.aspx (accessed September 14, 2008).
21. Sohail Inayatullah, "Alternative Futures for the Islamic Ummah," http://www.metafuture.org/Articles/AltFuturesUmmah.htm (accessed September 14, 2008).
22. Jorgen S. Nielsen, "New Centers and Peripheries in European Islam?" in *Shaping the Current Islamic Reformation*, ed. B.A. Roberson (London: Frank Cass, 2003), 64–81, 71.
23. See Hourani, *Arabic Thought in the Liberal Age*, 3.
24. Ibid.
25. See Kramer, *Political Islam*, 10–1.
26. Tanni Haas, "The Public Sphere as a Sphere of Publics," *Journal of Communication* 54, no. 1 (March 2004): 178–84.
27. See Roy, *Globalized Islam.*
28. Riaz Hassan, "Globalization's Challenge to Islam: How to Create One Islamic Community in a Diverse World," *Yale Center for the Study of Globalization*

(April 2003), http://www.yaleglobal.yale.edu/article.print?id=1417 (accessed September 14, 2008).

29. Nancy Fraser, "Rethinking the Public Sphere," in *Habermas and the Public Sphere*, ed. Craig Calhoun (Cambridge, MA: MIT Press, 1992), 109–42, 123.

30. Farhad Kazemi, "Perspectives on Islam and Civil Society," in *Islamic Political Ethics: Civil Society, Pluralism, and Conflict*, ed. Sohail H. Hashmi (Princeton, NJ: Princeton University Press, 2002), 38–53, 45.

31. Homi Bhabha, "Introduction," in *Nation and Narration*, ed. Homi Bhabha (London: Routledge, 1990), 1–7, 1.

32. Ernest Renan, "What Is a Nation?" in *Nation and Narration*, ed. Homi Bhabha (London: Routledge, 1990), 8–22, 19.

33. Dale Eickelman and James Piscatori, *Muslim Politics*, (Princeton, NJ: Princeton University Press, 2004), 48.

34. Ibid., 46.

35. See Roy, *Globalized Islam*, 38.

36. M. Raquibuz Zaman, "Islamic Perspectives on Territorial Boundaries and Autonomy," in *Islamic Political Ethics: Civil Society, Pluralism, and Conflict*, ed. Sohail H. Hashmi (Princeton, NJ: Princeton University Press, 2002), 79–101, 87.

37. Sulayman Nyang, "Religion and the Maintenance of Boundaries: An Islamic View," in *Islamic Political Ethics: Civil Society, Pluralism, and Conflict*, ed. Sohail H. Hashmi (Princeton, NJ: Princeton University Press, 2002), 102–12, 109.

38. Ibid.

39. See Hourani, *Arabic Thought in the Liberal Age*, 1.

40. Ibid.

41. Ibid., 3.

42. See Zaman, "Islamic Perspectives on Territorial Boundaries and Autonomy," 96.

43. Ibid.

44. Ibid., 97.

45. Ibid., 98.

46. See Kramer, *Political Islam*, 10.

47. Mona Abul-Fadl, *Islam and the Middle East: The Aesthetics of a Political Inquiry* (Herndon, VA: International Institute of Islamic Thought, 1990), 24.

48. Ibid.

49. Abdelwahab El-Affendi, "Democracy and Its (Muslim) Critics: An Islamic Alternative to Democracy?" in *Islamic Democratic Discourse: Theory, Debates, and Philosophical Perspectives*, ed. M.A. Muqtader Khan (Lanham, MD: Lexington Books, 2006), 227–56, 246.

50. See Hourani, *Arabic Thought in the Liberal Age*, 19.

51. Ibid., 4.

52. Ibid.

53. Ibid.

54. See Esposito, *Islam and Politics*, 4.

55. Ibid.

56. Ibid., 5.

57. Ibid.

58. Tareq Y. Ismael and Jacqueline S. Ismael, *Government and Politics in Islam* (New York: St. Martin's Press, 1985), 4.

59. Ibid.
60. Ibid.
61. See Hourani, *Arabic Thought in the Liberal Age,* 6–7.
62. Ibid., 7.
63. See Ismael, *Government and Politics in Islam,* 4.
64. See Hourani, *Arabic Thought in the Liberal Age,* 4.
65. See Ismael, *Government and Politics in Islam,* 10.
66. Ibid., 7.
67. Ibid.
68. Ibid., 8.
69. See Hourani, *Arabic Thought in the Liberal Age,* 5.
70. Ibid., 7.
71. Ibid.
72. Ibid.
73. See Hodgson, *The Venture of Islam,* 248.
74. Ibid.
75. See Hourani, *Arabic Thought in the Liberal Age,* 3.
76. See Zaman, "Islamic Perspectives on Territorial Boundaries and Autonomy," 88.
77. Ibid.
78. See Abul-Fadl, *Islam and the Middle East,* 24.
79. Ibid., 25.
80. Ibid.
81. Ibid.
82. See Ismael, *Government and Politics in Islam,* 3.
83. Ibid., 4.
84. Tamara Sonn, "Elements of Government in Classical Islam," in *Islamic Democratic Discourse: Theory, Debates and Philosophical Perspectives,* ed. M.A. Muqtader Khan (Lanham, MD: Lexington Books, 2006), 21–36, 21.
85. Ibid., 33.
86. See Abul-Fadl, *Islam and the Middle East,* 36.
87. Ibid., 35–6.
88. Ibid., 35.
89. Ibid., 36.
90. See Sonn, "Elements of Government in Classical Islam," 33.
91. See Abul-Fadl, *Islam and the Middle East,* 36.
92. Ibid.
93. See Gilsenan, *Recognizing Islam,* 18.
94. Ibid., 14.
95. Ibid., 18.
96. See Esposito, *Islam and Politics,* 30.
97. Ibid.
98. Ibid., 30–31.
99. Ibid., 30.
100. Sohail H. Hashmi, "Interpreting the Islamic Ethics of War and Peace," in *Islamic Political Ethics: Civil Society, Pluralism, and Conflict,* ed. Sohail H. Hashmi (Princeton, NJ: Princeton University Press, 2002), 194–216, 208.
101. See Abul-Fadl, *Islam and the Middle East,* 36–7.
102. Ibid., 37–8.
103. See Kramer, *Political Islam,* 20.
104. Ibid., 21.
105. Ibid.

106. Ibid., 21–2.
107. W. Montgomery Watt, *Islamic Fundamentalism and Modernity* (London: Routledge, 1988), 22.
108. Mahnaz Afkhami and Erika Friedl, "Introduction," in *Muslim Women and the Politics of Participation: Implementing the Beijing Platform*, ed. Mahnaz Afkhami and Erika Friedl (Syracuse, NY: Syracuse University Press, 1997), ix–xx, xii.
109. Ibid., xii–xiii.
110. See Gilsenan, *Recognizing Islam*, 15.
111. Ibid.
112. See Abul-Fadl, *Islam and the Middle East*, 38.
113. Ibid.
114. Ibid.
115. Ibid.
116. John L. Esposito, "Islam and Civil Society," in *Modernizing Islam: Religion in the Public Sphere in Europe and the Middle East*, ed. John L. Esposito and Francois Burgat (New Brunswick, NJ: Rutgers University Press, 2003), 69–100, 98.
117. John L. Esposito, "Introduction: Modernizing Islam and Re-Islamization in Global Perspective," in *Modernizing Islam: Religion in the Public Sphere in Europe and the Middle East*, ed. John L. Esposito and Francois Burgat (New Brunswick, NJ: Rutgers University Press, 2003), 1–14, 4.
118. Ibid.
119. Ibid.
120. Mansoor Moaddel, *Islamic Modernism, Nationalism, and Fundamentalism: Episode and Discourse* (Chicago: University of Chicago Press, 2005), 310–20, 338.
121. Ibid., 339.
122. Ibid.
123. Ibid., 340.
124. Ibid.
125. See Esposito, "Introduction: Modernizing Islam and Re-Islamization in Global Perspective," 1.
126. Connie Caroe Christiansen, "Women's Islamic Activism: Between Self-Practices and Social Reform Efforts," in *Modernizing Islam: Religion in the Public Sphere in Europe and the Middle East*, ed. John L. Esposito and Francois Burgat (New Brunswick, NJ: Rutgers University Press, 2003), 145–65, 165.
127. Andrea B. Rugh, "Reshaping Personal Relations in Egypt," in *Fundamentalism and Society*, ed. Martin E. Marty and R. Scott Appleby (Chicago: University of Chicago Press, 1993), 140–60, 151.
128. See Sonn, "Elements of Government in Classical Islam," 21.
129. Ibid.
130. M.A. Muqtedar Khan, "Preface," in *Islamic Democratic Discourse: Theory, Debates and Philosophical Perspectives*, ed. M.A. Muqtader Khan (Lanham, MD: Lexington Books, 2006), ix–x, ix.
131. Ibid.
132. Ibid.
133. M.A. Muqtedar Khan, "Introduction: The Emergence of an Islamic Democratic Discourse," in *Islamic Democratic Discourse: Theory, Debates and Philosophical Perspectives*, ed. M.A. Muqtader Khan (Lanham, MD: Lexington Books, 2006), xi–xxi, xii.

134. Ibid., xii–xiii.
135. Ibid., xiii.
136. Ibid., xv.
137. Ibid.
138. Samuel Huntington, "The Clash of Civilizations?" *Foreign Affairs 72*, no. 3 (Summer 1993): 22–49.
139. See Khan, "Introduction: The Emergence of an Islamic Democratic Discourse," xiii.
140. Ibid.
141. See Esposito, "Islam and Civil Society," 99.
142. Ibid.
143. Tariq Ramadan, "Ijtihad and Maslaha: The Foundations of Governance," in *Islamic Democratic Discourse: Theory, Debates and Philosophical Perspectives*, ed. M.A. Muqtader Khan (Lanham, MD: Lexington Books, 2006), 3–20, 11.
144. Ibid., 4.
145. Ibid.
146. Ibid.
147. See El-Affendi, "Democracy and Its (Muslim) Critics," 235.
148. Ibid., 234.
149. Ibid.
150. Ibid.
151. Ibid., 235.
152. See Khan, "Introduction," xi.
153. See Gilsenan, *Recognizing Islam*, 7.
154. See Esposito, "Islam and Civil Society," 92–3.
155. Ibid., 93.
156. Ibid., 100.
157. Ibid.
158. Peter Mandaville, *Global Political Islam* (London: Routledge, 2007), 302.
159. Dale F. Eickelman, "Islam and Ethical Pluralism," in *Islamic Political Ethics: Civil Society, Pluralism, and Conflict*, ed. Sohail H. Hashmi (Princeton, NJ: Princeton University Press, 2002), 115–34, 121.
160. Ibid., 115.
161. Ibid.
162. Ibid.
163. Ibid., 129.
164. Ibid.
165. See Esposito, "Islam and Civil Society," 94.
166. Ibid.
167. Ibid.
168. Ibid.
169. Ibid., 95.
170. Muhammad Khalid Masud, "The Scope of Pluralism in Islamic Moral Traditions," in *Islamic Political Ethics: Civil Society, Pluralism, and Conflict*, ed. Sohail H. Hashmi (Princeton, NJ: Princeton University Press, 2002), 135–47, 139.
171. Ibid.
172. Deniz Kandiyoti, "Beyond Beijing: Obstacles and Prospects for the Middle East," in *Muslim Women and the Politics of Participation: Implementing the Beijing Platform*, ed. Mahnaz Afkhami and Erika Friedl (Syracuse, NY: Syracuse University Press, 1997), 3–10, 4.

173. Ibid.
174. See Esposito, *Islam and Politics*, 2.
175. Ibid.
176. Ibid., 2–3.
177. See Kandiyoti, "Beyond Beijing: Obstacles and Prospects for the Middle East," 10.
178. Ibid.
179. Ibid.
180. Ibid.
181. Ibid., 6.
182. Ibid.
183. Ibid.
184. Ibid.
185. See Afkhami and Friedl, "Introduction," xi.
186. Ibid., xiii.
187. Ibid.
188. See Esposito, "Islam and Civil Society," 97.
189. Ibid.
190. See Afkhami and Friedl, "Introduction," xiii.
191. Ibid.
192. Ibid., xiv.
193. Azza M. Karam, "Women, Islamists, and State: Dynamics of Power and Contemporary Feminisms in Egypt," in *Muslim Women and the Politics of Participation: Implementing the Beijing Platform*, ed. Mahnaz Afkhami and Erika Friedl (Syracuse, NY: Syracuse University Press, 1997), 18–28, 24.
194. Ibid.
195. Ibid., 22.
196. Ibid.
197. Ibid., 21.
198. Ibid.
199. Ibid.
200. Ibid., 22.
201. See Esposito, "Introduction: Modernizing Islam and Re-Islamization in Global Perspective," 1.
202. Ibid.
203. See Gilsenan, *Recognizing Islam*, 18–19.
204. Ibid., 19.
205. Ibid.
206. Ibid.
207. Ibid., 20.
208. Sohail H. Hashmi, "Islamic Ethics in International Society," in *Islamic Political Ethics: Civil Society, Pluralism, and Conflict*, ed. Sohail H. Hashmi (Princeton, NJ: Princeton University Press, 2002), 148–72, 148.
209. Ibid.
210. Ibid., 149.
211. Ibid.
212. Ibid.
213. Saskia Witteborn, "The Situated Expression of Arab Collective Identities in the United States," *Journal of Communication* 57 (2007): 556–75, 565.
214. Ibid., 565–6.
215. See Eickelman, "Islam and Ethical Pluralism," 127.

216. Ibid.
217. Marc Lynch, "Dialogue in an Age of Terror," in *Islamic Democratic Discourse: Theory, Debates and Philosophical Perspectives,* ed. M.A. Muqtader Khan (Lanham, MD: Lexington Books, 2006), 193–225, 219.
218. Ibid., 219–20.
219. Bassam Tibi, "War and Peace in Islam," in *Islamic Political Ethics: Civil Society, Pluralism, and Conflict,* ed. Sohail H. Hashmi (Princeton, NJ: Princeton University Press, 2002), 175–93, 189.
220. See Esposito, "Islam and Civil Society," 95.
221. Ibid.
222. Muqtedar Khan, "The Politics, Theory, and Philosophy of Islamic Democracy," in *Islamic Democratic Discourse: Theory, Debates and Philosophical Perspectives,* ed. M.A. Muqtader Khan (Lanham, MD: Lexington Books, 2006), 149–71, 149.
223. Ibid., 149–50.
224. Ibid., 149.
225. Hasan Hanafi, "Alternative Conceptions of Civil Society: A Reflective Islamic Approach," in *Islamic Political Ethics: Civil Society, Pluralism, and Conflict,* ed. Sohail H. Hashmi (Princeton, NJ: Princeton University Press, 2002), 56–76, 74.
226. Ibid.
227. Ibid.
228. See Lynch, "Dialogue in an Age of Terror," 220.
229. Ibid., 205.
230. Ibid., 206.
231. Ibid.
232. See Eickelman, "Islam and Ethical Pluralism," 121.
233. See Esposito, "Islam and Civil Society," 96.
234. Ibid.

4 THE "VIRTUAL *UMMA*": COLLECTIVE IDENTITIES IN CYBERSPACE

1. Benedict Anderson, *Imagined Communities: Reflections on the Origin and Spread of Nationalism* (London: Verso, 2006), 6.
2. Michael Gilsenan, *Recognizing Islam: Religion and Society in the Modern Middle East* (London: I.B. Tauris, 2000), 18.
3. Ibid.
4. Ibid.
5. Dale F. Eickelman, "Islam and Ethical Pluralism," in *Islamic Political Ethics: Civil Society, Pluralism, and Conflict,* ed. Sohail H. Hashmi (Princeton, NJ: Princeton University Press, 2002), 115–34, 122–3.
6. Ibid., 123.
7. Michael Dartnell, "Communicative Practice and Transgressive Global Politics," *First Monday* 10, no. 7, (June 2005), http://www.firstmonday.org/issues/issue10_7/dartnell/index.html (accessed September 14, 2008).
8. Gary R. Bunt, *Virtually Islamic: Computer-Mediated Communication and Cyber Islamic Environments* (Cardiff: University of Wales Press, 2000), 17.
9. Ibid., 12.

10. Ibid.
11. Ibid.
12. Peter Mandaville, *Transnational Muslim Politics: Reimagining the Umma* (London: Routledge, 2001)
13. Ibid., 18.
14. Ibid., 18–19.
15. Ibid., 19.
16. Peter Mandaville, *Global Political Islam* (London: Routledge, 2007), 323.
17. Ibid., 323–4.
18. See Bunt, *Virtually Islamic*, 12.
19. Ahmad Yousif, "IT in the 21st Century: Benefits, Barriers & Concerns of Muslim Scholars," http://www.ifew.com/insight/15039net/infotech.htm (accessed September 14, 2008).
20. Gary Bunt, *The Islamic Internet Souq*, November, 2000, http://www.lamp.ac.uk/cis/liminal/virtuallyislamic/souqnov2000.htm (accessed September 14, 2008).
21. Ibid.
22. "Islam on the Internet," *National Public Radio*, http://www.npr.org/programs/watc/cyberislam/ideology/html (accessed September 14, 2008).
23. See Bunt, *Virtually Islamic*, 107.
24. Deborah Wheeler, "New Media, Globalization and Kuwaiti National Identity," *Middle East Journal* 54, no. 3 (Summer 2000): 432–44, 432.
25. Michael E. Samers, "Diaspora Unbound: Muslim Identity and the Erratic Regulation of Islam in France," *International Journal of Population Geography* 9 (2003): 351–64, 351–2.
26. Ibid.
27. Harry H. Hiller and Tara M. Franz, "New Ties, Old Ties and Lost Ties: The Use of the Internet in Diaspora," *New Media & Society* 6, no. 6 (2004): 731–52.
28. Ibid., 747.
29. Shahram Khosravi, "An Ethnographic Approach to an Online Diaspora," *Newsletter of the International Institute for the Study of Islam in the Modern World* (October, 2000): 13.
30. Karim H. Karim, "Mapping Diasporic Mediascapes," in *The Media of Diaspora*, ed. Karim H. Karim (London: Routledge, 2003), 1–17, 1.
31. Ibid.
32. Ibid., 2.
33. Ibid., 3.
34. Jocelyne Cesari, *When Islam and Democracy Meet: Muslims in Europe and in the United States* (New York: Palgrave Macmillan, 2004).
35. Ibid., 92.
36. Jon Anderson, "Cybernauts of the Arab Diaspora: Electronic Mediation in Transnational Cultural Identities," March 1997, http://www.naba.org.uk/content/articles/diaspora/cybernauts_of_the_arab_diaspora.htm (accessed September 14, 2008).
37. Ibid.
38. See Cesari, *When Islam and Democracy Meet*.
39. Ibid.
40. Peter Mandaville, "Reimagining the *Ummah*? Information Technology and the Changing Boundaries of Political Islam," in *Islam Encountering Globalization*, ed. Ali Mohammadi (London: Routledge, 2002), 61–90, 78.

41. Akbar Ahmed and Hastings Donnan, "Islam in the Age of Postmodernity," in *Islam, Globalization and Postmodernity,* ed. Akbar Ahmed and Hastings Donna (London: Routledge, 2002), 1–20.
42. Chantal Saint-Blancat, "Islam in Diaspora: Between Reterritorialization and Extraterritoriality," *International Journal of Urban and Regional Research* 26, no. 1 (March 2002): 138–51, 142.
43. Dale Eickelman and James Piscatori, *Muslim Politics* (Princeton, NJ: Princeton University Press, 2004), 38.
44. See Mandaville, *Transnational Muslim* Politics, 134.
45. See Mandaville, "Reimagining the *Ummah?*"
46. Ibid., 76.
47. Ibid., 85.
48. See Mandaville, *Transnational Muslim Politics,* 119.
49. Ibid., 151.
50. Lenie Brouwer, "Dutch-Muslims on the Internet: A New Discussion Platform," *Journal of Muslim Affairs* 24, no. 1 (April 2004): 47–55.
51. Shampa Mazumdar and Sanjoy Mazumdar, "The Articulation of Religion in Domestic Space: Rituals in the Immigrant Muslim Home," in *Contesting Rituals: Islam and Practices of Identity-Making,* ed. Pamela J. Stewart and Andrew Strathern (Durham, NC: Carolina Academic Press, 2005), 125–45, 125.
52. Ibid., 126.
53. Peter Mandaville, "Communication and Diasporic Islam: A Virtual *Ummah?*" in *The Media of Diaspora,* ed. Karim H. Karim (London: Routledge, 2003), 135–47.
54. Stuart Hall, "Cultural Identity and Diaspora," in *Identity: Community, Culture, Difference,* ed. J. Rutherford (London: Lawrence and Wishart, 1990), 222–37.
55. Carolina Acosta-Alzuru and Peggy J. Kreshel, "I'm an American Girl…Whatever *That* Means: Girls Consuming Pleasant Company's American Girl Identity," *Journal of Communication* 52, no. 1 (2002): 139–61, 143.
56. Ibid.
57. Stuart Hall, "The Work of Representation," in *Representation: Cultural Representations and Signifying Practices,* ed. Sturat Hall (London: Sage, 1997), 13–74.
58. Ibid.
59. See Acosta-Alzuru and Kreshel, "I'm an American Girl…Whatever *That* Means," 143.
60. Ibid.
61. Saskia Witteborn, "The Situated Expression of Arab Collective Identities in the United States," *Journal of Communication* 57 (2007): 556–75, 559.
62. Ibid.
63. Ibid.
64. Ibid., 571.
65. See Dahlberg, "The Internet and Democratic Discourse."
66. Mohammed Zayani, "Witnessing the Intifada: Al-Jazeera's Coverage of the Palestinian-Israeli Conflict," in *The Al-Jazeera Phenomenon,* ed. Zayani, M. (Boulder, CO: Paradigm, 2005), 171–82, 171–2.
67. Dale Eickelman and James Piscatori, *Muslim Politics* (Princeton, NJ: Princeton University Press, 2004), 15.
68. Jürgen Habermas, *Moral Consciousness and Communicative Action* (Cambridge, MA: MIT Press, 1990).

69. Robert C. Holub, *Jürgen Habermas: Critic in the Public Sphere* (London: Routledge 1991), 15.

70. Muhammad Khalid Masud, "Communicative Action and the Social Construction of Shari'a in Pakistan," in *Religion, Social Practice and Contested Hegemonies: Reconstructing the Public Sphere in Muslim Majority Societies*, ed. Armando Salvatore and Mark LeVine (New York: Palgrave Macmillan, 2005), 155–80, 156.

71. Lincoln Dahlberg, "The Internet and Democratic Discourse: Exploring the Prospects of Online Deliberative Forums Extending the Public Sphere," *Information, Communication & Society* 4, no. 4 (2001): 615–33.

72. John Esposito, "Islam and Civil Society," in *Modernizing Islam: Religion in the Public Sphere in Europe and the Middle East*, ed. John L. Esposito and Francois Burgat (Piscatawy, NJ: Rutgers University Press, 2003), 69–100, 72.

73. Anthony Giddens, *The Consequences of Modernity* (Palo Alto, CA: Stanford University Press, 1990), 92.

74. Tanni Haas, "The Public Sphere as a Sphere of Publics: Rethinking Habermas's Theory of the Public Sphere," *Journal of Communication* 54, no. 1 (2004): 178–84.

75. Seyla Benhabib, "Models of Public Space: Hannah Arendt, the Liberal Tradition, and Jürgen Habermas," in *Habermas and the Public Sphere*, ed. Craig Calhoun (Cambridge, MA: MIT Press, 1992), 73–98, 93.

76. Muhammad Qasim Zaman, "The 'Ulama of Contemporary Islam and Their Conceptions of the Common Good," in *Public Islam and the Common Good*, ed. Armando Salvatore and Dale Eickelman (Boston: Brill, 2006), 129–56, 147.

77. José Casanova, *Public Religions in the Modern World* (Chicago: University of Chicago Press, 1994), 25.

78. Ibid., 6.

79. Ibid., 228.

80. Ernest Gellner, "Foreword," in *Islam, Globalization and Postmodernity*, ed. Akbar Ahmed and Hastings Donna (London: Routledge, 2002), xi–xiv, xi.

81. Dale Eickelman and Jon Anderson, "Redefining Muslim Publics," in *New Media in the Muslim World: The Emerging Public Sphere*, ed. Dale Eickelman and Jon Anderson (Bloomington: Indiana University Press, 1999), 1–18, 5.

82. Ibid., 10.

83. Luke Goode, *Jürgen Habermas: Democracy and the Public Sphere* (London: Pluto Press, 2005), 47.

84. Ibid.

85. See Dahlberg, "The Internet and Democratic Discourse."

86. Craig Calhoun, "Concluding Remarks," in *Habermas and the Public Sphere*, ed. Craig Calhoun (Cambridge, MA: MIT Press, 1992), 462–79, 473.

87. Samuel Huntington, "The Clash of Civilizations?" *Foreign Affairs* 72, no. 3 (Summer 1993): 22–49.

88. Ibid.

89. See Eickelman and Piscatori, *Muslim Politics*, 162.

90. M. Karen Walker, "The Search for Community as Described in the Literature Addressing Identity Discourses in the Arab Public Sphere" (March 2007): 18, http://www.rhetoricalens.info/index.cfm?fuseaction=feature.display&feature_id=24 (accessed July 22, 2008).

91. Ibid.

92. Garbi Schmidt, "The Transnational Umma—Myth or Reality? Examples from the Western Diasporas," *Muslim World* 95 (October 2005): 575–86, 577.

93. Syed Ali, "Why Here, Why Now? Young Muslim Women Wearing *Hijab*," *Muslim World* 95 (October 2005): 515–30, 525.
94. See Cesari, "Where Islam and Democracy Meet," 91.
95. Ibid., 91–2.
96. See Mandaville, "Communication and Diasporic Islam: A Virtual *Ummah*?" 146.
97. Ibid.
98. Ibid.
99. Ibid., 147.
100. Ibid.
101. Marc Lynch, *Voices of the New Arab Public: Iraq, Al-Jazeera, and Middle East Politics Today* (New York: Columbia University Press, 2006), 83.
102. Ibid., 84.
103. Ibid.
104. See Bunt, *Virtually Islamic*, 102.
105. Ibid.
106. Ibid., 102–3.
107. Ibid., 103.
108. See Mandaville, "Communication and Diasporic Islam: A Virtual *Ummah*?" 135.
109. Ibid., 135–6.
110. Ibid., 136.
111. Ibid.
112. Jon Anderson and Yves Gonzalez-Quijano, "Technological Mediation and the Emergence of Transnational Muslims Publics," in *Public Islam and the Common Good*, ed. Armando Salvatore and Dale Eickelman (Boston: Brill, 2006): 53–71, 66.
113. Henry Jenkins, *Convergence Culture: Where Old and New Media Collide* (New York: New York University Press, 2006).
114. Ibid.
115. Alan McKee, *The Public Sphere: An Introduction* (London: Cambridge University Press, 2005), 35.
116. Ibid., 33.
117. Jamillah Karim, "Voices of Faith, Faces of Beauty," in *Muslim Networks: From Hajj to Hip Hop*, ed. Miriam Cooke and Bruce Lawrence (Chapel Hill: University of North Carolina Press, 2005), 169–88, 181.
118. Ibid., 181.
119. Ibid.
120. Ibid., 181–2.
121. See Dahlberg, "The Internet and Democratic Discourse," 625.
122. Ibid.
123. Jon Alterman, "Transnational Media and Social Change in the Arab World," *Transnational Broadcasting Studies Journal* 2 (Spring 1999): 1–2.
124. See Eickelman and Anderson, "Redefining Muslim Publics," 12.
125. Ibid.
126. See Dahlberg, "The Internet and Democratic Discourse," 623.
127. Keith Michael Baker, "Defining the Public Sphere in Eighteenth-Century France: Variations on a Theme by Habermas," in *Habermas and the Public Sphere*, ed. Craig Calhoun (Cambridge, MA: MIT Press, 1992), 181–211, 198.
128. Jürgen Habermas, "Further Reflections on the Public Sphere," in *Habermas and the Public Sphere*, ed. Craig Calhoun (Cambridge, MA: MIT Press, 1992), 421–61, 428.

129. Nancy Fraser, "Rethinking the Public Sphere," in *Habermas and the Public Sphere*, ed. Craig Calhoun (Cambridge, MA: MIT Press, 1992), 109–42, 123.
130. See Karim, "Voices of Faith," 181.
131. See Witteborn, "The Situated Expression of Arab Collective Identities in the United States," 562.
132. Ibid., 561.
133. Ibid., 571.
134. Ibid.
135. Ibid., 572.
136. Ibid., 570.
137. See Mandaville, "Communication and Diasporic Islam: A Virtual *Ummah?*" 136.
138. Ibid., 137.
139. Ibid., 136–7.
140. Ibid., 137.
141. John Thompson, *The Media and Modernity: A Social Theory of the Media* (Palo Alto, CA: Stanford University Press, 1995), 180.
142. See Bunt, *Virtually Islamic*.
143. Ibid., 104–5.
144. See Mandaville, *Transnational Muslim Politics*, 186.
145. See Bunt, *Virtually Islamic*, 132.
146. See Mandaville, "Reimagining the *Ummah?*"

5 ISLAMIC WEBSITES: DIVERGENT IDENTITIES IN CYBERSPACE

1. Carolina Acosta-Alzuru and Peggy J. Kreshel, "I'm an American Girl...Whatever *That* Means: Girls Consuming Pleasant Company's American Girl Identity," *Journal of Communication* 52, no. 1 (2002): 139–61, 143.
2. Ibid., 144.
3. Ibid.
4. Ibid.
5. Ibid., 157.
6. Lincoln Dahlberg, "The Internet and Democratic Discourse: Exploring the Prospects of Online Deliberative Forums Extending the Public Sphere," *Information, Communication & Society* 4, no. 4 (2001): 615–63, 623.
7. Ibid.
8. Ibid., 627.
9. Eileen Barker, "Crossing the Boundary: New Challenges to Religious Authority and Control as a Consequence of Access to the Internet," in *Religion and Cyberspace*, ed. Morten T. Højsgaard and Margit Warburg (London: Routledge, 2005), 67–85, 76.
10. See Dahlberg, "The Internet and Democratic Discourse," 623.
11. Lorne Dawson and Douglas Cowan, "Introduction," in *Religion Online: Finding Faith on the Internet*, ed. Lorne Dawson and Douglas Cowan (London: Routledge, 2004), 1–16, 2.
12. See Dahlberg, "The Internet and Democratic Discourse," 623.
13. Thomas McCarthy, "Practical Discourse: On the Relation of Morality to Politics," in *Habermas and the Public Sphere*, ed. Craig Calhoun (Cambridge, MA: MIT Press, 1992), 51–72, 60.

14. Gary Bunt, *Virtually Islamic* (Cardiff: University of Wales Press, 2000), 1.
15. Ibid., 106.
16. Peter Mandaville, *Transnational Muslim Politics: Reimagining the Umma* (London: Routledge, 2001), 4.
17. Ibid.
18. Ibid.
19. Ibid.
20. See Bunt, *Virtually Islamic*, 35–6.
21. Ibid., 36.
22. Ibid., 35.
23. Ibid.
24. Islamonline website, http://www.islamonline.net/discussione/rules.jsp (accessed September 14, 2008).
25. Jürgen Habermas, *The Structural Transformation of the Public Sphere: An Inquiry into a Category of Bourgeois Society* (Cambridge, MA: MIT Press, 1989).
26. John L. Esposito, "Islam and Civil Society," in *Modernizing Islam: Religion in the Public Sphere in Europe and the Middle East,* ed. John L. Esposito and Francois Burgat (New Brunswick, NJ: Rutgers University Press, 2003), 69–100, 95.
27. Jürgen Habermas, *Moral Consciousness and Communicative Action* (Cambridge, MA: MIT Press, 1990), 58.
28. Marc Lynch, "Dialogue in an Age of Terror," in *Islamic Democratic Discourse,* ed. M.A. Muqtader Khan (Lanham: MD, Lexington Books, 2006), 193–220, 220.
29. Ibid., 206.
30. Ibid.
31. See Dahlberg, "The Internet and Democratic Discourse," 623.
32. Ibid.
33. Karim H. Karim, "Mapping Diasporic Mediascapes," in *The Media of Diaspora,* ed. Karim H. Karim (London: Routledge, 2003), 1–17, 9.
34. Benjamin R. Barber, *Jihad vs. McWorld* (New York: Times Books, 1995).
35. See Acosta-Alzuru and Kreshel, "I'm an American Girl…Whatever *That* Means," 156.
36. Olivier Roy, *Globalized Islam: The Search for a New Ummah* (New York: Columbia University Press, 2004), 21.
37. Ibid., 20.
38. Ibid.
39. Peter Mandaville, "Communication and Diasporic Islam: A virtual ummah?" in *The Media of Diaspora,* ed. Karim H. Karim (London: Routledge, 2003), 135–47, 136.
40. Ibid., 137.
41. See Bunt, *Virtually Islamic*, 2.
42. Peter Mandaville, "Digital Islam: Changing the Boundaries of Religious Knowledge?" *Newsletter of the International Institute for the Study of Islam in the Modern World* (March, 1999): 1–23.
43. Dale Eickelman and James Piscatori, *Muslim Politics* (Princeton, NJ: Princeton University Press, 2004), 38.
44. See Roy, *Globalized Islam*, 154.
45. Ibid.
46. Gary R. Bunt, *Islam in the Digital Age: E-Jihad, Online Fatwas and Cyber Islamic Environments* (London: Pluto Press, 2003), 135.
47. Ibid.

48. Annabelle Sreberny, "Media, Muslims, and the Middle East: A Critical Review Essay," *Political Communication* 19, no. 2 (April 2002): 273–80.
49. Sheikh Samy Al-Sersawy, interviewed by authors, July 2008.
50. See, Esposito, "Islam and Civil Society," 94.
51. Ibid., 95.
52. Ibid., 97.
53. Saskia Witteborn, "The Situated Expression of Arab Collective Identities in the United States," *Journal of Communication* 57, no. 3 (September 2007): 556–75, 562.
54. Sahar Khamis, "Mulitple Literacies, Multiple Identities: Egyptian Rural Women's Readings of Televised Literacy Campaigns," in *Women and Media in the Middle East: Power Through Self-Expression,* ed. Naomi Sakr (London: I.B. Tauris, 2004), 89–108, 96.
55. Ibid.
56. Valerie Walkerdine, "Some Day My Prince Will Come: Young Girls and the Preparation for Adolescent Sexuality," in *Gender and Generation,* ed. Angela McRobbie and Mira Nava (London: Macmillan, 1984), 183–4.
57. Ronald L. Jackson, "Introduction: Theorizing and Analyzing the Nexus between Cultural and Gendered Identities and the Body," *Communication Quarterly* 50, no. 3 (2002): 245–50, 245.
58. Nancy Fraser, "Rethinking the Public Sphere: A Contribution to the Critique of Actually Existing Democracy," in *Habermas and the Public Sphere,* ed. Craig Calhoun (Cambridge, MA: MIT Press, 1992), 109–42, 124–5.
59. Ibid., 137.
60. See McCarthy, "Practical Discourse: On the Relation of Morality to Politics," 65.
61. Mohammed Zayani, "Witnessing the Intifada: Al-Jazeera's Coverage of the Palestinian-Israeli Conflict," in *The Al-Jazeera Phenomenon,* ed. Zayani, M. (Boulder, CO: Paradigm, 2005), 171–82, 173.
62. See McCarthy, "Practical Discourse: On the Relation of Morality to Politics," 60.
63. Ibid., 62.
64. Jürgen Habermas, "Further Reflections on the Public Sphere," in *Habermas and the Public Sphere,* ed. Craig Calhoun (Cambridge, MA: MIT Press, 1992), 421–61, 440.
65. Seyla Benhabib, "Models of Public Space: Hannah Arendt, the Liberal Tradition, and Jürgen Habermas," in *Habermas and the Public Sphere,* ed. Craig Calhoun (Cambridge, MA: MIT Press, 1992), 73–98, 88.
66. B.A. Roberson, "The Shaping of the Current Islamic Reformation," in *Shaping the Current Islamic Reformation,* ed. B.A. Roberson (London: Frank Cass, 2003), 1–19, 9.
67. See Zayani, "Witnessing the Intifada," 160.
68. See Habermas, *Moral Consciousness and Communicative Action,* 58.
69. See Esposito, "Islam and Civil Society," 92.
70. Ibid., 99.
71. See Witteborn, "The Situated Expression of Arab Collective Identities in the United States," 567.
72. Ibid., 565, 572.
73. See Mandaville, *Transnational Muslim Politics: Reimagining the Umma,* 10.
74. Ibid.
75. Ibid., 10–11.
76. Ibid., 11.
77. Ibid., 9.

78. Ibid.
79. See Witteborn, "The Situated Expression of Arab Collective Identities in the United States," 557.
80. Ibid., 558.
81. Ibid.
82. Ibid., 566.
83. Ibid., 572.
84. Ibid.
85. See Bunt, *Virtually Islamic*, 36.

6   VIRTUAL ISLAMIC DISCOURSES: PLATFORMS FOR CONSENSUS OR SITES OF CONTENTION?

1. Saskia Witteborn, "The Situated Expression of Arab Collective Identities in the United States," *Journal of Communication* 57, no. 3 (September 2007): 556–75, 571.
2. Ibid.
3. Ibid., 562.
4. Jürgen Habermas, *The Structural Transformation of the Public Sphere: An Inquiry into a Category of Bourgeois Society* (Cambridge, MA: MIT Press, 1989).
5. Lincoln Dahlberg, "The Internet and Democratic Discourse: Exploring the Prospects of Online Deliberative Forums Extending the Public Sphere," *Information, Communication & Society* 4, no. 4 (2001): 615–33.
6. Ibid., 622.
7. Ibid., 623.
8. Peter Mandaville, "Communication and Diasporic Islam: A Virtual Ummah?" in *The Media of Diaspora*, ed. Karim H. Karim (London: Routledge, 2003), 135–47, 137.
9. Henry Jenkins, *Convergence Culture: Where Old and New Media Collide* (New York: New York University Press, 2006), 2.
10. Ibid., 3.
11. Gerard A. Hauser, *Vernacular Voices: The Rhetoric of Publics and Public Spheres* (Columbia: University of South Carolina, 1999), 63.
12. Ibid.
13. Alan McKee, *The Public Sphere: An Introduction* (London: Cambridge University Press, 2005).
14. Ibid., 145.
15. Nancy Fraser, "Rethinking the Public Sphere" in *Habermas and the Public Sphere*, ed. Craig Calhoun (Cambridge, MA: MIT Press, 1992), 109–42, 115.
16. Ibid., 123.
17. See Dahlberg, "The Internet and Democratic Discourse," 625.
18. Ibid.
19. Ibid., 623.
20. Zizi Papacharissi, "The Virtual Sphere: The Internet as a Public Sphere," *New Media & Society* 1, no. 9 (2002): 9–27.
21. Dale F. Eickelman and Armando Salvatore, "The Public Sphere and Muslim Identities," *European Journal of Sociology* 43, no. 1 (2002): 92–115, 107.

22. Ibid.
23. M. Karen Walker, "The Search for Community as Described in the Literature Addressing Identity Discourses in the Arab Public Sphere," 23, http://www.rhetoricalens.info/index.cfm?fuseaction=feature.display&feature_id=24 (accessed June 2, 2008).
24. Gary R. Bunt, *Virtually Islamic: Computer-Mediated Communication and Cyber Islamic Environments* (Cardiff: University of Wales Press, 2000).
25. Hauser, *Vernacular Voices,* 77–80.
26. Ibid.
27. Ibid., 46.
28. Ibid., 51.
29. Ibid., 53.
30. Mohammed Abu-Nimer, "Framework for Nonviolence and Peacebuilding in Islam," in *Contemporary Islam: Dynamic, Not Static,* ed. Abdul Aziz Said, Mohammed Abu-Nimer, and Meena Sharify-Funk (London: Routledge, 2006), 132–72.
31. Sheikh Samy Al-Sersawy, interviewed by authors via telephone, July 2008.
32. Peter Mandaville, *Transnational Muslim Politics: Reimagining the Umma* (London: Routledge, 2001), 134.
33. Ibid., 183.
34. Dale Eickelman, "The Coming Transformation of the Muslim World," *Middle East Review of International Affairs* 3, no. 3 (September 1999) http://www.biu.ac.il/SOC/besa/meria/journal/1999/issue3/jb3n3a8.html (accessed September 14, 2008).
35. Islamonline discussion forum, http://www.islamonline.net/discussiona/message.jspa?messageID=101647&tstart=15 (accessed September 14, 2008).
36. See Al-Sersawy, personal interview.
37. See Dahlberg, "The Internet and Democratic Discourse," 623.

BIBLIOGRAPHY

Abdel Gawad, A. Personal Interview, Cairo, Egypt. February, 2011.

Abu-Nimer, Mohammed. "Framework for Nonviolence and Peacebuilding in Islam." In *Contemporary Islam: Dynamic, Not Static*, edited by Abdul Aziz Said, Mohammed Abu-Nimer, and Meena Sharify-Funk, 132–72. London: Routledge, 2006.

Abul-Fadl, Mona. *Islam and the Middle East: The Aesthetics of a Political Inquiry.* Herndon, VA: International Institute of Islamic Thought, 1990.

Acosta-Alzuru, Carolina, and Peggy J. Kreshel. "I'm an American Girl...Whatever That Means: Girls Consuming Pleasant Company's American Girl Identity." *Journal of Communication* 52, no. 1 (2002): 139–61.

Afkhami, Mahnaz, and Erika Friedl. "Introduction." In *Muslim Women and the Politics of Participation: Implementing the Beijing Platform*, ix–xx. Syracuse, NY: Syracuse University Press, 1997.

Ahmed, Akbar, and Hastings Donnan. "Islam in the Age of Postmodernity." In *Islam, Globalization and Postmodernity*, 1–20. London: Routledge, 2002.

Al-Anani, K. "Brotherhood Bloggers: A New Generation Voices Dissent." *Arab Insight: Bringing Middle Eastern Perspectives to Washington* 2, no. 1 (Winter 2008): 29–38.

Al-Gannoushi, R. Personal Interview, Doha, Qatar. March, 2011.

Ali, Syed. "Why Here, Why Now? Young Muslim Women Wearing *Hijab*." *Muslim World* 95 (October 2005): 515–30.

Alterman, Jon. "Transnational Media and Social Change in the Arab World." *Transnational Broadcasting Studies Journal* 2 (Spring 1999): 1–2.

Anderson, Benedict. *Imagined Communities: Reflections on the Origin and Spread of Nationalism.* London: Verso, 2006.

Anderson, Jon W. "'Cybarites,' Knowledge Workers and New Creoles on the Superhighway." *Anthropology Today* 11, no. 4 (August 1995): 13–15.

———. "Cybernauts of the Arab Diaspora: Electronic Mediation in Transnational Cultural Identities," March 1997, http://www.naba.org.uk/content/articles/diaspora/cybernauts_of_the_arab_diaspora.htm (accessed September 14, 2008).

———. "Internet Islam: New Media of the Islamic Reformation." In *Everyday Life in the Muslim Middle East*, edited by Donna Lee Bowen and Evelyn A. Early, 300–305. Bloomington: Indiana University Press, 2002.

———. "Is the Internet Islam's 'Third Wave' or the End of Civilization?" April 1997, http://www.usip.org/virtualdiplomacy/publications/papers/polrelander.html (accessed September 14, 2008).

———. "Muslim Networks, Muslim Selves in Cyberspace: Islam in the Post-modern Public Sphere," NMIT Working Papers, 2001, http://www.mafhoum.com/press3/102S22.htm (accessed September 14, 2008).

———. "New Media, New Publics: Reconfiguring the Public Sphere of Islam." *Social Research* 70, no. 3 (Fall 2003): 887–906.

———. "Technology, Media, and the Next Generation in the Middle East," September 28, 1999, http://www.mafhoum.com/press3/104T45.htm (accessed September 14, 2008).

———. "Wiring Up: The Internet Difference for Muslim Networks." In *Muslim Networks: From Hajj to Hip Hop*, edited by Miriam Cooke and Bruce Lawrence, 252–63. Chapel Hill: University of North Carolina Press, 2005.

Anderson, Jon W., and Yves Gonzalez-Quijano. "Technological Mediation and the Emergence of Transnational Muslims Publics." In *Public Islam and the Common Good*, edited by Armando Salvatore and Dale F. Eickelman, 53–71. Boston: Brill, 2006.

Arab Human Development Report: Building a Knowledge Society, 2003, http://hdr.undp.org/en/reports/regionalreports/arabstates/Arab_States_2003_en.pdf (accessed September 14, 2008).

Ayoob, Mohammed. "Deciphering Islam's Multiple Voices: Intellectual Luxury or Strategic Necessity?" *Middle East Policy* 12, no. 3 (2005): 79–90.

Barber, Benjamin R. *Jihad vs. McWorld*. New York: Times Books, 1995.

Barker, Eileen. "Crossing the Boundary: New Challenges to Religious Authority and Control as a Consequence of Access to the Internet." In *Religion and Cyberspace*, edited by Morten T. Hójsgaard and Margit Warburg, 67–85. London: Routledge, 2005.

Barzilai-Nohan, Karine, and Gad Barzilai. "Cultured Technology: The Internet and Religious Fundamentalism." *Information Society* 21 (2005): 25–40.

Benhabib, Seyla. "Models of Public Space: Hannah Arendt, the Liberal Tradition, and Jürgen Habermas." In *Habermas and the Public Sphere*, edited by Craig Calhoun, 73–98. Cambridge, MA: MIT Press, 1992.

Bhabha, Homi. "Introduction." In *Nation and Narration*, 1–7. London: Routledge, 1990.

Bohman, James. "Expanding Dialogue: The Internet, the Public Sphere and Prospects for Transnational Democracy." In *After Habermas: New Perspectives on the Public Sphere*, edited by Nick Crossley and John Michael Roberts, 131–55. Oxford: Blackwell, 2004.

Böttcher, Annabelle. "Sunni and Shi'i Networking in the Middle East." In *Shaping the Current Islamic Reformation*, edited by B.A. Roberson, 42–63. London: Frank Cass, 2004.

Bourdieu, Pierre. *Outline of a Theory of Practice*. London: Cambridge University Press, 2007.

Bowen, John R. "Beyond Migration: Islam as a Transnational Public Space." *Journal of Ethnic and Migration Studies* 30, no. 5 (September 2004): 879–94.

Brouwer, Lenie. "Dutch-Muslims on the Internet: A New Discussion Platform." *Journal of Muslim Affairs* 24, no. 1 (April 2004): 37–55.

Bunt, Gary R. *The Islamic Internet Souq*, http://www.lamp.ac.uk/cis/liminal/virtuallyislamic/souqnov2000.html (accessed September 14, 2008).

———. *Islam in the Digital Age: E-Jihad, Online Fatwas and Cyber Islamic Environments*. London: Pluto Press, 2003.

———. "Towards an Islamic Information Revolution." *Global Dialogue* 6, nos. 1–2 (2004): 107–17.

———. *Virtually Islamic: Computer-Mediated Communication and Cyber Islamic Environments*. Cardiff: University of Wales, 2000.

Calhoun, Craig. "Introduction." In *Habermas and the Public Sphere*, 1–48. Cambridge, MA: MIT Press, 1992.

Campbell, Heidi. "Considering Spiritual Dimensions within Computer-Mediated Communication Studies." *New Media & Society* 7, no. 1 (February 2005): 110–34.

———. *Exploring Religious Community Online: We Are One in the Network.* New York: Peterlang, 2005.

———. "Spiritualizing the Internet: Uncovering Discourses and Narratives of Religious Internet Usage." *Online Heidelberg Journal of Religions on the Internet* 1, no. 1 (September 2005).

Casanova, José. *Public Religions in the Modern World.* Chicago: University of Chicago Press, 1994.

Cesari, Jocelyne. *When Islam and Democracy Meet: Muslims in Europe and in the United States.* New York: Palgrave Macmillan, 2004.

Christiansen, Connie Caroe. "Women's Islamic Activism: Between Self-Practices and Social Reform Efforts." In *Modernizing Islam: Religion in the Public Sphere in Europe and the Middle East,* edited by John L. Esposito and Francois Burgat, 145–65. Piscataway, NJ: Rutgers University Press, 2003.

Cooke, Miriam, and Bruce Lawrence. "Introduction." In *Muslim Networks: From Hajj to Hip Hop,* 1–28. Chapel Hill: University of North Carolina Press, 2005.

Curran, James. "Rethinking the Media as a Public Sphere." In *Communication and Citizenship: Journalism and Public Sphere,* edited by Peter Dahlgren and Colin Sparks, 27–57. London: Routledge, 1997.

Dahlberg, Lincoln. "The Internet and Democratic Discourse: Exploring the Prospects of Online Deliberative Forums Extending the Public Sphere." *Information, Communication & Society* 4, no. 4 (2001): 615–33.

Dahlgren, Peter. "The Internet, Public Spheres, and Political Communication: Dispersion and Deliberation." *Political Communication* 22 (April–June 2005): 147–62.

———. "Introduction." In *Communication and Citizenship: Journalism and Public Sphere,* edited by Peter Dahlgren and Colin Sparks, 1–24. London: Routledge, 1997.

———. "The Public Sphere and the Net: Structure, Space, and Communication." In *Mediated Politics: Communication in the Future of Democracy,* edited by W. Lance Bennett and Robert M. Entman, 33–55. London: Cambridge University Press, 2001.

Dartnell, Michael. "Communicative Practice and Transgressive Global Politics." *First Monday* 10, no. 7 (June 2005).

Dawson, Lorne, and Douglas Cowan. "Introduction." In *Religion Online: Finding Faith on the Internet,* 1–16. London: Routledge, 2004.

Dow, Bonnie J., and Celeste M. Condit. "The State of the Art in Feminist Scholarship in Communication." *Journal of Communication* 55, no. 3 (2005): 448–78.

Eickelman, Dale F. "Clash of Cultures? Intellectuals, Their Publics, and Islam." In *Intellectuals in the Modern Islamic World: Transmission, Transformation, Communication,* edited by Stéphan Dudoigan, Komatsu Hisao, and Kosugi Yasushi, 289–304. London: Routledge, 2006.

———. "The Coming Transformation of the Muslim World." *Middle East Review of International Affairs* 3, no. 3 (September 1999): 16–20.

———. "Islam and Ethical Pluralism." In *Islamic Political Ethics: Civil Society, Pluralism, and Conflict,* edited by Sohail H. Hashmi, 115–34. Princeton, NJ: Princeton University Press, 2002.

Eickelman, Dale F., and Armando Salvatore. "The Public Sphere and Muslim Identities." *European Journal of Sociology* 43, no. 1 (2002): 92–115.

Eickelman, Dale F., and James Piscatori. *Muslim Politics*. Princeton, NJ: Princeton University Press, 2004.

Eickelman, Dale F., and Jon Anderson. "Preface." In *New Media in the Muslim World: The Emerging Public Sphere*, vii–ix. Bloomington: Indiana University Press, 1999.

———. "Redefining Muslim Publics." In *New Media in the Muslim World: The Emerging Public Sphere*, 2nd ed., 1–18. Bloomington: Indiana University Press, 2003.

Eisenstadt, Shmuel N. "Concluding Remarks: Public Sphere, Civil Society, and Political Dynamics in Islamic Societies." In *The Public Sphere in Muslim Societies*, edited by Miriam Hoester, Shmuel Eisenstadt, and Nehemia Levitzion, 139–61. Albany: State University of New York Press, 2002.

El-Affendi, Abdelwahab. "Democracy and Its (Muslim) Critics: An Islamic Alternative to Democracy?" In *Islamic Democratic Discourse: Theory, Debates, and Philosophical Perspectives*, edited by M.A. Muqtader Khan, 227–56. Lanham, MD: Lexington Books, 2006.

Esposito, John L. "Introduction: Modernizing Islam and Re-Islamization in Global Perspective." In *Modernizing Islam: Religion in the Public Sphere in Europe and the Middle East*, edited by John L. Esposito and Francois Burgat, 1–14. Piscataway, NJ: Rutgers University Press, 2003.

———. "Islam and Civil Society." In *Modernizing Islam: Religion in the Public Sphere in Europe and the Middle East*, edited by John L. Esposito and Francois Burgat, 69–100. Piscataway, NJ: Rutgers University Press, 2003.

———. *Islam and Politics*, 2nd ed. New York: Syracuse University Press, 1987.

Fairclough, Norman. *Analyzing Discourse: Textual Analysis for Social Research*. London: Routledge, 2003.

Fandy, Mamoun. "Information Technology, Trust, and Social Change in the Arab World." *Middle East Journal* 54, no. 3 (July 2000): 378–94.

Fernback, Jan. "The Individual with the Collective: Virtual Ideology and the Realization of Collective Principles." In *Virtual Culture: Identity & Communication in Cybersociety*, edited by Steven G. Jones, 36–54. London: Sage, 2002.

———. "There Is a There There: Notes toward a Definition of Cybercommunity." In *Doing Internet Research: Critical Issues and Methods for Examining the Net*, edited by Steve Jones, 203–20. London: Sage, 1999.

Foreign Policy, July–August 2008, 54–7.

Fraser, Nancy. "Rethinking the Public Sphere." In *Habermas and the Public Sphere*, edited by Craig Calhoun, 109–42. Cambridge, MA: MIT Press, 1992.

Gaffney, Patrick D. *The Prophet's Pulpit: Islamic Preaching in Contemporary Egypt*. Berkeley: California University Press, 1994.

Gellner, Ernest. "Foreword." In *Islam, Globalization and Postmodernity*, edited by Akbar Ahmed and Hastings Donna, xi–xiv. London: Routledge, 2002.

Gerholm, Tomas. "Two Muslim Intellectuals in the Postmodern West: Akbar Ahmed and Ziauddin Sardar." In *Islam, Globalization and Postmodernity*, edited by Akbar Ahmed and Donna Hastings, 1–20. London: Routledge, 2002.

Giddens, Anthony. *The Consequences of Modernity*. Palo Alto, CA: Stanford University Press, 1990.

Gilsenan, Michael. *Recognizing Islam: Religion and Society in the Modern Middle East*. London: I.B. Tauris, 2000.

Gitlin, Todd. "Public Sphere or Public Sphericules?" In *Media, Ritual and Identity*, edited by Tamar Liebes and James Curran, 168–74. London: Routledge, 1998.

Goode, Luke. *Jürgen Habermas: Democracy and the Public Sphere*. London: Pluto Press, 2005.

Gowing, N. "Time to Move On: New Media Realities—New Vulnerabilities of Power." *Media, War & Conflict* 4, no. 1 (April 2011): 13–19.

Gunaratne, Shelton A. "Public Sphere and Communicative Rationality: Interrogating Habermas's Eurocentrism." *Journalism Communication Monographs* 8, no. 2 (Summer 2006): 94–156.

Haas, Tanni. "The Public Sphere as a Sphere of Publics." *Journal of Communication* 54, no. 1 (March 2004): 178–84.

Habermas, Jürgen. *Moral Consciousness and Communicative Action.* Cambridge, MA: MIT Press, 1990.

———. *The Theory of Communicative Action.* Vol. 1, *Reason and the Rationalization of Society.* Boston: Beacon Press, 1984.

———. *The Structural Transformation of the Public Sphere: An Inquiry into a Category of Bourgeois Society.* Cambridge, MA: MIT Press, 1989.

Hall, Stuart. "Cultural Identity and Diaspora." In *Identity: Community, Culture, Difference,* edited by Jonathan Rutherford, 222–37. London: Lawrence and Wishart, 1990.

———. "Introduction." In *Paper Voices: The Popular Press and Social Change, 1935–1965,* edited by A.C.H. Smith, 11–24. London: Chatto and Windus, 1975.

———. "The Work of Representation." In *Representation: Cultural Representations and Signifying Practices,* 13–74. London: Sage, 1997.

Halliday, Fred. "The Politics of the *Umma*: States and Community in Islamic Movements." In *Shaping the Current Islamic Reformation,* edited by B.A. Roberson, 20–41. London: Frank Cass, 2003.

Hamelink, Cees. "The Decent Society and Cyberspace." In *Mediating Religion: Conversations in Media, Religion and Culture,* edited by Jolyon Mitchell and Sophia Marriage, 241–56. New York: T&T Clark, 2003.

Hanafi, Hasan. "Alternative Conceptions of Civil Society: A Reflective Islamic Approach." In *Islamic Political Ethics: Civil Society, Pluralism, and Conflict,* edited by Sohail H. Hashmi, 56–75. Princeton, NJ: Princeton University Press, 2002.

Harrison, Teresa M., and Timothy Stephen. "Researching and Creating Community Networks." In *Doing Internet Research: Critical Issues and Methods for Examining the Net,* edited by Steve Jones, 221–42. London: Sage, 1999.

Hashmi, Sohail H. "Islamic Ethics in International Society." In *Islamic Political Ethics: Civil Society, Pluralism, and Conflict,* edited by Sohail H. Hashmi, 148–72. Princeton, NJ: Princeton University Press, 2002.

Hassan, Riaz. "Globalization's Challenge to Islam: How to Create One Islamic Community in a Diverse World," April 2003, http://www.yaleglobal.yale.edu/article.print?id=1417 (accessed September 14, 2008).

Hauser, Gerard A. *Vernacular Voices: The Rhetoric of Publics and Public Spheres.* Columbia: University of South Carolina, 1999.

Helland, Christopher. "Online Religion as Lived Religion: Methodological Issues in the Study of Religious Participation on the Internet." *Online Heidelberg Journal of Religions on the Internet* 1, no. 1 (2005).

———. "Popular Religion and the World Wide Web: A Match Made in (Cyber) Heaven." In *Religion Online: Finding Faith on the Internet,* edited by Lorne Dawson and Douglas Cowan, 23–36. London: Routledge, 2004.

Hiller, Harry H., and Tara M. Franz. "New Ties, Old Ties and Lost Ties: The Use of the Internet in Diaspora." *New Media & Society* 6, no. 6 (2004): 731–52.

Hirschkind, Charles. "Civic Virtue and Religious Reason: An Islamic Counterpublic." *Cultural Anthropology* 16, no. 1 (2001): 3–34.

Hodgson, Marshall G.S. *The Venture of Islam: Conscience and History in a World Civilization.* Vol. 1, *The Classical Age of Islam.* Chicago: University of Chicago Press, 1974.

Hofheinz, Albercht. "The Internet in the Arab World: Playground for Political Liberalization," March 2005, http://library.fes.de/pdf-files/id/ipg/02941.pdf (accessed September 14, 2008).

Hójsgaard, Morten T. "Cyber-Religion: On the Cutting Edge between the Virtual and the Real." In *Religion and Cyberspace,* edited by Morten T. Hójsgaard and Margit Warburg, 50–63. London: Routledge, 2005.

Hójsgaard, Morten T., and Margit Warburg. "Introduction." In *Religion and Cyberspace,* 1–12. London: Routledge, 2005.

Holub, Robert C. *Jürgen Habermas: Critic in the Public Sphere.* London: Routledge, 1991.

Hooker, Richard. "Ummah Community." *World Civilizations* 1996, http://www.wsu.edu/~dee/GLOSSARY/UMMAH.HTM (accessed September 14, 2008).

Hoover, Stewart M. "Religion, Media and Identity: Theory and Method in Audience Research on Religion and Media." In *Mediating Religion: Conversations in Media, Religion and Culture,* edited by Jolyon Mitchell and Sophia Marriage, 9–19. New York: T&T Clark, 2003.

Hoover, Stewart M., and Knut Lundby. *Rethinking Media, Religion, and Culture.* London: Sage, 1997.

Hourani, Albert. *Arabic Thought in the Liberal Age, 1798–1939.* London: Cambridge University Press, 1993.

Huntington, Samuel. "The Clash of Civilizations?" *Foreign Affairs* 72, no. 3 (Summer 1993): 22–49.

Inayatullah, Sohail. "Alternative Futures for the Islamic Ummah," http://www.metafuture.org/Articles/AltFuturesUmmah.htm (accessed September 14, 2008).

"Islam on the Internet," http://www.npr.org/programs/watc/cyberislam/community.html (accessed September 14, 2008).

Ismael, Tareq Y., and Jacqueline S. Ismael. *Government and Politics in Islam.* New York: St. Martin's Press, 1985.

Jackson, Ronald L. "Introduction: Theorizing and Analyzing the Nexus between Cultural and Gendered Identities and the Body." *Communication Quarterly* 50, no. 3 (2002): 245–50.

Jenkins, Henry. *Convergence Culture: Where Old and New Media Collide.* New York: New York University Press, 2006.

Johnson, Sara. "Religion and the Internet: The Techno-Spiritual in Cyberspace," December 2002, http://www.umanitoba.ca/faculties/arts/anthropology/courses/478/religion.html (accessed September 14, 2008).

Kandiyoti, Deniz. "Beyond Beijing: Obstacles and Prospects for the Middle East." In *Muslim Women and the Politics of Participation: Implementing the Beijing Platform,* edited by Mahnaz Afkhami and Erika Friedl, 3–10. Syracuse, NY: Syracuse University Press, 1997.

Karam, Azza M. "Women, Islamists, and State: Dynamics of Power and Contemporary Feminisms in Egypt." In *Muslim Women and the Politics of Participation: Implementing the Beijing Platform,* edited by Mahnaz Afkhami and Erika Friedl, 18–28. Syracuse, NY: Syracuse University Press, 1997.

Karim, Jamillah. "Voices of Faith, Faces of Beauty." In *Muslim Networks: From Hajj to Hip Hop,* edited by Miriam Cooke and Bruce Lawrence, 169–88. Chapel Hill: University of North Carolina Press, 2005.

Karim, Karim H. "Mapping Diasporic Mediascapes." In *The Media of Diaspora*, 1–17. London: Routledge, 2003.

Khamis, Sahar. "Multiple Literacies, Multiple Identities: Egyptian Rural Women's Readings of Televised Literacy Campaigns." In *Women and Media in the Middle East: Power through Self-Expression*, edited by Naomi Sakr, 89–108. London: I.B. Tauris, 2004.

———. "The Role of New Arab Satellite Channels in Fostering Intercultural Dialogue: Can Al Jazeera English Bridge the Gap?" In *New Media and the NewMiddle East*, edited by Philip Seib, 39–51. New York: Palgrave Macmillan, 2007.

Khan, M.A. Muqtedar. "Introduction: The Emergence of an Islamic Democratic Discourse." In *Islamic Democratic Discourse: Theory, Debates and Philosophical Perspectives*, xi–xxi. Lanham, MD: Lexington Books, 2006.

———. "The Politics, Theory, and Philosophy of Islamic Democracy." In *Islamic Democratic Discourse: Theory, Debates and Philosophical Perspectives*, 149–71. Lanham, MD: Lexington Books, 2006.

———. "Preface." In *Islamic Democratic Discourse: Theory, Debates and Philosophical Perspectives*, ix–x. Lanham, MD: Lexington Books, 2006.

Khatib, Lina. "Communicating Islamic Fundamentalism as Global Citizenship." *Journal of Communication Inquiry* 27, no. 4 (2003): 389–409.

Khosravi, Shahram. "An Ethnographic Approach to an Online Diaspora." *The Newsletter of the International Institute for the Study of Islam in the Modern World* (October 2000): 13.

Kirli, Cengiz. "Coffeehouses: Public Opinion in the Nineteenth-Century Ottoman Empire." In *Public Islam and the Common Good*, edited by Armando Salvatore and Dale F. Eickelman, 75–97. Boston: Brill, 2006.

Kolko, Beth, and Elizabeth Reid. "Dissolution and Fragmentation: Problems in On-Line Communities." In *Cybersociety: Revisiting Computer-Mediated Communication and Community*, edited by Steven G. Jones, 212–30. London: Sage, 1998.

Krämer, Gudrun, and Sabine Schmidtke. "Introduction: Religious Authority and Religious Authorities in Muslim Societies: A Critical Overview." In *Speaking for Islam: Religious Authorities in Muslim Societies*, 1–14. Boston: Brill, 2006.

Kramer, Martin. "Political Islam." *Washington Paper* 3, no. 73. Washington, DC: Georgetown University Center for Strategic and International Studies, 1980.

Krüger, Oliver. "Discovering the Invisible Internet: Methodological Aspects of Searching Religion on the Internet." *Online Heidelberg Journal of Religions on the Internet* 1, no. 1 (September 2005): 1–27.

———. "The Internet as Distributor and Mirror of Religious and Ritual Knowledge." *Asian Journal of Social Sciences* 32, no. 2 (2004): 183–97.

———. "Methods and Theory for Studying Religion on the Internet: Introduction to the Special Issue on Theory and Methodology." *Online Heidelberg Journal of Religions on the Internet* 1, no. 1 (September 2005): 1–7.

Lapidus, Ira M. *A History of Islamic Societies*, 2nd ed. London: Cambridge University Press, 2002.

Larsson, Göran. "The Death of a Virtual Muslim Discussion Group: Issues and Methods in Analyzing Religion on the Net." *Online Heidelberg Journal of Religions on the Internet* 1, no. 1 (September 2005): 1–18.

Lawrence, Bruce B. "Allah On-Line: The Practice of Global Islam in the Information Age." In *Practicing Religion in the Age of the Media: Explorations of Media, Religion, and Culture*, edited by Stewart M. Hoover and Lynn Schofield Clark, 237–53. New York: Columbia University Press, 2002.

Lerner, Daniel. *The Passing of Traditional Society: Modernizing the Middle East.* Glencoe, IL: Free Press, 1963.

Linderman, Alf, and Mia Lövheim. "Internet, Religion and the Attribution of Social Trust." In *Mediating Religion: Conversations in Media, Religion and Culture,* edited by Jolyon Mitchell and Sophia Marriage, 229–40. New York: T&T Clark, 2003.

Lövheim, Mia. "Young People, Religious Identity, and the Internet." In *Religion Online: Finding Faith on the Internet,* edited by Lorne Dawson and Douglas Cowan, 59–73. London: Routledge, 2004.

———. "Young People and the Use of the Internet as Transitional Space." *Online Heidelberg Journal of Religions on the Internet* 1, no. 1 (September 2005).

Luckman, Thomas. *The Invisible Religion: The Problem of Religion in Modern Society.* New York: Macmillan, 1967.

Lynch, Marc. "Dialogue in an Age of Terror." In *Islamic Democratic Discourse: Theory, Debates and Philosophical Perspectives,* edited by M.A. Muqtader Khan, 193–225. Lanham, MD: Lexington Books, 2006.

———. *Voices of the New Arab Public Sphere: Iraq, Al-Jazeera, and Middle East Politics Today.* New York: Columbia University Press, 2006.

Maguire, Musa. "The Islamic Internet: Authority, Authenticity and Reform." In *Media on the Move: Global Flow and Contra-Flow,* edited by Daya Thussu, 237–50. London: Routledge, 2006.

Mandaville, Peter. "Communication and Diasporic Islam: A Virtual *Ummah?*" In *The Media of Diaspora,* edited by Karim H. Karim, 135–47. London: Routledge, 2003.

———. "Digital Islam: Changing the Boundaries of Religious Knowledge?" *International Institute for the Study of Islam in the Modern World* (March, 1999): 1–23.

———. *Global Political Islam.* London: Routledge, 2007.

———. "Reimagining the *Ummah?* Information Technology and the Changing Boundaries of Political Islam." In *Islam Encountering Globalization,* edited by Ali Mohammadi, 61–90. London: Routledge Curzon, 2002.

———. *Transnational Muslim Politics: Reimagining the Umma.* London: Routledge, 2001.

Masud, Muhammad Khalid. "The Scope of Pluralism in Islamic Moral Traditions." In *Islamic Political Ethics: Civil Society, Pluralism, and Conflict,* edited by Sohail H. Hashmi, 135–47. Princeton, NJ: Princeton University Press, 2002.

Mazumdar, Shampa, and Sanjoy Mazumdar. "The Articulation of Religion in Domestic Space: Rituals in the Immigrant Muslim Home." In *Contesting Rituals: Islam and Practices of Identity-Making,* edited by Pamela J. Stewart and Andrew Strathern, 125–45. Durham, NC: Carolina Academic Press, 2005.

McCarthy, Thomas. "Practical Discourse: On the Relation of Morality to Politics." In *Habermas and the Public Sphere,* edited by Craig Calhoun, 51–72. Cambridge, MA: MIT Press, 1992.

McKee, Alan. *The Public Sphere: An Introduction.* London: Cambridge University Press, 2005.

———. *Textual Analysis: A Beginner's Guide.* London: Sage, 2006.

Miles, Hugh. *Al-Jazeera: The Inside Story of the Arab News Channel That Is Challenging the West.* New York: Grove Press, 2005.

Moaddel, Mansoor. *Islamic Modernism, Nationalism, and Fundamentalism: Episode and Discourse.* Chicago: University of Chicago Press, 2005.

Mowlana, Hamid. *Global Communication in Transition: The End of Diversity?* London: Sage, 1996.

Mowlana, Hamid, and Laurie Wilson. *The Passing of Modernity: Communication and the Transformation of Society.* New York: Longman, 1990.

Naguib, S. "Islamism(s) Old and New." In *Egypt: The Moment of Change,* edited by El-Mahdi, R. and Marfleet, P., 103–119. London: Zed Books, 2009.

Nielsen, Jorgen S. "New Centers and Peripheries in European Islam?" In *Shaping the Current Islamic Reformation,* edited by B.A. Roberson, 64–81. London: Frank Cass, 2003.

Nomani, Asra. "Amr Khaled." *Time,* April 30, 2007, http://www.time.com/time/specials/2007/time100/article/0,28804,1595326_1615754_1616173,00.html (accessed September 14, 2008).

Norris, Pippa. *Digital Divide: Civic Engagement, Information Poverty, and the Internet Worldwide.* London: Cambridge University Press, 2006.

Norton, Augustus Richard. "The New Media, Civic Pluralism and the Slowly Retreating State." In *New Media in the Muslim World: The Emerging Public Sphere,* edited by Dale F. Eickelman and Jon Anderson, 19–28. Bloomington: Indiana University Press, 1999.

Ouis, Pernilla. "Islamization as a Strategy for Reconciliation between Modernity and Tradition: Examples from Contemporary Arab Gulf States." *Islam and Christian-Muslim Relations* 13, no. 3 (2002): 315–34.

Papacharissi, Zizi. "The Virtual Sphere: The Internet as a Public Sphere." *New Media & Society* 1, no. 9 (2002): 9–27.

Polat, R. K. "The Internet and Political Participation: Exploring the Explanatory Links." *European Journal of Communication* 20, no. 4 (2005): 435–59.

Poster, Mark. "Cyberdemocracy: The Internet and the Public Sphere." In *Virtual Politics: Identity and Community in Cyberspace,* edited by David Holmes, 212–28. London: Sage, 1997.

Postman, Neil. *Technopoly: The Surrender of Culture to Technology.* New York: Vintage Books, 1993.

Ramadan, Tariq. "Ijtihad and Maslaha: The Foundations of Governance." In *Islamic Democratic Discourse: Theory, Debates and Philosophical Perspectives,* edited by M.A. Muqtader Khan, 3–20. Lanham, MD: Lexington Books, 2006.

———. *In the Footsteps of the Prophet: Lessons from the Life of Muhammad.* New York: Oxford University Press, 2007.

Renan, Ernest. "What Is a Nation?" In *Nation and Narration,* edited by Homi Bhabha, 8–22. London: Routledge, 1990.

Rheingold, Howard. *The Virtual Community: Homesteading on the Electronic Frontier.* Cambridge, MA: MIT Press, 2000.

Roberson, B.A. "The Shaping of the Current Islamic Reformation." In *Shaping the Current Islamic Reformation,* 1–19. London: Frank Cass, 2004.

Roberts, John Michael, and Nick Crossley. "Introduction." In *After Habermas: News Perspectives on the Public Sphere,* 1–27. New York: Blackwell, 2004.

Rodman, George. *Mass Media in a Changing World.* Boston: McGraw Hill, 2007.

Roy, Olivier. *Globalized Islam: The Search for a New Ummah.* New York: Columbia University Press, 2004.

Rugh, Andrea B. "Reshaping Personal Relations in Egypt." In *Fundamentalism and Society,* edited by Martin E. Marty and R. Scott Appleby, 140–60. Chicago: University of Chicago Press, 1993.

Saint-Blancat, Chantal. "Islam in Diaspora: Between Reterritorialization and Extraterritoriality." *International Journal of Urban and Regional Research* 26, no. 1 (March 2002): 138–51.

Salvatore, Armando. "Public Religion, Ethics of Participation, and Cultural Dialogue." In *Contemporary Islam: Dynamic, not Static.* London: Routledge, 2006.

Salvatore, Armando, and Dale F. Eickelman. "Muslim Publics." In *Public Islam and the Common Good,* 3–27. Boston: Brill, 2006.

Salvatore, Armando, and Mark LeVine. "Introduction." In *Religion, Social Practice and Contested Hegemonies: Reconstructing the Public Sphere in Muslim Majority Societies,* 1–25. New York: Palgrave Macmillan, 2005.

Samers, Michael E. "Diaspora Unbound: Muslim Identity and the Erratic Regulation of Islam in France." *International Journal of Population Geography* 9 (2003): 351–64.

Schmidt, Garbi. "The Transnational Umma—Myth or reality? Examples from the Western Diasporas." *Muslim World* 95, no. 4 (October 2005): 575–86.

Schudson, Michael. "Why Conversation Is Not the Soul of Democracy." *Critical Studies in Mass Communication* 14 (December 1997): 297–309.

Seib, Philip. "New Media and Prospects for Democratization." In *New Media and the New Middle East,* 1–17. New York: Palgrave Macmillan, 2007.

Sheikholeslami, A. Reza. "From Individual Sacrament to Collective Salvation." In *Contemporary Islam: Dynamic, Not Static,* edited by Abdul Aziz Said, Mohammed Abu-Nimer, and Meena Sharify-Funk, 49–63. London: Routledge, 2006.

Skovgaard-Peterson, Jakob. "The Global Mufti." In *Globalization and the Muslim World: Culture, Religion and Modernity,* edited by Birgit Schaebler and Leif Stenberg, 153–65. New York: Syracuse University Press, 2004.

Slevin, James. *The Internet and Society.* London: Polity, 2000.

Sonn, Tamara. "Elements of Government in Classical Islam." In *Islamic Democratic Discourse: Theory, Debates and Philosophical Perspectives,* edited by M.A. Muqtader Khan, 21–36. Lanham, MD: Lexington Books, 2006.

Sparks, Colin. "Is There a Global Public Sphere?" In *Electronic Empires: Global Media and Local Resistance,* edited by Daya Thussu, 108–24. London: Arnold, 1998.

Sreberny, Annabelle. "Media, Muslims, and the Middle East: A Critical Review Essay." *Political Communication* 19, no. 2 (April 2002): 273–80.

Stenberg, Leif. "Islam, Knowledge, and 'the West': The Making of a Global Islam." In *Globalization and the Muslim World: Culture, Religion and Modernity,* edited by Birgit Schaebler and Leif Stenberg, 93–110. New York: Syracuse University Press, 2004.

Thompson, John. *Ideology and Modern Culture: Critical Social Theory in the Era of Mass Communication.* Palo Alto, CA: Stanford University Press, 1990.

———. *The Media and Modernity: A Social Theory of the Media.* Palo Alto, CA: Stanford University Press, 1995.

Tibi, Bassam. "War and Peace in Islam." In *Islamic Political Ethics: Civil Society, Pluralism, and Conflict,* edited by Sohail H. Hashmi, 175–93. Princeton, NJ: Princeton University Press, 2002.

Utvik, Björn Olav. "The Modernizing Face of Islamism." In *Modernizing Islam: Religion in the Public Sphere in Europe and the Middle East,* edited by John L. Esposito and Francois Burgat, 43–68. Piscataway, NJ: Rutgers University Press, 2003.

Van Der Veer, Peter. "Secrecy and Publicity in the South Asian Public Arena." In *Public Islam and the Common Good,* edited by Armando Salvatore and Dale F. Eickelman, 29–51. Boston: Brill, 2006.

Walker, M. Karen. "Proposing a Joint Enterprise for Communication and Terrorism Studies: An Essay on Identity Formation and Expression within the Arab Public Sphere." *Review of Communication* 7, no. 1 (January 2007): 21–36.

————. "The Search for Community as Described in the Literature Addressing Identity Discourses in the Arab Public Sphere." http://www.rhetoricalens.info/index.cfm?fuseaction=feature.display&feature_id=24 (accessed September 14, 2008).

Walkerdine, Valerie. "Some Day My Prince Will Come: Young Girls and the Preparation for Adolescent Sexuality." In *Gender and Generation*, edited by Angela McRobbie and Mira Nava, 162–84. London: Macmillan, 1984.

Warner, Michael. *Publics and Counterpublics*. New York: Zone Books, 2002.

Watt, W. Montgomery. *Islamic Fundamentalism and Modernity*. London: Routledge, 1988.

Wellman, Barry, and Milena Gulia. "Virtual Communities as Communities: Net Surfers Don't Ride Alone." In *Communities in Cyberspace*, edited by Marc A. Smith and Peter Kollock, 167–94. London: Routledge, 2003.

"What Is the Muslim Understanding of 'Ummah?'" *The Christian Broadcasting Network*, http://www.cbn.com/spirituallife/onlinediscipleship/understandingislam/What_is_the_Muslim_understanding_of_Ummah.aspx (accessed September 14, 2008).

Wheeler, Deborah L. "The Internet and Youth Subculture in Kuwait." *Journal of Computer Mediated Communication* 8, no. 2 (January 2003): 133–62.

————. *The Internet in the Middle East: Global Expectations and Local Imaginations in Kuwait*. Albany: State University of New York Press, 2006.

————. "New Media, Globalization and Kuwaiti National Identity." *Middle East Journal* 54, no. 3 (Summer 2000): 432–44.

White, Jenny B. "Amplifying Trust: Community and Communication in Turkey." In *New Media in the Muslim World: The Emerging Public Sphere*, edited by Dale F. Eickelman and Jon Anderson, 162–79. Bloomington: Indiana University Press, 1999.

Williams, D. "Bloggers Bucking the Brotherhood in Egypt." *The New York Times*. Retrieved from: http://www.nytimes.com/2008/10/28/world/africa/28ihtletter.1.17303886.html (accessed October 28, 2008).

Wilkins, Karin G. "Communication and Transition in the Middle East." *Gazette, the International Journal for Communication Studies* 66, no. 6 (December 2004): 483–96.

Wise, Lindsay. "Words from the Heart: New Forms of Islamic Preaching in Egypt." Unpublished Masters Thesis, St. Anthony's College: Oxford University, 2003.

Witteborn, Saskia. "The Situated Expression of Arab Collective Identities in the United States." *Journal of Communication* 57, no. 3 (September 2007): 556–75.

Yousif, Ahmad F. "IT in the 21st Century: Benefits, Barriers & Concerns of Muslim Scholars." http://www.ifew.com/insight/15039net/infotech.htm (accessed September 14, 2008).

Zaman, M. Raquibuz. "Islamic Perspectives on Territorial Boundaries and Autonomy." In *Islamic Political Ethics: Civil Society, Pluralism, and Conflict*, edited by Sohail H. Hashmi, 79–101. Princeton, NJ: Princeton University Press, 2002.

Zaman, Muhammad Qasim. *The 'Ulama in Contemporary Islam: Custodians of Change*. Princeton, NJ: Princeton University Press, 2002.

————. "The 'Ulama of Contemporary Islam and Their Conceptions of the Common Good." In *Public Islam and the Common Good*, edited by Armando Salvatore and Dale F. Eickelman, 129–56. Boston: Brill, 2006.

Zayani, Mohammed. "Witnessing the Intifada: Al-Jazeera's Coverage of the Palestinian-Israeli Conflict." In *The Al-Jazeera Phenomenon: Critical Perspectives on New Arab Media*, 171–82. Boulder, CO: Paradigm, 2005.

Zeghal, Malika. "Religion and Politics in Egypt: The Ulema of Al-Azhar, Radical Islam, and the State." *International Journal of Middle East Studies* 31, no. 3 (August 1999): 371–99.

INDEX

CPSIA information can be obtained at www.ICGtesting.com
Printed in the USA
BVOW040721291011

274772BV00002BA/2/P